CHANGING THE SELF

D1617155

SUNY Series, Studying the Self
Richard P. Lipka and Thomas M. Brinthaupt, Editors

CHANGING THE SELF

Philosophies, Techniques, and Experiences

edited by

THOMAS M. BRINTHAUPT
and RICHARD P. LIPKA

State University
of New York
Press

Published by
State University of New York Press, Albany

© 1994 State University of New York

All rights reserved

Production by Susan Geraghty
Marketing by Terry Swierzowski

Printed in the United States of America

No part of this book may be used or reproduced
in any manner whatsoever without written permission
except in the case of brief quotations embodied in
critical articles and reviews.

For information, address State University of New York
Press, State University Plaza, Albany, N.Y., 12246

Library of Congress Cataloging-in-Publication Data

Changing the self : philosophies, techniques, and experiences / edited
  by Thomas M. Brinthaupt and Richard P. Lipka.
      p.   cm. — (SUNY series, studying the self)
    Includes bibliographical references and indexes.
    ISBN 0-7914-1867-7 (alk. paper). — ISBN 0-7914-1868-5 (pbk.
  alk. paper)
      1. Change (Psychology)   2. Self.   3. Self-help techniques.
  I. Brinthaupt, Thomas M., 1958–   .   II. Lipka, Richard P.
  III. Series.
  BF637.C4C43   1994
  155.2'5—dc20   93-10522
                                                                CIP

CONTENTS

CONTRIBUTORS

Darren C. Aboyoun
Department of Psychology
University of Scranton
Scranton, Pennsylvania

Roy F. Baumeister
Department of Psychology
Case Western Reserve University
Cleveland, Ohio

James A. Beane
National College of Education
Madison, Wisconsin

Linelle M. Blais
Cancer Prevention Research Consortium
University of Rhode Island
Kingston, Rhode Island

Joseph M. Boden
Department of Psychology
Case Western Reserve University
Cleveland, Ohio

Thomas M. Brinthaupt
Department of Psychology
Middle Tennessee State University
Murfreesboro, Tennessee

Carlo C. DiClemente
Department of Psychology
University of Houston
Houston, Texas

John M. Dodd
Department of Special Education and Reading
Eastern Montana College
Billings, Montana

Martin Gold
Institute for Social Research
University of Michigan
Ann Arbor, Michigan

Diane Grimley
Cancer Prevention Research Consortium
University of Rhode Island
Kingston, Rhode Island

Don Hamachek
Counseling and Educational Psychology
Michigan State University
East Lansing, Michigan

Bonnie Henderson Hofland
Department of Special Education and Reading
Eastern Montana College
Billings, Montana

Ralph W. Hood, Jr.
Psychology Department
University of Tennessee at Chattanooga
Chattanooga, Tennessee

Richard P. Lipka
Center of Educational Services, Evaluation and Research
Pittsburg State University
Pittsburg, Kansas

J. Ron Nelson
Eastern Washington University
Cheney, Washington

John C. Norcross
Department of Psychology
University of Scranton
Scranton, Pennsylvania

James O. Prochaska
Cancer Prevention Research Consortium
University of Rhode Island
Kingston, Rhode Island

Dianne M. Tice
Department of Psychology
Case Western Reserve University
Cleveland, Ohio

S. Kay Toombs
Philosophy Department
Baylor University
Waco, Texas

P. J. Watson
Psychology Department
University of Tennessee at Chattanooga
Chattanooga, Tennessee

Wayne F. Velicer
Cancer Prevention Research Consortium
University of Rhode Island
Kingston, Rhode Island

Charles Zastrow
Social Work Department
University of Wisconsin - Whitewater
Whitewater, Wisconsin

INTRODUCTION

Thomas M. Brinthaupt
Richard P. Lipka

The self has become a major contemporary concern of both the academic and lay communities. Over the past several decades, a great deal of theory and research has been directed at this difficult-to-define concept. The professional interest in the self is reflected by the large number of published studies on some variant of the self and self-related processes, as well as by the dozens of academic books on the subject.

Concurrently, the "person in the street" has come to be preoccupied with self, identity, and related constructs. There seem to be several reasons for this historical trend (e.g., Baumeister, 1986, 1987; Cushman, 1990). Preoccupation with the self is easily seen in the number of popular "self-help" books, the multimillion-dollar "self-help" business, and the frequency of self- or identity-related maladies associated with problems of adjustment, psychopathology, and social problems (Levin, 1987; Rosen, 1987; Starker, 1989; Zilbergeld, 1983).

While the academic knowledge providers labor at identifying the factors involved in changing the self and the usefulness of various techniques designed to facilitate that process, dramatic (and often exaggerated and unsubstantiated) claims are made by the merchants of self-change (Gambrill, 1992; Gross, 1978). For the intelligent consumer of the latest self-related information, there are two choices. On the one hand, one can leaf through the un-

1

documented, overgeneralized, cheerleaderlike claims made in the mass market paperbacks. On the other hand, one can trudge through the massive scientific literatures on the self that are often so abstruse as to resemble a foreign language.

A clearer consideration of the issues related to changing the self is in order. How do we know when change in the self has occurred? Measuring change of any kind is not an easy thing, and it is especially difficult when what it is that is alleged to have changed is so elusive a concept as the self. The present collection of essays takes a much-needed step toward linking the concerns of the academic self-researcher and the consumer of research pertaining to changing the self. It is organized around the related themes of the philosophies, techniques, and experiences of changing the self.

Developmental psychologists have long been interested in change in the self. When, how, and why the self develops as it does has been a major part of most theories of personal development (Lipka & Brinthaupt, 1992). But there are other ways to think about the self and self-change. In addition to taking a developmental perspective, we can consider the intentional—or inadvertent—changing of the self. The purpose of this volume is to examine the varieties of self-change and the factors that can influence it.

When we speak of changing the self, many questions arise. For example, what exactly must be changed? Must the individual change, or will changes in the environment bring about changes in the self? Why should the self change, and why is it that we conceive of the self as changeable? How is self-change brought about? How do we know when changes in the self have occurred? Does volunteering to change one's self differ from being forced to change the self? The contributors do not purport to be able to answer all of these questions. They each do, however, address one or more of them.

Interest in changing the self is so prevalent across differing disciplines that there is an almost unlimited number of content areas from which to choose. We have assembled contributions from many disciplines with the hope that a clearer idea about the usefulness of the self construct would emerge. In the process, we also wanted to clarify how different disciplines consider what is involved in changing the self.

In Part 1, the contributors address the issue of what self-change is and introduce some of the explanations and philosophies for the process of changing the self. In Part 2, specific techniques and strategies of changing the self are discussed. In Part 3, some of the results and experiences of changes in the self are presented.

PART 1. PHILOSOPHIES OF CHANGING THE SELF

There are many issues involved with the notion of changing the self. Among the most basic of these issues are questions such as: How does the self change and what happens to it as it changes? How are poor or unhealthy changes in the self prevented or reversed? As the self has come to assume increased importance in Western culture, what approaches to changing the self have emerged? In addressing these questions, the first section of the book considers some of the different philosophies of changing the self.

What does it actually mean to change the self? In the first chapter of this section, Hamachek plots the developmental trajectory of the self by following the framework provided by Erikson's (1963, 1980) stages of psychosocial development. As he notes, for those who are interested in changing the self, a knowledge of its development is crucial. After differentiating among the concepts of self, self-esteem, and self-concept, Hamachek presents a detailed model of how the self develops. As he does this, he illustrates the importance of mental health professionals being aware of the specific functions and characteristics of the self as they plan strategies for change. For example, behavioral problems involving one stage of the self's development may be influenced by unresolved issues in some other developmental stage.

The psychosocial developmental framework provides useful guidelines for considering the question of changing the self. One of the points stressed by Hamachek is that problems with the self should be seen as an imbalance or as an unfavorable ratio of negative to positive self-attributes. This means that the ideal self is not one that is free from mistrust, self-doubt, guilt, or feelings of inferiority. Rather, for proper development to occur, these characteristics need to be experienced and incorporated into the self along with their opposites of trust, autonomy, or industry.

Especially interesting is Hamachek's argument that the various therapeutic approaches in psychology may be more appropriate for specific stages of the self's development. For instance, when a person is suffering from a lack of basic trust, a Rogerian therapist may be most effective. On the other hand, excessive feelings of shame, self-doubt, or guilt—which are associated with a different developmental stage—may be more easily and appropriately changed by means of a cognitive-behavioral therapeutic approach. For persons in the later stages of development, an eclectic strategy to changing the self may be most appropriate. Thus a key theme that comes though Hamachek's chapter is the importance of recognizing that how the self can—or should—be changed depends upon the person's level of self-development, not only in childhood or young adulthood but throughout the life span. This is important to keep in mind when examining the recommendations of the other contributors.

One of the areas in which concern with the self has had a very strong impact and a relatively long history is the schools. How have schools addressed issues pertaining to changing the self? In the next chapter, Beane details the past and present efforts of schools to enhance the self-perceptions of students. As indicated by the title of his chapter, these efforts have been far from systematic and sensible. Historically, the emergence of the humanistic branch of psychology led to an increase in attention to the individual and to the self in the schools. As Beane documents, this attention has waxed and waned over the past several decades and has garnered its share of criticism, with recent attacks on the practice of using schools to change the self. He shows how political and social agendas have always affected efforts to enhance self-perceptions.

Beane identifies three basic arguments for why the schools have been concerned with changing the self. These include providing skills to students in order to cope with life's problems, enhancing school-related achievement outcomes, and playing a role in the development of feelings of personal dignity and social efficacy. As he notes, these arguments involve prevention, in the sense of providing students with feelings of self-esteem or self-worth and other tools for living in contemporary society. That is, they are primarily means rather than ends.

In the latter part of his chapter, Beane describes some of the specific approaches used by schools to enhance self-perceptions and some of their advantages and disadvantages. Among these approaches are exercises in self-disclosure and self-affirmation, structured self-esteem programs, and "ecological" views that take into account aspects of the school as a whole, including institutional features and characteristics of teaching and curriculum. Beane closes his chapter by addressing the current controversy over the proper role of schools. As he notes, the claim that the schools' purpose is to foster the economic competitiveness and future of the country minimizes the importance of and need for a focus on the self. However, he finds little reason to think that this is more important than the historically "child-centered" impulse to mold and change the self by establishing human dignity and personal and social efficacy.

In the question of changing the self, it is important to distinguish between development (the occurrence of change in a structured, predictable manner), prevention (inhibiting the occurrence of abnormal or pathological changes), and rehabilitation (fixing something that's "broken"). In his chapter, Hamachek describes the developmental implications of changes in the self. In his chapter, Beane reviews the efforts of the school to mold or alter the self primarily for purposes of society. In the next chapter, Gold describes some of the implications of the self gone awry. He presents a self-related perspective on juvenile delinquency that begins with a discussion of how the self is implicated in this problem behavior and ends with suggestions for rehabilitating the delinquent self.

For Gold, a crucial aspect of the self is its agentic property, or its connection to feelings of competence and volition. Tying the self to the experiences of intimacy, identification, and alienation, he reviews previous theory and research on delinquency as providing a way to defend against the threat of a derogated self. Concerns with such a derogated self and the need for restoring self-esteem can explain why delinquent behavior is embraced. An important part of this process is the development of a "delinquent subculture" that provides an appreciative and esteem-enhancing audience for delinquent performances.

In the latter part of his chapter, Gold describes some of the self-related educational interventions that might be effective in preventing delinquent behavior and rehabilitating those individuals who have found it to be rewarding. The problem is to replace delinquent with nondelinquent behavior that is esteem-enhancing. He describes alternative school programs, similar to those discussed by Beane, that lessen feelings and experiences of failure and provide a warm and supportive relationship. These programs alter normal role relations between teacher and student, permit greater flexibility in classroom rules and norms, and focus more on the agentic selves of students than traditional educational programs. Thus Gold's philosophy of changing the self is to provide healthy alternatives to the unhealthy external circumstances of young people. In this way, a positive sense of self-agency might be acquired.

Since the fall in importance and prevalence of religion as a cultural institution, one of the most popular and influential philosophies of changing the self has come to be psychotherapy. With this shift in emphasis, the relationship between psychotherapy and religion has been an intimate and controversial one over the years. In the final chapter in this section, Watson addresses what is probably the most important aspect of this relationship—how each thinks about the self and changing the self. As he notes, both religion and psychology deal with similar problems and issues, providing ideas and technologies designed for the "ordering of the internal life." However, to the extent that the two areas conflict with one other about what it means to be psychologically healthy and about the nature of the person, different philosophies of changing the self are offered. Should psychology and psychotherapy address religious issues, and if so, how? To examine this question, Watson contrasts the religious self with the psychological self and discusses the social construction of each. Which camp is correct? Is the "religious self" a fundamental and positive aspect of the person, or is it tangential and potentially damaging?

In his chapter, Watson addresses the clash of belief systems that arises when the religious self is the topic. He discusses the claim made by some psychologists, especially Albert Ellis, that certain religious belief systems are associated with psychological maladjustment and mental health problems. For Ellis, effective therapy serves to rid a client of the religious self by supplanting irrationality with rationality. Individuals should thus be directed towards a psychologically healthy ideal self which consists of the characteristics of tolerance, flexibility, self-acceptance, and so on.

For Watson, however, the issue is much more complicated. There are times, for example, when the religious self lessens rather than increases emotional distress, such as when it uses the concept of sin to promote constructive sorrow or personal responsibility instead of feelings of guilt or self-punitiveness. He also points to the importance of carefully defining and measuring the religious self and notes that, when this is done, claims that the healthy self is incompatible with religiousness do not receive strong empirical support.

Throughout his analysis, Watson points out that therapy (and any effort to change the self) raises basic ideological issues. One of these issues is the difference between the philosophy and practice of religious ideas as they apply to changing the self. Another issue concerns the role of therapy in changing a person's belief structure versus accepting or working with those beliefs. Can this be done when one is attempting to help bring about positive change in another person? That is, should the religious self be abandoned or fostered? As Watson demonstrates, such questions are too infrequently addressed by those whose job it is to help others change themselves. When it comes to changing the self, psychotherapy and religion are not necessarily incompatible in theory or practice.

PART 2. TECHNIQUES OF CHANGING THE SELF

What happens when people are dissatisfied with something about themselves? What can they do about it? In the second section of this book, some of the many specific techniques of changing the self are described. If individuals are sufficiently motivated or their behaviors sufficiently dysfunctional, there are several options available to them. A person might, for example, seek (or be given) professional help, receive guidance from friends or acquaintances, read a book relevant to the problem, or perhaps even do nothing at all. Another option is to try to change a problematic aspect of oneself by escaping from it. It is this latter option that is the focus of the first chapter in this section.

In their chapter, Baumeister and Boden consider the costs associated with the excessive self-attention accompanying modern identity. They propose that a major way to escape from the discomfort of this self-awareness is to reduce the size and scope of that part of the self that is present in awareness. One can, as they put it, try to focus on a "narrow and unproblematic slice of the self-concept." Baumeister and Boden discuss the circumstances that might give rise to such an attempt, including calamitous or distressing events, chronic everyday life stresses, and even efforts to achieve ecstasy. These can bring about the motivation to shrink or escape from the self in an effort to provide at least temporary relief from the burdens of modern selfhood.

As Baumeister and Boden note, in practice, people cannot completely rid themselves of their selves. Short of making permanent changes (which are often quite difficult, as other contributors note), the best people can do is to direct their attention to a small and safe part of the self-concept. This can be accomplished through a process that the authors call "cognitive deconstruction" or "mental narrowing." They note that one of the most effective ways to accomplish this is to think of oneself as a mere biological specimen, in essence escaping from identity into body. This is attractive because it can remove normal inhibitions, reduce the need to plan or think about personal responsibilities, and perhaps also create a state of emotional numbness.

In the remainder of their chapter, Baumeister and Boden describe several of the major ways that individuals shrink the self. These include alcohol use and abuse, suicide, sexual masochism, binge eating, and religious mysticism. All of these can be thought of as attempts to change the "phenomenal" or experienced sense of self by reducing awareness of it. Unlike the changes in the self considered by other contributors to this collection, however, the changes here take the form of temporary—though often repeatable—escape. Baumeister and Boden are showing that there is a whole new range of behaviors through which the self and issues pertaining to changing the self can be implicated. We might include delinquency as described by Gold and mysticism as conceived by Hood (in a later chapter) as also being consistent with the analysis of Baumeister and Boden.

In the next chapter, Zastrow describes a specific technique designed to bring about positive changes in the self. This approach to changing the self, based on Ellis's (1979) rational-emotive therapy, is concerned with the interesting tendency we have to "talk" to ourselves. For Zastrow, faulty (that is, irrational) self-talk accounts for many of the problems people encounter in their lives. By "self-talk," Zastrow means the evaluative thoughts that we have about our behavior and the things that happen to us. He argues that such internal conversations are the key element of our self-concept and how it is developed and maintained. The major implication of this view is that when we talk about changing the self, we need to look toward changing the self's talk.

According to Zastrow, the way to get around the problems created by dysfunctional self-talk is through the rational management of the thoughts people tell themselves. The basic principle revolves around the notion that, whereas people cannot change the unpleasant events that have occurred, they can change what they tell themselves about those events. The approach is essentially an effort to change the self by restructuring thinking. Much of Zastrow's chapter is an attempt to illustrate how this can be accomplished in a controlled and systematic manner.

As a self-change technique, this cognitive-emotional approach tries to get a person to become his or her own therapist or counselor, in a sense bringing the external change agent "inside." Thus the person is encouraged to identify conclusions or interpretations that are irrational or illogical, actively consider alternatives, and come up with counterexamples, much as a therapist might do when working with that person. Zastrow uses examples of interpersonal problems and criminal rehabilitation to illustrate how the approach can be used. However, there are some possible difficulties with the successful utilization of this self-talk approach. For example, some self-talk may be "automatic" or difficult to recognize by the person. In the final part of his chapter, Zastrow discusses this and other potential limitations of the approach.

Not surprisingly, most of the interest in and attention to changing the self has been shown by psychotherapists. In fact, it is probably accurate to describe the trained psychotherapist as a "change expert." The role of the therapist is usually to provide the client with insight about his or her problem and with techniques to change the problem for the better. Of course, the emphasis of a therapist can be quite varied. For example, insight-oriented approaches, such as psychoanalysis or client-centered therapy, might require a good deal of time devoted to the client's "ego" or "self" and the things that have led to its current characteristics. On the other hand, a cognitive-behavioral therapist might spend more time considering a client's behavior and how the self affects that behavior or vice versa.

Some approaches to change focus almost entirely on behavior, without any necessary reference to the "self" or related constructs. The next chapter in this section, by Grimley and her colleagues, represents an example of this latter approach. They describe the transtheoretical model of change that primarily deals with how and when change occurs in the therapeutic setting, especially as applied to addictive behaviors, such as smoking. Their model consists of five stages of change—precontemplation, contemplation, preparation, action, and maintenance.

Grimley and colleagues emphasize different change processes at different stages. For example, during the precontemplation stage, individuals have no intention of changing their maladaptive behavior. Such persons can move to the contemplation stage of change through "consciousness raising," or by having their awareness of themselves and their problem increased through observation, confrontation, interpretation, and so on. Grimley and colleagues also discuss the pros and cons of specific problem behaviors and the effects these have both within and across the different stages of change.

Throughout their chapter, Grimley and her colleagues argue that to talk of changing the "self" is not particularly useful. Instead, to bring about lasting personal change, particularly with regard to maladaptive or harmful behaviors, the behaviors themselves are what need to change. To the extent that the self is involved in this process, it seems at most a distant observer. Thus they propose that most problematic behaviors are not intimately tied to the self and its reverberations, as Baumeister and Boden argue. In fact, they suggest that when the levels of change are "self-related," the determinants of the problem behavior are increasingly removed from individual awareness. They report an impressive array of research on problem behaviors that is consistent with their transtheoretical model.

Does this mean that changes in behavior do not bring about changes in the self? Even if behavioral changes do affect the self, Grimley and colleagues suggest that this is not an important issue. However, for the next contributor, when and how behaviors change the self is a very important issue. Tice is especially interested in specifying those conditions that lead to changes in the self and the processes that produce such changes. She proposes that our self-concepts will change in order to incorporate the results and implications of behaviors into our private sense of self. This process, which she calls internalization, rests on the notion that persons are unlikely to change their selves unless they actively cooperate in the process. This is normally a gradual rather than a sudden process. However, as she notes, changes in the self might occur more quickly if a person fails to recognize or resist pressures to change or if facets of that person's self are in flux or are not clearly defined.

Tice illustrates some of the cognitive and interpersonal factors that seem to influence the process of behavioral internalization. For example, through self-perception processes, individuals may change their self-views based on the way they have behaved and the circumstances surrounding their behavior. Much of her discussion concerns situations in which behavior has implications for the public and private aspects of the self. One of the most common of those situations arises when behavior is performed in the presence of other people. Tice describes several studies that support the idea that public performance tends to magnify the effects of certain behaviors in changing the self.

Part of the reason for this effect is that when we behave in front of other people, such actions cannot easily be ignored, forgotten, or covered up. An important implication, therefore, is that behavior performed in the eyes of important other people (that is, behaviors involving the "public self") may be an especially effective way to change the internal, private self. Other people can provide valuable data in the form of social comparison information, allowing standards on which changes in the self can be based. Thus, for Tice, the interpersonal context can be very influential in bringing about changes in the self. This is less consistent with the primarily intrapersonal, self-talk approach advocated by Zastrow than it is with the behavioral approach described by Grimley and her colleagues. Tice's analysis also helps to give a clearer account of the ways that the "delinquent subculture" discussed by Gold can provide the conditions for changes in the self-concepts of young people.

PART 3. EXPERIENCES OF CHANGING THE SELF

In Part 2 of this book, our contributors describe some of the ways that changes in the self might be brought about. Given the assumption that such changes in the self (or in behavior) do occur, what happens to the "self"? What are the conditions that bring about self-change, and what are the effects of such changes? How such questions are answered depends on factors like why the change occurred—was it voluntary or involuntary, planned or unplanned?—

and whether it came about on one's own or with the help or coercion of others. In the third section of this book, we present some alternative perspectives on these issues.

In the first chapter, Norcross and Aboyoun examine the self-change efforts of the change experts themselves. How do those who are professionally trained to help others change—that is, psychotherapists—change themselves and deal with their own personal problems and distress? How are these self-change efforts related to the therapists' efforts to help others to change? Are there differences in approaching a particular problem when it is presented by clients as opposed to when the therapists themselves are experiencing it?

Among the issues addressed by Norcross and Aboyoun are the experiences and handling of personal difficulties by therapists (often concerning interpersonal problems or experiences of loss) and the success of their efforts to change themselves. One of their many interesting findings is that therapists tend to rely on a wider variety and more complete repertoire of self-change techniques and strategies than laypeople, meaning that therapists are more successful in changing themselves. Laypersons seem to be "caught up in themselves" and depend more on self-focused activities and internal cognitive approaches than do therapists. Thus it seems that the "change experts" are good not only at helping others to change but also at helping themselves to change.

Another interesting finding concerns the many different schools of therapeutic change. Norcross and Aboyoun point out that when they are working with their clients, psychotherapists tend to employ techniques that are consistent with their particular theoretical orientation. However, when it comes to their own efforts to change themselves, therapists apparently are not strongly influenced by the theories in which they were trained. Norcross and Aboyoun spend some time speculating about what might account for this disparity. For example, actor-observer effects may be operating, therapists may make less favorable assumptions about their clients' problems than their own, there may be differential expectations for the success of self-change efforts, and so on. By examining these and other issues, Norcross and Aboyoun give us additional insight into the experiences of self-change shown by those who are most closely tied to helping others change themselves.

When we talk about changing the self, the issues usually involve moving from a negative to a more positive state. After all, if the characteristics of the self were positive, what would there be to change about the self? Of course, the nature of the self is such that there are probably always parts of it that can, should, or must be changed. Despite this emphasis, there is another way of looking at changing the self. In particular, is it actually possible to lose or get rid of the self? What does this mean, and what is the experience when this happens?

In fact, there are some traditions that advocate a loss of the self. In their chapter, Baumeister and Boden describe some of the techniques through which we can shrink or escape from the self. In the next chapter in this section, Hood discusses one of the most prominent of these traditions, religious mysticism, and the implications this has for changing the self. He begins by comparing and contrasting the traditional religious and social scientific views of the self. From the religious perspective, the "egoless" state or the state of "nonself" is a desired end. That state is what commonly accompanies the mystical experience.

Relying on empirical research based on his own scale of mysticism, Hood attempts to analyze the nature of the mystical experience systematically. An important distinction in the realm of mysticism is that between extrovertive and introvertive experiences. In both cases, the self is "lost." With extrovertive experiences, the self seems to be expanded as the person becomes "one with the entire field of perception." With introvertive experiences, the self seems to shrink into an undifferentiated, contentless reality of pure consciousness. Hood describes the frequency of these experiences and the characteristics of the persons who report them. One of his findings is that mystical experience seems to be a capacity of many healthy, normal persons and is not necessarily something that falls into the realm of the pathological.

In the latter part of his chapter, Hood describes some of the conditions that can trigger mystical experiences. Among these triggers are sexual experiences, sensory isolation, and the use of drugs. Some of these triggers give rise to extrovertive mystical experiences, and some of them lead to introvertive experiences. A common attribute of these triggers is the presence of what he calls "incongruities." These refer to circumstances in which the person is aware of unusual, atypical perceptions or in which there is a transcendence of routine information processing. By describing these triggers and the resulting experience of loss of self, Hood provides a picture of the self changed in the extreme. In so doing, he also suggests a possibly fruitful link between self psychology and religious mysticism.

Those who study the self often point out the importance of group and ethnic identification to the establishment of a clear, positive sense of identity. Our social groups clearly play a powerful role in defining who we are. It is common to think of and define ourselves as members of specific groups, and we are often quick to respond if these groups are attacked by others. Our culture has strong links to our self-perceptions and self-identifications. What happens to the self when this culture goes through changes? Baumeister and Boden touch on some of the implications of historical change on the self. In the next chapter of this section, Dodd, Nelson, and Hofland focus directly on this issue by considering the effects of social, cultural, and historical changes on the self and identity of a specific group that has been much discriminated against—Native Americans.

What have been the effects of the long-term repression and neglect of the Native American people on their sense of self and identity? What is the result of externally imposed and involuntary changes in self forced upon this group? Dodd and his colleagues address this question by describing the present-day experiences of Native Americans, including their experiences with language, cultural conventions concerning time, school experiences and outcomes, family structure and attitudes toward children, and the problems of disability and suicide. They finish their chapter by addressing the issue of what can be done to clarify the self-concepts of Native Americans and to enhance their feelings of self-esteem. Given the nature of the changes in self that have occurred over the decades, this issue is not one that is easily resolved.

Underlying Dodd and colleagues' discussion is the notion of a clash of cultures, one of which values community and strong ethnic identity, the other of which values extreme individualism and the rejection of ethnic identity. The latter view, advocated by the larger American culture, conceives of a self that clashes with the traditions of the Native American. The nature of this clash is well illustrated by the authors' very interesting analysis of how differences in behavior can be interpreted in completely opposite ways by the two cultures. More generally, Dodd and colleagues illustrate how changes in one's group can lead to changes in the sense of self that is so intimately tied to that group. As history has shown with Native Americans, simply changing the self will not change the situation of the group. If anything, the opposite approach seems warranted, given the importance of the group to one's personal identity and sense of selfhood.

What it is like to have changed the self? Dodd and colleagues give a detailed answer to this question for Native Americans. The changes in the self experienced by most people (and discussed by most of the contributors to this book) involve either positive or negative shifts in behavior, personality, social behaviors, physical appearance or capabilities, ideas and values, and so on. Most of these shifts are likely to be gradual and small but cumulative. If positive, changes in the self can bolster a person's self-esteem and feelings of accomplishment and success. If negative, a person may suffer from a negative self-evaluation and seek to reverse the change, often with the help of other people. When the changes are negative, we nonetheless assume that the opportunity to change for the better is always available to us, even if we do not immediately take advantage of that opportunity or see the circumstances for change to be favorable.

In either the positive or negative case, changes in the self are often thought to be attributable to something the person has done correctly or incorrectly. That is, when we talk about changing the self, we often give credit or blame to the person who has experienced the change. There are times, however, when the self is changed suddenly, dramatically, or irreversibly. As Dodd and colleagues note in their discussion of Native Americans, similar attributions will often be made in these cases as well. When a change is chronic, permanent, or outside of one's control, the self is presented with a unique challenge. If the possibility of reversing a negative personal change is taken away, as in the case of a disabling physical condition, what effect does this have on the self?

In the final chapter of this section, Toombs provides a powerful discussion of the experience of physical disability and its effects on the self, made more compelling by her own personal experiences. Fundamental to her discussion is the notion that disability brings about a profound transformation of the self. Based on the ideas of the phenomenologists concerning the bodily self, Toombs illustrates how, with a disability, the body is more closely tied to consciousness than usual and becomes much more of an "insistent presence."

It is typical for a person to take his or her body and its orientational and intentional contributions for granted with minimal awareness. For example, we do not often think about our ability to maintain our balance as we go about our daily lives. As Toombs shows, however, with the loss of motility comes an increasing awareness of that which we take for granted most of the time. With a disability, she argues, we come to show a new bodily perception which she calls a "seeing-through-the-body." As she puts it, the body becomes "thematic to consciousness." Toombs highlights how the experience of the self changes with the loss of motility. This includes changes in the perception of time and effort, feelings of at-homeness in one's own body, disruptions in the interpersonal and social arenas, the accompanying threats to life goals, and so on.

In the later parts of her chapter, Toombs addresses the failure of the nondisabled to recognize the changes wrought by a disability. She focuses especially on those in the medical community whose approach to disability has been to ignore the changes in the lived body (and the self). As she puts it, "To ignore the transformation of the self is to discount the major impact of disability." Toombs describes several implications of her analysis (and her personal experiences) for medical practice, including recognizing that disability represents a total disruption of one's being-in-the-world, and the need to acknowledge the effects of disability on one's sense of the present and the future.

Unlike the cases described by Baumeister and Boden, a disability forces an involuntary shrinking of or "escaping" from the self. Here is a case where, because the body has changed for the worse, the self must also change. However, as Toombs notes, the changes in the self need not necessarily also be for the worse. She proposes that disability does not so much diminish the self as it leads to the acquisition of a new identity, with the possibility that the self can be newly and continuously defined. She asks for the understanding and support of the helping professions in recognizing this possibility.

In summary, we have brought together in this book a collection of individuals who have concerned themselves with the theme of changing the self. Although that theme is common to the effort of each contributor, its expression is quite varied, and their conclusions do not necessarily agree with one another. Where there is consensus, however, is that understanding and accounting for change in the self is vitally important across a wide range of human experience.

REFERENCES

Baumeister, R. F. (1986). *Identity: Cultural change and the struggle for self*. New York: Oxford University Press.

———. (1987). How the self became a problem: A psychological review of historical research. *Journal of Personality and Social Psychology,* 52:163–176.

Cushman, P. (1990). Why the self is empty: Toward a historically situated psychology. *American Psychologist, 45:*599–611.

Ellis, A. (1979). Rational-emotive therapy. In *Current psychotherapies* (2nd ed.), edited by R. Corsini (pp. 185–229). Itasca, IL: F. E. Peacock.

Erikson, E. H. (1963). *Childhood and society* (2nd ed.). New York: Norton.

———. (1980). *Identity and the life cycle*. New York: Norton.

Gambrill, E. (1992). Self-help books: Pseudoscience in the guise of science? *Skeptical Inquirer, 16:*389–399.

Gross, M. L. (1978). *The psychological society*. New York: Simon & Schuster.

Levin, D. M. (1987). *Pathologies of the modern self: Postmodern studies on narcissism, schizophrenia, and depression*. New York: New York University Press.

Lipka, R. P., & Brinthaupt, T. M. (Eds.). (1992). *Self-perspectives across the life span*. Albany, NY: State University of New York Press.

Rosen, G. M. (1987). Self-help treatment books and the commercialization of of psychotherapy. *American Psychologist, 42:*46–51.

Starker, S. (1989). *Oracle at the supermarket: The American preoccupation with self-help books*. New Brunswick, NJ: Transaction Books.

Zilbergeld, B. (1983). *The shrinking of America: Myths of psychological change*. Boston, MA: Little, Brown.

PART 1

Philosophies of Changing the Self

CHAPTER 1

Changes in the Self from a Developmental/Psychosocial Perspective

Don Hamachek

Mental health specialists, because they wish to enhance their effectiveness as change agents, have always had a vested interest in understanding personality development. One way of working toward this goal is through a deeper understanding of the behavioral changes that occur in the self as it evolves along a continuum of differential growth stages and shifting cultural expectations. The purpose of this chapter is to present an outline for doing this with a self-concept frame of reference that incorporates the basic tenets of psychosocial theory. I am drawn to Erikson's psychosocial theory because it not only clearly defines a developmental continuum from birth to the later years but is also broad enough to allow for the incorporation of other views that can further our understanding and interpretation of the self's growth and change over time.

In keeping with this volume's focus on strategies for changing the self, I will attempt to accomplish four objectives in this chapter: (a) to examine briefly the interrelatedness of self, self-concept, and self-esteem (to help us see how changes in one may affect the other two); (b) to present a schematic model for how the self develops (which may help us to see better how to change it); (c) to review the major tenets and the eight major stages of psychosocial theory (to provide a view of the foundation on which one's ego and sense of self are constructed), and (d) to examine the implications of the foregoing discussion in terms of approaches to changing the self.

INTERRELATEDNESS OF SELF, SELF-CONCEPT, AND SELF-ESTEEM

Each of these terms is an outgrowth of a self-concept frame of reference within personality theory, a view that begins with the idea that each person has (a) a *self* (a sense of personal existence), (b) a *self-concept* (an idea of personal identity), (c) a certain level of *self-esteem* (feelings of personal worth), and (d) an *ego* (a barometer of psychological and emotional strength).

As the self has evolved in psychological literature, it has come to have two distinct meanings, self-as-doer and self-as-object, both first introduced by William James (1890) in his seminal chapter "The Consciousness of Self." These meanings evolved into the now familiar *I-me* dichotomy, in which the total self (or person) is differentiated into two "discriminated aspects": (a) the self as the "doer" (the self whose functions include perceiving, performing, thinking, and remembering, through which it is the "knower," the "I"), and (b) the self as object (the self that has certain physical, social, emotional, and intellectual attributes through which it becomes the "known," the "me"). Thus, such statements as "I am hungry," "I am disappointed in myself," or "I am not as skilled as you" express a curious duality. One can stand outside the self and look at it as an object, describe it, evaluate it, respond to it, but the object one perceives, evaluates, and responds to is one's own self. The "I" comes to know the "me."

It is this capacity for self-consciousness, this ability to look at the self from the outside as an object, that enables one to develop one's self-concept. Basically, a self-concept is that particular cluster of ideas and attitudes we have about ourselves at any given moment. It is the organized cognitive structure we have of ourselves derived from the sum of all our experiences. From these experiences grow the ideas (concepts) of the kind of person we see ourselves as being, which constitutes our own private mental image of ourselves, a collection of beliefs about the kind of person we are (Hamachek, 1992).

Whereas self-concept is an indicator of what people *think* about themselves (the cognitive component of the self), self-esteem is the emotional barometer of how people *feel* about themselves (the affective component of the self). Self-esteem is a reflection of how one evaluates the self, which Coopersmith (1967) referred to as "an attitude of approval or disapproval, and indicates the extent to which an individual believes himself to be capable, significant, successful, and worthy" (p. 4).

The terms *ego* and *self* are frequently used interchangeably, each a synonym for the other. These terms are difficult to separate from each other because the ego is actually part of the self. In psychoanalytic theory, for example, the self has generally been described as the more inclusive construct, with the ego, superego, and id being component parts. In its evolution, what we refer to as "ego" seems to have reference to the strength and resiliency of our self, self-concept, and self-esteem. For example, we cannot see another person's self-concept—that is private—but we can see expressions of that self-concept in behavior, which can be interpreted as reflections of an individual's overall personal strength and resiliency. A person might say, for example, "Joni has a strong ego; she can handle criticism" or "John has a fragile ego; he cracks easily under pressure." That person would probably not say, "Joni has a strong self" or "John has a fragile self." The self is something the other person already has; the ego is something added to it, usually by way of assessment of strength or weakness.

The term *ego qualities,* as it will be used in this chapter, refers to the particular polarities associated with each of Erikson's eight stages, such as trust/mistrust, initiative/guilt, intimacy/isolation, and so forth. Each of these ego qualities can be associated with characteristic behaviors and attitudes, which we will examine later.

THE SELF'S DEVELOPMENT

Figure 1.1 is a schematic overview of the self's development. Basically, it is an effort to summarize and visually reduce an enormously long and complex process to its simplest and most basic components. I have taken some of the most frequently mentioned and commonly discussed aspects of the self and attempted to show how they relate and interconnect along a developmental continuum.

As shown in Figure 1.1, the beginnings of the self occur through four primary input channels: auditory cues, physical sensations, body image cues, and personal memories. These input channels provide the emotional medium that allows the self to grow along the lines of Cooley's (1902) "looking-glass self," within the framework of Mead's (1934) "socially formed self," and in

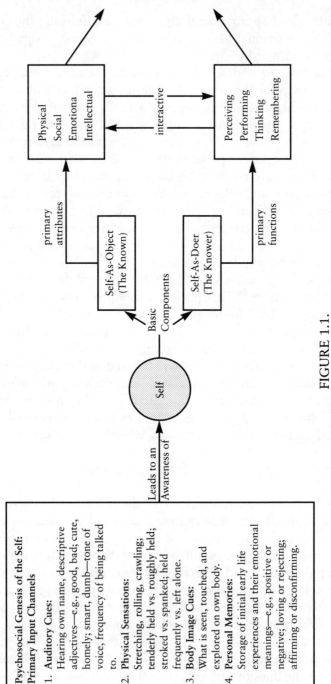

FIGURE 1.1.

Schematic overview of the self's development

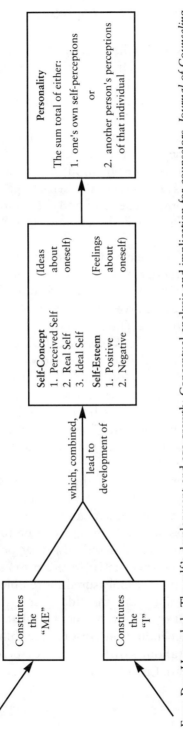

From Don Hamachek, The self's development and ego growth: Conceptual analysis and implication for counselors, *Journal of Counseling and Development,* 64(1985):136–142. Copyright ACDA. Reprinted with permission. No further reproduction authorized without written permission of American Counseling Association.

the context of Sullivan's (1947) interpersonal framework of "reflected appraisals."

Self-awareness develops when young children begin to recognize the distinction between self and not-self, between their bodies and the remainder of their visible environment. For example, Mahler's (1979) clinical observations suggest that infants initially go through a stage of differentiation, when they slowly separate (differentiate) themselves from parents, and then gradually move through the final phase of separation, roughly between 24 and 30 months of age, when a "consolidation of individuality" usually occurs. Self-awareness and eventually self-image are very much associated with body image cues and body sensations, as was documented carefully by Fisher and Cleveland (1968) and L'Ecuyer (1992).

When personal experience widens and intellectual functioning expands, the self differentiates further as one gains increased abilities both to understand the outside world more fully (to be the "knower" or "doer") and to see oneself as an object in the outside world (to be the "known"). The self-as-object involves attributes that are physical (how one looks), social (how one relates), emotional (how one feels), and intellectual (how one thinks). These attributes interact with that aspect of the self that comes to know through its perceiving, performing, thinking, and remembering functions. The component of the self that is the knower constitutes the "I" or the "agent of experience," and that dimension of the self that is the known constitutes the "me" or "the content of experience."

The interactive combination of these attributes and functions leads to the development of two core ingredients of the self, namely, self-concept (ideas about oneself) and self-esteem (feelings and evaluations about oneself). Self-concept can be more specifically differentiated into the perceived self (the way people see themselves) and into what Horney (1950) referred to as the "real" self (the way a person really is, as measured more objectively through tests or clinical assessments) and the "ideal" self (the way a person would like to be). Out of all of this emerges what might be called personality, which, depending on who is describing it, can be either the sum total of (a) one's own internal self-perceptions, or (b) another person's external perceptions of that individual.

CONSIDERING THE SELF'S DEVELOPMENT WHEN
PLANNING CHANGE STRATEGIES

As seen in Figure 1.1, the self is more than just a mass of amorphous psychological potential. Rather, it can be conceptualized as having specific interactive attributes and functions that are observable, measurable components of one's being. An awareness of how this interactive machinery works can be helpful to mental health workers as they develop therapeutic strategies for helping people change their behaviors, their views of themselves, or both.

Included in every mental health worker's training is the basic idea of understanding the "whole" person, a view they are encouraged to keep in mind when planning treatment or intervention strategies. By operating within a psychological framework that enables them to see that the self has certain specific functions and attributes, mental health personnel can be taught that the self is made up of certain interactive components, which, when conceptualized as part of a larger picture, allow one to see not only the "whole" person more clearly, but the parts that constitute the whole.

Not only does the self have certain interactive functions and attributes, but it is constantly developing and changing. It keeps developing in terms of its experience and knowledge. And it changes not so much in terms of its overall color as in its hue. The basic self remains more or less the same, but its expression may be modified.

Conceptualizing the self in this manner can be helpful in two ways. One, it alerts us to the possibility that problems experienced in one of the components of the self may be triggered by unresolved issues in the other. As an illustration, it may be that a student falling below academic expectations is doing so not because of deficits in performing, thinking, or remembering (primary functions of the self-as-doer), but because of concerns related to self-doubts related to intellectual ability (an attribute of the self-as-object). Thus, counselors would not only want to help students like this to develop more effective study skills, but they would also want to find ways to help those students develop a more realistic and positive self-concept. The problem may not be a lack of ability, but in the belief *about* ability.

Secondly, conceptualizing the self as a system of interacting functions and attributes enables one to see that the self keeps growing, changing, and developing in response to different life stages, each of which has its own challenges, expectations, and conflicts. A way of thinking about these life stages is to do so within the developmental framework of psychosocial theory.

PSYCHOSOCIAL THEORY AS A FRAMEWORK
FOR UNDERSTANDING CHANGES IN THE SELF

Because Erikson's (1963, 1982) psychosocial theory acknowledges changes in both the expression and capacity for physical, social, emotional, and intellectual functioning along a continuum of behavioral possibilities, it provides a helpful frame of reference for understanding psychological growth at any given point in time. Also, because the theory is built around the idea that emotional-social growth progresses through different stages, each with its own unique ego accomplishments, it provides a natural conceptual framework for helping to explain and understand the self's development further.

Although Erikson's ideas build solidly on Freudian analytic theory, an important departure is that it is the ego, not the id, that is the life force of human development. Consistent with this departure is the emphasis on the continuity of interpersonal experience involving functions of the ego that go beyond those of Freud's sexual (libidinal) developmental progression. According to Erikson (1963, 1982), the ego, the affective components of life, and the innate, inner self, rather than unconsciously motivated libidinal strivings, relate to society. In reinforcing this idea, psychosocial theory stresses the interlinkage of biological, psychological, and social development by giving equal weight to each of these dimensions and by accenting their shared participation in the development of an individual.

Three basic contributions to the study of the human ego have been provided by Erikson (1963). First, psychosocial stages of ego development, in which individuals have to establish new, basic orientations to themselves and their social world, exist side by side with the psychosexual stages described by Freud (the oral, anal, phallic, genital, Oedipal, and pubertal). Second, personality development continues throughout the entire life cycle. Finally, each stage of development has positive as well as negative ego qualities.

PSYCHOSOCIAL STAGES AS RELATED TO THE SELF'S DEVELOPMENT AND EGO GROWTH

According to Erikson (1963, 1980, 1982), each individual passes through a succession of eight psychosocial stages, beginning at birth and ending in the retirement years. Five of those stages are experienced during the first twenty years of life and the remaining three during adulthood. The eight psychosocial stages and the approximate time span usually associated with each are as follows:

1. Trust versus mistrust (birth to 18 months)
2. Autonomy versus shame and doubt (18 months to 3 years)
3. Initiative versus guilt (3 to 6 years)
4. Industry versus inferiority (6 to 12 years)
5. Identity versus identity confusion (12 to 20 years)
6. Intimacy versus isolation (20 to 35 years)
7. Generativity versus self-absorption (35 years to retirement)
8. Integrity versus despair (retirement years)

Erikson observed that each state represents a "psychosocial crisis" or turning point when both potential and vulnerability are greatly increased, a time when things may go either well or not well depending on one's life experiences. In all people, there is probably a certain ratio between the positive and negative qualities associated with each state. A more positive ratio will help them in coping with later crises.

The idea of acquiring a healthy ratio between positive and negative ego qualities is an important one; sometimes, however, the focus is almost entirely on the positive outcomes of each psychosocial stage. According to Erikson (Evans, 1981):

> When these stages are quoted, people often take away mistrust and doubt and shame and all of these not so nice, "negative" things and try to make an Eriksonian achievement scale out of it all, according to which in the first stage trust is "achieved." Actually, a certain ratio of trust and mistrust in our basic social attitude is the critical factor. When we enter a situation, we must

be able to differentiate how much we can trust and how much we must mistrust, and I use mistrust in the sense of a readiness for danger and an anticipation of discomfort. (p. 15)

It is desirable that there be more positive ego qualities than negative ego qualities. However, if positive ego qualities are all that are considered when assessing the overall health of the self's development, one could easily overlook the possible value to be found in the negative ego qualities associated with each stage. For example, a certain amount of mistrust helps people to be less gullible and more cautious (stage 1); a certain readiness to feel shame and doubt helps people behave appropriately and pursue assertively goals that are important to them (stage 2); the capacity to feel guilt helps people make correct moral judgments and behave responsibly (stage 3); experiencing feelings of inferiority from time to time helps people stay motivated to do their best (stage 4); and a certain degree of identity confusion helps people sharpen their self-perceptions and make new adjustments in light of new experiences and changing life circumstances (stage 5). Feelings of isolation may be the very thing that motivates certain people to reach out to others and expand their social boundaries (stage 6); a certain amount of self-absorption from time to time may be just what people need in order to stay in touch with their inner lives so as not be swept away by outside demands (stage 7); and feelings of despair now and then may help people remain vigilant to avenues they can take to retain their sense of productiveness and integrity (stage 8).

Behavioral Expression Tables Associated with Each Psychosocial Stage

The self's development can be either enhanced or inhibited during any of the psychosocial stages, depending on the particular constellation of one's life experiences. We do not always know what those experiences have been, but we can see some of the behavioral consequences of those experiences once we know what to look for.

Tables 1.1 to 1.8 depict some of the characteristic behaviors and implicit attitudes that can be logically and clinically deduced from Erikson's (1950, 1959, 1963, 1968, 1980, 1982; Erikson, Erikson, & Kivnick, 1986; Evans, 1981; Hall, 1987) discussions of the psychodynamics associated with each of the eight stages. Each table represents an effort to extract from Erikson's formulations some practical clinical meanings that mental health workers can use to evaluate clients' self-concept and ego growth along a developmental continuum. The behaviors and implicit attitudes in the left column of each table reflect some of the positive outcomes of the ego resolutions associated with each stage, and those in the right column, some of the less healthy possibilities.

The validity of the eight behavioral expression tables can be argued on the basis of their "closeness of fit" with Erikson's own descriptive and clinical analyses of the behaviors associated with each of the psychosocial stages. I endeavored to express the central polarities of each stage (such as trust versus mistrust, industry versus inferiority) as ten observable behaviors and three implicit attitudes.

Rather than viewing the behavioral expression tables as containing a series of positive and negative characteristics associated with the ego polarities of each stage, I think it would be most helpful (and accurate) to see them as reflecting a *continuum* of behavioral possibilities, as opposed to either-or expressions. For example, there are not many people who have *either* a capacity for intimacy *or* feelings of isolation (Table 1.6); most people tend to express some blend of each.

Furthermore, it is not my intent to convey the idea that only those behaviors associated with the positive ego qualities on the left side of each table can lead to healthy psychological development. As mentioned earlier, it is a matter of balance.

I do not believe that any single statement on any of the eight behavioral expression tables is by itself a reliable index of the directions of psychological growth of particular individuals. However, when a person reflects three, four, or more behaviors resembling those suggested in a given table, then there is reason to suspect that he or she might be displaying expressions of positive or negative ego development, as the case may be.

Each stage builds on the psychological outcomes of the previous stage(s), although not according to a rigid timetable. For example, when development proceeds normally, with no outstanding traumatic events to derail its progress, the attitude of basic trust that develops during stage 1 helps children feel safe enough to expand the range and diversity of their experiences and, in the process, develop an attitude of autonomy in stage 2. Trusting their environment and feeling the necessary autonomy to move freely in

it, children reinforce the attitude of initiative associated with stage
3. This freedom encourages the industry of stage 4, an attitude that
emerges as children learn to control their lively imaginations and
apply themselves to formal education. With the basic groundwork
laid (basic trust, autonomy, initiative, and industry), young people
are ready for the monumental challenges of stage 5—establishing
an identity, a sense of who they are as individuals.

How the final three stages unfold in one's life depends to some
extent on how the ego qualities of the previous stages have evolved
and developed. If, for example, there were breakdowns during any
of the first five stages, in particular, then we might expect that the
individuals involved may have acquired a higher ratio of any one or
more negative ego qualities, such as mistrust, shame and doubt,
guilt, inferiority, or identity confusion, which may predispose them
to problems in their adult lives. Erikson underscored the crucial
importance of the early stages by giving more painstaking attention to stage 1—trust versus mistrust—and stage 5—identity versus identity confusion—than to the other six stages combined.

With Erikson's discussions and descriptions of each stage as a
frame of reference, I addressed myself to two basic questions: (a)
What behaviors would one likely see among people with high trust
or low trust, or with a sense of autonomy or shame and guilt, and
so on through each of the eight stages? (b) What implicit undercurrent attitudes would one likely see reflected in people in each polarity of each stage? Although I do not believe that these are the
only polarities of behaviors and attitudes that could be associated
with each stage, I do believe that they are representative of and
consistent with the basic psychodynamic themes projected in Erikson's thinking.

These basic themes to which I am referring are illustrated in a
few brief examples of how Erikson himself described the central
issues in each of the eight stages. Regarding the stage 1 theme of
trust versus mistrust (Table 1.1), Erikson (1980) observed that "in
adults the impairment of basic trust is expressed as *basic mistrust.*
It characterizes individuals who withdraw into themselves in particular ways when at odds with themselves and with others" (p.
58). The capacity to trust is basic to the development of positive
ego qualities in subsequent stages. An emotionally consistent environment allows children to grow up and to grow away because

they have learned from an early age that the world around them and the people in it can generally be counted on—trusted.

In regard to the stage 2 theme of *autonomy versus shame and doubt* (Table 1.2), Erikson (1980) noted that this is "the stage for experimentation with two simultaneous sets of social modalities— holding on and letting go" (p. 72). Also, this stage "can be decisive for the ratio between . . . the freedom of self-expression and its suppression. From a sense of self-control without loss of self-esteem comes a lasting sense of autonomy and pride; from a sense of . . . loss of self-control, and of parental over-control comes a lasting sense of doubt and shame" (pp. 70–71). Thus autonomy is accompanied by feelings of confidence, positive self-esteem, and a capacity for independent thinking, whereas feelings of doubt and shame tend to lead to low self-esteem and doubts about one's abilities and personal worth.

The theme of stage 3 is *initiative versus guilt* (Table 1.3), about which Erikson (1980) observed, "It is at this stage . . . that the great governor of initiative, namely, conscience, becomes firmly established. . . . The consequences of guilt aroused at this stage . . . keeps an individual from living up to his inner capacities. . . . Only a combination of early prevention and alleviation of hatred and guilt in the growing being . . . permits a peaceful cultivation of initiative, a truly free sense of enterprise" (pp. 84–86). Feelings of initiative help one to reach out, take risks, and explore potential for growth. Guilt tends to keep a person in one place, fearful of making mistakes.

The theme of stage 4, revolving around the idea of *industry versus inferiority* (Table 1.4), is a time when, according to Erikson (1980), all children "sooner or later become dissatisfied and disgruntled without a sense of being useful, without a sense of being able to make things and make them well and even perfectly; this is what I call the sense of industry. . . . [The child] now learns to win recognition by producing things" (p. 91). Erikson also noted that "there is an enormous curiosity during this stage of life—a wish to learn, a wish to know" (Evans, 1981, p. 26). Whereas feelings of initiative have to do with planning and getting started, a sense of industry has more to do with finishing and going on for more. The inferiority side of this continuum reflects not only one's fear of making mistakes, but the deeper fear of *being* a mistake.

TABLE 1.1
Behavioral Expressions of a Sense of Trust and Mistrust—Stage 1

Characteristic Behaviors of People Who Have a High Sense of Basic Trust	Characteristic Behaviors of People Who Have a Low Sense of Basic Trust
1. They are able to ask others for help or emotional support without overdoing it.	1. They tend to have trouble asking others for help or emotional support.
2. They are inclined to believe that others will come through for them, unless there is good reason not to believe that.	2. They are inclined to believe that others will not come through for them, even when there is no reason to believe that.
3. They start with the assumption that people are generally good.	3. They start with the assumption that people are generally bad or evil.
4. They tend to focus on the positive aspects of others' behavior.	4. They tend to focus on the negative aspects of others' behavior.
5. They tend to behave in a relatively disclosing and open manner when around others.	5. They tend to behave in a relatively guarded and closed manner when around others.
6. They find it relatively easy to receive (favors, compliments, gifts, etc.) from other people, but prefer a balance of giving and receiving.	6. They find it rather difficult to receive (favors, compliments, gifts, etc.) from other people, and find it easier to be the giver than the taker.

7. They have no trouble sharing their possessions, the "things" in their lives with other people.
8. They are not particularly fearful of disclosing themselves, even their more negative qualities, to other people.
9. They tend to have a generally optimistic worldview without being Pollyannaish or unrealistic about it.
10. They are inclined to believe that other people know what is best for themselves, even though they may privately feel differently about others' choices.

Implicit Attitude:

1. You're O.K.
2. Life is generally fair and good to me.
3. I'm willing to share what I have.

7. They have problems sharing their possessions, the "things" in their lives with other people.
8. They are very hesitant about disclosing themselves, particularly their negative qualities, to other people.
9. They tend to have a generally pessimistic worldview even when things are going well and sometimes *particularly* when things are going well.
10. They are inclined to believe that other people usually do not know what is best for themselves, and prefer to tell others what to do.

Implicit Attitude:

1. You're not O.K.
2. Life is generally unfair and unkind to me.
3. I'm not willing to share what I have.

Source: Don Hamachek, Evaluating self-concept and ego development within Erikson's psychosocial framework, *Journal of Counseling and Development*, 66(1988): 354–360.
Source: Don Hamachek, Evaluating self-concept and ego status in Erikson's last three psychosocial stages, *Journal of Counseling and Development*, 68(1990): 136–142. (©) ACA. Table reprinted with permission. No further reproduction authorized without written permission of American Counseling Association.

TABLE 1.2

Behavioral Expressions of a Sense of Autonomy and Shame and Doubt—Stage 2

Characteristic Behaviors of People Who Have a Sense of Autonomy	*Characteristic Behaviors of People Who Have a Sense of Shame and Doubt*
1. They like to make their own decisions, particularly about manners important to them.	1. They prefer being told what to do rather than make their own decisions.
2. They are able to say no to requests made of them without feeling guilty.	2. They have problems saying no to requests made of them.
3. They are inclined to express themselves in terms of what they "will" do or "want" to do.	3. They are inclined to express themselves in terms of what they "should" do or "ought" to do.
4. They tend to resist being dominated by people wanting to control them.	4. They tend to allow themselves to be dominated by others, even though they may not like it.
5. They are able to work well by themselves or with others, depending on the situation.	5. They are not comfortable working by themselves, particularly when they know work will be judged or evaluated.
6. They are inclined to get on with what needs to be done and remain task-persistent until finished.	6. They have trouble getting started with what needs to be done: procrastination may be a key feature of personality.

7. They can work easily with either open-ended or structured work assignments, although they may prefer more open-endedness.
8. They are able to listen to their own inner feelings when deciding what is right or wrong, appropriate or inappropriate.
9. They tend to feel relatively un-self-conscious and at ease when in group situations.
10. They tend to want a certain amount of order and organization in their lives to reinforce feelings of personal control and self-approval.

Implicit Attitude:

1. I think I can do it.
2. This is what needs to be done.
3. I have something of value to offer.

7. They have problems working with open-ended work assignments, preferring more structure and direction.
8. They have difficulty listening to their own inner feelings when deciding what is right or wrong, appropriate or inappropriate.
9. They tend to feel uneasy and self-conscious, even embarrassed, when in group situations.
10. They tend to want things "just so" as one way of avoiding others' disapproval and criticism.

Implicit Attitude:

1. I don't think I can do it.
2. Tell me what needs to be done.
3. I have little of value to offer.

Source: Don Hamachek, Evaluating self-concept and ego development within Erikson's psychosocial framework, *Journal of Counseling and Development,* 66(1988): 354–360.
Source: Don Hamachek, Evaluating self-concept and ego status in Erikson's last three psychosocial stages, *Journal of Counseling and Development,* 68(1990): 136–142. (©) ACA. Table reprinted with permission. No further reproduction authorized without written permission of American Counseling Association.

TABLE 1.3

Behavioral Expressions of a Sense of Initiative and Guilt—Stage 3

Characteristic Behaviors of People Who Have a Sense of Initiative	Characteristic Behaviors of People Who Have a Sense of Guilt
1. They prefer to get on with what needs to be done to complete the task at hand.	1. They tend to postpone, put off, put aside, and generally procrastinate starting.
2. They like accepting new challenges now and then.	2. They are inclined to resist new challenges.
3. They tend to be fast self-starters.	3. They tend to be slow self-starters.
4. They tend to be effective leaders when in that position.	4. They tend to be ineffective leaders when in that position.
5. They tend to set goals and then set out to accomplish them.	5. They may set goals but have problems getting them accomplished.
6. They tend to have high energy levels.	6. They tend to have low energy levels.
7. They have a strong sense of personal adequacy.	7. They have a weak sense of personal adequacy.

8. They seem to enjoy "making things happen."	8. They prefer to remain in the background, preferring not to stir things up.
9. They are able to emotionally appreciate the idea that initiative begins and ends with the person, not the production it generates.	9. They may try to outrun their guilt with a tireless show of accomplishment, believing that efficient production may compensate for being a deficient person.
10. They have a balanced sense of right and wrong without being overly moralistic.	10. They tend to focus moralistically on those things in life that are "wrong."
Implicit Attitude:	Implicit Attitude:
1. I will start now.	1. I will start tomorrow.
2. I enjoy new challenges.	2. I prefer sticking with what I know.
3. This is what needs to be done and I will do it.	3. This is what needs to be done, but who will do it?

Source: Don Hamachek, Evaluating self-concept and ego development within Erikson's psychosocial framework, *Journal of Counseling and Development,* 66(1988): 354–360.
Source: Don Hamachek, Evaluating self-concept and ego status in Erikson's last three psychosocial stages, *Journal of Counseling and Development,* 68(1990): 136–142. (©) ACA. Table reprinted with permission. No further reproduction authorized without written permission of American Counseling Association.

TABLE 1.4

Behavioral Expressions of a Sense of Industry and Inferiority—Stage 4

Characteristic Behaviors of People Who Have a Sense of Industry	Characteristic Behaviors of People Who Have a Sense of Inferiority
1. They enjoy learning about new things and ideas.	1. They do not particularly enjoy learning about new things and ideas.
2. They reflect a healthy balance between doing what they *have* to do and what they *like* to do.	2. They tend to concentrate mostly on what they believe they *have* to do, neglecting what they *like* to do.
3. They reflect strong curiosities about how and why things work the way they do.	3. They are not terribly curious about why and how things work.
4. They enjoy experimenting with new combinations, new ideas, and arriving at new syntheses.	4. They prefer staying with what is known; new ways do not attract them so much as do proven ways.
5. They are excited by the idea of being producers.	5. They tend to be threatened, even guilty, about the idea of being producers.

6. They like the recognition that producing things brings, which reinforces sense of industry.
7. They develop a habit of work completion through steady attention and persevering diligence.
8. They have a sense of pride in doing at least one thing well.
9. They take criticism well and use it to improve their performance.
10. They tend to have a strong sense of persistence.

Implicit Attitude:

1. I'm a pretty good learner.
2. Being a producer excites me.
3. I'll work hard to succeed.

6. They would like the recognition that production brings, but sense of inferiority stands in the way.
7. They develop a habit of work delay by ongoing procrastinations.
8. They have problems taking pride in their work, believing it is not worth it.
9. They take criticism poorly and use it as a reason to stop trying.
10. They tend to have a weak sense of persistence.

Implicit Attitude:

1. I'm not a very good learner.
2. Being a producer frightens me.
3. I'll work hard to avoid failing.

Source: Don Hamachek, Evaluating self-concept and ego development within Erikson's psychosocial framework, *Journal of Counseling and Development*, 66(1988): 354–360.
Source: Don Hamachek, Evaluating self-concept and ego status in Erikson's last three psychosocial stages, *Journal of Counseling and Development*, 68(1990): 136–142. (©) ACA. Table reprinted with permission. No further reproduction authorized without written permission of American Counseling Association.

The theme of stage 5, *identity versus identity confusion* (Table 1.5), is an especially important one for Erikson. In his words, "The ego values accrued in childhood culminate in what I have called a sense of ego identity. [This] is the accrued confidence that one's ability to maintain inner sameness and continuity (one's ego in the psychological sense) is matched by the sameness and continuity of one's meaning for others. Thus, self-esteem, confirmed at the end of each major crisis, grows to be the conviction that one is . . . developing a defined personality within a social reality that one understands" (Erikson, 1980, pp. 94–95). A sense of identity is an outgrowth of the first four psychosocial stages, an outcome that enables one to consolidate a self-concept, a sense of self that fits. Identity confusion is more likely to be the case with people whose earlier developmental stages may have been marked by excessive negative ego resolutions, thereby causing them to feel less optimistic about their chances in life and less certain about who they are and what they can do.

Stage 6, *intimacy versus isolation* (Table 1.6), represents the first of the three psychosocial stages Erikson devoted to adulthood. Although Erikson's views about adult development were somewhat similar to those of other adult development theorists, in terms of the general outcomes of each stage, he showed the greatest difference—the most uniqueness, I would say—in his conception of young adulthood. Whereas theorists like Gould (1978) focused on young adults' roles and responsibilities, Levinson (1978) on exploring possibilities for adult living and developing a stable life structure, and Vaillant (1977) on career consolidation, Erikson concentrated on interpersonal/intrapsychic issues like intimacy and feelings of isolation. Thus Erikson's discussions about this stage tended to focus on the importance of people fusing, bonding, coming together, forming relationships.

Erikson (1963) was quite specific about possible consequences when the capacity for intimacy fails to develop: "The avoidance of such experiences because of a fear of ego loss may lead to a deep sense of isolation and consequent self-absorption. . . . The danger of this stage is that intimate, competitive, and combative relations are experienced with and against the self same people" (p. 264). The overall psychological significance of this stage is that it is a time when people can expand their concept of self to include others, when they can take larger risks in work, friendship, and love relationships, when they are able to perceive and practice mutuality in relationships, and when, in a broader sense, they develop their capacities to love.

The psychosocial crisis of stage 7, *generativity versus stagnation* (Table 1.7) occurs somewhere between 30 to 65. In Erikson's words (Evans, 1981), generativity occurs when

> one begins to take one's place in society, and to help in the development and perfection of whatever it produces. And one takes responsibility for that. I know that generativity is not an elegant word, but it means to generate in the most inclusive sense. . . . I use the word "generativity" because I mean everything that is generated from generation to generation: children, products, ideas and works of art. (p. 51)

Thus generativity is a broadly conceived ego quality that has the potential for showing its generative possibilities in the production of outcomes as specific as children, or in expressions as abstract as the creation of ideas and art. Although Erikson (1963) believed that there is an instinctual wish to have children, particularly among women, he also recognized that "the mere fact of having or even wanting children does not 'achieve' generativity" (p. 267). Reflecting his early psychoanalytic training, he believed that it is possible to sublimate one's procreative drive into many healthy channels. For example, during an interview with Erikson, Hall (1987) observed that she could see how childless artists or writers or teachers could sublimate generativity in their work, but, she wondered, "How does a plumber do it?" Erikson reflected the breadth of the possibilities for generativity in his reply: "Don't underestimate the generative contributions of a good plumber. Also, he or she may be a church member who can do something for all the children in his community. And he or she is still a voter" (p. 134).

However it is expressed, generativity is a positive ego quality of middle adulthood that grows out of the strengths of earlier periods of development: hope, will, purpose, competence, loyalty, and love. The basic strength of stage 7 is *care,* a word Erikson (Evans, 1981) used to express the ideal that it is during this stage that one develops the capacity to care "in a sense that includes 'to care to do' something, to 'care for' somebody or something, 'to take care of' that which needs protection and attention, and 'to take care not to' do something destructive" (p. 53).

TABLE 1.5

Behavioral Expressions of a Sense of Identity and Identity Confusion—Stage 5

Characteristic Behaviors of People Who Have a Sense of Identity	*Characteristic Behaviors of People Who Have a Sense of Identity Confusion*
1. They have a stable self-concept that does not easily change.	1. They tend to have an unstable self-concept marked by ups and downs.
2. They are able to combine short-term goals with long-range plans.	2. They tend to set short-term goals, but have trouble establishing long-range plans.
3. They are less susceptible to the shifting whims of peer pressure influences.	3. They are more susceptible to the shifting whims of peer pressure influences.
4. They tend to have reasonably high levels of self-acceptance.	4. They tend to have rather low levels of self-acceptance.
5. They are able to make decisions without undue wavering and indecisiveness.	5. They are apt to have trouble making decisions, fearing that they will be wrong.

6. They tend to be optimistic about themselves, others, and life generally.	6. They tend to have a somewhat cynical attitude about themselves, others, and life generally.
7. They tend to believe that they are responsible for what happens to them, good or bad.	7. They tend to believe that what happens to them is largely out of their hands, a matter of fate or breaks.
8. They are able to seek self-acceptance directly by being their own person.	8. They are inclined to seek self-acceptance indirectly by being what they believe others want them to be.
9. They are able to be physically and emotionally close to another person without fearing a loss of self.	9. They are inclined to have trouble being physically and emotionally close to another person without being either too dependent or too separate.
10. They tend to be cognitively flexible; their sense of self does not depend on being "right."	10. They tend to be cognitively inflexible; their sense of self resides heavily on being "right."
Implicit Attitude:	*Implicit Attitude*
1. I am this kind of person	1. I am not sure who I am as a person.
2. I'm not perfect, but I'm still O.K.	2. I should be much better/more than I am.
3. I can accept your shortcomings because I can accept my own.	3. I have trouble accepting your shortcomings just as I have trouble accepting my own.

Source: Don Hamachek, Evaluating self-concept and ego development within Erikson's psychosocial framework, *Journal of Counseling and Development,* 66(1988): 354–360.
Source: Don Hamachek, Evaluating self-concept and ego status in Erikson's last three psychosocial stages, *Journal of Counseling and Development,* 68(1990): 136–142. (©) ACA. Table reprinted with permission. No further reproduction authorized without written permission of American Counseling Association.

TABLE 1.6
Behavioral Expressions of a Sense of Intimacy and Isolation—Stage 6

Characteristic Behaviors of People Who Have a Sense of Intimacy	*Characteristic Behaviors of People Who Have a Sense of Isolation*
1. They have been able to establish a firm sense of their own identity.	1. They have not been able to establish a firm sense of their own identity.
2. They tend to be tolerant and accepting of the differences perceived in other people.	2. They tend not to be particularaly tolerant or accepting of differences perceived in other people.
3. They are willing and able to trust others and themselves in the relationships they form.	3. They are not particularly willing to trust either themselves or others in the relationships they form.
4. They are able to form close emotional bonds without fearing the loss of their own identity.	4. They are hesitant to form close emotional bonds because of fear of losing self-identity.
5. They tend to develop cooperative, affiliative relationships with others.	5. They tend to develop competitive relationships with others, making cooperative efforts more difficult.

6. They find satisfaction in their affiliation with others but can comfortably isolate themselves and be alone when they choose.	6. They tend to prefer more separation from others; they feel uncomfortable when affiliations with others are too close.
7. They are willing and able to commit themselves to relationships that demand sacrifice and compromise.	7. They have difficulty committing to relationships that may demand sacrifice and compromise.
8. They are inclined to perceive relationships as something one gives to.	8. They are inclined to perceive relationships as something one takes from.
9. They tend to perceive sex as a means of both achieving physical closeness and expressing love; partner is seen as a person.	9. They tend to perceive sex as a means of achieving physical satisfaction but not necessarily expressing love; partner is seen more as an object.
10. They are able to express their caring feelings in a variety of ways and to say the words "I love you" without fear.	10. They have difficulty expressing their caring feelings for others and find the words "I love you" hard to verbalize.

Implicit Attitude	Implicit Attitude
1. I'm okay and others are, too.	1. I'm okay, but others are not okay.
2. Others can generally be trusted.	2. Others cannot generally be trusted.
3. Life can be difficult, but through mutual interdependence we can make it.	3. Life can be difficult, and people have to learn to take care of themselves.

Source: Don Hamachek, Evaluating self-concept and ego status in Erikson's last three psychosocial stages, *Journal of Counseling and Development,* 68(1990): 136–142. © ACA. Table reprinted with permission. No further reproduction authorized without written permission of American Counseling Association.

TABLE 1.7

Behavioral Expressions of a Sense of Generativity and Stagnation—Stage 7

Characteristic Behaviors of People Who Have a Sense of Generativity	Characteristic Behaviors of People Who Have a Sense of Stagnation
1. They feel personally concerned about others, their immediate family, which includes future generations and the nature of the world in which those generations will live.	1. They are concerned primarily with themselves and show little interest in future generations.
2. They reflect varying degrees of involvement with enhancing the welfare of young people and making the world a better place for them to live and work.	2. They show little by way of involvement with the welfare of young people and helping to make the world a better place to live and work.
3. They have an interest in producing and caring for children of their own.	3. They have little interest in producing or caring for children of their own.
4. They reflect a parental kind of concern for the children of others.	4. They show little by way of a parental kind of concern for the children of others.
5. They tend to focus more on what they can *give* to others rather than on what they can *get*.	5. They tend to focus more on what thet can *get* from others rather than on what they can *give.*

6. They tend to be absorbed in a variety of activities outside of themselves.
7. They are interested in leading productive lives and in contributing to society.
8. They display other-centered values and attitudes.
9. They are interested in enhancing what is known, even if it means changing the status quo.
10. They feel a strong inclination to develop some unique talent or to express themselves creatively.

Implicit Attitude

1. What can I give to others?
2. Risks I would like to take include . . .
3. I enjoy being productive and creative.

6. They tend to be absorbed primarily in themselves and their own needs.
7. They are not particularly interested in being productive or in contributing to society.
8. They display self-centered values and attitudes.
9. They are interested in maintaining and preserving what is known in order to conserve the status quo.
10. They do not feel any particular inclination to develop some unique talent or to express themselves creatively.

Implicit Attitude

1. What can I get from others?
2. Risks I would like to avoid include . . .
3. I prefer routine and sameness.

Source: Don Hamachek, Evaluating self-concept and ego status in Erikson's last three psychosocial stages, *Journal of Counseling and Development,* 68(1990): 136–142. © ACA. Table reprinted with permission. No further reproduction authorized without written permission of American Counseling Association.

Stagnation, the negative ego quality of this stage, is what can happen to people whose efforts on behalf of generativity may be so minimal that they are not able to enjoy the fruits of either a productive life or the rewards of a caring one. In a broad sense, when people live in a generative mode, they tend to reflect behaviors that indicate caring and concern for others, along with an interest in living productive, contributory lives. When in a stagnation mode, however, people tend to show less by way of caring or concern for others and do not seem particularly interested in productivity and achievement.

Stage 8, when the psychosocial crisis is between *integrity versus despair* (Table 1.8), is a time when people begin to reflect back on their lives, review their ups and downs, and in the process consolidate their memories and experiences into a coherent package of beliefs about themselves and the world around them.

In Erikson's (1963) view, resolution on the side of integrity is achieved when there is "acceptance of one's one and only life cycle as something that had to be and that, by necessity, permitted no substitutions . . . " (p. 268). In a way, people inherit their integrity from themselves, in the sense that people's integrity reflects all that they have been and done and achieved. Integrity, it would seem, is an ego quality that allows one to express the feeling that, "Yes, I have made mistakes, but given the circumstances and who I was at the time, the mistakes were inevitable. I accept responsibility for them, along with the good things that have happened in my life."

Despair, as described by Erikson (1963), "is signified by fear of death . . . [and] expresses the feeling that the time is now short, too short for the attempt to start another life and to try out alternate roads to integrity" (pp. 268–269). Disgust sometimes hides a deeper despair, which may be reflected in a lack of patience for the struggles and failings of others. According to Erikson (1980, p. 105), people in this stage who feel this way may, at a deeper level, be reflecting their contempt for themselves.

The emerging ego strength of stage 8 is wisdom, which is described "as a kind of informed and detached concern with life itself in the face of death itself" (Erikson, 1982, p. 6). Although Erikson talked about the accumulation of wisdom as being both possible and necessary in one's later years, he cautioned people not to carry this ideal so far as to "make it too darn wizard like" (Hall, 1987, p. 135). Describing this stage in a later writing (Erikson,

Erikson, & Kivnick, 1986), Erikson and his colleagues observed that "it is through this last stage that the life cycle weaves back on itself in its entirety, ultimately integrating maturing forms of hope, will, purpose, competence, fidelity, love and care, with a comprehensive sense of wisdom" (pp. 55–56).

A Word of Caution

Erikson's speculations about the development of trust versus mistrust, autonomy versus shame and doubt, and so on through each of the eight psychosocial stages are similar to people's own experiences and correspond closely to their knowledge about human development. There is, however, a noteworthy caution about Erikson's psychosocial framework. Miller (1989), for example, suggests that "Erikson's theory is a loose connection of observations, empirical generalizations, and abstract theoretical claims [which] are laden with interpretations that are difficult to evaluate" (p. 193). This is a fair criticism, and thus it seems prudent to keep in mind that Tables 1.1 to 1.8 are highlighting expressions of behavior that are *likely* to be associated with the ego polarities of each stage. In addition, the behaviors and attitudes emphasized in these tables may *not* be crucial in the development of all people in the same way, and types of behavior mentioned may be of more or less significance, depending on the person and circumstances. Questions remain to be tested. For example, are the behaviors associated with the ego qualities of each polarity equally applicable to men and women? Are they fair to all groups? How seriously do ego impairments in the early stages interfere with healthy ego development in later stages? Can early ego development damage be undone or "fixed" later on?

IMPLICATIONS FOR ASSESSING AND CHANGING THE SELF

An awareness of the continuum of positive and negative ego qualities associated with the self's development at each psychosocial stage, as suggested in Tables 1.1 to 1.8, may be useful in helping mental health workers detect areas of strengths and weaknesses in one's self-concept in five ways: (a) as a way of helping them to recognize clusters of behavioral possibilities associated with the ego polarities of each stage, (b) as an aid in helping them frame the

TABLE 1.8

Behavioral Expressions of a Sense of Integrity and Despair—Stage 8

Characteristic Behaviors of People Who Have a Sense of Integrity	Characteristic Behaviors of People Who Have a Sense of Despair
1. They reflect many of the positive ego qualities associated with earlier stages, such as trust, autonomy, initiative, industry, and identity.	1. They reflect many of the negative qualities associated with earlier stages, such as mistrust, shame, guilt, inferiority, and identity confusion.
2. They believe that who they are and what they have become are largely the consequences of their own choices.	2. They are inclined to believe that who they are and what they have become is not something over which they have had much control.
3. They accept the idea that this is their one and only life and that what has happened to it is largely of their own doing.	3. They have trouble accepting the idea that this is their one and only life and that what has happened to it is largely of their own doing.
4. They accept death as an inevitable part of the life cycle.	4. They show signs of fearing death and do not accept it as part of the life cycle.
5. They are able to admit to themselves and others that, for the most part, they have no one but themselves to blame for whatever troubles or failures they have experienced.	5. They tend to blame others for whatever troubles or failures they have experienced.

6. They are ready and able to defend the dignity of their own life-styles against all physical economic threats, that is, they are not easily pushed around.
7. They are able to look back on their lives with feelings of pleasure, gratefulness and appreciation.
8. They tend to be reasonably happy, optimistic people, satisfied with their lives.
9. They approach the final stage of their lives with a sense of personal wholeness.
10. They are able to integrate their past experiences with current realities, and in this way generate a kind of "wisdom" about how to live one's life and cope successfully.

Implicit Attitudes

1. I have much to be thankful for.
2. I am in control of my life.
3. I accept myself for who I am, and I accept others for who they are.

6. They offer little resistance to physical and economic threats to their life-styles, that is, they are easily pushed around.
7. They tend to look back on their lives with feelings of displeasure, regret, and depreciation.
8. They tend to be fairly unhappy, pessimistic people, dissatisfied with their lives.
9. They approach the final stage of their lives with a sense of personal fragmentation, an incompleteness.
10. They seem stuck at the level of blame and disappointment, which makes it difficult for them to learn from their mistakes.

Implicit Attitudes

1. I have little to be thankful for.
2. I have little control over what happens to me.
3. I do not accept myself for who I am, and I wish others could be different.

Source: Don Hamachek, Evaluating self-concept and ego development within Erikson's psychosocial framework, *Journal of Counseling and Development,* 66(1988): 354–360.
Source: Don Hamachek, Evaluating self-concept and ego status in Erikson's last three psychosocial stages, *Journal of Counseling and Development,* 68(1990): 136–142. (©) ACA. Table reprinted with permission. No further reproduction authorized without written permission of American Counseling Association.

right kind of probing questions in the early phases of therapeutic contact to facilitate diagnostic efforts, (c) as a way of identifying quickly the psychosocial stage(s) in which clients have experienced greatest difficulty, (d) as a way of isolating in at least a general way the developmental periods that may be associated most strongly with a client's personal and/or interpersonal difficulties, and (e) as an aid to planning appropriate treatment strategies and relationship modalities.

The epigenetic principle, upon which psychosocial theory is based, reminds us that each new developmental stage is influenced by, and connected to, each of the earlier stages. This is a particularly important idea to keep in mind because it is a reminder to keep the *totality* of a person's development in focus when assessing psychological status and thinking about treatment modalities. Thus, to be maximally helpful, a mental health worker's knowledge about a client has to go beyond knowing only about the ego qualities a person is reflecting in his or her current stage of development to include an awareness of that person's experiences in previous psychosocial stages.

Along with using the behavioral expression tables as guides to assess the course of the self's development and change, it is advisable to examine the behavior being considered with three questions in mind: (a) How *appropriate* is the behavior? (b) How *intense* is it? and (c) What has been its *duration?* For example, statement 5 in Table 1.1 suggests that people with a high sense of basic trust tend to behave in a relatively disclosing and open manner around others. Assume that a person is observed who has a habit of talking in very revealing ways about himself with people he meets for the first time. He is disclosing himself, but is it appropriate given the length of time he has known his listeners? Do the intensity and duration of his disclosing statements suggest that he is basically a trusting person, or one whose social insecurities trigger massive displays of emotional exhibitionism? When his behavior is examined more closely, it may be seen that it is not so much a sign of positive ego resolution in the trust area as it is a symptom of negative ego resolution along the lines of shame and doubt in stage 2 or inferiority in stage 4.

At first sight, any given behavior observed may seem appropriate enough, but its intensity across many situations is so strong that one may have reason to wonder whether it is as appropriate as it originally seemed. For example, as noted in statement 4 of Table 1.2, a possible sign of autonomy is that people tend to resist being dominated by others. Assume that an 18-year-old high school student is observed resisting the authoritarian dictates of one of her teachers. Given the developmental state she is in and the teacher's personality, one might view her behavior as appropriate for the situation and her age. But suppose she resists the reasonable requests of democratic teachers and constantly argues with peers and parents over trivial issues. In light of the undifferentiated intensity and consistency of the protestations, one may begin to suspect that the trigger for her resistance does not stem so much from positive ego resolution favoring autonomy in stage 2, but perhaps more from negative ego resolutions related to trust and identity issues in stages 1 and 5.

Thus, when using the behavioral expression tables (or any other diagnostic tool) as a guideline for evaluating the nature of a person's self-concept development, it may be helpful to consider the *appropriateness, intensity,* and *duration* of particular behaviors to enhance the possibility of interpreting correctly the various expressions of the self's behavior at any point along the growth continuum.

Planning Strategies for Change

When considering therapeutic strategies for helping people change, sensitivity to behaviors associated with different ego resolutions can be useful in a number of ways. For example, if mental health workers observe clients manifesting a high frequency of the negative ego qualities associated with low trust in stage 1, they can be alerted to the possibility that developing a relationship may take more time and that it will be tested in more ways. Because a healthy ratio of trust to mistrust is so basic to positive ego resolutions in subsequent stages of psychosocial development, mental health workers also can be alerted to the possibility that when the stage 1 ratio is on the side of too much mistrust, it may be more difficult to achieve positive resolutions in subsequent stages. Thus therapists can be sensitive to the necessity of doing as much as possible to remediate stage 1 damage to help clients work toward the positive attributes of later stages. Establishing the classical Rogerian (1951) climate of unconditional positive regard may be one way of working toward the development of basic trust in those who struggle with this issue.

Suppose that certain clients are observed exhibiting high frequencies of the negative ego qualities shame and doubt in stage 2 or high levels of the negative ego quality guilt in stage 3. Clients (and most other people, for that matter) who experience such feelings frequently have trouble making decisions and getting started. Counselors may find cognitive-behavioral approaches particularly helpful with these people because of the emphasis on problem definition and concentration on specific behavioral change (Meichenbaum, 1985).

If behavioral signs and other indications suggest that a client's growth has been blocked or inhibited by a sense of inferiority, the negative ego resolution associated with stage 4, counselors may find it therapeutically beneficial to use approaches incorporating Adlerian methods, a counseling framework that helps clients arrive at insights into how feelings of inferiority and dependence develop and teaches them how much feelings are frequently based on faulty, subjective self-evaluations (Dinkmeyer, Pew, & Dinkmeyer, 1979).

Symptoms of identity confusion, which are associated with stage 5, are the accumulative by-products of excessive negative ego resolutions made during the four preceding stages. Identity confusion is more than not just knowing who one is (identity); it is not knowing for sure what one can do (initiative, industry), not knowing whether one can do what needs to be done (autonomy), and, in some instances, not knowing whether anyone can be counted on to help (trust). Thus, treatment approaches with clients exhibiting identity confusion behaviors need to be established (a) within a framework of caring and carrying through (to provide evidence of trust), (b) within an emotional medium of support and caring (to encourage autonomy), (c) with an attitude of positive but realistic expectations (to build a sense of initiative and industry), and (d) with a spirit of unconditional acceptance (for the exploration of positive identity).

Let's turn our attention now to the last three stages and some examples of how, through an awareness of behaviors associated with the psychosocial stages, people can be assisted in their efforts to change. Consider, first of all, the case of a 66-year-old woman— Rochelle, I will call her—who exhibited many of the signs found in stage 8 (Table 1.8) that might be characteristic of people who have a sense of despair. Rochelle was inclined to feel that she had little control over her life, she tended to blame others for her troubles, and she felt unhappy and dissatisfied much of the time. Recognizing that too many negative ego resolutions in previous stages can trigger problems in one's current psychosocial stage, her therapist began by probing Rochelle's experiences in stages 6 and 7. Ordinarily, healthy people are able to strike a balance between intimacy and isolation in stage 6 (Table 1.6) and between generativity and stagnation in stage 7 (Table 1.7). Because she knew what to look for, the psychologist discovered quickly that Rochelle felt very lonely and isolated since her husband died of a heart attack when she was 40 years old. After his death, Rochelle found a job as a secretary and plodded through the next twenty-five years, sustained emotionally by her work and periodic vacation sojourns with friends. Within one session the therapist was able to learn enough about Rochelle to know that her despairing, depressed behavior was linked to a deep sense of loss related to not having a family and children of her own. Failing to move beyond her hurts and disappointments, Rochelle had grown increasingly more self-absorbed and self-centered, thus nurturing the seeds of stagnation in her middle years that eventually grew into the despair she was beginning to feel in her retirement.

The therapist decided quickly that talking, although important, was less crucial to Rochelle than action. A plan was worked out for Rochelle to attend a weekly senior citizens' group that focused on interpersonal issues (to help with her feelings of isolation—stage 6) and to become involved in two volunteer groups, one of which worked with children (to help her develop a sense of generativity—stage 7). These experiences, in combination with bimonthly counseling sessions, served as a package of therapeutic experiences designed to provide as many opportunities as possible for the development of ego qualities associated with a sense of integrity (stage 8).

Consider now the case of a 29-year-old man I will call William, who hesitantly sought professional help because of problems he had in sustaining long-term relationships with women. He seemed to fit many of the behavioral patterns of people in stage 6 (Table 1.6) who have a sense of isolation. Characteristic of people whose emotional capacity for intimacy is poorly developed, he seemed somewhat confused about who he was and what he stood for. He was not very trusting and grew uncomfortable when relationships got too close. He was more of a taker than a giver. These behaviors, gleaned from both observation and conversation, disclosed important facets about his current status, but they revealed little about the emotional factors and life conditions that led to his current sense of isolation.

Through an awareness of the general behavioral patterns associated with the ego polarities of earlier psychosocial stages, however, the therapist was able to quickly piece together the developmental puzzle that revealed some of the deeper issues behind William's concerns. Knowing, for example, that problems with trust can go deep into one's past, the therapist soon discovered that emotionally inconsistent parenting might have nurtured the beginnings of low trust in William (stage 1). Probing further, it was noted that William's early feelings of mistrust were compounded by feelings of shame and doubt (stage 2), because he had been raised in a shame-based environment. Repeated exposures to shame experiences nurtured in William a chronic sense of guilt (stage 3). Recognizing how William's earlier psychosocial experiences affected his life, the therapist understood readily why William emerged from adolescence with feelings of identity confusion (stage 5) and moved into young adulthood unprepared emotionally for the development of intimacy (stage 6).

Although a therapist would want to remain fully cognizant of William's presenting problem—relationship difficulties with women—treatment approaches would have to take into considerations not just surface manifestations, but undercurrent dynamics that may be driving the observable behavior. I realize that most approaches to counseling and psychotherapy do take a client's history into consideration. What I am suggesting here is that another and perhaps even more clinically fruitful way to do this is within the framework of psychosocial stage theory and the behaviors that can be related to those stages.

In William's case, for example, it might be easy enough to help him develop simple behavioral skills or assertiveness techniques that would be helpful to him in establishing relationships and getting them started. And perhaps, if his fears and emotional deprivations did not have deep roots, those skills and techniques would be enough. However, if his feelings of isolation are the outgrowth of a significant imbalance of negative ego qualities in prior psychosocial stages, then it is more imperative to consider those imbalances in treatment plans. In a case like William's, a therapeutic relationship that is basically supportive and accepting seems an important prerequisite to helping him understand how his deeper feelings of mistrust and guilt have contributed to the interpersonal problems he faces.

I am hesitant to recommend or promote specific therapeutic modes that mental health workers might use to achieve particular outcomes primarily because the empirical literature related to therapeutic work points to a dominant finding: Although there is ample evidence to show that a therapeutic experience is helpful to most people who try it (Garfield, 1981; Smith, Glass, & Miller, 1980), there is equally strong evidence showing that there are few important differences in effectiveness among many quite different types of psychotherapy (Landman & Dawes, 1982; Smith & Glass, 1977). This may be one of the reasons why, in recent yeas, there has been a movement away from strong loyalty to individual schools of thought and a corresponding move toward integrating different approaches to therapy (Beitman, Goldfried, & Norcross, 1989; see also Chapter 7 in this volume by Grimley and colleagues). In two surveys in the 1980s of psychologists' theoretical orientations, it was found that the greatest proportion of respondents described themselves as eclectic in their approaches (Norcross & Prochaska, 1982; Smith, 1982).

With increasing numbers of mental health workers turning to eclectic approaches to counseling and therapy, it is not surprising to find that some therapists, such as Lazarus (1989), with his multimodel therapy model, have even developed systematic approaches to being eclectic. The advantage of this, of course, is that it enables mental health workers to creatively blend different approaches to therapy and counseling, depending on the client's psychodynamics and psychosocial history.

HOW CHANGEABLE IS THE SELF?

Longitudinal research findings related to human behavior suggest that behavior is marked by both stability *and* change. On the side of behavioral stability, Kagan and Moss (1962), for example, found that many of the behaviors exhibited by children between the ages of 3 and 6 were moderately good predictors of their behaviors at age 29, a finding that was especially true for aggressive behavior in boys and dependency behavior in girls.

Other evidence has shown that the self's basic characteristics remain remarkably stable from young adulthood into the later years. For example, Costa and McCrae (1980, 1986) in two separate studies collected personality test data on such overall dimensions as extraversion and neuroticism as well as on more specific traits, such as gregariousness, assertiveness, anxiety, and depression. In one study, over 400 men, ranging in age from 25 to 82, filled out a test battery in the mid-1960s and then completed another battery ten years later, in the mid-1970s. In a second study, more than 200 men between the ages of 20 and 76 completed test batteries three times, separated by six-year intervals. Three major personality dimensions emerged in which people show the greatest consistency between young adult and later adult years:

1. *Extraversion and introversion:* The highest degrees of stability, ranging from .70 to .84, were found for these two dimensions, which assess gregariousness, warmth, and assertiveness. Men who were more extraverted in their younger days—outgoing, active, excitement seeking, and people-centered—were very likely to be so in their later years. On the other hand, those who were more introverted in their younger days—solitary, quiet, less people-centered—were likely to be so in their later years as well.

2. *Neuroticism:* Almost as much stability was found in the domain of "neuroticism," which includes such specific traits as depression, anxiety, hostility, and impulsiveness. Those scoring high in neuroticism (compared to those scoring low) typically reveal signs of being more anxious, more often depressed, more self-conscious, more impulsive, and more hostile, and they are inclined, it appears, to end up that way, too. Neurotics are likely to be complainers throughout life. The less neurotic person reacts to life's problems with greater equanimity.

3. *Openness to experience versus rigidity:* Evidence for consistency on this dimension is the weakest of the three, but there is enough to support the possibility that some people are consistently more "open to experience," in the sense of being willing to try new things, to take risks, and to make big changes. This

dimension represents a rather broad continuum, which may be why it shows the weakest consistency.

Impressive evidence for behavioral stability deep into life and over a 40-year span emerged from a unique longitudinal study by Maas and Kuypers (1974). For this study, in-depth interviews were conducted with 95 women and 47 men (average age 70) to gather information about the kind of persons they had become, their health, and how they were living. This information was then compared with survey data from the Institute of Human Development at the University of California (Berkeley) that had been gathered from the same persons for a project started in 1929. Some of the major findings emerging from this study are the following:

1. "Pathology" in old age has more visible roots in early adulthood than does "strength." However, early adulthood pathology does *not* lead inevitably to pathology in old age.

2. There was strong evidence that many of the persons interviewed who were found to lead a similar life-style or to have a similar personality in their later years were also alike in their young adulthood.

3. Old age does not usher in problems that are necessarily new but tends, if anything, to highlight or underscore problems that have long-term antecedents.

Both of these studies suggest that one's attitude toward life is apparent in early adulthood (its roots no doubt go deeper) and remains fairly stable over time, particularly if it is negative. We can only speculate, but perhaps one reason for this has to do with the idea that negative attitudes (outlooks, points of view, beliefs) are essentially defensive in nature, designed to protect one from anxiety, opposing points of view, and the unexpected. To give them up is to feel unprotected and exposed, something that for some people may be a scary possibility. Hence, there is readiness to both expect and see the worst in case evasive action is necessary.

Overall, both Costa and McCrae's and Maas and Kuyper's research findings suggest that those afflicted with more physical or psychological health problems in their later years are likely to be those who are pessimistic, self-blaming, and hostage to the idea that there is little they can do to change their lives or their circumstances. Thus we may see somewhat less change in their behavior.

All in all, the studies we've just reviewed, along with findings from other research (Conley 1985; Costa, McCrae, & Arenberg, 1980; Eichorn, Clausen, Haan, Honzik, & Mussen, 1981; McClelland, 1981), indicate that behavior tends to be reasonably stable over time. All things being equal, the person we are in our younger years resembles the person we become in later years. In fact, Finn's (1986) analysis of 459 men over a thirty-year period suggests that, as we age, behavioral patterns stabilize and personality traits grow increasingly more resistant to change.

It is important to remember, however, that personality can and does have the capacity to change. The findings do *not* indicate that personality characteristics are *completely* formed during childhood and adolescence. Also, even though a general dispositional trend may be established early, the manner in which it is expressed, indeed, whether it is expressed directly at all, may continue to be quite susceptible to change. Clinical and psychotherapeutic literature, for example, abounds with evidence suggesting that adults can change not only their general life-styles but specific behavior as well (Garfield, 1981). Whereas basic aspects of personality such as anxiety or emotionality, friendliness, and eagerness for novel experiences tend to remain relatively stable throughout life, other traits, such as alienation, morale, and feelings of satisfaction, can change greatly. In his analysis of data collected on 388 men and women over a forty-five-year period, Conley (1985) found that these traits change so much that there is virtually no relationship between their levels when adults are in their 20s and when they are in their 60s. Perhaps a reason for this is that these are traits that are more likely to be influenced by external conditions. Thus they are more subject to change as life conditions change.

Levinson's (1981) research is another case in point. His findings suggest that each adult moves through alternating periods of stability *and* change. During the stable periods, we create what Levinson calls a *life structure*, a network of roles and relationships, including work and family ties, inner feelings about ourselves (self-concepts), and aspirations that fit together in an overall picture. It is during the transitions that change is most likely to occur as we reexamine our life structure and decide whether to modify it or maintain it.

Although not all researchers in human development agree with either Levinson's methodology (he bases his findings on extensive interviews with small samples of men and is doing similar research with women) or his findings, his pioneering efforts have caused professionals and laypersons alike to question the idea that there is little change in our basic personality once the pattern has been established.

Although stability of personality was a major finding emerging from a forty-year longitudinal study involving 521 people conducted at the Institute of Human Development at the University of California (Berkeley), one of the institute's psychologists, Norma Haan (1972), found that many healthy individuals do adjust their personalities and values to reflect changes throughout the life cycle. One of the most striking results emerging from research that has focused on behavioral change and stability is the evidence of the tremendous adaptability of human beings. MacFarlane (1974), for example, one of the institute's researchers, noted that many of the most outstanding mature adults in the groups studied had overcome difficult situations even though "their characteristic responses during childhood and adolescence seemed to us to compound their problems." MacFarlane went on to note that she and her associates had failed to appreciate the maturing utility of many painful, strain-producing, and confusing experiences. On the other hand, many subjects who "early had had easy and confidence-inducing lives" and who had been free from severe strains and had exhibited very promising abilities and talents were "brittle, discontented, and puzzled adults" (pp. 115–126).

CONCLUSION AND IMPLICATIONS FOR CHANGING THE SELF

As a psychological entity, this phenomenon we call the "self," broadly defined as one's sense of personal existence, evolves from its amorphous and undifferentiated beginnings in infancy into a highly differentiated and complex psychic structure in adulthood. Understanding the various phases of its growth along a developmental continuum not only helps us see the specific ego components that contribute to one's sense of self at any point in time, but may help us appreciate in an even deeper way the idea that the human organism is always more than the sum of its parts. Thus it is not enough to know that one has a high or low sense of trust, or a strong sense of autonomy or an excessive amount of shame, or healthy feelings of industry or deep feelings of inferiority, as the case may be; more importantly, we want some idea about how these various ego components of the self interact.

One way of keeping the big picture in mind, the whole person, is through the psychosocial framework presented by Erikson over forty years ago and refined in various publications since that time. Psychosocial theory has been enormously important in helping mental health workers see why one's self-concept is positive in some areas but negative in others, and why there are great variations in ego strength and resiliency among individuals, depending upon the emotional and social demands placed upon them. Psychosocial theory acknowledges that humans are biological *and* social *and* psychological and that it is the interactive mix of these inner and outer forces that, along a continuum of developmental stages, shapes the human psyche. That has been its strength. A weakness, I believe, has been in the ambiguity surrounding what behaviors to look for during any particular growth stage that would allow one to evaluate a person's psychosocial growth more specifically. I have tried to extend the usefulness of Erikson's formulations by identifying certain behaviors and implicit attitudes that might be logically and clinically associated with each of the psychosocial stages, as these stages were discussed by Erikson. Further work needs to be done. For example, research designed to compare the behavioral expressions suggested in the tables with people who are known to have high or low trust, a sense of autonomy or feelings of shame and guilt, and so forth, as determined by personality tests and clinical interviews or observations, will provide more information about the validity of these criteria.

A word of caution: Throughout this chapter reference has been made to the developmental continuum over which the self must travel to achieve its particular psychosocial outcomes. In addition, there are many references to the eight "stages" of psychosocial development that humans experience. It is important, I think, to keep in mind that one's progress along any developmental continuum is highly individualized in terms of when certain "stages" of growth are experienced. For example, some people in their late 20s may still be psychologically adolescent and still going through identity formation, whereas others in their teen years are emotionally advanced enough to experience issues and concerns normally reserved for adulthood.

Over time, human behavior is characterized by both stability and change. The longitudinal research that leads up to this conclusion points clearly to the idea that although the self reflects a high degree of stability and consistency, changes in its expression and intrapsychic content are possible. How much the self changes or whether it changes at all depends in part on the psychosocial stage that one is in, and it also depends on the motivation of the self's owner, a motivation that can be significantly influenced by the degree of personal disequilibrium that is felt. Many times, people do not change until the emotional discomfort of remaining in their current condition exceeds the pain that may be involved in modifying their behavior. Thus, we hear stories about people getting, for example, divorced or ceasing some kind of self-destructible behavior because they couldn't bear it any longer; they had hit the bottom of the barrel.

At other times, people may change some aspect of their behavior because they are experiencing the kind of security and personal stability that allows them to feel uncommonly courageous and, thus, ready to take new risks and subject themselves to new ventures.

Helping people change, even those who are motivated to do so, is not easy. Once the self's core is molded and shaped by experience and feedback, it does not change easily. It tends to conserve its form and protect its expression through the use of countless defense mechanisms designed for that purpose. However, as we have seen, change is possible. Mental health workers may find that they can be even more skillful facilitators of that process by developing their awareness of some of the healthy and unhealthy behaviors and attitudes that may be associated with each of the psychosocial stages.

REFERENCES

Beitman, B. D., Goldfried, M. R., & Norcross, J. C. (1989). The movement toward integrating psychotherapies: An overview. *American Journal of Psychiatry, 146*:138–147.

Conley, J. (1985). Longitudinal stability of personality traits: A multitrait-multidimensional analysis. *Journal of Personality and Social Psychology, 19*:1266–1284.

Cooley, C. H. (1902). *Human nature and the social order.* New York: Scribner's.

Coopersmith, S. (1967). *The antecedents of self-esteem*. San Francisco: Freeman.

Costa, P. T., Jr., & McCrae, R. R. (1980). Still stable after all these years: Personality as a key to some issues in adulthood and old age. In *Some issues in adulthood and old age*, edited by P. B. Bates & O. G. Brim, Jr. New York: Academic Press.

———. (1986). Personality stability and its implications for clinical psychology. *Clinical Psychology Review, 6*:407–423.

Costa, P. T., Jr., McCrae, R. R., & Arenberg, D. (1980). Enduring dispositions in adult males. *Journal of Personality and Social Psychology, 38*:793–800.

Dinkmeyer, D. C., Pew, W. L., & Dinkmeyer, D. C., Jr. (1979). *Adlerian counseling and psychotherapy*. Monterey, CA: Brooks/Cole.

Eichorn, D. H., Clausen, J. A., Haan, N. , Honzik, M. P., & Mussen, P. H. (Eds.). (1981). *Present and past in middle life*. New York: Academic Press.

Erikson, E. H. (1950). *Childhood and society*. New York: Norton.

———. (1959). Identity and the Life Cycle. *Psychological Issues, 1*(1). New York: International Universities Press.

———. (1963). *Childhood and society* (2nd ed.). New York: Norton.

———. (1968). *Identity: Youth and crisis*. New York: Norton.

———. (1980). *Identity and the life cycle*. New York: Norton.

———. (1982). *The life cycle completed: A review*. New York: Norton.

Erikson, E. H., Erikson, J. M., & Kivnick, H. O. (1986). *Vital involvement in old age*. New York: Norton.

Evans, R. I. (1981). *Dialogue with Erik Erikson*. New York: Praeger.

Finn, S. E. (1986). Stability of personality ratings over 30 years: Evidence of age/cohort interaction. *Journal of Personality and Social Psychology, 50*:813–818.

Fisher, S., & Cleveland, S. E. (1968). *Body image and personality* (2nd ed.). New York: Dover.

Garfield, S. L. (1981). Psychotherapy: A 40-year appraisal. *American Psychologist, 36*:174–183.

Gould, R. L. (1978). *Transformations: Growth and change in adult life*. New York: Simon & Schuster.

Haan, N. (1972). Personality development from adolescence to adulthood in the Oakland growth and guidance studies. *Seminars in Psychiatry, 4*:399–414.

Hall, E. (1987). *Growing and changing*. New York: Random House.

Hamachek, D. (1992). *Encounters with the self* (4th ed.). Fort Worth, TX: Harcourt Brace Jovanovich.

Horney, K. (1950). *Neurosis and human growth*. New York: Norton.

James, W. (1890). *Principles of psychology* (vol. 1). New York: Holt.

Kagan, J., & Moss, H. A. (1962). *From birth to maturity: A study of psychological development.* New York: John Wiley.

Landman, J. T., & Dawes, R. M. (1982). Smith and Glass' conclusions stand up under scrutiny. *American Psychologist, 37:*504–516.

Lazarus, A. A. (1989). Multimodel therapy. In *Current psychotherapies,* edited by R. J. Corsini & D. Weddings. Itasca, IL: F. E. Peacock.

L'Ecuyer, R. (1992). An experiential-developmental framework and methodology to study transformations of the self-concept from infancy to old age. In *The self: Definitional and methodological issues,* edited by T. M. Brinthaupt & R. P. Lipka. Albany, NY: State University of New York Press.

Levinson, D. J. (1978). *The seasons of a man's life.* New York: Knopf.

———. (1981). Exploration in biography: Evolution of the individual life structure in adulthood. In *Further explorations in personality,* edited by A. I. Rabin, J. Aronoff, A. M. Barclay, & R. A. Zucker. New York: John Wiley.

MacFarlane, J. L. (1974). Perspectives on personality consistency and change from the guidance study. *Vita Humana, 7:*115–126.

Mahler, M. S. (1979). *The selected papers of Margaret Mahler* (vols. 1–2). New York: Jason Aronson.

Maas, H. S., & Kuypers, J. A. (1974). *From thirty to seventy.* San Francisco: Jossey-Bass.

McClelland, D. C. (1981). Is personality consistent? In *Further explorations in personality,* edited by A. I. Rubin, J. Aronoff, A. M. Barclay, & R. A. Zucker (pp. 87–113). New York: John Wiley.

Mead, G. H. (1934). *Mind, self, and society.* Chicago: University of Chicago Press.

Meichenbaum, D. (1985). Cognitive-behavioral therapies. In *Contemporary psychotherapies: Models and methods,* edited by S. J. Lynn & J. P. Garske. Columbus, OH: Merrill.

Miller, P. H. (1989). *Theories of developmental psychology* (2nd ed.). San Francisco: Freeman.

Norcross, J. C., & Prochaska, J. O. (1982). National survey of clinical psychologists: Affiliations and orientations. *Clinical Psychologist, 35:*1, 4–6.

Rogers, C. R. (1951). *Client-centered therapy.* Boston: Houghton Mifflin.

Smith, D. (1982). Trends in counseling and psychotherapy. *American Psychologist, 37:*802–809.

Smith, M. L., & Glass, G. V. (1977). Meta-analysis of psychotherapy outcomes. *American Psychologist, 32:*752–760.

Smith, M. L., Glass, G. V., & Miller, T. I. (1980). *The benefits of psychotherapy.* Baltimore, MD: Johns Hopkins University Press.

Sullivan, H. S. (1947). *Conceptions of modern psychiatry: The first William Alanson White lectures*. Washington, DC: William Alanson White Foundation.

Vaillant, G. E. (1977). *Adaptation to life*. Boston: Little, Brown.

CHAPTER 2

Cluttered Terrain:
The Schools' Interest in the Self

James A. Beane

The past two decades have been marked by a virtual explosion of interest among educators in the self-perceptions of young people. In fact, hardly a conference program or journal issue can get by these days without some attention to this topic. Yet it should be a mistake to think that all of the school-based efforts to enhance self-perceptions are sound or, in some cases, even sensible. The fact is that this area is one of considerable confusion and contradiction as well as tension. In this paper I want to lay out the lines of reasoning typically used to support the idea of enhancing self-perceptions in schools, some of the approaches used for this purpose, and the grounds upon which the very idea of doing so is being challenged.

One of the problems in such an analysis is language confusion, particularly the interchangeability in school talk of "self"-related terms such as *self-concept, self-esteem, self-worth,* and the like. Partly for theoretical reasons (Beane & Lipka, 1986) and partly to find a way out of that confusion, I will use the term *self-perceptions* as an overall organizing reference for the many specific types of self-thinking. The term *self-concept* will refer specifically to descriptive, nonevaluative thinking about the self ("I am a fourth grader," "I take social studies"), and *self-esteem* will refer to evaluative judgments of the self-concept dimensions ("I am a successful student," "I work well in groups").

Its recent popularity aside, placing self-perceptions on the school agenda is hardly a new idea. If we understand that self-perceptions are one aspect of the larger area of "affect" and that they are integrated with social attitudes and behaviors, then it is fair to conclude that perceptions of the self were at least implied in both the lessons of the early religious schools and the arguments for "moralizing" young people that helped initiate the public, common school in the United States (Beane, 1990a). On that same basis, we can trace implications for self-perceptions across the twentieth century through movements for character education, social efficiency, progressive education, values education, moral education, and virtually every other event that has been of note.

However, the current serious and explicit attention to self-perceptions in schools has its roots in the work of perceptual psychologists that emerged around midcentury. Of particular note here is the landmark volume *Perceiving, Behaving, Becoming* (Combs, 1962), which included papers by Earl Kelley, Carl Rogers, Abraham Maslow, and Arthur Combs as well as an analysis of schools in terms of their relation to self-perceptions. The focus on the individual continued to be buoyed by the humanistic education movement of the late 1960s and early 1970s as well as by the larger trends toward human relations, social sensitivity, and self-realization.

Though never far from the surface, the prominence of self-perceptions waned considerably in the 1970s as the "back-to-basics" and religious fundamentalist movements gained ascendance. The former considered (and still does consider) work on self-perceptions to be an unnecessary frill in schooling and anathema to the "hard work" ethic of basic achievement. The latter, of course, viewed (and still does view) virtually any person-centered activity to be contrary to the centrality of religious values and therefore a part of "secular humanism."

By the mid-1980s, however, educators rediscovered self-perceptions as they were linked to more and more self-destructive behaviors among young people, school achievement, "at-risk" populations, and a number of other social and educational issues. Publication of *Toward a State of Esteem* (California Task Force, 1990) catapulted self-esteem into the national media and provoked a debate over the entire topic. As renewed attention was focused on this area, a number of arguments for enhancing self-perceptions in schools emerged, as did several general types of approaches.

ARGUMENTS FOR ENHANCING SELF-PERCEPTIONS
IN SCHOOLS

The arguments for enhancing self-perceptions in schools typically run along three lines. One focuses on coping with life conditions or problems. The second foregrounds correlations between self-esteem and various school-related purposes. The third casts the school in a role in which it contributes to a larger sense of personal and social efficacy. Unpacking each of these sheds some light on the current confusion and controversy regarding self-perception efforts in the schools.

Most observers of the current scene agree that we are living in an age of ambiguity and ambivalence, of discontinuity and disbelief. The postmodern age, based as it is on increasing awareness of the social construction of realities, may fairly be characterized by the crumbling of certainty and the recognition of the illusory and reified content of long-standing beliefs. While some yearn for the "good old days" of common values and conventional customs, others are exploring alternative life-styles. At the same time, the coupling of increased cultural diversity, the economic problems of advanced capitalism, the inequitable distribution of wealth, power, and justice, and so on has created a sense of social dissonance and problematic living conditions for many people.

In such a time, it is hard for many people to find anything certain to hang on to in terms of stability and consistency in their lives. In this context, one may interpret youth statistics regarding substance abuse, crime, pregnancy, depression, attempted and actual suicides, and other self-destructive behaviors as symptoms of confusion and alienation. Society is thus posed as a maze of potentially harmful booby traps which young people are forced to negotiate if they are to survive. Since people who like themselves are presumably not inclined to hurt themselves or to place themselves in dangerous situations, a strong, positive self-esteem is seen by some as the best possible antidote for life in contemporary society and the armor necessary to be resilient in self-threatening situations.

In this way, then, enhancing self-esteem in schools is seen as a moral obligation of educators. The school itself is, in turn, seen as a kind of self and social "Maginot Line" of last defense or, as the Carnegie Council put it, as "the last best chance" (Carnegie Council on Adolescent Development, 1989). Such reasoning, of course, does not ask about the schools' power in the larger society or exactly which side of the "Maginot Line" the school is on, both matters that I will take up later.

The second argument for enhancing self-perceptions in schools is based upon the widely touted correlation between self-perceptions and various ends which the school seeks to accomplish (Beane & Lipka, 1986; Byrne, 1984; Purkey, 1970; Rosenberg, 1979). Foremost among these, and the one that drives much of the present school-based interest in self-perceptions, is the correlation with academic achievement. Beyond this, research suggests similar correlations with participation in school activities, school completion, prosocial behavior in the school setting, and self-direction in school tasks. Research aside, common sense suggests that young people are more likely to succeed in these areas if they believe they will than if they do not.

This second argument has a particular kind of appeal because it suggests that all people in the school ought to be concerned with self-perceptions even if they are unwilling to swallow the moral argument. So it is that concern for self-perceptions is not relegated only to guidance counselors or those teachers who choose to do "affective" activities with young people. Rather, it now must concern all adults, from mathematics class to physical education, from club advisors to the assistant principal in charge of discipline. In every case, adults must pay attention to the sense young people have of their ability to succeed, a sense which the correlations suggest has a lot to do with their actual achievement.

Simple as this reasoning might seem, it becomes complicated by misunderstanding and misperception in the school. In the first place, many educators are confused about the kind of self-perceptions involved in the reputed correlations. The latter, of course, become stronger as situations become more specific (Marsh, Byrne, & Shavelson, 1992); that is, the correlation between self-confidence in one's ability and achievement in mathematics (or some other area) is strongest in mathematics situations (or that other area). On the other hand, we can expect that self-confidence in one's ability in physical education will not correlate that strongly with mathematics achievement, nor will the global sense of self. Given the misunderstanding about such situation-specific contexts, it is not surprising that many educators are confused when self-confidence in one's ability in one area fails to carry over to another or when global verbal praise ("you are a nice person") is not followed by a noticeable rise in test scores.

A second misunderstanding has to do with the nature of research itself. Most studies of the self, like studies of groups in general, suggest group tendencies rather than predict the actual behavior of every person in the sample. For this reason, educators are likely to point out one or a few young people they have known whose behavior contradicts research and, at times, to even use such variations as grounds for rejecting research outright. There is a certain kind of irony in such conclusions, since we might expect those who are interested in self-perceptions to understand that they are highly personal and individualized; in other words, such people should be more surprised with group tendencies.

A third misunderstanding arises from a failure to fully explore meanings behind the correlations. For example, although educators often claim that extracurricular activities, especially sports, build self-esteem, and thus understand the "participation" correlation that way, it is far more likely that those who have self-confidence would choose to participate in such activities in the first place. Hence, although the correlation does exist, it is likely to be a consequence of prior attitudes.

Another misunderstanding has to do with the "school completion" correlation or, more precisely, with the desire to universalize the issue of school dropouts so that a single intervention might be involved. Popular rhetoric on dropouts, as well as on "at-risk" young people, suggests that they have poor self-esteem. Although it may be true that many have poor academic self-esteem as a result of long-term negative feedback, it is also the case that some have a clear self-concept and positive self-esteem (Beane & Lipka, 1986); that is, they know what they want and are satisfied with their choices. It is just that they do not see the school as helping them get where they want to go. I will have more to say about this later in looking at how the school places responsibility for problems. Suffice it to say here that the possibility of placing the dropout issue in the context of self-esteem largely absolves the school of problems of its own making.

Finally, the correlation between self-perceptions and various school goals, particularly academic achievement, has become particularly problematic as educators have argued over the "chicken or egg" question: which comes first, self-confidence in ability or achievement itself? Those who argue for self-perceptions seem likely to seek out instances of success wherever they may be found and to emphasize the need for a positive and "inviting" school climate (Purkey & Novak, 1978). Those who argue for achievement seem likely to want to demand more from young people by way of achievement and to withhold any positive feedback until those demands are met. Again, as we shall see later, such differences of opinion have led to both confusion and tension in efforts to exploit the correlation between self-perceptions and school success.

The third argument for enhancing self-perceptions in schools emphasizes a philosophical and sociological line of reasoning over the clearly psychosocial lines of the first two. Here, self-perceptions are situated in the context of human dignity, of which self-esteem is a defining feature (Beane, 1990a). Put simply, human beings, including the young, are entitled to a sense of dignity. Therefore, any social institution has the obligation to sponsor experiences that extend the possibility of human dignity and to avoid those that may detract from it.

Although this argument has not enjoyed the popularity of the other two, it has far more potential to open up possibilities for enhancing self-perceptions in the school because it is based upon the overriding question of what makes for a fulfilling life. For this reason, it makes no assumptions about the "need" to cope with unsavory conditions in society, nor does it tie young people's self-perceptions to the accomplishment of purposes that others have set out for them without their consent. Thus those who argue this case are free to explore authentic meanings of self-esteem and to open up questions about such issues as justice, equality, equity, democracy, and cultural diversity as these may function inside and outside the school context.

Whereas the first two lines of reasoning differ largely in terms of the context of situational coping, the "human dignity" argument transcends coping and suggests possibilities for social reconstruction; that is, positive self-esteem is extended into a sense of efficacy whereby the individual might be moved to seek a change in social conditions rather than simply cope with them. Moreover, the sense of individual efficacy is expanded by pursuing a sense of social or collective efficacy that empowers groups rather than only individuals. Without such a vision the notion of the school as a "Maginot Line" is reduced to a matter of self-interest rather than expanded to a larger sense of common good based upon collective action.

A good example of this is the multiple ways in which self-esteem is situated in arguments for multicultural education (Banks, 1989; Grant & Sleeter, 1989). At one level, the inclusion of multicultural stories in the curriculum is seen as a way to help minority individuals feel that their culture has a place on the school's agenda. At another level, the stories of culturally nonprivileged groups are seen as a starting point for collectively overcoming the hegemony of the dominant culture and transforming social structures (see Chapter 11 by Dodd, Nelson, and Hofland in this volume). That multicultural education is so strongly resisted may well indicate that the possibility of personal and collective efficacy leading to action is not invisible to those who have a high stake in the dominant culture.

The place of collective self-esteem and the possibility for action in this third line of reasoning should not be taken lightly because they set this argument apart from the other two. Whereas self-esteem advocates have long argued that social transformation begins with individuals who have positive self-esteem (Combs, 1962), there is, in the first two lines of reasoning, the impending threat of pitting the individual against the group and recreating the kind of Social Darwinism that has led to gross social inequities. And it is those inequities that detract from human dignity in the larger world and thus threaten to wash away whatever salutary effect school-based self-esteem efforts might have. In contrast, as the individual "sees his [or her] stake in others" (Kelley, 1962), the threat of purely individualistic uses of self-esteem is assuaged.

The common failure of educators to come to grips with this idea arises largely out of two problems. One is the fact that school-based self-esteem efforts occur in an institution that reflects (if not reproduces) the individualistic philosophy of the larger society. The second is that too many school-based self-esteem advocates fail to recognize that self-perceptions, particularly self-esteem, are formed on the basis of values. I will be kind in suggesting that this failure leads to an unconscious failure to examine the values that the school promotes and/or that are implicit in self-esteem programs. However, it is more than a little probable that many educators, including some who are vocal advocates for the "coping" and "achievement" arguments for work on self-esteem, themselves subscribe to the individualistic and socially problematic values that schools so often reinforce.

LOCUS OF CONTROL AND THE USES
OF SELF-PERCEPTIONS

If we look inside the three lines of reasoning that typically support work on school-based self-perceptions, it is clear that, with the exception of the outright human dignity argument, self-esteem is not viewed as an end but as a means. In other words, even when school goals speak to developing one's self-concept or self-esteem, that development is done for some larger purpose: to cope with difficult life situations, to improve achievement of school purposes, or to undergird the transformation of debilitating social structures. In straightforward terms, this means that the idea of enhancing self-perceptions in the school amounts to asking young people to change themselves or the way they think about themselves so that they are more likely able to do something else.

Putting matters this way begins to reveal some metaphors about young people that lurk just beneath the surface of work on school-based self-perceptions. And it is these metaphors that are the subtext of such work and the lens through which educators look at young people. In the "moral" argument presented by the first line of reasoning, we meet the "coping self," who may be one of two types. The first is the "self-destructive self," who is struggling to stay afloat in a difficult world. The other is the "vulnerable self," who may not be in trouble now but who will surely face tough times down the road. Although these metaphors may be appropriate at a given moment for particular young people, they are problematic as a general theory; that is, such metaphors suggest that the status quo of the larger world is unchangeable and that young people simply need to learn how to survive. This is hardly the kind of optimistic scenario that one imagines holding up positive self-esteem.

The "achievement" argument presented by the second line of reasoning offers up a different metaphor. Here we meet the "boot-strap" self, whose problems with school success can be overcome if only she or he would feel more confident. Unfortunately, in too many schools there is little that would suggest to young people that they ought to have confidence in themselves, since virtually everything about their lives, including judgments about the quality of their work, is in the hands of adults. Worse yet, for some young people such factors as class, race, and gender bias in the school suggest that there is not much to be confident about anyway.

Finding the subtextual metaphors in the "human dignity" line of reasoning is more difficult in that it depends upon the larger view that surrounds self-perception work. Just scratching the surface of the many conditions in school and society that detract from human dignity can so overwhelm our hopes that we begin to create a "powerless self" metaphor. It is hard to imagine the "liberating self" that this line of reasoning wants to call forth. Lacking the connection of the individual to the collective and without a realistic, manageable site for action, the "liberating self" will almost surely become the "powerless" one.

Before examining various approaches to enhancing self-perceptions in schools, we need to add one more variable to the mix we have already considered. This variable involves situating the responsibility for the formation of self-perceptions and their change. Because I am speaking from a humanistic/developmental position, it is important to note that, ultimately, individuals form and alter their own self-perceptions and that only they themselves can do this. But this is not the same as fixing responsibility for formation and change. Here we are confronted with two possibilities. The first is that individuals are responsible for their own self-perceptions as well as for any alteration in them. The second is that self-perceptions are most powerfully informed by one's environment; therefore, changing or enhancing self-perceptions involves altering the environment.

Now there is little question that the formation and alteration of self-perceptions occur as the individual reflects upon interactions with and feedback from the surrounding environment. The question is: Which is more powerful, the individual or the environment? The answer here, I think, is that, with few exceptions, particularly in the case of young people, the environment is more powerful. Again, both the environment and the individual play a role in self-perceptions, but the equation of their relations is not balanced. This is easily understood if we simply remember that young people depend almost entirely on adults for both the necessities of subsistence and the credentials for fuller access to society. Perhaps it is even easier to understand if we think about how powerfully conditions like poverty, racism, and social injustice, which are not of young peoples' own making, enter into their lives and their identities. We cannot underestimate the importance of this concept since it must figure largely into how one approaches enhancing self-perceptions in schools as well as our analysis of the various approaches that are already in practice.

APPROACHES TO ENHANCING SELF-PERCEPTIONS IN SCHOOLS

To their credit, educators have increasingly recognized the need to attend to self-perceptions; in fact, *self-concept* and *self-esteem* have become "buzzwords" in popular educational circles over the past two decades. For the most part, educators seem to approach the idea of enhancing self-perceptions in three ways, and a fourth has only recently emerged.

The first approach has its roots most clearly in the "pop" psychology notion of self-revelation and affirmation. The best way to understand what this means is to picture a teacher or counselor with a group of young people sitting in a circle talking about themselves: who they are, how they feel, what they like or fear or wish, and so on. The group's role is to affirm what individuals say and generally reassure each other that all are good persons who ought to like themselves. Attached to this is a general atmosphere in which adults persistently tell young people how much they like them and how they ought to like themselves and, often, clever posters whose slogans exhort young people to have positive self-esteem.

This approach, of course, operates upon some very tenuous assumptions. One is that a young person, or anyone for that matter, will actually reveal himself or herself in a group situation. A second is that people will feel good about themselves simply by having other people tell them they should. A third is that school adults are high-level significant others in the lives of young people— high enough that young people will pay any attention to their opinions.

Although no one who seriously understands the workings of self-perception would want to take such practices too seriously, this approach, or at least its spirit, ought not to be rejected outright. After all, there is much to be said about people being "nice" to one another, especially when "mean" adults have so often filled the lives of young people. Moreover, the notion of the group at least recognizes that peers are more apt to be significant others than adults. Yet although being surrounded by nice people may be helpful in forming positive self-perceptions, it is certainly not sufficient. Taken alone, this approach is surely not all it is cracked up to be by its advocates. Fortunately, most educators have realized this and moved beyond such a simplistic approach. Those who have not are likely to be under attack from fundamentalist groups, who see this approach as one of the defining types of "secular humanism."

The second approach, and clearly the most popular of all, is the self-esteem "program." Whenever a new "need" or topic is identified for the schools, educators almost always want to establish a new program for it, and self-esteem is no exception. During the 1980s, as *self-esteem* become a buzzword in schools, programs for enhancing self-esteem appeared with terrifying frequency. Middle schools in particular embraced this approach and even gave a title to it, namely, the "advisory" program.

In the "program" approach, time is set aside each day (or less frequently) for small groups of young people to engage in various activities, from self-analysis worksheets to discussion, aimed at enhancing self-esteem. In many cases, the materials are purchased as part of a commercial package, the developers of which may claim that if their program is regularly used, young people will stop using drugs, stop committing crimes, stop getting pregnant, stop attempting suicide, and get good grades in school. In 1970, Weinstein and Fantini suggested that there were at least 350 such programs known, involving some three thousand "affective exercises and techniques," and there is no reason to believe that there are any fewer today when locally developed programs are included in the total. I estimate that there are about thirty to thirty-five packaged programs that are widely known and used in schools and a larger number of popular consultants who conduct workshops on program development and who draw suggested activities from both nationally and locally developed sources.

The growth of this approach, and particularly the purchase of commercially packaged programs, is not surprising. After all, the

1980s were marked by the commodification of the self—"I am what I buy." The step to buying a package for self-esteem is not that far beyond. But the problems with the separate program approach run more deeply than that. Beginning with the classic character education studies by Hartshorne and May in the 1920s and continuing with those on values clarification and moral development programs (Lockwood, 1978), educators have had ample evidence to suggest that set-aside programs do not seem to transfer outside the programs themselves. Nor is there any evidence to warrant the claims about effects made by the developers of self-esteem packages (Strein, 1988).

The plain fact of the matter is this: Educators may do all kinds of things related to self-esteem, personal decision making, goal setting, and so on in separate programs, but there is no guarantee that anyone else in the school outside of that particular room will care one wit about any of it. So it is that whatever salutary effects may be gained within the program are at risk of being washed away in the rest of the school, to say nothing about conditions outside the school itself. Once again, though, we do not want to completely reject these programs, since there may be a place for the direct study of self-perceptions. But to make a difference, the spirit of these programs would need to stretch across the entire school so that the matter of self-esteem counts for more than one time slot in the day.

Worse yet, the separate program approach is evidence of educators' failure to recognize the levels at which self-perceptions function. To imagine that the global and social aspects of the self which these programs emphasize would influence a specific situation such as achievement in one or another subject in the school not only ignores research but defies common sense. To imagine that they will somehow create the "bootstrap self" out of nonprivileged "at-risk" young people is just another version of "Horatio Alger" fiction.

To that point, this approach raises the more serious question related to the lines of reasoning previously described. It is here that we meet head-on the "self as coper" or "survivor" in a cruel world. Again, this metaphor is dangerous because it suggests that the status quo is intransigent and that people are powerless to change it. How ironic it is that an approach that is basically humanistic should end up leaving humans in "ideologically frozen relations of dependence" on the very conditions that dehumanize them (Habermas, 1971, p. 310).

The third approach to enhancing self-perceptions in schools is the "ecological" one. In the previous two the responsibility for forming and altering self-perceptions was left to the individual; that is, if we want change then we must look inside the individual. The ecological approach takes a quite different slant on the issue by looking outside the individual at the environment that informs the self. In this way it pays attention to the previously mentioned disproportionate power of the environment relative to the individual.

The ecological approach begins with the question of whether the school as a whole is a self-enhancing place and then proceeds to examine every aspect of the school in light of that question, including both institutional features and curriculum and teaching (Beane & Lipka, 1986, 1987). It is interesting to note that, in identifying possibilities for action, this approach draws from a variety of research sources, in some of which effects on self-perceptions are not the central concern. Table 2.1 shows a number of possibilities for working toward a self-enhancing school that this approach promotes.

Although the "ecological" approach has much to offer in light of self-perception theory, it has enjoyed nowhere near the popularity of the two previously described approaches. In a sense, it offers a parallel structure in which the ecological theory is an overarching theme that might be brought to life in many, diverse ways. But because it does not say exactly what and when things should be done, it is not attractive to those educators who are seeking a quick and precisely specified recipe for action. In other words, there are no lesson plans, ready-to-wear worksheets, or glossy handouts. The ecological approach calls for nothing less than difficult and thoughtful deliberation and action by educators themselves.

The one real shortcoming of this approach is that, like the others, it does not clearly speak to conditions outside the school that enter into the ongoing formation and alteration of self-perception. Although its advocates have suggested that educators must begin in the school, where they have some certain control over things, this is a theory that needs to be stretched into political action on behalf of young people. On the other hand, even the

TABLE 2.1
Moving toward the Self-Enhancing School

From	To
Low priority on self-perceptions	Self-perceptions as a focus
Custodial climate	Humanistic climate
Attribute grouping	Variable grouping
External control	Self-direction
Self-isolation	Peer interaction
Age isolation	Multiage interaction
Accepting failure	Expecting and assuring success
Avoiding or blaming parents	Working with parents
Negative expectations	Positive expectations
Debilitating teacher self-perceptions	Enhancing teacher self-perceptions
Vague self-perception goals	Clear self-perception goals
Confusion about learners	Clear understanding of learner characteristics
Vague learning constructs	Learning constructs to enhance self-perceptions
Subject-centeredness	Life centeredness
Teacher-exclusive planning	Teacher-student planning
Textbooks and tests	Problems and projects
Maintenance of the status quo	Continuous development

Source: Reprinted by permission of the publisher from Beane, James A. and Lipka, Richard P., Self-Concept, Self-Esteem and the Curriculum (New York: Teachers College Press, © 1986 by Teachers College, Columbia University. All rights reserved.), Table 5.1, page 180.

school focus of the approach risks being so broad that individuals may evade the need for action. Stretching ouside the school only exacerbates that risk, especially since so many educators want to believe that the source of school-related self-perceptions has nothing to do with their actions inside the school.

The fourth approach, and one that has only recently emerged, takes the matter of self-perceptions out of separate programs, off the edges of school deliberations, and places it squarely into the ongoing curriculum of the school. In doing so, it honors the "ecological" theory's call for empowering young people but presses it further. In what I will call the "integrated" approach, the curriculum is centered on helping young people search for self and social meaning in their lives. I have written more thoroughly about this approach elsewhere (Beane, 1990b, 1991a, 1992) and will only sketch it in broad strokes here.

Planning of the curriculum begins with young people identifying questions and concerns they have about themselves and the larger world in which they (and we) live. Common questions and concerns are shared in small groups, and an attempt is made to connect questions about self with related questions about the world; for example, issues about personal health are connected to concerns about environmental problems. Clusters of questions are organized by themes, and the whole group then decides upon activities they will do to address the themes and answer the questions. Themes that have emerged from such planning have included "living in the future," "jobs, careers, and money," "sex, health, genetics," "conflict, gangs, and violence," "cultures," and many more.

It does not take much imagination to see how self-perceptions are at the very center of such a curriculum. More than that, this kind of curriculum brings questions of the self into connection with the larger world, thus integrating self and social interests. And giving young people a powerful voice in planning the curriculum is a direct attempt to develop authentic efficacy: what young people have to say counts for something. Furthermore, young people will be in a continuing process of constructing personal and social meanings rather than having themselves and their world defined exclusively for them by adults.

Initial work with this kind of curriculum is being conducted in middle schools in various places around the country, though it is hoped that eventually other levels will take it on since they are implicated in its possibilities as well. When this approach is combined with the "ecological" one, schools have available to them a comprehensive and compelling framework for enhancing self-perceptions. Certainly the "pop psychology" and "separate program" approaches pale in comparison to this one.

ILLUSION AND POSSIBILITY

Having explored the lines of reasoning typically used to argue for enhancing self-perceptions in schools and some of the approaches that are often used, I now want to turn to the current debate that surrounds this topic (Beane, 1991b). From the previous discussion it should be clear that this kind of work has a checkered history in schools, marked as it is by confusion and misinterpretation as well as by the search for simplistic solutions.

In the past few years, however, a controversy has arisen over the very idea of enhancing self-perceptions in schools. The grounds for this controversy follow along two lines. First, the 1980s were a decade of proposed reform for schools. The main theme of proposals has been fixed (or fixated) on the place of the United States in world economic competition and the role of schools in preparing youth as workers who can supposedly help the United States regain its dominant status. Most of the proposals have called for substantially increasing the standards for success in school and also for increasing the achievement of nonprivileged young people so as to expand the labor pool, which has been depleted by the decline in the number of youth in the country.

Such a scenario has very interesting implications for self-perceptions if we understand school efforts to enhance those perceptions as related to the values the school seeks to promote. In this case the pertinent value has to do with the school's relation to economic competition. By implication, then, the quality of young peoples' self-esteem presumably should depend upon the degree to which they are contributing, through their achievement, to the economic future of business and industry. When this condition of self-esteem is imposed upon nonprivileged young people, who have suffered the most in the current economic climate, it amounts to "blaming the victims," hardly the sort of theory that supports positive self-esteem. Moreover, those who favor this approach do not strongly believe that self-esteem, as a dimension of human dignity, is an entitlement of (young) people, or that they have their own aspirations.

Valuing economic competition in this way is only one aspect of the larger Conservative Restoration that continues in the 1990s and that questions the idea of privileging self-perceptions in the school. Visible critics such as Leo (1990) and Krauthammer (1990) want us to conjure up a picture of thousands and thousands of teachers throwing away standards in an orgy of baseless affirmation of young people. Moreover, they find little that is desirable in multicultural programs that honor anything but Western, male activity, thus depriving those outside the dominant culture of a sense of place in the curriculum. Add to these attitudes narrow behavior prescriptions and salvos tossed against sex education and recognition of diverse family patterns, and this package is revealed as the secular version of religious fundamentalism that gained ascendance in the 1980s.

Now this point may seem far afield from the central issue of this paper, but, in fact, it is in these broad, political terms that we are able to understand that the very idea of enhancing self-perceptions in schools, as well as young people's aspirations and identities, is under attack. And the confusion and contradictions about self-perceptions among educators have only made this area of work more vulnerable to such criticism. Certainly I have not painted a pretty picture of how self-perceptions are addressed in schools, but even in the most careless of approaches we must recognize that there is usually the good-spirited, "child-centered" impulse that historically has been a central feature in this area.

So it is that the idea of enhancing self-perceptions is of continuing interest to educators, even when they are under attack from critics of their work. The real challenge in this area of schooling is to clear up the confusion and reduce the contradictions so that efforts to enhance self-perceptions can become authentic and meaningful. This means moving beyond the "fluff" and the quick-fix program toward a genuine remaking of the schools so that they are self-enhancing places where human dignity and personal and social efficacy are central themes in every corner of the institution.

REFERENCES

Banks, J. A. (1989). Multicultural education: Characteristics and goals. In *Multicultural education: Issues and perspectives,* edited by J. A. Banks & C. A. McGee Banks. Needham Heights, MA: Allyn & Bacon.

Beane, J. A. (1990a). *Affect in the curriculum: Toward democracy, dignity, and diversity.* New York: Teachers College Press.

———. (1990b). *A middle school curriculum: From rhetoric to reality.* Columbus, OH: National Middle School Association.

———. (1991a). The middle school: The natural home of integrated curriculum. *Educational Leadership, 49*(2):9–13.

———. (1991b). Sorting out the self-esteem controversy. *Educational Leadership, 49*(1):25–30.

———. (1992). Turning the floor over: Reflections on *A Middle School Curriculum*. *Middle School Journal, 23*(3):34–40.

Beane, J. A., & Lipka, R. P. (1986). *Self-concept, self-esteem and the curriculum*. New York: Teachers College Press.

Byrne, B. M. (1984). The general/academic self-concept nomological network: A review of construct validation research. *Review of Educational Research, 54:427–456.*

California Task Force on Self-Esteem and Social Responsibility. (1990). *Toward a state of esteem*. Sacramento: State of California.

Carnegie Council on Adolescent Development. (1989). *Turning points: Preparing American youth for the 21st century*. New York: Carnegie Corporation.

Combs, A. W. (Ed.). (1962). *Perceiving, behaving, becoming: A new focus for education*. Washington, DC: Association for Supervision and Curriculum Development.

Grant, C. A., & Sleeter, C. E. (1989). Race, class, gender, exceptionality, and educational reform. In *Multicultural education: Issues and perspectives,* edited by J. A. Banks & C. A. McGee Banks. Needham Heights, MA: Allyn & Bacon.

Habermas, J. (1971). *Knowledge and human interests*. New York: Beacon.

Kelley, E. C. (1962). The fully functioning self. In *Perceiving, behaving, becoming: A new focus for education,* edited by A. W. Combs. Washington, DC: Association for Supervision and Curriculum Development.

Hartshorne, H., & May, M. A. (1928, 1929, 1930, respectively). *Studies in the nature of character: Volume 1: Studies in deceit, Volume 2 (with F. K. Shuttleworth): Studies in service and self control, Volume 3: Studies in the organization of character*. New York: Macmillan.

Krauthammer, C. (1990). Education: Doing bad and feeling good. *Time,* February 5, p. 78.

Leo, J. (1990). The trouble with self-esteem. *U.S. News and World Report,* April 2, p. 16.

Lockwood, A. L. (1978). The effects of values clarification and moral development curricula on school-age subjects: A critical review of research. *Review of Educational Research, 48:325–364.*

Marsh, H. W., Byrne, B. M., & Shavelson, R. J. (1992). A multidimensional, hierarchical self-concept. In *The Self: Definitional and methodological issues,* edited by T. M. Brinthaupt and R. P. Lipka. Albany, NY: State University of New York Press.

Purkey, W. W. (1970). *Self-concept and school achievement*. Englewood Cliffs, NJ: Prentice-Hall.

Purkey, W. W., & Novak, J. (1978). *Inviting school success: A self-concept approach to teaching and learning.* Belmont, CA: Wadsworth.
Rosenberg, M. (1979). *Conceiving the self.* New York: Basic Books.
Strein, W. (1988). Classroom-based elementary school affective education programs: A critical review. *Psychology in the Schools,* 25:288–296.
Weinstein, G., & Fantini, M. D. (1970). *Toward humanistic education: A curriculum of affect.* New York: Praeger.

CHAPTER 3

Changing the Delinquent Self

Martin Gold

Self has become a central explanatory concept in contemporary theories of the causes of juvenile delinquency. Regnant theory proposes that delinquency is a function of the balance between provocations (motivation, strain) to commit delinquent acts on the one hand and social controls that inhibit such behavior on the other. The motive to defend against threats of derogation of the self is weighed heavily in the balance on the side of provocation. In this chapter, I ground this explanation for delinquency in a formal definition of *self*, review the evidence for the usefulness of this definition, and discuss an experimental delinquency treatment program based on this approach.

A DEFINITION OF *SELF*

Thinking about *self* makes me feel queasy. It is like standing between two facing mirrors, my reflection reflected, and reflected again, in infinite regress. Who is doing this thinking? Myself? Who just thought about who is thinking about the self? Who . . . ? And so on. I need some psychological distance to think constructively about the apparently vital idea of self, and formal theory provides that necessary distance.

Let us assume that the function to be served by the concept of *self* is to help explain *purposive* behavior, that is, action. Suppose

I want to thank Elizabeth Douvan, Marita Roesch Inglehart, and the editors for their helpful comments on a draft of this paper.

that most human behavior is action in this sense, that it is moti-vated. It is intended to attain certain more or less specific goals. An explanation of such behavior then covers a great deal of human behavior.

In order that the concept of *self* may perform its explanatory function, let us define *self* as *that which responds exclusively to one's will.* More specifically, call this *self* the *agentic self,* nominat-ing it as the devoted servant to one's motives. Let us further posit that nothing else is so totally devoted to helping one reach one's goals. Anything less totally devoted is not, by definition, *self.* Thus, should one find oneself unwillingly serving the will of another, one's self is thereby diminished. And thus, should one find another totally and dependably devoted to one's own will, that other will be psychologically absorbed into one's self.

A good deal of theorizing about *self* has conceptualized it as *object* rather than as agent, as "me" rather than as "I." This seems intuitively useful, for we often find ourselves regarding our selves. Furthermore, the hypothesis that delinquency serves the function of defending against threats of a derogated self implies the idea of self-as-object. The meaning of self-as-object may be derived from the concept of the agentic self. Its meaning as object is in relation to its function as agent, couched primarily in terms of its effective-ness in enabling one to attain one's goals. Effectiveness is not the only dimension of meaning of self-as-object, however. Two other dimensions fill out its meaning—the energy with which the agent applies its resources and the morality of the goals to which it devotes its energies. These three dimensions of meaning, it should be noted, correspond to the dimensions of meaning of any object, as identified by Osgood, Suci, and Tannenbaum (1957): power, activity level, and goodness.

It follows that *self-esteem* is desirable. It is tautological that people want to attain their goals. The *self* is evaluated as to its capacities to attain one's goals, the energy with which it employs these capacities, and the worthiness of one's ends. Thus, a positive evaluation—self-esteem—connotes self-confident striving for re-spectable goals.

Other terms commonly used in discussions of *self* can be found within this framework. Some examples: *Self-alienation* refers to the diminishment of self mentioned earlier; it is the belief that no agent is actively devoted to the attainment of one's own goals, a belief inevitably accompanied by a feeling of dismay. *Identification,* the fantasy that one is another, results from the belief that one's own goals and the goals of the other are substantially the same; thus the other becomes a component of one's self. *Intimacy* or *friendship* depends on this kind of identification, this fusing of selves without a sense of alienation or diminishment of self.

Other authors in this volume have argued that *self* is a relatively recent phenomenon, that it did not always exist as a psychological or sociocultural reality (see Chapter 2 by Beane and Chapter 5 by Baumeister and Boden). Defining *self* in agentic terms implies the psychological and cultural conditions that create *self.* Inasmuch as *self* depends upon the belief that individuals can effect attainment of their goals, it implies fate control.

Contrast the belief in personal fate control to a belief that an intractable (not necessarily malevolent) natural or supernatural force controls what happens to anyone. The idea of an agentic self is incompatible with this belief. Only an experiencing self is conceivable under this condition, a self as object that responds emotionally and behaviorally to the will of another.

From this perspective, one can identify the historical/cultural conditions that give rise to the phenomenon of an agentic self. An agentic self is conceivable when the technology and ideology of a culture empower individuals to effect their wills, either by independent action or by successfully persuading tractable powers. When whimsical gods, cold despots, and oppressive collectivities lose control and legitimacy, *self* becomes possible.

THE SELF IN THEORY ABOUT DELINQUENCY

The idea that juvenile delinquency is provoked by a derogated self was introduced into theory about the causes of delinquency by A. K. Cohen in his book *Delinquent Boys* (1955). Cohen intended to explain, not individual differences in delinquency, but the location of a delinquent subculture among lower- rather than middle- or higher-class boys. However, his theory rests upon assumptions regarding the psychological dynamics of self-esteem.

Cohen posited that the socialization of lower-class boys tends to disable them in competition with higher-class boys in attaining the Good Life. Lower-class boys are more likely than their higher-status peers to conclude that they are not competent to achieve their goals, most notably in scholastic competition, where the performance of secondary school students is compared to "all comers." Those most severely struck by this belief share a common problem, self-derogation; and they are, by virtue of attending the same schools and living in the same neighborhoods, in communication with another. These two conditions satisfy the prerequisites for the development of a culture.

According to Cohen, the delinquent subculture develops and is maintained to solve the common problem. The subculture is characterized by its disparagement of conventional striving, exemplified by doing one's schoolwork, getting a part-time job, and other legitimate ways to gain status. It values instead the daring defiance of social norms, exemplified by such behavior as fighting, stealing, doing drugs, and engaging in promiscuous sexuality. In this cultural context, one proves one's self-worth with delinquency. An additional satisfaction is that those others who are perceived as disparaging one's self are discomfited by the delinquent behavior.

It need only be mentioned for the purposes of the present discussion that Cohen's theory foundered on empirical rocks. Since the theory aimed to explain why the delinquent subculture is typically found among lower-class boys, it followed that lower-class boys were more delinquent than their higher-class peers. Neither the fact to be explained nor the fact that followed from the explanation now appears true. When the methods for measuring delinquency began to include self-reports instead of relying exclusively on the records of the juvenile justice system, the location of the delinquent subculture among lower-class boys and their disproportionate delinquency were cast into great doubt. It appears now that whatever relationship there may be between social class and delinquency is quite small and limited to the frequency of assaultive behavior, mostly among peers (Elliott & Huizinga, 1983; Gold, 1970; Nye, Short, & Olson, 1958; Williams & Gold, 1972).

Nevertheless, the underlying psychological dynamics posited by Cohen remain plausible. There are data that document them. It appears only that the conditions for these dynamics are not conditions of life more prevalent among lower-class boys: they are just as much the experience of middle- and upper-class youth. Consider, for example, scholastic failure. The average grades of students do not vary much from one high school to another (Hauser, 1969), even though students in rather homogeneously higher-class schools may be more proficient scholastically. Students apparently meet "all comers" *within their schools*. Obviously, every high school has its bottom 5 percent achievers, and in many schools, these poor achievers' families may be quite well off. Moreover, the goals that higher-status youth are encouraged to achieve may be higher than those set for lower-class youth. Achievement and competence are relative. Thus felt incompetence and self-derogation as a condition for the formation of a delinquent subculture and a cause of individual recruitment into a delinquent way of life are not necessarily associated with lower socioeconomic status.

The notions that delinquency serves the function of raising self-esteem and that it is imbedded in a delinquent subculture imply a particular characterization of delinquency. It is useful to think of delinquent behavior as a *performance:* it is a way of "showing off." To characterize it thus is not meant to minimize its sometimes harmful nature; it can be extremely destructive and cruel. However, this conception may be more valid as to the causes of delinquency and more useful for devising prevention and treatment than other common characterizations are. It suggests, for example, that delinquency is not necessarily aggressive in its intent, even when it inflicts personal injury. "Performance" also suggests that the rewards of delinquency lie elsewhere than in material gain, even when valuable objects are stolen.[1] Nor do the satisfactions of delinquency lie primarily in its thrills, even when car thieves elude pursuing police. To characterize delinquency as performance is meant to assert that its reward is applause, the enhancement of self-esteem by an appreciative audience.

The data describing delinquent behavior support the idea that it is a performance. More than 80 percent of delinquent acts are committed in the company of others, and of the remaining solo acts, more than half are shortly thereafter recounted to peers (Gold, 1970). Why should this be so? The vast majority of delinquent acts do not require assistance. Objects stolen jointly need to be shared. Lone offenders are more likely to escape detection, and telling someone about one's crime increases one's chances of apprehension. Nevertheless, if delinquency is performance in the service of self-esteem, then these facts about its companionate nature fall into place.

Why is it that boys are invariably found to be markedly more delinquent than girls? The only offense that girls commit about on a par with boys is running away from home (Gold, 1970; Williams & Gold, 1972). The idea of delinquency as self-enhancing performance suggests that delinquency is not so self-enhancing for girls as it is for boys. Morris (1964) found that this is indeed the case: The same delinquent behavior described to adolescents as committed by a girl is more likely to be regarded by them as "crazy" than when it is attributed to a boy. An American girl does not get the applause for delinquent behavior that a boy would get.

The reason for this is that delinquent behavior does not demonstrate a competent self for girls as it does for boys. Insofar as their sex roles assign boys and girls different tasks, their goals are normatively expected to differ. Their peers do not perceive that delinquent behavior serves girls' purposes. They therefore conclude that delinquent girls must have lost self-control, that is, must be "crazy." Thus, unable ordinarily to obtain self-affirmation of competency through delinquency, girls are less delinquent than boys are.

Some findings inexplicable by an obvious cost-benefit analysis make sense if delinquency is understood as performance. Stuart, Quire, and Krell (1976) observed the incidence over time of self-reported use of marijuana by high school students in three small midwestern cities. In the course of three years, the penalty for being caught in possession of marijuana in one of the cities fluctuated from a heavy fine and the possibility of detention to a negligible fine of five dollars and then back to the heavier penalty. Meanwhile, the more severe penalty remained constant at the other sites. Over the period of observation, reported use of marijuana increased in the communities with the constant, more severe penalties. However, the negligible penalty in the one community had the effect of inhibiting use; when it was in force, fewer students reported smoking pot than did before and after. Why? One plausible explanation is that smoking pot when the penalty is merely a five dollar fine gains youths no more applause in the delinquent subculture than if they let their parking meters run out.

DELINQUENCY AND SELF-ESTEEM

That delinquency is provoked by self-derogation and functions to restore self-esteem is indicated by the findings of three different kinds of studies. In one, Gold and Mann (1972) hypothesized that the conscious self-esteem of more delinquent youth would be as high as that of their less delinquent peers, but that the former would exhibit lower levels of unconscious self-evaluation. Their reasoning was based on the supposition that delinquency is for many youth an adequate psychological defense against felt self-derogation, but that continuing delinquent behavior is driven by abiding self-derogation at an unconscious level. The researchers found that self-esteem measured by the ideal-self discrepancy method did not distinguish the self-reported more than the less delinquent youth. Rather, the more delinquent youth exhibited significantly lower self-evaluations on a projective test of self-esteem (Ziller, Hagey, Smith, & Long, 1969).

In the second kind of research, Oyserman and Markus (1990) compared the "possible selves" of youths more and less delinquent, according to their self-reports. They found that the more delinquent youths projected significantly more negative than positive possibilities of what they would be like and what they would be doing in the future. It is especially relevant here that a negative imbalance between "getting along in school" and "not getting along well in school" was among the projected self-descriptions that distinguished the groups most sharply.

In the third, Kaplan (1980) measured the self-esteem and self-reported deviant behavior of junior high school students three times over the course of two years. Kaplan sought to clarify cause-effect relationships by observing change in the variables. He found that the more students' self-esteem declined during the first year, the more their deviant behavior increased during the second year. Furthermore, increasing deviant behavior among those initially low in self-esteem was associated with an increase in their subsequent self-esteem. Thus this study is the most nearly unequivocal of the three cited in establishing that low self-esteem provokes delinquent behavior and that delinquent behavior can enhance self-esteem.

EXPERIMENTS ON DELINQUENCY AND SELF

Carefully controlled experimental interventions reveal causal relationships most definitively at the same time that they test the worth of hypothetically ameliorative programs. In the present context, a program would aim to enhance the self-esteem of heavily delinquent youth while they are under continuing observation to determine if their self-esteem increases and their delinquent behavior declines. If it is true that scholastic failure is a major cause of self-derogation that leads to delinquency, then intervention in the schools is indicated. This theoretical approach posits that an effective educational intervention would have two essential characteristics: students would not fail, and they would enjoy a warm, supportive relationship with their teachers and school staff. In fact, the experimental findings of two such interventions have been reported, with promising results.

Bowman and Liddle (1959) randomly assigned 61 at-risk ninth graders to two special classrooms or a control group. These students were judged to be at risk for dropping out of school and delinquency on the basis of their scholastic performance: their tested IQs were below normal, largely in the range of 75 to 89, and they were failing in most of their classes. Eighteen percent of them had juvenile court records, 28 percent had been nominated as among the worst behavior problems in their schools, and 41 percent were rated as seriously maladjusted by school staff.

The authors described the experimental program thus: "Endeavoring to create a warm, relaxed, and informal classroom climate which would allow freedom not permissible in larger academically-geared classrooms, we adopted a kind of a code which said in effect: 'Here there are no rules. You may do much as you like, as long as you do not infringe upon the rights of others within the group, within the total school society, or the rights of the classroom teacher'" (p. 21). This approach, in social organizational terms, increased the *informality* of the classroom.

The definitive feature of an "informal" organization is that its constituent role relationships may be negotiated by the role occupants. In "formal" organizations, roles are prescribed by others—in documents, by a superior, and so on—and role occupants must conform to the prescriptions. Of course, organizations may differ in the degree of their formality, being neither totally formal or informal. Ordinarily, secondary schools are quite formal, and the relationships between teachers and students are minimally negotiable.

In the Quincy, Illinois, program described by Bowman and Liddle, a classroom social organization was created that permitted more negotiation, thereby taking into account each student's styles, needs, and interests. Much of the learning experiences consisted of individual and group projects, and scholastic grades were based on individual progress. Thus the students' agentic self could act in the student role. Furthermore, the emotional warmth of the teachers implied a favorable evaluation of the students' selves. The import of this kind of program for the selves of the students is that it functions to affirm self-worth and the program is cast as an ally of the agentic self.

The program proved effective in important ways. After two years, the students in the special classes attended school significantly more often than did those in the control group, and the former were significantly less delinquent than the latter, according to official records. No significant treatment or control differences were found in scholastic achievement, whether measured by grades awarded in conventional classes or in standard scholastic achievement tests.

In the second field experiment, Gold and Mann (1980) observed secondary school students in three suburban alternative school programs and comparison groups of students who had been referred to the programs but could not be enrolled because there was no more room. All of these students were facing expulsion or suspension from school because of their disruptive behavior. When asked in a confidential interview about their delinquent behavior, they reported substantially more recent delinquent acts than a comparable national sample of American teenagers had. The research followed the students through a year of the alternative school experience of the treatment group and then through the subsequent school term when all the students were supposed to attend the conventional school.

Although the three programs seemed quite different, they were selected for study because they shared two characteristics: students pursued individualized curricula, and their teachers were especially warm and supportive. Otherwise, one program featured a daily group meeting at which students' social and emotional problems were discussed; another focused partly on teaching students to cope with difficult interpersonal situations by means of classroom exercises in social skills; and the third seemed quite conventionally scholastic. The two common characteristics were thought to be essential, however, to affect the youths' sense of themselves. They served to sharply reduce experiences of scholastic failure and to keep the students willingly in their program.

By tailoring each student's study to his or her interests and skills levels, the alternative programs gave their students opportunities to experience scholastic success. Students worked on "contracts" that specified, for example, which books they would read in a given period of time and how many math workbooks they would complete. They also contracted, individually or sometimes in small groups, to complete art and building projects or reports on library research. Not only could students see themselves completing their projects and moving through graded workbooks and such, but the evaluative feedback that they got from their teachers was solely in terms of comparisons with their own earlier performance. They were not held up to universal norms for their age and year in school. Their school grades reflected their progress.

It was important that the alternative school teachers provided more social and emotional support to their students than is typical in a conventional secondary school, especially at first. These problematic youth came to the alternative programs after years of conflict and failure at school. Many were suspicious and hostile toward teachers, and they doubted their capacity to succeed. Assuring them that their selves were safe from bruising encouraged the students to keep coming to school. This was done by partly suspending the conventional teacher-student role relationships, making them more informal. Rather than the students changing teachers each class period as they passed from room to room, the same team of teachers was present for most of a student's day. This frequently included those periods devoted to physical education, so that the teams of teachers would play games with their students. The teachers also participated in outings and overnight camping trips with their classes. Interaction in many different kinds of social settings served to encourage informality, reducing the predetermined regulated role relationships that typically prevail between secondary school teachers and students. It became common for students to call their teachers by their first names. There was also more physical touching between teachers and students than one commonly observes in a conventional secondary school.

These relationships were designed to demonstrate that the teachers believed their students were good people. Consequently, when the researchers asked the alternative school students about their attitudes toward their teachers, it was not uncommon for students to describe their teachers as their "friends."

One should not underestimate the potentiality of teachers for affirming adolescents' selves. Despite the rapidly changing physical, cognitive, and social forces that impel adolescents toward greater conformity with peer influence, the influence of adults remains important. This is especially true in matters that transcend taste and style in music, clothes, and such—portentous matters of skills and values. Interaction with teachers and the grades that teachers give matter. In large part, youth turn to peers for self-affirmation to the degree that teachers and other responsible adults do not provide it.

Students at the alternative schools were substantially better behaved there than they had been at conventional schools. Nevertheless, disruption was more common at the alternative schools than at the conventional schools. Students often had to be admonished by a glance or a word. They had to be "talked to" quietly at their desks. Sometimes thay had to be hauled bodily out of the classroom. Parents were sometimes called to school for conferences. In all cases, punishment was avoided. Inappropriate behavior was dealt with, but in ways intended to preserve as much as possible students' feelings of autonomy and to maintain relationships that testified to the worth of each student's self.

The way truancy was often treated is a good example of how the alternative school programs applied discipline gentle to the self. Truancy had been a major problem with the students who were referred to these programs. Although attendance improved considerably during the year at the alternative school, students still did not always show up or call in excused absences at the start of the school day. On these occasions, it was frequently the practice to go get them. A staff member would drive out to a truant student's home, and, by cajoling, insisting, or threatening to call the attendance officer, persuade the student to come to school. Once there, the student would first be stoked up with coffee or milk and a doughnut and then sent off to class. Later that day, the student was obliged to negotiate some arrangement to make up the time missed, and this arrangement was enforced. Throughout this procedure, the alternative school staff stressed that they wanted the student to attend school regularly because it was important to his or her own welfare.

In these ways, then, this kind of alternative school affirms its students' selves. When assured of scholastic success, troubled and troublesome students receive unaccustomed evidence of a critical competency. At the same time, teachers' socioemotional support affirms the general worth of their students, thus also testifying to the students' ability to achieve social approval from important authorities.

Another self-enhancing characteristic of the alternative school program deserves some mention, although it is probably not as essential as assuring success and giving students warm social and emotional support. The staffs at the three participating alternative schools tended to be somewhat subversive of the conventional school system. We researchers spent many hours in informal conversation with them, and this theme was struck frequently. The staffs were self-selected, committed to working with difficult students. Many expressed the belief that their alternative school program was the right one, not only for difficult students but for schools generally. They aspired to be in the vanguard of general school reform.

This educational philosophy was part of the staffs' occupational culture. For the students, who undoubtedly became aware of it, this culture implied that they were not responsible for the conflict and failure they had experienced in conventional schools. "The System" was at fault, not themselves. They came to believe that they could make it in the conventional school if they learned to cope with its faults. This belief of the students was confirmed by the feedback of progress they were making at the alternative school and contributed to their confidence in themselves as students.

The results of all three programs were positive. According to the teachers at the conventional school to which they returned, the alternative school students performed better scholastically and behaved better than students in the comparison group did. Indeed, most of the alternative school students came within the normal range of conventional students in these respects.

Certain psychological changes appear to have been critical to the effectiveness of the alternative school programs. First, it was important that the students recognized that their teachers and the program would adapt to their needs, a variable that the researchers labeled "flexibility." The alternative school students perceived their schools to be significantly more flexible than the conventional school comparison group did, and a path analysis of the data showed that this perception was pivotal to other changes. In terms of the general theory of self outlined earlier, the alternative school students recognized that the teachers and the programs were to some greater degree responsive to their wills, that is, allied with their agentic selves. Those that did not believe this were not as a group significantly more successful conventional school students later.

Perceiving greater flexibility of the alternative schools, students tended to change some of their attitudes. They reported that they were more confident of themselves as students, and they expressed more interest in continuing their education. These data are the most relevant to the theoretical links among school experiences, feelings about the self, and delinquent behavior. For those students who gave this evidence of greater confidence in their scholastic competency were those who were later less disruptive and more successful students.

It should be pointed out that neither ideal-self discrepancy nor projective measures of self-esteem distinguished the treated from the comparison groups; nor did they relate to success at the conventional school in the follow-up data. The evidence for change in self resides in the measures of confidence as a student and interest in school.

SELF, SCHOOL, AND SOCIETY

The kind of alternative school described here contrasts sharply with delinquency treatment programs that neglect the self-enhancing motivation for delinquency. Indeed, some of these programs may intentionally or unintentionally threaten youth's self-esteem.

One such program is Scared Straight. This program, now out of favor, would expose delinquent youth or youth "at risk" of delinquency to adult prisoners. In dramatic sessions at the prisons, convicts described the dreadful conditions of incarceration and warned the youth of the dangers awaiting them should they be imprisoned. The idea of Scared Straight was to enhance social control by demonstrating the terrible costs of deviance.

In contrast to the glowing reviews the program received in some of the popular media, careful research on Scared Straight (Finckenour, 1979; Heeren & Shichor, 1984) revealed that it did not decrease delinquency. In fact, those exposed to the program may have become more delinquent on account of it. Scared Straight might very well have challenged youths' sense of competency. Youth may have taken the program as a dare, in the same way that it seems youth observed by Stuart et al. (1976) regarded increased penalties for possessing marijuana. To have retreated from delinquency in the face of the convicts warnings may have been regarded as "chicken."

Another example of a program that threatens rather than affirms delinquent youths' self-esteem is the "boot camp." This intervention emphasizes strict obedience to authority and challenges the limits of youths' physical stamina. It is modeled on basic military training.

Basic training anticipates lethal combat as a potential situation in military service. In that situation, strict discipline and physical stamina are highly functional. This rationale is not appropriate for delinquents. It is likely that youth interned in boot camps, deliberately commanded to subjugate their wills to the staff, and sometimes humiliated and intimidated experience the program as an attack on their selves.

Does the physical challenge of boot camp programs have the potential to enhance youth's self-esteem? To the degree that the challenge is modulated by individual differences and ensures youth's success, it may, although it is not clear that such modulation actually occurs.

Other delinquency treatment programs also present physical challenges in order to enhance youths' self-esteem. For example, Outward Bound (Kelly & Baer, 1971; Baer, Jacobs, & Carr, 1975) offers rock climbing, spelunking, and such, and teaches youth the skills to meet these challenges successfully. Garrett's (1985) meta-analysis of delinquency treatment programs led her to conclude that this kind of program is promising. Evaluations of this program have not been rigorous, however, inasmuch as they have not employed control groups.

I doubt that these programs have the impact of alternative schools. It is unlikely that experiences of success in outdoor programs effect lasting changes in many youths' sense of competence, because only a rare youth regards such activities as relevant to "career."

The power of the kind of alternative school program that I have described derives from the centrality of the school system in our society. Schools are proving grounds and a sorting mechanism. They are designed to serve our society, aping in many ways the social structure of work and leisure in the adult years. It is widely believed, among students as among the rest in our culture, that how well youths perform in school is indicative of their vocational and avocational competence. And this of course implies what quality of life-style they may enjoy for the rest of their lives. Success or failure at school is therefore a telling experience, affecting evaluation of self.

Proven competence outside of the scholastic domain, in such activities as Outward Bound, seldom is so telling. In order for it to have the effect that proven scholastic ability has, it must seem relevant to career, in a broad sense, and to reference groups that witness an individual's career or career potential. By social consensus, success in other activities does not convey so well the affirmation that scholastic competence enjoys. Still, some delinquent youths may adopt reference groups that do appreciate demonstrated competence of some other sort, and these references may replace peer reference groups for them. Lacking widespread social recognition, however, these sources of self-esteem do not have the potential for changing the self that schools do.

This raises the troubling question of how to treat youth who for some reason do not appear capable of acquiring minimal scholastic competence and, by implication, social respectability in the future. Are many of these inevitably bound to a heavily delinquent adolescence? Are they fated as adults to the myriad problems to which delinquent adolescents are prone (Robins, 1966)? The prospects for these youth are not so dim. It should be pointed out that, according to standard scholastic achievement tests, the scholastic competence of the alternative school students studied by Bowman and Liddle and by Gold and Mann did not improve significantly relative to the comparison groups. However, their course grades improved, their confidence in their ability as students increased, and their behavior got better. What seemed to matter was that their selves became "normal," that is, adequate to attain normal goals. The special programs enabled them to employ what talent they had to surmount the hurdle of adolescence and send them on more benign ways.

The psychological importance of a normally competent self has been demonstrated by the findings of an exemplary Headstart program (Schweinhart, Berrueta-Clement, Barnett, Epstein, & Weikart, 1985). The specifics of the intervention need not concern us here. Suffice it to say that it seemed critical to the program's effectiveness that caregivers learned to engage in intellectually enriching interaction with their preschoolers and that the preschool teachers encouraged the children to initiate inquiry and activity. Compared with a control group, the children in the program demonstrated superior scholastic competence for the next several years of school, but that superiority faded. Nevertheless, the program's students behaved better and performed better through high school.

The researchers note especially that the children who had been in this Headstart program were significantly less likely than the control group to be referred in primary school to special classes for the emotionally maladjusted or learning disabled. In other words, their teachers found them to be more normal. One interpretation of this is that their early experiences of competence at school created a foundation of self-confidence that enabled the students to satisfy the norms of their school. Their motivation to do so was not blunted by discouragement. Growing up believing that their agentic self was adequate to achieve socially respectable goals, these youth did not then strike out on other, troublesome paths.

If belief in at least a normally competent self is important for youths' behavior, what then is the effect of being sent to a special school during adolescence? The potential problem of stigma was addressed explicitly both by Bowman and Liddle and by Gold and Mann. Neither found stigma to be a problem for the youths. Students in both programs initially expressed some concern about appearing "weird," "bad," and such, but that concern soon diminished as their morale increased. It was replaced by personal pride in the gains they were making and in the belief in the superiority of their school.

SUMMARY

I have offered a definition of *self* that is centered on competence. *Self* is defined as *that which is exclusively responsive to one's will;* that is, it is the ultimate agent which must realize an individual's purposes. Evaluation of the self is therefore based primarily on how effective that agent is for achieving goals, and a positive evaluation—self-esteem—is desirable.

From this base is derived a theory of juvenile delinquency. Delinquent behavior is hypothesized to be a performance for the purpose of raising self-esteem. By means of delinquency, youth demonstrate a kind of competency to themselves and to others and, at the same time, reject the value of the goals which they judge themselves incompetent to achieve. Much of the data describing delinquent behavior, its preconditions, and its consequences fall into coherent place within this framework.

Failure at school is identified as a major cause of self-derogation. The importance of scholastic performance flows from the centrality of school as a social institution: it is both a training site and proving ground for the styles and skills necessary to the attainment of those goals which youth are ordinarily socialized to desire. It follows from this that a scholastic program in which students do not fail will raise youths' self-esteem and reduce their delinquent behavior. Several such programs have proved effective.

Whether the theory and data of alternative schools for heavily delinquent and disruptive youth indicate that they should be models for schools generally is arguable. I have observed that the many staff members of alternative schools believe that their philosophy and practice should be adopted widely. This proposal has not received adequate theoretical and empirical attention, so what follows should be taken as my speculation.

The argument is keenest in the secondary schools. Primary schools in the United States already at least voice a particularistic philosophy of "teaching the child, not the subject." Secondary schools are markedly more impersonal (Eccles & Midgley, 1989).

My own inclination is to favor the impersonality and normative evaluation prevalent in comprehensive U.S. secondary schools. Schools function to prepare youth for adulthood in their society. However much some may lament the impersonality and competitiveness of contemporary U.S. society, schools have not historically been the vanguard of social change, so opinions about what constitutes the Good Society are beside the point here. Adolescents are better prepared for contemporary American adulthood by learning to cope with an impersonal social organization and universalistic evaluation. The vast majority of our youth succeed in this environment; few are crushed by it.

The current typical levels of impersonality and universalism should be tempered, however, in two instances. First, students should not have to make the transition from primary to secondary school cold turkey. The transition should be more gradual. This is essentially the philosophy of the "middle school" in contrast to the "junior high school." Middle school philosophy calls for blending the primary and secondary school approach along just those two dimensions that distinguish effective alternative schools, graduating the change from particularistic to universalistic evaluation of performance and from socioemotional support to impersonality.

Second, secondary schools should accommodate themselves as much as possible to individual student differences in readiness for the secondary school orientation within the comprehensive high school. Accommodation is limited, however; and for this reason, Gold and Mann (1980) have argued for separate physical facilities for alternative schools for extremely troubled and troublesome students. Nevertheless, greater accommodation than is usually afforded within the conventional secondary school is in order for those students who are having difficulty coping with the program. Referral to a separate alternative school should not be made prior to other remedial efforts because alternative schools necessarily entail a delay in students' social development. Besides, alternative schools are costly.

This discussion, focusing as it has on the way *self* is implicated in provocations to delinquent behavior, has neglected the other side of the delinquency equation, social control. Specifically, I have not discussed the function that the social institution of the family plays in restraining delinquency, through its caregiving and socializing (Snyder & Patterson, 1987; Weintraub & Gold, 1991). Although caregivers may also provoke delinquency by derogating their wards, it is probably the case that families contribute to youths' delinquency mainly by losing control over them. In other words, families may afford youth the opportunity to defend their self-esteem by means of delinquency. This subject requires separate treatment and cannot be pursued here. Suffice it to point out that the alternative school programs I described have proved effective without attempting to deal with their students' problems at home. It may be necessary, however, to deal with these problems in order to reach the very anxious and depressed students with whom these programs are not effective.

In conclusion, I want to underscore what I hope will prove to be the major contribution of this chapter. I want to emphasize its base in the theory about *self* from which the ideas about the cause and treatment of delinquency have been derived. I believe that the definition of *self* as agent is a useful one, one which organizes a great deal of the theory and data about *self*, including theoretical and practical problems not connected to juvenile delinquency. I have tried to show that conceiving of *self* as agent also sharpens our understanding of how we regard our selves as objects. Moreover, this approach specifies the relationship between self and society, locating it in the socialization process by which goals and the means for attaining them are approved or disapproved.

NOTE

1. Marita Roesch Inglehart has pointed out to me that juvenile drug addicts indeed steal to support their habit. This is true, but drug addicts are rare among even heavily delinquent juveniles. Furthermore, I hypothesize that juveniles' initial use of drugs is, like other delinquent behavior, typically a performance for their peers.

REFERENCES

Baer, D. J., Jacobs, P. J., & Carr, F. E. (1975). Instructors' ratings of delinquents after Outward Bound survival training and their subsequent recidivism. *Psychological Reports, 36:*547–553.

Bowman, P. H., & Liddle, G. P. (1959). *Slow learners in the secondary schools.* Chicago: University of Chicago Quincy Youth Development Project.

Cohen, A. K. (1955). *Delinquent boys: The cultures of the gang.* Chicago: Free Press.

Eccles, J. S., & Midgley, C. (1989). Stage/environment fit: Developmentally appropriate classrooms for early adolescents. In *Research on education,* edited by R. E. Ames & C. Ames (vol. 3, pp. 139–186). New York: Academic Press.

Elliott, D. S., & Huizinga, D. (1983). Social class and delinquent behavior in a national youth panel. *Criminology, 21:*149–177.

Finckenour, J. O. (1979). Scared crooked. *Psychology Today, 13*(3):6–11.

Garrett, C. J. (1985). Effects of residential treatment on adjudicated delinquents: A meta-analysis. *Journal of Research in Crime and Delinquency, 22:*287–308.

Gold, M. (1970). *Delinquent behavior in an American city.* Belmont, CA: Brooks/Cole.

Gold, M., & Mann, D. W. (1972). Delinquency as defense. *American Journal of Orthopsychiatry*, 42:463–479.

———. (1980). *Expelled to a friendlier place*. Ann Arbor, MI: University of Michigan Press.

Hauser, R. (1969). Schools and the stratification process. *American Journal of Sociology*, 74:587–611.

Heeren, J., & Shichor, D. (1984). Mass media and delinquency prevention: The case of "Scared Straight." *Deviant Behavior*, 5:375–386.

Kaplan, H. B. (1980). *Deviant behavior in defense of self*. New York: Academic Press.

Kelly, F. J., & Baer, D. J. (1971). Physical challenge as a treatment for delinquency. *Crime and Delinquency*, 17:437–445.

Morris, R. R. (1964). Female delinquency and relational problems. *Social Forces*, 43:82–89.

Nye, F. I., Short, J. F., & Olson, V. J. (1958). Socioeconomic status and delinquent behavior. *American Journal of Sociology*, 63:381–389.

Osgood, C. E., Suci, G. J., & Tannenbaum, P. H. (1957). *The measurement of meaning*. Urbana, IL: University of Illinois Press.

Oyserman, D., & Markus, H. R. (1990). Possible selves and delinquency. *Journal of Personality and Social Psychology*, 59:112–125.

Robins, L. N. (1966). *Deviant children grown up*. Baltimore, MD: Williams & Wilkins.

Schweinhart, L. J., Berrueta-Clement, J. R., Barnett, W. S., Epstein, A. S., & Weikart, D. P. (1985). The promise of early childhood education. *Phi Delta Kappan*, 66:548–553.

Snyder, J., & Patterson, G. R. (1987). Family interaction and delinquent behavior. In *Handbook of juvenile delinquency*, edited by H. C. Quay. New York: John Wiley.

Stuart, R. B., Quire, K., & Krell, M. (1976). Penalty for the possession of marijuana: An analysis of some of its concomitants. *Contemporary Drug Problems* (Winter):553–563.

Weintraub, K. J., & Gold, M. (1991). Monitoring and delinquency. *Criminal Behaviour and Mental Health*, 1:268–291.

Williams, J. R., & Gold, M. (1972). From delinquent behavior to official delinquency. *Social Problems*, 20:209–229.

Ziller, R., Hagey, J., Smith, M., & Long, B. (1969). Self-esteem: A self-social construct. *Journal of Consulting and Clinical Psychology*, 33:84–95.

CHAPTER 4

Changing the Religious Self and the Problem of Rationality

P. J. Watson

Psychotherapeutic attempts to change the religious self most simply occur as an encounter between client and therapist. Yet, as Browning (1987) notes, they also represent "a cultural problematic of great general significance" (p. 2). The difficulty is that both religion and the modern psychologies "provide concepts and technologies for the ordering of the interior life" (Browning, p. 2), and like moral philosophies generally (MacIntyre, 1981, pp. 50–51), clinical psychologies begin with some definition of "fallen" or pathological forms of "human nature," specify some *telos* or goal toward which the individual should strive, and then employ the practical reasoning and experience of therapy to move a client from the former to the latter condition. In short, "significant portions of the modern psychologies, and especially the clinical psychologies, are actually instances of religio-ethical thinking" (Browning, p. 8).

Some psychotherapists may try to ignore this "cultural problematic" by demanding to see the self as a culturally nonspecific psychological process. This is not an uncontroversial strategy, however. Self-concept can be described "as a multifaceted phenomenon—as a set of images, schemas, conceptions, prototypes, theories, goals, or tasks," and in much contemporary research, "there is a consensus that . . . [these aspects of the self] are social products" (Markus & Cross, 1990, p. 577). Some selves therefore crystallize into internal structures that are derived from religious social environments. For these individuals, religion supplies the schemas, goals, and other structures that serve as the raw

materials of a self. The crucial question is whether psychotherapists can dismiss the religious construction of such selves and instead concentrate on a more generic and hypothetical psychological self.

In answering this question, this chapter first will claim that
conflicts between religious and therapeutic conceptualizations of
the self reveal that religious issues cannot be ignored. Next, it will
be argued that recent developments in understanding the scientific
method, rationality, and the self reveal that there are no simple
solutions to the problem. A promising approach nevertheless will
appear in research that remains sensitive to the manner in which
community-specific forms of "rationality" can lead both to the
formation of a self and to the creation of new psychological knowledge. Such a sensitivity will be illustrated in recent studies examining psychotherapeutic critiques of traditional religion. More generally, the promotion of "conversations" among individuals on all
sides of an issue will be described to be the most defensible response to this "cultural problematic." Such interchanges should
promote deeper understandings of the self in general and of the
religious self in particular.

CONFLICTS OF THE "CULTURAL PROBLEMATIC"

A common grounding in religio-ethical thinking could operate as a
"cultural problematic" only if some conflict were involved. A
Christian who tries "to turn the other cheek" must confront the
undesirable consequences of his unassertiveness (Sanders & Malony, 1982). A young woman finds herself drawn to feminist
thought, but experiences a growing sense of loneliness within her
church (Rayburn, 1985). A college student is troubled by his inability to eliminate depression through prayer and Bible study
(Grosch, 1985). A victim of post-traumatic stress disorder struggles with how his actions in Vietnam proved to be incompatible
with his religious beliefs (Wick, 1985). An abused wife is paralyzed
between desires to leave her husband and to remain true to her
marriage vows (Liaboe, 1985). In each instance, psychological discomfort reveals a need for change, and the presenting problem
unavoidably implicates religious issues. For some therapists, it undoubtedly would be clear that religious beliefs conflict with mental
health and consequently should be eliminated.

The claim that mental health and religion are incompatible is not new, of course. Theorists prominent in the history of psychology have been famous for their antipathy toward organized religion. In the best-known example, Freud evaluated religion as "a delusional remolding of reality" (1961b/1930) and as a "universal neurosis" that spared believers "the task of constructing a personal one" (1961a/1927, p. 44). Jung, as Rieff (1966, pp. 128–129) points out, "presented a God who strangely resembled the Christian devil"; and Fromm (1947, pp. 18–24) differentiated rational humanistic forms of ethics from the supposedly antidemocratic and guilt-ridden spirit of traditional beliefs. For Skinner (for example, 1953, p. 351), faith could be reduced to superstitious behavior, and on the basis of his own research, Maslow (1970) discovered little opportunity for an individual to be both self-actualized and committed to any religion that included "the supernatural element and institutional orthodoxy" (p. 169).

More recent theorists have offered even more severe critiques. Within Branden's biocentrism, for example, "faith is a malignancy that no system can tolerate with impunity. . . . When one turns from reason to faith . . . one's mind becomes an organ one cannot trust anymore" (1969, p. 240). With regard to more specific beliefs, Branden further claims that religious notions about sin and the atonement are "as monstrous an injustice, as profound a perversion of morality as the human mind can conceive" (Branden, 1983, p. 221).

In clarifying rational-emotive therapy, Ellis similarly contends that religion, especially in its more theologically conservative forms, "is in many respects equivalent to irrational thinking and emotional disturbance" (1980, p. 637). Much like Branden, he also argues that the "concept of sin is the direct and indirect cause of virtually all neurotic disturbance" (1962, p. 146) and that "unbelief, skepticism, and thoroughgoing atheism are practically synonymous with mental health" (Ellis, 1983, p. 1).

Given such antagonisms, critical reactions within the wider religious community probably come as no great surprise. Christian commentators, for example, caution against the "seductions" of the modern psychological emphasis on the self. Such theories, it is argued, foster "the very antithesis of a workable society where each one submits to a pattern of mutual duty" and degrade social life into "an abrasive collection of selves, each one pressing his claim to the limit" (Kilpatrick, 1983, p. 46). More generally, an analysis of the modern psychologies as antisocial and antireligious "cults of self-worship" (Vitz, 1977) has received an increasingly sympathetic reading in works designed for a broader Christian audience (for example, Bobgan & Bobgan, 1987; Brownback, 1982; Hunt & McMahon, 1985).

Other indictments of psychotherapy have had a wider cultural impact. Lasch (1979, p. 13), for instance, has portrayed contemporary therapies as "antireligions" that undergird a narcissism that supposedly dominates Western social arrangements. Bellah and his colleagues complain that the therapeutic mentality undermines forms of obligation essential to a sense of community, and they go on to "wonder if psychological sophistication has not been bought at the price of moral impoverishment" (Bellah, Madsen, Sullivan, Swidler, & Tipton, 1985, p. 139). Finally, MacIntyre (1981, p. 71) has identified the therapist as one of the central characters of modernity, the one most easily deceived both by the "moral fictions" of the age and by a faith in therapy.

What these contentious views make clear is that therapy for the religious self can occur as a cultural conflict. A culture, in Browning's terms, is "a system of symbols and norms which guides a society or group by providing general images of the nature of the world, the purpose of life, and at least some of the basic principles by which life should be lived" (p. 5). In therapy, the religious self may struggle with the moral philosophies of two warring cultures, one religious and one psychological. Battle lines may be drawn between incompatible assumptions about ultimate causes, about reasonable forms of interpersonal obligation, about the nature of morally acceptable needs, about the social forces that should organize community structures, and about the rules and roles that should govern daily life (Browning, 1987, pp. 8–15, 238–239). Clearly, therapeutic attempts to change the religious self cannot ignore religious issues. How can this kind of cultural conflict be resolved, so embedded as it is in more subjective value commitments?

UNACCEPTABLE ANSWERS

If a satisfactory response to this cultural problematic is defined as one that maintains an appropriate sensitivity to the concerns of all sides, then unsatisfactory solutions are much easier to describe. Again, some psychotherapists might be tempted to deny the existence of the problem in the first place. These therapists could contend that they "restrict themselves to the realms in which rational agreement is possible—that is, of course from their point of view to the realm of fact, the realm of means, the realm of measurable effectiveness" (MacIntyre, 1981, p. 29). By characterizing applied psychologies as mere technologies that say nothing about the proper ends of adjusted self-functioning, defenders of this position could dismiss the notion that therapy has anything at all to do with ethics.

This position suffers from the most obvious difficulty that it represents a commitment to the "facts" that misreads the "facts." "Rational agreement" does not exist. Modern psychologies can have a great deal to say about the "pathology" of religious ends. Objections to religious belief are not imposed upon an "applied" psychology by a wider culture that condemns religion. In the United States, at least, the populace overwhelming believes in God (for example, Bergin, 1980a, p. 99), and therapeutic complaints against religion clearly emerge from a logic intrinsic to the psychological theories themselves.

But perhaps this position could be defended in a prescriptive rather than a descriptive form. Even if they fail to do so, psychotherapists *should* restrict themselves to treatment objectives about which there is rational agreement. The "facts" of particular problems and the effectiveness of therapy could then be assessed objectively, and empirical research could be constrained within boundaries properly sensitive to Hume's warnings against deriving "ought" from "is." That a particular condition exists says nothing about whether it ought to exist. Just because a measure of self-actualization predicts both adaptive self-functioning and a rejection of orthodox notions about sin, for example, does not mean that the religious self ought to be more self-actualized and less orthodox. Science is about "facts." Concerns about the "values" of a religious self should fall within the purview of other, more appropriate experts—moral philosophers and theologians perhaps. The cultural problematic should be resolved by exempting the religious self from psychological critique.

A first difficulty with this approach is that values historically have been an unavoidable concern in psychotherapy. Jung, for example, complained that Western societies too much demand the development of extraversion (1971/1928). For him, the cultural promotion of extraversion obscured the essential contributions of introversion to a more balanced self-functioning. Even largely non-religious aspects of the personality like extraversion therefore can be criticized relative to values associated with other largely non-religious facets of the self like introversion. If largely nonreligious attributes cannot be spared from critiques that are based upon values, then why should religious beliefs be exempted?

A second problem is that attempts to transfer values-related issues to moral philosophy and theology cannot yield a noncontroversial elimination of empirical evidence from ethical questions. In MacIntyre's (1978) reading of Hume, for example, Hume wished only to dismiss "a religious foundation for morality" and sought to offer a replacement "foundation in human needs, interests, desires, and happiness" (p. 121), all of which can be examined empirically. Indeed, if ethical systems begin with assumptions about "human nature," then the social sciences clearly supply data which have an impact on the moral conduct of daily life (Frank, 1988; Schwartz, 1986).

Furthermore, at least some positions in contemporary moral philosophy assume an epistemological and metaphysical continuity between science and ethics (Stout, 1988, p. 297). Evidence made available by the social sciences would have a crucial role in this approach to ethics. MacIntyre (1981, p. 70), for example, "finds something deeply mistaken in the notion enforced by the conventional curriculum that there are two distinct subjects or disciplines—moral philosophy, a set of conceptual enquiries, on the one hand and the sociology of morals, a set of empirical hypotheses and findings, on the other." The conceptual and the empirical cannot be separated. From this perspective, "ethics is not to be sharply distinguished from social science" (Stout, 1988, p. 47).

Most importantly, a prohibition against psychological challenges to the religious self would dictate complicity in forms of life that some therapists would find unconscionable. That the religious self sometimes should change would be for these therapists, and for many other as well, an undeniable fact of history. Indeed, the Enlightenment origins of more secularized and antireligious psychologies probably can be traced to justifiable reactions against the violent religious intolerance of the premodern era (Stout, 1988, p.

161; Toulmin, 1990, pp. 45–71). For those who see most religions as "sexist, patriarchical . . . enemies of human progress" (Albee, 1984, p. 83) and who claim that religious beliefs promote "spiritual murder" (Branden, 1969, p. 245), demands that the religious self be protected from psychological critique must seem like an enforced professional incompetence. Like Ellis (1962, p. 119), these theorists would argue that "basic constructive personality change . . . seems to require fundamental modifications in the ideologies and value systems of the disturbed individual."

Perhaps, then, an opposite solution makes sense. Therapeutic responses to the religious self should be guided solely by the rational and empirical approaches of the social sciences. As Freud (1961a/1927, p. 54) once stressed, "nothing can withstand reason and experience," and empirical evidence presumably would validate his further contention that "the contradiction which religion offers to both is all too palpable." Within this framework, social scientific research could offer an increasingly more precise picture of the pathologies of the religious self. Minor details in understanding might change, of course, but no fundamental reversals would be expected because "transformations of scientific opinion are developments, advances, not revolutions" (Freud, 1961a/1927, p. 55). By refusing to ground itself in reason and experience, the religious self necessarily would reveal its foundations in illusion; "science," in contrast, "is no illusion" (Freud, 1961a/1927, p. 56).

Fromm (1947) exemplified this confidence in reason and experience. Using reason to derive first principles of an "objectivistic humanistic ethics," he identified the *"aim of man's life . . .* as *the unfolding of his powers according to the laws of his nature"* (p. 29, emphasis his). A "science of man" was needed to study human nature. "But this science does not start out with a full and adequate picture of what human nature is; a satisfactory definition of its subject matter is its aim, not its premise" (pp. 32–33). Human nature "is a theoretical construct which can be inferred from empirical study" (p. 3), and objective evidence should reveal how "man's life" should proceed. In theory, reason and experience should discover an ideal self as the proper goal of each individual's development, and a rejection of this *telos* by any religious self would unmask religious "illusion" and "irrationality." In other words, the cultural problematic should be resolved by encouraging a psychological critique of the religious self.

No doubt some social scientists see wisdom in this argument, but recent intellectual developments have conspired to make its conceptual foundations look like an "illusion" (Bernstein, 1983, p. 72). What seemed so clear to Freud over a half-century ago is no longer obvious. Contemporary philosophy of science suggests that revolutions do occur in science; that competing positions can be "rational," "empirical," and "incommensurable"; and that scientific "objectivity" depends upon paradigms with often unsuspected moorings in "subjectivity" (Kuhn, 1970). Like, though not necessarily "just like" religion, "science itself turns out to be a surprisingly pluralistic affair, and some of those who talk about its methods even use terms like 'faith' and 'conversion'" (Placher, 1989, p. 14). Science apparently "begins with assumptions and operates within a tradition or traditions," and the implications seem obvious, "No one can escape the problems of pluralism and discover 'universality' and 'objectivity' simply by appealing to scientific method" (Placher, 1989, pp. 14–15).

Understandings of "reason" have suffered a similar fate. The Cartesian dream of a neutral rationality now seems to have evaporated (Bernstein, 1983, pp. 16–20). The anthropological literature, in particular, has suggested that different cultures and traditions operate according to their own forms of rationality (compare Placher, 1989, pp. 53–73). What a society accepts as plausible will determine to some important degree what is in fact plausible (for example, Berger & Luckmann, 1966, pp. 64–65). At one time, "objective" Enlightenment reason may have appeared to be a reliable guide to indubitable first principles, but now it turns out to have been a cultural construction designed to cope with the upheavals of a specific time and place (Stout, 1988; Toulmin, 1990). Indeed, some theorists have concluded that "all species of objectivism almost inevitably turn into vulgar or sophisticated forms of ethnocentricism in which some privileged understanding of rationality is falsely legitimated by claiming for it an unwarranted universality" (Bernstein, 1983, p. 19).

Such an analysis, however, does not mean that standards of reason have ceased to exist. Instead, the crucial insight is that reason now seems inextricably embedded in the social practices of specific circumstances. That which makes sense within a particular tradition still makes sense, but an external, transcultural Archimedian point of "sense making" no longer seems likely. In the words of MacIntyre (1988, p. 7), "What we need now to recover is . . . a conception of rational enquiry as embodied in traditions, a conception according to which the standards of rational justification themselves emerge from and are part of a history." A tradition constructs its reason as much as reason constructs the tradition in which it operates. Fromm, for example, did not merely rely upon reason to derive first principles of a humanistic ethics. He also used humanistic ethics to derive the principles of his reason.

Relative to Freud's time, therefore, "reason" and "experience" seem much less able to supply unassailable guidance in how to change the religious self. A final and perhaps most surprising difficulty has appeared in contemporary arguments against long-standing conceptualizations of the "self." Implicit in the distinction between a more general psychological self and a religious self is the notion that an essential psychological self can be distilled from the particularities of social circumstances. Illusion and irrationality presumably result when undesirable values enter in as contaminants, and a pristine self uncorrupted by specific commitments should offer the appropriate standard against which the religious self can be evaluated. Within this framework, the happiness of each man "rests upon his courage to be himself and to be for himself" (Fromm, 1947, p. 251).

The existence of such an essential self is increasingly challenged (for example, Sandel, 1982). In social constructionist approaches to psychology, the "self is a social artifact" created by dominant forms of cultural life (Cushman, 1991, p. 208), and a devoutly religious self would not be a self with a lot of religion added to it. Instead, this kind of self would be religious through and through. Similarly, the self-contained and masterful ideal self of humanistic psychology could not be the discovery of an "objectivistic" social science (Sampson, 1977, 1988); rather, such a self would be its product. In other words, this analysis suggests that humanistic ethics, as a received tradition with its own authorities and supporting forms of life, "used" Fromm to work out aspects of its reason.

For some, the social constructionist perspective therefore means that psychology must fail in all attempts to define an essential psychological self. Every self is a "citizen of somewhere," and all attempts to discover the ideal "citizen of nowhere" will be conditioned by the narrow assumptions of a particular time and place (MacIntyre, 1988, pp. 345, 388). In short, conceptual developments in understanding scientific experience, reason, and the self can support a conclusion about traditional religion that is very different from the one offered by Freud. "Far from denying or neglecting reason and experience, orthodoxy wishes to embody them in and through a living tradition" (Oden, 1979, p. 157).

In summary, some commentators undoubtedly believe that the religious self should be protected from psychological critique while others claim that a hypothetical psychological self should serve as the standard against which the religious self should be evaluated. Neither position is fully defensible, however. For some, faith seems too irrational and nonempirical, and for others, reason and science seem too strongly based upon a kind of faith. The situation points toward two most obvious and presumably unacceptable solutions— a mindless relativism or an intellectual authoritarianism of one type or another. What is needed instead is an approach that holds all selves—religious, objectivistic, and otherwise—somehow accountable for their construction and that also acknowledges the limited "objectivity" of the social sciences.

MENTAL HEALTH AND THE IDEOLOGICAL SURROUND

If attempts to change the religious self have a cultural dimension, then "objectivity" would seem to require an explicit awareness of this important "subjective" factor. One place to begin might be with the admission that therapy necessarily raises ideological issues.

Ideology is a word with a long and controversial history; therefore, any meaningful use of the term requires a clear definition. MacIntyre (1978) argues that an ideology has three essential features. First, it has foundations that are somewhat nonempirical. An ideology "attempts to delineate certain general characteristics of nature or society or both, characteristics which do not belong only to particular features of the changing world which can be investigated only by empirical inquiry" (p. 5). Christian beliefs that God created the universe, for example, refer to the real world, but they also speak about events that seem well beyond any easy confirmation or falsification. Evaluation of such beliefs consequently is problematic relative to "the truth or falsity of scientific or historical claims about the character of empirically investigable processes and events" (p. 6).

Second, an ideology has a normative component. It is "an account of the relationship between what is the case and how we ought to act, between the nature of the world and that of morals, politics, and other guides of conduct" (p. 6), including, presumably, psychotherapy. An important linkage exists here because an ideology "does not merely tell us how the world is *and* how we ought to act, but is concerned with the bearing of the one upon the other" (p. 6, emphasis his). Assumptions about events that are beyond empirical inquiry determine beliefs about proper behavior and vice versa.

Finally, an ideology has a sociological dimension. This is true because "it is not merely believed by members of a given social group, but believed in such a way that it at least partially defines for them their social existence. . . . There is a Christian account of why Christians are Christians and the heathens are not" (p. 6), for example. In short, attempts to change the religious self may operate within a somewhat nonempirical, normative, and sociological surround. The nonempirical element may be especially noteworthy because the ideal self of any particular therapeutic encounter could receive no ultimate defense through appeal to more "objective" social scientific data.

However, to say that an ideal self cannot be offered an ultimate defense is not to say that it cannot be defended. Logically, any self can be held accountable to two basic kinds of standards. First, a self can be evaluated according to the standards involved in its own social construction. Since they are normative by definition, ideologies will specify how an ideal self should operate within a particular, somewhat nonempirical understanding of the universe. Ideologies therefore offer a hypothesis about the ideal self. "If a self remains properly oriented within this ideological surround, then it should function in this normatively specified manner." Such hypotheses presumably are open to empirical confirmation.

Second, a self can be evaluated according to the standards built into the ideologies underlying the social construction of other selves. Since they have a sociological dimension, ideologies offer a description of both "us" and "them." Ideological understandings of "them" can be viewed as hypotheses as well. "If the self exhibited by 'them' is analyzed within the assumptions maintained by 'us,' then 'their' weaknesses will be uncovered." Such hypotheses can also be tested.

Nevertheless, efforts to test these hypotheses will need to remain sensitive to current understandings of science, reason, and the self. Most importantly, perhaps, it will be necessary to acknowledge that research operationalizations are the social constructions of particular forms of life. This means that social scientific measurement devices may have a built-in circularity that guarantees the "creation" of what is supposed to be "discovered." As Cushman (1991, p. 207) indicates, "A culture delineates which topics are important to study, which in turn influence the overall strategy of study, which in turn influences what is proper data, which in turn influences how the data are collected and analyzed." In other words, all social scientists will be the representatives of a particular culture, and their empirical work will define domains of interest in terms that are compatible with their cultural assumptions. Within this circularity, assumptions will determine data as much as data will determine assumptions.

A concrete illustration of the "circularity" problem may appear in recent warnings about the dangers of using personality questionnaires to study personality (Nicholls, Licht, & Pearl, 1982). Researchers can operationalize constructs in a manner that virtually ensures a confirmation of hypotheses. A psychologist might argue, for example, that "masculinity" promotes "self-esteem," but by definition, "masculinity" can also include healthy self-esteem. To define masculinity in this manner thus can lead to the development of a "masculinity" scale that contains items monitoring healthy self-esteem. Hence, a positive correlation of the masculinity scale with self-esteem might not confirm the initial hypothesis so much as reflect the constructed data of a particular theoretical orientation. "Given some overlap, we must entertain the hypothesis that the correlation between the scales reflects, to a greater or lesser degree, overlap or equivalence of item content and individual consistency in self-report" (Nicholls et al., 1982, pp. 573–574).

These kinds of difficulties may be common in social scientific investigations and may present an important challenge to the "objectivity" of research. Caution may therefore be required. "It is reasonable to ask what belongs in a construct. Should nurturance, for example, be considered an aspect of femininity? One cannot answer that question with a femininity scale that refers to nurturance" (Nicholls et al., 1982, p. 578).

Such circularity problems can also appear in tests of hypotheses focusing on a conflict between ideologies. For instance, the Personal Orientation Inventory (POI: Shostrum, 1974) is a well-known measure of self-actualization and is based upon the writings of prominent humanistic psychologists. This instrument could be used to test Maslow's claim that traditional religiosity correlates inversely with self-actualization, but the problem is that at least some POI items make explicit reference to religious beliefs. Most obviously, perhaps, one forced-choice item asks a respondent to pick between being "orthodoxly religious" and "not orthodoxly religious." Orthodox commitments are scored as incompatible with self-actualization, and the circularity problem should be obvious. Should rejection of orthodoxy be considered an aspect of self-actualization? One cannot answer that question with a self-actualization scale that refers to a rejection of orthodoxy.

In summary, selves can be held accountable to two kinds of standards, those that go into their own social construction and those that are involved in the social construction of other selves. Such standards can be translated into research hypotheses, but the empirical questions operate within an ideological surround. Researchers may need to understand that somewhat nonempirical, normative, and sociological "meanings" assume a "constitutive" role in social life. "We have to admit that intersubjective social reality has to be partly defined in terms of meanings; that meanings as subjective are not just in causal interaction with a social reality made up of brute data, but that as intersubjective they are constitutive of this reality" (Taylor, 1987/1971, p. 59). All attempts to change the religious self may need to be guided by a more interpretative social science, one that is sensitive to intersubjective meanings.

AN EXAMPLE: THE RATIONAL-EMOTIVE CRITIQUE OF RELIGION

The potential importance of ideological factors in social science can be illustrated by recent controversies over the mental health consequences of religious commitment. In opposition to positive evaluations of religion (Bergin, 1980a, 1980b), Albert Ellis, the founder of rational-emotive therapy (RET), has argued that more conservative, theistic belief systems essentially promote mental disturbance (for example, 1980, 1986). Ellis's critique is framed within a very explicit understanding of the self, science, and rationality that makes his arguments especially apropos for exploring problems associated with the ideological surround.

With regard to the self, Ellis offers the broad recommendation that an ideal self should be based upon a socialized hedonism (1962, pp. 363–364). This first translates into a basic commitment to self-interest: "Emotionally healthy people are primarily true to themselves" (1983, p. 2). They also are self-directed, avoiding excessive dependencies while maintaining a normal gregariousness. Tolerance, flexibility, and acceptance of uncertainty are other key traits, as are risk taking, self-acceptance, and a deep involvement in outside causes or in the lives of other persons (for example, 1983). Although admitting that any description of mental health is debatable, Ellis nevertheless emphasizes that therapists generally support this analysis. "Not all mentally healthy individuals possess the highest degree of these traits at all times. But when people seriously lack them or when they have extreme opposing behaviors, we often consider them to be at least somewhat emotionally disturbed" (1983, p. 2). A normative psychological self therefore can be identified and defended across time and place.

Scientific thinking is another essential aspect of the ideal self, and incidentally of RET as well. Psychologically healthy individuals "not only construct reasonable and empirically substantiated theories relating to what goes on in the surrounding world . . . but they also, if they follow the teachings of RET, are able to apply the rules of logic and of the scientific method to their own lives" (1983, p. 4). Science requires hypotheses capable of empirical falsification, and only empiricism can be trusted to solve important problems that actually have any solution at all. Science is the lone reliable guide to more objective, positive facts.

Finally, "rationality" assumes a pivotal role because Ellis's foundational assumption is that reason and emotion cannot be separated (1962, p. 39). They represent two perspectives on the same phenomenon, an idea illustrated most simply in his A-B-C model of psychopathology (for example, Ellis, 1973). Individuals experiencing mental distress typically explain their difficulties in terms of an activating event (A) causing an unpleasant emotional consequence (C). (See Chapter 6 in this volume by Zastrow.) A salesman may say, "I was fired from my job (A), and that made me depressed (C)." RET assumes, however, that the event alone can never explain the emotional effect. Some belief (B) must translate the activating event into its consequence. The unemployed salesman may irrationally conclude that being fired means that he is a total failure or that his career is over. Such irrationalities, rather than being fired, actually cause the depression. RET thus defends a Stoic view of rationality, and Ellis (1962, p. 54) in fact quotes with admiration the advice of Epictetus: "Men are disturbed not by things, but by the views which they take of them."

Within this perspective, Ellis sees religious orthodoxy as completely indefensible. His position can be summarized most simply as suggesting that conservative forms of theism supply irrational beliefs that necessarily translate the activating events of life into pathological emotional consequences. Particular religious assumptions deserve special condemnation because, as noted previously, Ellis joins others in evaluating the notion of sin as especially dangerous. "The concept of sin," he has argued, "is so humanly inhumane that it would be difficult to conceive a more pernicious technique for keeping mankind moral" (Ellis, 1962, p. 142). Rather than self-interest, "masochistic self-sacrifice" follows from this belief (Ellis, 1983, p. 2). Belief in sin also yields self-blaming, and "the states of anxiety created in an individual by his self-blaming tendencies induce concomitant breakdown states in which he cannot think clearly of anything, least of all constructive changes in himself" (Ellis, 1962, p. 139).

More generally, religious commitments work in every way against a realization of the psychologically healthy ideal self. Rather than self-direction, religion promotes dependencies on hypothetical gods and church authorities. Religious persons do not have a healthy social interest, but "tend to sacrifice human love for godly love (agape) and to withdraw into monastic and holy affairs at the expense of intimate interpersonal relations" (Ellis, 1983, p. 2). Tolerance is "anathema," acceptance of uncertainty is precluded by a neurotic defensiveness, and flexibility is replaced by narrowness and bigotry. Transcendent assumptions make scientific thinking impossible, and indeed, "we could contend that the more devout one is, the less scientific one tends to be" (1983, p. 4). Religious commitments also seem to be "obsessive-compulsive" rather than healthy, and believers are too fearful of failure to take many risks. Finally, believers do not really accept themselves, but make their positive self-attitudes vulnerable to the approval of their god and of the members of their church (Ellis, 1983).

In short, those with orthodox religious commitments think irrationally, and an effective therapy would undermine such beliefs. "The elegant therapeutic solution to emotional problems is to be quite unreligious and have no degree of dogmatic faith that is unfounded or unfoundable in fact" (Ellis, 1980, p. 637). Still, the RET promotion of what seems to be a transcultural ideal self, its confidence in the ability of science to discover purely empirical foundations for a sustainable social life, and its advocacy of an essentially Stoic form of rationality all suggest a form of commitment, a kind of faith that criticizes religion from within a very particular ideological surround.

ANALYSIS WITHIN AN IDEOLOGICAL SURROUND

When the RET critique of religion is placed within an ideological surround, two forms of evidence become relevant. Relative to the issues emphasized by Ellis, how does the religious self hold itself accountable to the standards of it own construction? Second, how does the religious self fare when evaluated according to the standards of RET? The first of these questions can be illustrated by examining the religious understanding of "sin." Within a social constructionist perspective, the meaning of a belief like "sin" may change when moved from one ideological surround to another. What makes "sense" within RET may be "non-sense" within a religious frame of reference, and vice versa.

Social scientific efforts to analyze traditional beliefs in sin in fact have supported this possibility. "Sin" is a central Christian doctrine, of course, and at least some Christian understandings of sin must surely promote emotional distress. The key question, however, is whether any orthodox approaches to sin can be associated with relative mental health. Confirmation of this possibility would document the importance of the "intra-ideological" meanings of the term.

Instead of emphasizing guilt, traditional Christian interpretations of sin focus on an individual's rebellion against God or against the laws laid down by God (Ramm, 1985; Vitz & Gartner, 1984). Seen in this light, the purpose of believing in sin is not to encourage emotional guilt reactions, but to understand what God has commanded. Ramm clarifies the concept by pointing out the Greek origins of the word *repentance*. To "repent" one's sins simply means to "rethink" things in terms of the perfection of God. "Our first opinion is our own and it is an approving opinion. When confronted with the perfection of God, we form a second opinion about sin, which is God's opinion" (Ramm, 1985, p. 95). Repentence consequently refers to a change in mind based on an understanding of what God requires.

Remorse may follow from such thoughtful reconsiderations, of course, but such an effect may not be all bad. Bergin (1983b, p. 10) suggests that a "sensitive but non-neurotic guilt response is a helpful signal that the individual's behavior may be violating someone else's welfare." Similarly, Narramore (1984) talks about reactions to sin in terms of a "constructive sorrow." This kind of response is "a love-motivated emotion closely related to guilt feelings yet radically different. Whereas psychological guilt is a self-punitive process, constructive sorrow is a love-motivated desire to change that is rooted in concern for others" (p. 33). As Paul suggests, "For the sorrow that is according to the will of God produces a repentence without regret, leading to salvation, but the sorrow of the world produces death" (2 Corinthians 7:10, New American Standard [NAS]). A belief in sin therefore should promote personal responsibility and empathic concern, not pathological guilt.

Even when distressing emotions do follow from repentence, a harmonious solution to the problem may exist in the traditional doctrine of "grace." It is the Christian position that a freely available forgiveness for sin is open to all those who accept the atoning death of Christ. "There is therefore now no condemnation for those who are in Christ Jesus" (Romans 8:1, NAS). In theory, since all is forgiven, a psychological transformation should occur because fear should no longer attend the admission of wrongdoing (for example, Cassier, 1988, pp. 119–169). As Oden (1980) notes, "Christian consciousness experiences itself in a curious sense as liberated to fail" (p. 117). Unhealthy guilt responses should be alleviated by strengthening beliefs in grace, not by removing beliefs in sin.

Within a Christian ideological surround, therefore, sin-related beliefs operate in ways either unsuspected or dismissed by RET (Ellis, 1983, p. 6). Such beliefs may not be defensible when removed from their framing assumptions, yet they still suggest hypotheses about how the Christian self should be held accountable to the standards of its own construction. If a self maintains a sensitivity to the traditional meanings of sin, then that self should be more caring in its relationships with others. Furthermore, if emotional distress results from a reconsideration of wrongful actions, then psychological relief should be available in a sense of grace.

Tests of these hypotheses have employed indices of "unhealthy" guilt reactions (Guilt Scale) and of a personal experience of grace (Grace Scale). Guilt was recorded through agreement with such statements as the belief that "nobody in the world is really good, least of all, am I." A sense of grace included the idea that "knowing that I am sinful and that I am forgiven for my sins gives me the strength to face my faults and be a better person." As preliminary operationalizations, these instruments had marginal internal reliabilities, and they also were employed with university students displaying heterogeneous forms of largely though not exclusively Christian commitment. Statistically significant outcomes therefore were not especially robust. Nevertheless, hypotheses framed within a Christian ideological surround received empirical support. With regard to a sensitivity to others, for example, Grace displayed an inverse linkage with narcissistic exploitativeness (Watson, Hood, Foster, & Morris, 1988) and a direct tie with emotional empathy (Watson, Morris, & Hood, 1988a, 1989a).

Explorations of the interaction between guilt and grace centered on what can be described as a "progression" model (Watson, Morris, & Hood, 1988a). Some religious individuals might need to "progress" from the experience of guilt to a sense of grace. Reconsideration of wrongful actions might lead initially to a dominant guilt response. Then in a second stage of reaction, the individual might cope with the emotional discomfort by placing guilt within the context of grace. Finally, personal religious beliefs could produce an alleviation of the emotional distress through a confidence in the availability of grace.

Within this model, Guilt more than Grace should predict maladjustment, and Grace more than Guilt should be associated with mental health. Complexities seem unavoidable, however, for Guilt and Grace presumably would correlate directly. The maladaptive consequences of Guilt therefore might be softened by the adaptive influences of Grace, and vice versa. This covariance might also result in associations of Guilt with healthy self-functioning that were mediated by Grace and of Grace with unhealthy self-functioning that were mediated by Guilt. Guilt therefore should appear to be more unhealthy in partial correlations controlling for Grace, and Grace should seem even healthier following removal of the variance explained by Guilt. In addition, no Guilt associations with adjustment should remain after controlling for Grace, and no Grace linkages with maladjustment should survive the statistical removal of Guilt.

All of these "progression model" hypotheses have received at least some confirmation in an extended series of studies (Watson, Morris, & Hood, 1988a; 1989a, 1989b, 1989c). Grace, for example, displayed reliable connections with lower levels of depression, and when Guilt produced the same result, this effect was mediated by Grace. In fact, a statistically significant inverse Guilt relationship with depression was transformed into a significant positive correlation through the partial correlational procedure (Watson, Morris, & Hood, 1989a). Also noteworthy was the observation that the pattern of outcomes varied with the religious commitment represented within a sample. For predictions congruent with a Christian ideological surround, hypotheses received stronger support in samples containing a larger percentage of sincere believers (Watson, Morris, & Hood, 1989a). Data therefore were somewhat ideology-dependent.

In summary, predictions that a community makes about itself can be tested. Confirmation that traditional beliefs can be correlated with mental health does not mean that the RET critique of religion suddenly collapses, however. Ideological surrounds— Christian, RET, and otherwise—can receive no empirical justification *by definition*. Analyses conducted within an ideological surround nevertheless accomplish two important objectives. First, they hold a community accountable to its own standards. All communities presumably would agree that they should be judged by what they advocate, and a failure to live up to internal standards would challenge the viability of any form of life. Second, such analyses hold other communities responsible for their criticism. Arguments against other ideological surrounds presumably should reflect a fair and comprehensive description of verifiable difficulties.

ANALYSIS OF CONFLICTS
BETWEEN IDEOLOGICAL SURROUNDS

Any attempt to hold the religious self accountable to the standards of other ideological surrounds must respond to two most important challenges. First, operationalizations of religiosity must be chosen carefully. All communities must have both strengths and weaknesses, and the discovery of weaknesses would surely represent a worthwhile contribution. Still, the question remains whether the ideal self of an ideological surround can also be challenged on empirical grounds. Defenders and critics alike probably would agree that the strongest evidence against an ideological surround would follow from the identification of flaws in its ideal self.

Efforts to measure "healthy" religiousness have a long and controversial history in the psychology of religion. The American psychologist Gordon Allport offered one influential approach when he differentiated intrinsic from extrinsic forms of religious motivation. Intrinsicness theoretically represents a sincere commitment in which religion becomes the master motive in a believer's life. Extrinsicness, in contrast, is conceptualized as the use of religion as a means to more selfish ends. Allport and Ross (1967) devised scales to measure both orientations, and research generally supports the idea that intrinsicness is largely adaptive whereas extrinsicness is largely maladaptive (Bergin, 1983a; Donahue, 1985).

Favorable interpretations of the Intrinsic Scale have not gone unchallenged, however. A key difficulty is that intrinsicness predicts agreement with traditional Christian doctrines. Such linkages have led to the claim that "the Intrinsic Scale probably measures something quite different from what Allport intended; it probably measures intense, rigid devotion to orthodox religious beliefs and practices" (Batson & Ventis, 1982, pp. 146–147). Among other things, this controversy indicates that the Intrinsic Scale may be especially useful in testing RET hypotheses about religiosity. From the standpoint of Christianity, the Intrinsic Scale seems to record something very close to the ideal self. From the perspective of RET, intrinsicness may also monitor the "pathogenic irrationality" that Ellis associates with devout orthodoxy.

The second challenge associated with holding a religious self accountable to the standards of other ideological surrounds has been mentioned previously. Circularity in the operationalization of constructs might artifactually create relationships between religion and maladjustment. Again, a self-actualization scale can include rejection of orthodoxy as a defining feature of self-actualization. At least in theory, orthodox individuals might have the opportunity to appear self-actualized only if they self-reported that they were not orthodoxly religious. Recent explorations of such potential circularity problems have rested upon the development of more interpretative methodologies that can be described as rational partitioning, correlational marker, and direct interpretation assessment procedures.

For example, Ellis laments that religious individuals cannot tolerate ambiguity or uncertainty: "Just because life is so uncertain and ambiguous, and because millions of people think that they cannot bear its vicissitudes, they invent absolutistic gods, and thereby pretend that there is some final invariant answer to human problems" (1983, p. 3). The Avoidance of Existential Confrontation Scale (AECS: Thauberger, Ruznisky, & Cleland, 1981) records tendencies to hide from unpleasant ontological realities, and it consequently measures a trait very similar to what Ellis identifies as a weakness in the religious self. The expectation therefore would be for a positive correlation between intrinsicness and the AECS, which in fact has been observed ($r = .20$, $p < .05$: Watson, Hood, & Morris, 1988).

Still, a sensitivity to the ideological surround makes it clear that the AECS includes traditional religious beliefs as indicators of an inability to face existential truths. These beliefs include the ideas that "God exists," that "there is much certainty about the existence of God," and that "it is quite certain what happens after death." Perhaps the AECS correlation merely reveals that only by not believing in God could those who believe in God prove themselves to be innocent of an inability to confront reality.

Analysis of this possible circularity problem centered on the use of a rational partitioning procedure. All AECS items were analyzed rationally and partitioned into separate religious and nonreligious categories based upon their meaning. Religious (AECS-R) and nonreligious (AECS-N) subscales were then constructed and correlated with other variables. Subscale correlations most importantly revealed a significant Intrinsic Scale association with the AECS-R ($r = .51$, $p < .001$), but not with the AECS-N (r

= .06, $p > .05$). AECS-R and AECS-N also did not correlate directly. Data for the full AECS therefore resulted from circularity effects.

The correlational marker procedure has been exemplified in studies of self-actualization (Watson, Morris, & Hood, 1987, 1989b). For Ellis (1980, p. 636), a self-actualization that remains properly sensitive to the rights of others is an important clinical-therapeutic value, but the orthodoxly religious "are so overconcerned whether their god loves them, and whether they are doing the right thing to continue in this god's good graces, that they sacrifice some of their most cherished and enjoyable interest to supposedly appease their god" (Ellis, 1983, p. 2). Sincere religious commitments therefore should correlate inversely with self-actualization. Yet, as previously noted, a measure like the POI identifies orthodoxy as a symptom of unactualized self-functioning. The question remains, however, whether all humanistic articulations of self-actualization are incompatible with religion.

When the correlational marker procedure was used to explore this problem, the Intrinsic Scale served as a "marker" of the ideal and therefore actualized religious self (Watson, Morris, & Hood, 1989b). Intrinsicness then was correlated with each item from the POI. This procedure determined if at least some humanistic understandings of self-actualization could correlate directly with a "marker" of sincere religiousness. The observation of such outcomes would suggest that "antireligious" items within the POI might obscure linkages that actually do exist between religious faith and some aspects of self-actualization.

In fact, both "proreligious" and "antireligious" POI items were discovered. Separate measures were constructed out of these two types of items, and they in fact correlated oppositely with a number of other constructs. Most notably, perhaps, the antireligious items predicted higher levels of the interpersonal manipulativeness of Machiavellianism, and the proreligious dimensions of self-actualization were associated with lower levels of this trait. In addition, the antireligious items combined together correlated negatively with the proreligious items ($r = -.14$, $p < .05$), and all these effects appeared while the Intrinsic Scale failed to display a significant association with the full POI.

In short, these findings confirmed that self-actualization was not wholly incompatible with religiousness, and the Machiavellianism data suggested that antireligious articulations of self-actualization may not foster the sensitivity to others that Ellis recommends. Furthermore, failures of the Intrinsic Scale to predict self-actualization may indeed have reflected an antireligious ideological bias built into the overall instrument. This conclusion received its clearest support in the inverse linkage between the antireligious and the proreligious items. Psychometric standards of internal consistency demand that this correlation be strongly positive, not significantly negative (see also Watson, Morris, & Hood, 1990).

Finally, an attempt to control for circularity effects can be based upon the direct interpretation of questionnaire items by religious respondents. The Irrational Beliefs Test (IBT) of Jones (1968) measures ten basic irrationalities that Ellis (1962) diagnoses as pathogenic, and among these is a Dependency measure that is especially relevant to the supposed pathologies of the religious self. Ellis (1983, p. 2) argues, "Mentally healthy people largely assume responsibility for their own lives, enjoy the independence of mainly working out their own problems." Religionists, however, are necessarily handicapped, "To be true to orthodoxies, they first must immolate themselves to their god or god-like hero; second, to the religious hierarchy that runs their church or organization; and third, to all the other members of their religious sect, who are eagle-eyedly watching them." In brief, Ellis concludes, "For humans to be true believers and to also be strong and independent is well nigh impossible."

Many items from the Dependency subscale in fact include "irrationalities" with which the intrinsically religious presumably would feel compelled to agree. These include the ideas that "people need a source of strength outside themselves" and that "everyone needs someone he can depend on for help and advice." People with a sincere faith in God almost by definition would maintain these kinds of assumptions, and within Ellis's A-B-C model of psychopathology, such beliefs should connect the important activating events of life with disturbing emotional consequences. Not surprisingly, therefore, correlations between the Intrinsic Scale and Dependency are highly replicable and reliable (p's < .001: Watson,

Folbrecht, Morris, & Hood, 1990; Watson, Morris, & Hood, 1988c, in press).

Nevertheless, a sensitivity to the ideological surround suggests that practical rationalities for RET might be practical irrationalities for religion and vice versa. In an exploration of this possibility, religious respondents defined for themselves what was rational and what was irrational. Research participants first responded to all Dependency items according to standard instructions. They then reacted to these same statements once again, but this time evaluating the degree to which each was consistent or inconsistent with personal religious commitments. Religious meanings therefore were assessed directly and were analyzed in a way that revealed where RET and Christian ideological surrounds offered the same or different interpretations of each specific belief (Watson, Morris, & Hood, 1988c).

Statistical analyses therefore offered an empirically based definition of the religious rationality employed by the sample. The Dependency subscale then was rescored so that it operationalized the construct both as a religious and as an RET irrationality. Once these two "readings" of Dependency were created, their comparative validities were ascertained by examining correlations with other self-report measures. For subjects examined thus far, the religious meaning of Dependency has proven to be more valid. For example, the RET scoring of Dependency has suggested that it is "rational" to display high levels of interpersonal manipulativeness, an alienated normlessness, depression, low levels of empathy, and little community concern. In contrast, a religious definition of Dependency has tended to produce the opposite, presumably more defensible recommendations (Watson, Morris, Hood, & Folbrecht, 1990; Watson, Morris, & Hood, in press).

In short, by looking only at IBT correlations with the Intrinsic Scale, researchers might conclude that religiousness predicts a pathogenic dependency. However, direct interpretation assessment procedures suggest something entirely different. RET understandings of rationality may be "irrational" when applied to religious individuals. Such a conclusion does not mean that the RET definition of beliefs is necessarily invalid for everyone. With more antireligious populations, the IBT might yield data more congruent with Ellis's position. Nor do such results mean that religious rationalities are without liabilities. Religion may promote a largely adaptive interdependency without sufficiently stressing the occasional need for an individual to stand separate from the group (Watson, Morris, & Hood, in press). More importantly, however, these data plus those obtained with rational partitioning and correlational marker procedures confirm that "rationality" may have community-specific elements that cannot be ignored when examining mental health issues.

CONCLUSION

Psychotherapeutic attempts to change the religious self most simply occur as an encounter between client and therapist, but they also represent "a cultural problematic of great general significance" (Browning, 1987, p. 2). In some ways, a careful analysis of this cultural problematic reveals that the position of the religious self in therapy is not unique. All efforts to change a self, whether that self be religious or otherwise, occur within the context of normative and sociological assumptions that have somewhat nonempirical groundings.

In a pluralistic culture, however, therapy for the religious self in particular can be complicated by a conflict between the ideologies of the therapist and of the client. In an attempt to resolve this conflict, the religious self could be accepted noncritically on its own terms, but history clearly demonstrates that the religious self can and sometimes should change even relative to the standards of its own construction. Alternatively, some social scientific definition of the ideal self could be accepted as the "objective" and universal criterion of adjustment, but such definitions now seem based upon nonempirical assumptions very much like those of religion. They are "instances of religio-ethical thinking" (Browning, 1987, p. 8), and an excessive confidence in the social sciences could betray an ethnocentrism.

Still, where pluralism is an undeniable characteristic of society, then objectivity would seem to require a pluralistic social science. Different social scientists could examine the attempts of their own and of other communities to socially construct an ideal self. These different constructions could then be interpreted according to ideals both within and between ideological surrounds. Such a social science would open a community and a self to positive changes that proved to be compatible both with its own and with other ideological assumptions (see, for example, Bergin, 1985), but it also would afford a community and a self with the opportunity to defend itself against the perhaps unsuspected ethnocentricism of a different system of belief.

At a practical level, such a general approach to changing the religious self may seem frustrating. It does not yield an easy "technical" solution to the problem, nor does it culminate in any simple recommendation. Beliefs about sin and grace, for example, seem to work within a religious ideological surround. Should therapists therefore promote religion in all clients? Certainly not; many therapists and clients would object vehemently to this kind of recommendation. Does it mean instead that therapists should always see things from the religious client's perspective and accept all beliefs that have demonstrably positive effects? Not necessarily; some therapists might complain that these positive effects are isolated within the broader negative consequences of a religious ideological surround.

The direction of the interpretation can also be reversed. A commitment to self-interest appears to work within a more "secular" ideological surround. Should therapists therefore promote secular perspectives in all clients? Religious therapists and clients could not accept that suggestion. Should religious therapists instead always see things from the perspective of their secular clients and accept all beliefs that have documented beneficial effects? Not necessarily; religious therapists might complain that such positive effects are isolated within the broader negative consequences of secular ideological surrounds.

When efforts to change the religious self are placed within an ideological surround, a more general recommendation emerges. It is a commonplace claim that therapists should see things from the perspective of their clients. To this advice should be added the further suggestion that therapists must also be aware of their own ideological assumptions. Therapy may include the "ideological transferences" of the client and the "ideological countertransferences" of the therapist (Strunk, 1985). The nature of such processes may mean that certain therapists are unsuited for certain clients. In addition, progress in changing the religious self may require that therapists enlist the collaboration of clients in gaining insight into the ideological dimensions of both psychological problems and of psychotherapy. Therapists experienced in the process presumably could be more "rational" in their treatment of all clients. Perhaps this possibility can be read into ideas once expressed by Jung (1971/1916, p. 297):

> The present day shows with appalling clarity how little able people are to let the other man's argument count, although this capacity is a fundamental and indispensable condition for any human community. Everyone who proposes to come to terms with himself must reckon with this basic problem. For, to the degree that he does not admit the validity of the other person, he denies the "other" within himself the right to exist—and vice versa. The capacity for inner dialogue is a touchstone for outer objectivity.

More generally, all attempts to change the religious self should be informed by a broader cultural conversation in which advocates of different ideologies "move past self-consciousness and self-aggrandizement into joint reflection upon the subject matter of the conversation" (Tracy, 1981, p. 101). This conversation should seek to clarify the nature of all forms of ideal selfhood and should be guided by an understanding that science "has become again both historical and hermeneutical" (Tracy, 1987, p. 33; see also Evans, 1989). Because different communities have contrasting ideological boundaries, "experience" and "rationality" may have important limiting conditions. Beyond these initial stipulations, however, it presumably could be agreed that nothing should be accepted "that is unfounded or unfoundable in fact" (Ellis, 1980, p. 637).

REFERENCES

Albee, G. W. (1984). Reply to Lantz. *American Psychologist, 39:82–84.*

Allport, G. W., & Ross, J. M. (1967). Personal religious orientation and prejudice. *Journal of Personality and Social Psychology, 5:432–443.*

Batson, C. D., & Ventis, W. L. (1982). *The religious experience.* New York: Oxford University Press.

Bellah, R. N., Madsen, R., Sullivan, W. M., Swidler, A., & Tipton, S. M. (1985). *Habits of the heart.* New York: Harper & Row.

Berger, P. L., & Luckmann, T. (1966). *The social construction of reality.* Garden City, NY: Anchor Books.

Bergin, A. E. (1980a). Psychotherapy and religious values. *Journal of Consulting and Clinical Psychology, 48:95–105.*

————. (1980b). Religious and humanistic values: A reply to Ellis and Walls. *Journal of Consulting and Clinical Psychology, 48:642–645.*

_____. (1983a). Religiosity and mental health: A critical reevaluation and meta-analysis. *Professional Psychology: Research and Practice, 14*:170–184.

_____. (1983b). Values and evaluating therapeutic change. In *Therapeutic behavior modification,* edited by N. J. Helms & A. E. Bergin (pp. 9–14). Berlin: VEB Deutscher Verlag der Wissenschaften.

_____. (1985). Proposed values for guiding and evaluating counseling and psychotherapy. *Counseling and Values, 29*:99–116.

Bernstein, R. J. (1983). *Beyond objectivism and relativism.* Philadelphia: University of Pennsylvania Press.

Bobgan, M., & Bobgan, D. (1987). *Psychoheresy.* Santa Barbara, CA: Eastgate.

Branden, N. (1969). *The psychology of self-esteem.* New York: Bantam Books.

_____. (1983). *Honoring the self.* New York: Bantam Books.

Brownback, P. (1982). *The danger of self-love.* Chicago: Moody Press.

Browning, D. S. (1987). *Religious thought and the modern psychologies.* Philadelphia: Fortress.

Cassier, H. W. (1988). *Grace and law.* Grand Rapids, MI: Eerdmans.

Cushman, P. (1991). Ideology obscured. *American Psychologist, 46*:206–219.

Donahue, M. J. (1985). Intrinsic and extrinsic religiousness: Review and meta-analysis. *Journal of Personality and Social Psychology, 48*:400–419.

Ellis, A. (1962). *Reason and emotion in psychotherapy.* Secaucus, NJ: Citadel.

_____. (1973). *Humanistic psychotherapy.* New York: McGraw-Hill.

_____. (1980). Psychotherapy and atheistic values: A response to A. E. Bergin's "Psychotherapy and religious values." *Journal of Consulting and Clinical Psychology, 48*:635–639.

_____. (1983). *The case against religiosity.* New York: Institute for Rational-Emotive Therapy.

_____. (1986). Do some religious beliefs help create emotional disturbance? *Psychotherapy in Private Practice, 4*:101–106.

Evans, C. S. (1989). *Wisdom and humanness in psychology.* Grand Rapids, MI: Baker Book House.

Frank, R. H. (1988). *Passions within reason.* New York: Norton.

Freud, S. (1961a/1927). *The future of an illusion,* translated by J. Strachey. New York: Norton.

_____. (1961b/1930). *Civilization and its discontents,* translated by J. Strachey. New York: Norton.

Fromm, E. (1947). *Man for himself.* New York: Fawcett Premier.

Grosch, W. N. (1985). The psychotherapist and religious commitment. In *Psychotherapy and the religiously committed patient,* edited by M. Stern (pp. 123–127). New York: Haworth.

Hunt, D., & McMahon, T. A. (1985). *The seduction of Christianity.* Eugene, OR: Harvest House.

Jones, R. G. (1968). A factored measure of Ellis' irrational belief system with personality and maladjustment correlates. *Dissertation Abstracts International, 29:*4379B. (University Microfilms No. 69-6443)

Jung, C. G. (1971/1916). The transcendent function. In *The portable Jung,* edited by J. Campbell (pp. 273–300). New York: Penguin.

_____. (1971/1928). The spiritual problem of modern man. In *The portable Jung,* edited by J. Campbell (pp. 456–479). New York: Penguin.

Kilpatrick, W. K. (1983). *Psychological seduction.* Nashville, TN: Thomas Nelson.

Kuhn, T. S. (1970). *The structure of scientific revolutions* (2nd ed.). Chicago: University of Chicago Press.

Lasch, C. (1979). *The culture of narcissism.* New York: Warner Books.

Liaboe, G. P. (1985). The place of wife battering in considering divorce. *Journal of Psychology and Theology, 13:*129–138.

MacIntyre, A. (1978). *Against the self-images of the age.* Notre Dame, IN: University of Notre Dame Press.

_____. (1981). *After virtue.* Notre Dame, IN: University of Notre Dame Press.

_____. (1988). *Whose justice? Which rationality?* Notre Dame, IN: University of Notre Dame Press.

Markus, H., & Cross, S. (1990). The interpersonal self. In *Handbook of personality,* edited by L. A. Pervin (pp. 576–608). New York: Guilford.

Maslow, A. H. (1970). *Motivation and personality* (2nd ed.). New York: Harper & Row.

Narramore, S. B. (1984). *No condemnation.* Grand Rapids, MI: Zondervan.

Nicholls, J. G., Licht, B. G., & Pearl, R. A. (1982). Some dangers of using personality questionnaires to study personality. *Psychological Bulletin, 92:*572–580.

Oden, T. C. (1979). *Agenda for theology.* San Francisco: Harper & Row.

_____. (1980). *Guilt free.* Nashville, TN: Abingdon.

Placher, W. C. (1989). *Unapologetic theology.* Louisville, KY: Westminster/John Knox Press.

Ramm, B. (1985). *Offense to reason: A theology of sin.* San Francisco: Harper & Row.

Rayburn, C. A. (1985). The religious patient's initial encounter with psychotherapy. In *Psychotherapy and the religiously committed patient,* edited by M. Stern (pp. 35–45). New York: Haworth.

Rieff, P. (1966). *The triumph of the therapeutic*. New York: Harper & Row.

Sampson, E. E. (1977). Psychology and the American ideal. *Journal of Personality and Social Psychology, 35:767–782.*

———. (1988). The debate on individualism. *American Psychologist, 43:15–22.*

Sandel, M. J. (1982). *Liberalism and the limits of justice.* Cambridge: Cambridge University Press.

Sanders, R. K., & Malony, H. N. (1982). A theological and psychological rationale for assertiveness training. *Journal of Psychology and Theology, 10:251–255.*

Schwartz, B. (1986). *The battle for human nature.* New York: Norton.

Shostrum, E. L. (1974). *Manual for the personal orientation inventory.* San Diego: Educational and Industrial Testing Service.

Skinner, B. F. (1953). *Science and human behavior.* New York: Free Press.

Stout, J. (1988). *Ethics after Babel.* Boston: Beacon Press.

Strunk, O., Jr. (1985). Dealing with proceptive countertransference-like issues: The factor of psychotherapeutic ideology. In *Psychotherapy and the religiously committed patient,* edited by M. Stern (pp. 129–134). New York: Haworth.

Taylor, C. (1987/1971). Interpretation and the sciences of man. In *Interpretive social science: A second look,* edited by P. Rabinow & W. M. Sullivan (pp. 33–81). Berkeley, CA: University of California Press.

Thauberger, P. C., Ruzinsky, S. A., & Cleland, J. F. (1981). Avoidance of existential-ontological confrontation: A review of research. *Psychological Reports, 49:747–764.*

Toulmin, S. (1990). *Cosmopolis.* New York: Free Press.

Tracy, D. (1981). *The analogical imagination.* New York: Crossroad.

———. (1987). *Plurality and ambiguity.* San Francisco: Harper & Row.

Vitz, P. C. (1977). *Psychology as religion.* Grand Rapids, MI: Eerdmans.

Vitz, P. C., & Gartner, J. (1984). Christianity and psychoanalysis, Part 1: Jesus as the anti-Oedipus. *Journal of Psychology and Theology, 12:4–14.*

Watson, P. J., Folbrecht, J., Morris, R. J., & Hood, R. W., Jr. (1990). Values, "irrationality," and religiosity. *Journal of Psychology and Theology, 18:348–362.*

Watson, P. J., Hood, R. W., Jr., Foster, S. G., & Morris, R. J. (1988). Sin, depression, and narcissism. *Review of Religious Research, 29:295–305.*

Watson, P. J., Hood, R. W., Jr., & Morris, R. J. (1988). Existential confrontation and religiosity. *Counseling and Values, 33:47–54.*

Watson, P. J., Morris, R. J., & Hood, R. W., Jr. (1987). Antireligious humanistic values, guilt, and self esteem. *Journal for the Scientific Study of Religion,* 26:535–546.

———. (1988a). Sin and self-functioning, Part 1: Grace, guilt, and self-consciousness. *Journal of Psychology and Theology,* 16:254–269.

———. (1988b). Sin and self-functioning, Part 2: Grace, guilt, and psychological adjustment. *Journal of Psychology and Theology,* 16:270–281.

———. (1988c). Sin and self-functioning, Part 3: The psychology and ideology of irrational beliefs. *Journal of Psychology and Theology,* 16:348–361.

———. (1989a). Sin and self-functioning, Part 4: Depression, assertiveness, and religious commitments. *Journal of Psychology and Theology,* 17:44–58.

———. (1989b). Sin and self-functioning, Part 5: Antireligious humanistic values, individualism and the community. *Journal of Psychology and Theology,* 17:157–172.

———. (1990). Intrinsicness, self-actualization, and the ideological surround. *Journal of Psychology and Theology,* 18:40–53.

———. (in press). Mental health, religion, and the ideology of irrationality. In *Research in the social scientific study of religion (vol. 5),* edited by D. O. Moberg & M. L. Lynn. Greenwich, CT: Jai Press.

Watson, P. J., Morris, R. J., Hood, R. W., Jr., & Folbrecht, J. (1990). Dependency, "irrationality," and community. *Journal of Psychology and Theology,* 18:334–347.

Wick, E. (1985). Lost in the no-man's-land between psyche and soul. In *Psychotherapy and the religiously committed patient,* edited by M. Stern (pp. 13–33). New York: Haworth.

PART 2

Techniques of Changing the Self

CHAPTER 5

Shrinking the Self

Roy F. Baumeister
Joseph M. Boden

The self-concept is a large and complex entity—much too large and complex to fit into consciousness at any given time. As a result, self-awareness is inevitably a merely partial self-awareness. When people think about themselves or turn attention to their self-conceptions, only a limited part of the self-concept can be encompassed. To put it another way, the same person may have a different self-awareness from one occasion to the next, not only because the self changes, but because different parts of the self become the focus of self-awareness.

The result of this limitation in awareness is that it is necessary to distinguish between the full self-concept and that limited part of it that is present in awareness at any given time. The latter portion, sometimes called the "phenomenal self" (Jones & Gerard, 1967), has attracted increasing attention from researchers during recent years. The fluctuations and shifts in self-awareness have been shown to have a substantial impact on thought processes, feelings, and behavior. Most of this research has focused on people's shifts from being aware of one part of the self-concept to being aware of a different part. This chapter, however, will focus on a different aspect of the shifts in the phenomenal self, namely, shifts designed to shrink it—that is, shifts in which people become aware of a smaller and more meaningless portion of the self-concept. Such shifts are extremely important; as we shall see, they are implicated in a broad range of human behavior and experience, ranging from religious ecstasy to dieting, from athletics to alcoholism, and from sexuality to suicide.

WHY SHRINK THE SELF?

The very notion of shrinking the self seems, at first blush, to run contrary to the main motives and desires that modern individuals associate with the self. Modern society is fascinated, even obsessed, with individual selfhood, and this fascination has helped spur an elaboration of our conceptions about selfhood and personal identity into something far more complex, intricate, and mythical than what our ancestors understood (see Baumeister, 1986, 1987). The modern interest in selfhood has resulted in an expansion of self, in the sense that people have come to believe that the contents of the self and the scope of the inner self contain an astonishing assortment of phenomena, including the basis for finding personal values, latent wellsprings of creativity, personality traits that may be hidden from everyone and may even be in contradiction to the person's behavior, latent preferences, the keys to satisfaction and fulfillment, unique capabilities and potentialities, and a goal or destiny that is specially designated for that individual.

Moreover, the modern growth of selfhood has included a love affair with it. Whereas, for centuries, morality and self-interest were regarded as mortal enemies, the modern individual has increasingly linked the self to positive values (see Baumeister, 1991b). Finding oneself, knowing oneself, cultivating oneself, and benefiting oneself are seen not only as moral rights but even, increasingly, as moral duties. This stunning reversal of self-ish motives, from morally depraved to morally elevated, has encouraged people to embrace a cult of selfhood in a frank and enthusiastic fashion that would certainly embarrass earlier generations. The latest fad in this series is the modern obsession with self-esteem. The popular discourse in modern society, ranging from talk shows to government commissions, seems to assume that people should think well of themselves and, further, that it would be desirable for society if everyone simply came to hold a higher, more favorable opinion of himself or herself. Obviously, we have come a long way from the cultural perspective that condemned self-love as two (pride and vainglory) of the seven deadly sins (see Clebsch, 1979), as the mortal error of hubris, as a mark of heresy (Zweig, 1980), or even just as the unattractive interpersonal trait of conceitedness.

The sanction for self-love has helped people feel a kind of fulfillment in self-absorption (Baumeister, 1991b). Braudy's (1986) history of fame concluded that modern society has democratized the glorification of self, offering the dream and perhaps the promise of fame to anyone and everyone. And, indeed, there are many times when people enjoy being aware of themselves in broad and meaningful ways. At the peak of success, when enjoying celebrity status, or on similar occasions people seek and cultivate self-awareness.

At other times, however, people find such broad self-awareness burdensome, stressful, distressing, or troubling, and it is these times with which we are concerned. In such cases, people want to escape from broad, meaningful self-awareness. Everyday experience, clinical insight, and even laboratory experiments have confirmed that people sometimes desire to forget themselves (see, for example, Duval & Wicklund, 1972; Dixon & Baumeister, 1991; Gibbons & Wicklund, 1976; Greenberg & Musham, 1981; Steenbarger & Aderman, 1979).

Unfortunately, self-awareness cannot simply be turned off like a lamp. Escaping from self-awareness cannot generally be accomplished by an act of will. The effort to shut self-awareness down may even be paradoxical, because as one monitors one's efforts to forget oneself, the very monitoring directs attention to the self. This is therefore the core problem of escaping the self.

The most common solution to this core problem is to shrink the phenomenal self. Rather than banishing the self from awareness, the person simply reduces the size and scope of that part of self that is present in awareness. By focusing on a narrow and unproblematic slice of the self-concept, many of the aversive aspects of self-awareness can be successfully avoided. Reducing the phenomenal self to its bare minimum turns out to be sufficient to overcome most of the troubling or undesirable aspects of self-awareness.

The desire to shrink the self, therefore, can be regarded as a more limited but more promising version of the goal of escaping from self-awareness. But what gives rise to the desire to escape from self-awareness? There is unfortunately no single answer to that question, but the many possible answers can be grouped into three broad categories (Baumeister, 1991a). We shall now examine each of these in turn.

Calamity

The first, and most easily understood, reason to want to escape from self-awareness is that the portion of the self-concept that is present in awareness is bad, that is, incompetent, unattractive, guilty, or otherwise deficient. More to the point, these undesirable aspects of self are linked to unpleasant emotional states, such as anxiety, remorse, guilt feelings, embarrassment, humiliation, shame, and so forth. When thinking about oneself brings emotional distress, people want to stop thinking about themselves.

This motivation for escaping from self-awareness can be classified as the calamity pattern, because most often it is set in motion by some crisis, misfortune, or setback. There is a standard pattern to the calamity motivation, although of course many exceptions and variations are possible. The pattern, as outlined by Baumeister (1990), begins with some event that falls short of expectations. It is well known that people have standards, norms, values, and other expectations about how events are supposed to go. Actual events may disappoint them. Sometimes the disappointment is caused by unrealistically high expectations, whereas in other cases it is an unusually negative outcome that causes it, but in either case the key is the discrepancy between what one expected and what one got. When that discrepancy is large, it is fair to speak of a calamity, even though other people (with different expectations) might not regard that same outcome as a calamity.

The second step in the calamity pattern involves attributing the cause to the self. Failure or misfortune does not lead to a need to escape the self as long as it can be blamed on other people, bad luck, or other external factors. But when people blame their misfortunes on themselves, then their self-concepts are drawn into the problem.

The third step involves high self-awareness. As Duval and Wicklund (1972) made clear (see also Carver & Scheier, 1981), self-awareness is not simply the noticing of the self, but rather it typically involves comparing the self to various standards. After a calamity that is blamed on the self, self-awareness will generally be negative and aversive. Thus, not only events, but also the self, has fallen short of expectations.

The fourth step is emotional distress. Negative affect, whether depression, anxiety, guilt, anger, or something else, will arise from being aware of oneself as deficient (see Higgins, 1987). Thus, by this point, some bad event has been blamed on the self, resulting in an awareness of self as deficient and in a corresponding rise of unpleasant emotional states. The more the person thinks about himself or herself, the more common and intense these emotional states become, and so people will want to escape from self-awareness. Shrinking the self to a bare minimum may be effective at shutting down the emotional distress and permitting a measure of peace.

Ego Stress

Not all urges to shrink the self arise from a particular calamity. They may also arise from what may be called "ego stress." The ego stress model is derived from several key findings from stress research that illuminate the essential nature of stress. Although people naively tend to assume that stress is the occurrence of calamities, they are quite mistaken, and in fact someone can be under considerable stress even if nothing bad ever happens. The *anticipation* of calamity is at least as important as the actual occurrence of it (see, for example, Monat, Averill, & Lazarus, 1972). Furthermore, stress is increased if there is uncertainty about whether something bad will actually occur, by a lack of control over it, and by constant threat, that is, if there are periods of relative safety and security between threats, the total stress is immensely reduced.

The core to the ego stress model is the somewhat counterintuitive hypothesis that *the modern self is a source of stress* (Baumeister, 1991a). This hypothesis is the flip side of the glorification of selfhood that we described earlier in this chapter. Just as the value of the self has risen, so has its cost—or, to put it another way, the burden of maintaining a modern identity has become much greater. To develop a modern self, to discover its nature, to know it and cultivate its potentialities, and to maintain a high level of self-esteem can be a demanding job.

As a contrast, consider the nature of identity in the Middle Ages. Who you were was heavily determined at birth: factors such as the social position of your parents, your gender, and your geographical home were powerful determinants of your life course. These remained fixed throughout your life and there was little you could do to alter them. Today, however, these things matter much less, and a life course is built on an identity that is constantly subject to alteration and renegotiation. Family connections no longer arrange an occupation, but rather one's education and personal choices define it. Likewise, parents no longer arrange one's marriage, but rather opportunity, social attractiveness, and personal choice determine who one will marry. Instead of being firmly established at birth, identity is constructed and reconstructed by the individual at adolescence and, to a lesser extent, throughout life. With this increased freedom and flexibility, however, comes increasing difficulty in defining the self. The value of the self is no longer firmly rooted in a family tradition going back several generations; instead, it depends on one's own achievements, and these have to be renewed frequently lest one become a "has-been" despite one's accomplishments. Moreover, competition in achievement means that other people are often trying to take away one's public esteem, and so one has to keep fighting.

The result is a kind of constant threat or vulnerability. The value of the self is dependent on the recognition of others for one's achievements, and that recognition can disappear for many reasons. Projecting the right image and sustaining a good reputation have become preoccupations of the modern individual, with good reason. The point is not that these are shallow or neurotic concerns, but simply that they produce stressful demands. A single failure, a single embarrassment, even a single remark can undo a lifetime's worth of work by destroying one's image. As a vivid example of this, consider the case of Al Campanis, the vice president of the Dodgers baseball organization who in 1987 made one remark on television that was interpreted as racist, which ended up ruining his career and necessitating his resignation.

As stated earlier, however, it is not necessary that anything bad actually happen. The mere vulnerability is enough to cause stress. The self can be compared to a garden that can be made into something magnificent but that is constantly threatened by weeds, bugs, storms, drought, wildlife, and other dangers, only some of which can be predicted and controlled by the gardener. The threat is always there, even if no catastrophe materializes.

There is probably no way for the majority of modern citizens to remove the stressful demands of identity entirely. These stressful demands can be reduced substantially, however, by various means. The means that concern us here involve another principle of stress research. Specifically, interruptions in threat or vulnerability—safe periods—greatly reduce the wear and tear of stress. People can handle many problems, setbacks, hassles, and dangers if these are interspersed with periods of relative safety and security. It is when the danger is there all the time that one gets ulcers or shows other signs of stress. Combat stress (first called shell shock) is indicative of this pattern. A soldier may break down when confronted with dangers that are not discernibly different from what he has faced and survived before; but when these dangers are relentlessly present, with no interruption and no end in sight, they produce a much higher level of stress (Hackworth & Sherman, 1989; Keegan, 1976).

Putting these two lines of reasoning together, it becomes clear why shrinking of the self may be desirable and even beneficial for modern individuals. The self is a source of stress, and stress is reduced by interruption, so modern citizens will be much better off if they can forget themselves now and then. A temporary escape is all that is needed, but it *is* needed. Just as an occasional week's vacation will greatly improve a worker's ability to cope with the stressful demands of his or her occupation, so an occasional escape from self-awareness will increase one's ability to keep up with the demands of modern identity.

Ecstasy

Thus far, we have focused on motives to escape the self that emphasize getting away from something, but escape can also be escape *to* something. Even if there is no particular problem with the self-concept, people may sometimes want to escape from self-awareness as a means of entering into desired, extraordinary experiences. This pattern of motivation can be labeled as the pursuit of ecstasy, because the term *ecstasy* is derived from Greek roots that literally mean "to stand outside of oneself," and because such escape from self is often understood to be a prerequisite for the blissful experiences that form the modern definition of ecstasy.

The idea that self-awareness is an antidote to some forms of bliss is far from new. The major Western and Eastern religions have railed against the self for centuries, arguing that the supreme human joys require shedding the shackles of individual selfhood (see Baumeister, 1991b). Mystical enlightenment, salvation, and divine grace are among the religious conceptions of the ultimate human experience, and all of them require the individual to leave petty egotism, selfishness, and other self-oriented concerns behind. Modern psychological research has confirmed this ancient view in a variety of ways. Love, sex, creative work, peak performance, and other "peak" or "flow" experiences (see Csikszentmihalyi, 1982, 1990; Maslow, 1968) appear to require a forgetting of self or a transcending of self-awareness.

HOW TO SHRINK THE SELF

Regardless of what motivates someone to try to shrink the self, the process of escaping the self follows roughly the same psychological path. Again, the core problem is that the person wants to lose self-awareness, but no act of will can enable a person to shut himself or herself out of his or her own mind. The best one can do, therefore, is often to work on the phenomenal self—to direct one's attention to a small and safe part of the self-concept.

The essence of shrinking the self is a mental process that can be called "mental narrowing" (Baumeister, 1991b) or "cognitive deconstruction" (Baumeister, 1990). It is based on Vallacher and Wegner's (1985, 1987) influential theory of action identification. Drawing on the philosophy of action, Vallacher and Wegner have analyzed how any given unit of behavior can be understood at multiple levels, ranging from broadly meaningful ones to narrow, mechanistic ones. For example, a student may think about what she is doing as *making marks on paper* or *moving her fingers* (low levels), *taking an examination* or *proving her knowledge* (middle levels), or *getting an education, preparing for her career,* or *participating in the transmission of cultural knowledge* (high levels). The higher levels are marked by long-range time spans and elaborate, meaningful contexts; the low levels emphasize the here and now and strip away meaning to focus instead on process. At high levels, one has meaningful action and experience; at low levels, one has merely movement and sensation.

Applying this analysis to the self, one can be aware of oneself at broadly meaningful levels, such as being a citizen of a certain nation and culture, an individual pursuing a particular life plan and maintaining a certain reputation, enmeshed in certain obligations and relationships, and so forth—or, at the opposite extreme, one can be aware of oneself as a living, breathing animal, eating and sleeping, sitting or walking, here and now. Obviously, most people would not be content to think of themselves as merely a lump of protoplasm or as merely another biological specimen pursuing the standard needs of food, drink, and warmth—most of the time. But shrinking the self brings just such a view of self to the fore, and it does provide an appealing way to take a break from the stresses and concerns that come with the complex, intricate, committed, obligated identity that the modern individual constructs.

Perhaps the best way to summarize this temporary transformation of self-awareness is to present it as an *escape from identity into body* (Baumeister, 1991a). The totality of the self can be thought of as a combination of the physical body plus an identity, which is an accumulation of meaningful, socially constructed definitions. There is perhaps no way to get rid of one's body, but one can certainly blot all these complex definitions of self out of one's mind by focusing awareness on the merely physical. Identity is a construct, and so it can be deconstructed.

Another way of understanding the essence of escaping the self is that it involves a rejection of meaningful thought. Recall the calamity pattern of motivation: the problem lies with meaning, that is, in the implications of recent events about the self in relation to various standards and expectations. Self-awareness is aversive only on the basis of some fairly complex, meaningful calculations, such as "Because this client chose to replace me, I must have performed poorly, which means that I am losing my abilities or perhaps never really had them, and soon probably my boss will decide that I am not as good as he previously thought, and maybe I will lose my job, and my spouse and the neighbors will lose respect for me, and . . ." If one can stop engaging in meaningful thought, all those implications will be blotted out. Instead, one becomes aware of self as merely a body sitting in a chair, watching television, consuming fluids, feeling warm and relaxed.

The hallmarks of mental narrowing include an altered sense of time which focuses narrowly on the here and now; attention to rigid, concrete matters rather than abstract or complex thought; and when thinking is necessary, it follows simple, standard, familiar patterns and formulas rather than examining anything new. Movement and sensation replace action and experience.

There are several consequences of shrinking the self and achieving a mentally narrow state. First, one's normal inhibitions are removed, because inhibitions are meaningful guidelines about possible actions, and so when meaningful thought is prevented and action becomes mere muscle movement, inhibitions are not recognized. Second, initiative is largely diminished and the person becomes passive, because to act in a meaningful way is to implicate the self and take responsibility, which is exactly what the person wants to avoid. The person may passively do little or nothing, or, in some cases, there may be a preference for random, casual, impulsive, or even compulsive actions which help distract the mind but do not invoke planning or responsibility.

Third, mental narrowing is generally accompanied by a kind of emotional numbness. Emotions are typically based on meaningful appraisals, and the reduction of meaningful thought removes the basis for emotion. Indeed, the emotional numbing is often a central reason for shrinking the self, because the person wants to escape from emotional distress. One can easily get anxious or depressed about one's professional reputation or one's chances for attracting a suitable mate, but if one can reduce self-awareness to being a physical organism walking to the kitchen to get a glass of water, there is much less to be upset about.

Fourth, shrinking the self creates a kind of mental vacuum that may occasionally manifest itself in bizarre fantasy, irrational thought or action, inconsistency, or apparent transformation of self. Few minds really remain empty, and the rejection of meaningful thought leaves room for new ideas or beliefs. Of course, the person is not usually looking for these new thoughts, because to do so would involve creative playing with ideas or thoughtful exploration, but if such ideas are introduced—for example, in the form of a religious cult—the mentally narrow person may be unusually receptive. Critical thinking is at a minimum, and so simple ideas may be accepted more readily than usual, even if they are unusual, strange, or even dangerous when considered from a normal perspective.

The mental vacuum brings up one additional and important point about mental narrowing: it is unstable, in the sense that people do not find it easy to remain in that state. The modern human mind is almost inevitably driven to resume thinking. Even if people succeed in shutting down meaningful thought, they find that the mind will soon begin to work again. For someone who is merely seeking a brief escape, this may present no serious problem, but for people who are desperately trying to avoid acute emotional distress by shrinking the self, the instability of the state is a serious problem. Each time the mind begins to think in meaningful terms again, the aversive self-awareness and the emotional distress may come back, and the result may be a frantic quest for strong means of sustaining the numb, narrow state.

The broader point is that once the self has been shrunk to meaninglessness or insignificance, it is possible for a new version or image of self to emerge. This does not necessarily happen, but it is possible, just as Vallacher and Wegner (1985) noted that shifting down to the lowest levels of action identification can pave the way for new understandings of one's actions to emerge. As we shall see, sexual masochists and suicidal individuals dream of having a new identity, and spiritual seekers actually feel themselves transformed into a new self. Shrinking the self does create the possibility for new images of self to replace the old ones.

SOME PRINCIPAL MEANS OF ESCAPE

We shall now turn to consider briefly several of the ways people use to shrink the self. Obviously, a full description and analysis of any one of these phenomena would require a long article or even a book in its own right, so only an overview can be provided here. Interested readers may, however, pursue a topic with the aid of some of the principal references and literature reviews (Baumeister, 1988, 1989, 1990, 1991a; Heatherton & Baumeister, 1991; Hull, 1981; Steele & Josephs, 1990).

The question of what prompts a person to choose one means of escape instead of another is an extremely difficult one. To be sure, this is a difficult question for many psychological problems: What prompts one person to prefer one flavor of ice cream over another, to seek out a particular romantic partner instead of others, to choose one hobby out of the many that are available? It seems plausible that accidental discovery of strongly reinforcing efforts may be a major mechanism for steering different people into different forms of escape. The most important point is that the different motives for escape (calamity, ego stress, and ecstasy) generate slightly different patterns of escapist needs, and so people will be most satisfied with a means of escape that corresponds to their precise needs. Thus, for example, someone needing a readily available and extremely powerful means of escape is not likely to be satisfied with a tentative foray into masochistic sexuality, especially if (as is usually the case) no similarly inclined partner is present, and someone who wants a frequent and moderate means of achieving relief from the stressful burden of self is not likely to find suicide attempts to be a viable option.

Still, there is considerable overlap in the satisfaction that the different forms of escape provide. This is perhaps best indicated by evidence of correlations among the different escapist activities. Such evidence is reviewed in Baumeister (1991a), and it is not extensive, but some examples can be listed. Thus, alcoholics have high suicide rates, and binge eaters are prone to engage in deviant sexual patterns.

Alcohol Use and Abuse

People have been drinking alcohol for many centuries, and yet the appeal of this popular drug has not been easy to explain. Recent work by Hull (1981) and by Steele and Josephs (1990) has shed important light on alcohol use, however, and their work suggests that escaping from self-awareness may be a crucial piece of the puzzle.

Hull (1981) proposed that one major effect of alcohol is to reduce self-awareness. In a compelling series of research studies, he and his colleagues provided multifaceted support for his theory. They showed that people who consume alcohol are less aware of themselves than people who consume nonalcoholic drinks, even including people who believe they are receiving alcohol but actually receive drinks without alcohol (which indicates that it is the effect of the alcohol itself, rather than the person's beliefs about alcohol, that reduces self-awareness) (Hull, Levenson, Young, & Sher, 1983). They showed that failure experiences that produce aversive self-awareness cause people to consume greater quantities of alcohol (Hull & Young, 1983). They showed that detoxified alcoholics relapse faster if they suffer from aversive self-awareness than if their self-awareness is either low or pleasant (Hull, Young, & Jouriles, 1986).

More recent work by Steele and Josephs (1990) has clarified the mechanism by which alcohol reduces self-awareness, and it appears to conform to the broad outlines of mental narrowing. Steele and Josephs use the term *alcohol myopia* to capture these effects: alcohol makes one nearsighted, as it were. They note that alcohol reduces peripheral attention and focuses the mind on a single stimulus. As long as this stimulus is something unconnected to the self, escape may be facilitated, but if the drinker begins to dwell on his or her troubles, depression or distress may increase.

Alcohol is of special interest for the theory of mental narrowing because all three motivational patterns have been implicated. Some people drink on the calamity pattern, such as when one recent setback or problem makes a person go out and get radically intoxicated. Others drink on the ego stress model, perhaps having a martini or two every day unless there is a particular need to remain sober. And alcoholic drinks, particularly wine, have been used to facilitate the pursuit of ecstasy in everything from religious ceremonies to sexual pleasure.

Alcohol has physiological effects that impair the capacity for meaningful thought, making it an effective means of mental narrowing. People who want to stop thinking find that alcohol makes it possible for them to achieve that goal, at least until they sleep it off and recover from the hangover.

The consequences of alcohol use likewise conform to those we have identified for shrinking the self. The myopia described by Steele and Josephs often extends to a reduction in emotion, although if the emotional event happens to become the central focus of the intoxicated person's attention it can seem to be intensified rather than numbed. Alcohol's disinhibiting effects are well known. Consistent with our analysis, alcohol does not produce new, spontaneous, creative desires; it merely removes inner blocks, making the person more willing to do something that he or she wanted to do but felt inhibited about doing (Steele & Southwick, 1985). The mental vacuum and receptivity to new ideas that we have suggested as arising from mental narrowing have not been widely studied, but anecdotal evidence suggests that they do indeed sometimes result from alcohol use, such as in cases where people do irrational things and later say that "it seemed like a good idea at the time."

Suicide

Suicide has been a favorite topic of research for over a century, and many theories have been put forth to explain it. A recent review of the literature suggests, however, that the patterns and manifestations of suicide fit the theory of shrinking the self better than other theories (Baumeister, 1990); indeed, the study of suicide was instrumental in developing the theory about escape from self (see also Baechler, 1979). Because of the immense wealth of data available about suicide, it is possible to be more careful and thorough in understanding it than with any of the other phenomena covered in this chapter, although that amount of information also rules out any possibility of a detailed coverage in these pages. To prevent these pages from being filled with several hundred references, we shall cover only the broad outlines and refer interested readers to the comprehensive review in Baumeister (1990).

Suicide conforms, obviously, to the calamity model. Even attempted suicide is likely to be a one-time response to a major personal crisis rather than a regular means of coping with stress or a means of achieving ecstasy. Suicide typically begins with a major personal setback, problem, or disappointment. Studies have indicated that either unrealistic expectations or exceptional problems can result in a suicide attempt. For example, a study of the intimate relationship patterns of suicidal women found that, contrary to the researcher's hypothesis that abusive husbands would be the most common pattern, these relationships most commonly took either of two forms (Stephens, 1985). In one, the woman's expectations for closeness, intimacy, and communication were approximately normal, but the husband remained aloof and withdrawn, thus frustrating her desires. In the other, the husband's behavior was approximately normal, but the woman's expectations for intimacy were extremely, excessively high, so that again she was disappointed. Thus, neither the man's behavior nor the woman's expectation was the cause for the suicide—rather, it was the size of the discrepancy between the two.

Attribution of problems to the self was the second step outlined earlier in this chapter in the calamity model, and it is well documented in suicide. People who manage to blame their problems on external factors do not tend to commit suicide. Suicidal individuals have been shown to be full of self-blame and other signs of internalization of responsibility for problems and failures (Maris, 1981). Low self-esteem accompanies this tendency to blame oneself for one's misfortunes (Rothberg & Jones, 1987; Tishler, McKenry, & Morgan, 1981).

Levels of self-awareness are difficult to document among suicides, but the available evidence suggests that suicide does go with high self-awareness. Careful quantitative analysis of suicide notes has revealed an unusually high frequency of references to self, more even than is found among notes left by people who are dying from external causes or among simulated suicide notes (Henken, 1976; see also Ogilvie, Stone, & Schneidman, 1983). The indirect evidence is also consistent: over and over, one finds that groups known to have high rates of self-consciousness (such as adolescents, depressed people, and members of individualistic cultures) also have high suicide rates (see Baumeister, 1990, or Hendin, 1982, for reviews).

Emotional distress is the fourth step in the calamity model. It would probably not surprise anyone to discover that people who commit suicide have been suffering from emotional distress. Ironically, though, this distress was the hardest of the escape hypotheses to verify with suicidal individuals. People who have distressing experiences such as divorce or loss of employment have high suicide rates, but actual observations on these individuals (at least, on the ones who survive the suicide attempt) have generally not found high levels of emotion. The reason for this may be that one consequence of shrinking the self is emotional numbness, so that the suicidal mental state has often effectively kept the emotional distress at bay. Another, less impressive reason for the absence of observed emotion is that suicide survivors are sometimes studied soon after the attempt, when they are being kept in a hospital or institution and may have been tranquilized.

Mental narrowing is well documented among suicidal people (see Baumeister, 1990, 1991a). They show an intense narrowing of time perspective, more extreme even than that of hospitalized mental patients. Their thoughts are austerely concrete, in sharp contrast to what people imagine. Thus, although the stereotype of suicide notes involves philosophical reflections on one's failed life and references to the future lives of the surviving significant others, actual suicide notes generally focus on specific, pragmatic, banal concerns (Henken, 1976). The thinking of suicidal people is also marked by excessive rigidity, so much so that for decades cognitive rigidity was considered to be a trait that predisposed people toward suicide. This view was only undermined when Perrah and Wichman (1987) showed that, many months after the suicide attempt, suicide attempters are no more cognitively rigid than the average nonsuicidal person; the rigidity is only found near in time to the suicide attempt. Rigidity is thus a state, not a trait, that goes with suicide, which fits well with the hypothesis that suicide attempts result from an inner reaction to exceptional circumstances. The consequences of shrinking the self are particularly relevant to suicide. The loss of inhibitions may be instrumental in making the suicide attempt possible. It is safe to assume that most people would never take their own lives, and for those who do make the attempt it seems likely that they have somehow overcome a variety of inner barriers (see Linehan, Goodstein, Nielsen, & Chiles, 1983).

Passivity is a well-documented feature of suicidal individuals, and it sheds an interesting light on many treatments of suicide. In the final analysis, a suicide is both a murderer and a victim, combining the active and the passive roles; but most treatments of suicide have emphasized either the active or the passive aspect. Legal and religious approaches to suicide have generally emphasized the active aspect (it is wrong to kill; therefore, it is wrong to kill oneself). Likewise, Freudian and other theories have focused on the active role, regarding the suicide as resulting from a wish to kill someone else, which is inhibited and turned against the self. In contrast, people who commit suicide, and those close to them (see Buksbazen, 1976) tend to assimilate the suicidal person to the passive, victim's role. In their own minds, suicidal people are victims, not murderers.

The suppression of emotion has already been mentioned. Suicidal individuals show a great deal of affective numbness. An important study by Williams and Broadbent (1986) began with the prediction that suicidal individuals would respond with unpleasant emotional memories faster than nonsuicidal people, indicating that they were full of emotional distress, but would not differ from normals with respect to pleasant emotional memories. The results were quite different from what the researchers had predicted, however: with bad emotions, suicidals were found to be no different from control subjects, and with good emotions suicides were slower to respond. Moreover, suicidal subjects overall were more likely than nonsuicidal subjects to respond to questions by saying they were unable to recall any emotional memories at all. These results fit the view that suicidal subjects are simply trying to shut down their emotional systems and have managed to succeed to a substantial degree.

The fourth consequence of mental narrowing is the mental vacuum and resultant tendency toward irrationality or fantasy.

Irrational thinking has been found among suicidal individuals, not surprisingly, but the most relevant finding has to do with fantasy. In a large survey, subjects were asked whether they ever wished to be someone else. Although nonsuicidal subjects never expressed that wish, a significant minority of suicidal individuals said they had that wish (Maris, 1981). Becoming someone else is an extreme kind of escape from self, and so this finding is a striking confirmation that suicide is concerned with just such an escape.

As we noted, the mentally narrow or deconstructed state tends to be unstable, and that instability may be vital to understanding why people actually try to kill themselves. Following a calamity, people may begin with merely psychological efforts to become numb. Ideally this numbness is a temporary stage, and later the person reconstructs new interpretations of self and world that incorporate the calamity and allow them to resume participation in life. Some people, however, are unable to make these reinterpretations, and so they remain trapped in the wake of the calamity. If they could remain numb indefinitely, they might eventually recover, but the mind begins too soon to resume meaningful thought, which in their case takes them back to the calamity and its devastating implications. These people are thus caught in a hellish oscillation between two states: one numb and empty, the other full of troubling thoughts and acute emotional distress. Because numbness is better than suffering, they may seek with escalating depression for means that will facilitate their mental narrowing, and suicide lies at the end of this escalation.

This view of suicide differs from previous theories in multiple respects, including the nature of the appeal of suicide. In contrast to views that have presented suicide as an aggressive catharsis, a self-punishment for guilt, or a cry for help, escape theory proposes the appeal of suicide to be oblivion. It is in a sense the ultimate step in shrinking the self, and if successful it does shrink it down to nothing. Even an unsuccessful suicide attempt, however, may be a successful means of escape, because the suicide survivor is typically removed from the distressing circumstances, treated with gentle solicitude by others, and so forth. The actual attempt is typically reported to be a powerful means of narrowing attention to the here and now, focusing the mind on immediate lethal activities rather than on things that might remind one of one's problems and feelings.

Masochism

Masochism has puzzled psychologists for decades, and like suicide it has been the target of a variety of theories. The term was originally used to refer to a pattern of sexual behavior, but Freud and others began to use it in a more general sense to refer to any behavior pattern that seems to lead to one's own suffering, failure, or misfortune. These usages are metaphors and analogies, however, and because they may be based on a misunderstanding of the basic (sexual) form of masochism, they may be misleading. At present, what is needed is a clearer understanding of sexual masochism, and once that is fully understood it may be appropriate to begin generalizing to other behavior patterns.

Shrinking the self is an essential aspect of sexual masochism. Indeed, all aspects of masochism seem designed to undermine and thwart individual selfhood. Whereas maximizing control and self-esteem are two of the fundamental pillars of selfhood (Taylor & Brown, 1988), masochistic techniques are systematically designed to reduce control and esteem. Masochists submit to being bound, gagged, given orders, and generally dominated by a partner who exercises all authority, initiative, and control. Likewise, masochists endure (and enjoy) a wide variety of practices designed to make self-esteem and dignity impossible. Among male masochists, these include symbolic conversion into a female, being called demeaning names, being treated as a baby or dog, kissing the feet or anus of the dominant partner, and being cuckolded. For female masochists, the indignities focus more on embarrassment through being displayed naked. For both sexes, too, being spanked often carries a significant element of embarrassment or humiliation in addition to the pain.

And what about pain? The apparent enjoyment of pain is perhaps the greatest of the various puzzles in masochism. Although part of its appeal may be the symbolism of submitting to the partner's will and being humiliated, there are also direct effects of pain that may facilitate the loss of self. As Scarry's (1985) analysis of the experience of pain has made clear, pain deconstructs the world, reducing awareness to mere sensation in the immediate present and often preventing meaningful, complex, or abstract thought. We have described shrinking the self as an escape from identity into body, and it is difficult to surpass pain for focusing awareness on the body.

The masochistic use of pain has misled other theorists because they have assumed that a desire for pain must mean a desire for injury, loss, failure, and other forms of suffering. Actual observations of masochism contradict this mistake strongly, however (Scott, 1983; Weinberg & Kamel, 1983). Masochists desire pain but eschew injury, and in fact the manuals and workshops that teach people how to engage in sadomasochistic sex uniformly turn out to emphasize advice about how to administer pain without causing injury. Masochists want carefully measured and limited doses of pain, administered by a trusted (and preferably loved) partner, without harm or risk. Some masochists like the illusion of danger or injury, but they do not want to be hurt.

Pain functions thus like a drug to help them escape from their normal identities and enter into their scene of sexual play. Regarded as a mild drug, pain thus can be understood as an appealing tool for shrinking the self, particularly in the ego stress pattern. Unlike the calamity pattern, masochists do not seek out a single, intense experience of pain following a particular crisis or setback in their personal lives. Rather, they tend to engage in their sexual activities on a regular or occasional basis (provided they can find a partner, which is often difficult), repeating favorite practices, and gradually moving to more intense or sophisticated patterns. The troubles that go with ego stress vanish from the mind when physical pain is applied. When being whipped, presumably, one's mind does not wander back to deadlines, pressures, long-range problems, financial worries, and other troubles. "A whip is a great way to get someone to be here now," wrote one bisexual woman with ample experience on both sides of sadomasochism. "They can't look away from it, and they can't think about anything else" (Califia, 1983).

It should be obvious by this point that our analysis applies to masochism and not sadism. If anything, sadism is the opposite of masochism, and it may expand the self rather than shrink it, at least if the person takes seriously the role of being served and worshiped by slaves. In other respects, however, sadism is not a proper opposite of masochism, and people who routinely take the dominant role in sadomasochistic sex games may have a variety of motivations and satisfactions (see Baumeister, 1989). For present purposes, it is sufficient to caution against generalizing our discussion to sadists.

Several of the consequences of shrinking the self are quite relevant to masochism. Passivity is obviously a central aspect of masochism; it seems certain that part of the appeal of being bound and gagged is that no initiative is possible and so one is forced to become a passive participant in all activities. Disinhibition makes people more willing to engage in bizarre sexual practices, which may help explain why masochists seem to move gradually toward more intense and extreme experiences. Sometimes group sex or homosexual practices are also done for the first time during masochistic scenes, which suggests that the operation of disinhibition goes beyond the submissive sexuality itself.

Lastly, the element of fantasy and irrationality that follows deconstruction is also central to masochism. Anyone who talks with masochists quickly perceives that they know their actions are bizarre, and not only that, they embrace and enjoy this bizarreness. Masochism is clearly the acting out of fantasy, and masochists do not mind the unreality of it—indeed, Baumeister (1989) has proposed that they prefer the unreality of it and would probably reject any scene that contained too strong an element of reality.

We noted that suicidal people are more likely than the average person to express a wish to be someone else, which can be described as an ultimate form of identity change. Masochists apparently have the same wish and fantasy. In their scenes, they shed their normal identities and enter into a game with an entirely new role, such as a sex slave, captive, or harem girl. The identity change sometimes extends to having a new name, a new position in society, new interpersonal relationships, and even a new gender. Masochism temporarily shrinks identity down to almost nothing, and at least in play it is possible to replace the departed identity with a new one.

Although we have presented masochism in terms of the ego stress model, it is worth noting that there may be an element of the ecstasy model too, and for some masochists the ecstasy may be (or become) the main attraction. The essence of ecstatic escape is that losing self-awareness allows one to enjoy certain potential pleasures more fully. Sexual pleasure appears to conform to that model. As Baumeister (1988, 1989) has described, masochistic practices have multiple parallels to the practices that sex therapists use to enhance sexual response and pleasure (Masters & Johnson, 1970). Egotism is apparently a great deterrent to sexual pleasure, whether one is worrying about making a good impression, showing off, accumulating ego boosts through conquests, or testing one's qualifications as a full-fledged man or woman. Masochistic scenes typically end with sexual pleasure, and masochists routinely claim that these pleasures are stronger and more satisfying than what can be achieved with conventional sexual activities. It is of course quite difficult to evaluate these claims and to know if they would apply to everyone, but the parallel with sex therapy makes them plausible. The point is that shedding self-awareness may enable masochists to achieve sexual ecstasy. If so, then it is not surprising that masochists keep coming back for more.

Other Escapes

Alcohol use, suicide, and masochism have been presented in some detail because they are reasonably well understood, clear-cut examples of shrinking the self. Before concluding, however, it is worth considering briefly several other means of escape, because they reveal the range of behavior patterns that are moved by the desire to lose oneself.

Binge eating is a behavior problem that has attracted increasing attention and concern in recent years, possibly because the problem is becoming more widespread. A voluminous literature on eating patterns has contributed substantial light to understanding this phenomenon, and that literature appears to support the view that shrinking the self is a core aspect of what binge eating is all about (see Heatherton & Baumeister, 1991).

The term *binge eating* encompasses a wide range of phenomena, from the occasional overindulgence that violates a diet plan and sets one's weight-loss goals off schedule, to the pathological extreme of bulimia (in which alternating phases of dieting and binge eating become sufficiently extreme so as to endanger one's health). Binge eating appears to be driven by some combination of the calamity and ego stress models—in most cases, it is neither a single intense binge nor a regular activity, but it is a pattern that may be repeated periodically, often in response to minor stresses, setbacks, and problems. Binge eaters are typically women who subject themselves to high standards and expectations and suffer acute emotional distress when they fall short. Personal failures make them painfully aware of themselves as inadequate, incompetent, or unattractive.

The eating binge itself tends to conform to the broad outlines of deconstruction and mental narrowing (see also Baumeister, 1991a). Attention is narrowly focused on the sensations of chewing, tasting, and swallowing, thereby removing long-range concerns and problems to a great distance. Some individuals describe their eating binges as akin to trance states, thus making clear the narrowing of attention and the altered sense of the passage of time.

The consequences, too, conform to what we have proposed as typical of shrinking the self. Disinhibition is once again central to the phenomenon, for both dieters and bulimics have strong rules about controlling their food intake, and these rules must be broken in order for an eating binge to occur. Indeed, the irony of binge eating is not that the dietary rules are broken in the first place, but that once they are broken the person goes to the extreme of consuming vast quantities of food. That is also, of course, the key to their self-defeating nature. An occasional extra candy bar would not seriously disrupt one's diet if one stopped there, but when the candy bar is followed by a pizza, a gallon of ice cream, and a cake the diet is indeed ruined. Bulimic efforts to undo this damage by induced vomiting only lead to a different set of health problems. And although eating would seem to be an active behavior, binge eaters describe their binges in passive terms, particularly invoking a sense of losing control. For them, apparently, the self is identified with restraint, and once that restraint is overcome the eating occurs almost passively.

Binge eating resembles alcohol abuse and suicide as ultimately self-destructive activities, but shrinking the self is not necessarily destructive. It is therefore particularly valuable to consider the role of shrinking the self in religious, spiritual activities, because these activities are often regarded as among the highest, best, and most fulfilling experiences available to humankind. Although the outcome may be self-fulfillment rather than self-destruction, the process of escaping the self is in many ways identical with what we have already covered.

Spiritual aspects of changing the self are covered elsewhere in this volume, and so a few words will suffice here. Buddhist, Christian, Moslem (Sufi), and other major religions have long treated self-oriented motives as harmful to spiritual progress (Clebsch,

1979; Goleman, 1988; Kapleau, 1980; Shafii, 1988). The blissful states achieved through mystical devotions require the transcendence of the individual ego, including the overcoming of selfish desires and motives. The peak religious experiences themselves are often described as involving a merging of self with the cosmos, with God, or with all life. The popular term *ego dissolution* expresses this experience metaphorically, comparing the transcendence of selfhood with the way a sugar cube dissolves in a glass of water.

It is worth noting that the spiritual shrinking of the self may often be experienced as, paradoxically, an expansion of self. Mystics have often noted the inadequacy of the metaphors used to describe religious experiences in popular terms, but these metaphors seem to suggest both expansion and contraction. The expanded self, however, is fundamentally transformed and goes beyond what is normally regarded as the self or ego; it typically recognizes a communion with divine beings or with universal life. Again, the dissolution metaphor may be the best. The cube of sugar is dropped into water, and it quickly shrinks and disappears—yet is also in an important sense expanded to become as large as the glassful of water. For present purposes, the important aspect is the initial part of shrinking the old, familiar self in order to get rid of it. Once the old self has been sufficiently shrunk, the person can discover a new way to be aware of a transcendent selfhood.

The techniques for spiritual progress seem geared to deconstruct one's worldview and achieve mental narrowing. Meditation is perhaps the best studied of these. Meditative exercises often begin by having the individual concentrate attention on breathing, which obviously brings awareness down to one of the lowest possible levels of action identification. Breathing is a simple, short-term, largely passive activity that occurs in the immediate present and invokes almost no meaningful contexts or implications.

Other spiritual techniques resemble masochistic submission. Religious monks, nuns, and other initiates must often endure a regimen designed to induce humility, such as shaving one's head, ritual prostrations, and begging for food or alms, and extending in some cases to verbal abuse and insults. To focus the mind, some spiritual practices involve pain, ranging from flagellation to the simple soreness of legs that comes from sitting motionless in a zazen posture. There is also in many cases a deliberate relinquishing of control to one's spiritual guide or master that parallels the masochist's submission to his or her dominant partner.

The ecstatic benefits of shrinking the self are not limited to spiritual exercises. Csikszentmihalyi (1990) has concluded from many years of studying people's happiest experiences that a loss of self-awareness is an essential part of what he calls the "flow" experience, in which people become immersed in an activity. They lose track of time, other people, and external factors while happily absorbed in what they are doing. Usually these activities involve some kind of exercise of skill or efficacy, so the passive loss of control we have identified with shrinking the self is not consistent with Csikszentmihalyi's observations, but the loss of self-awareness is nonetheless a key aspect.

Indeed, self-awareness can produce extremely disruptive and harmful consequences when it intrudes on the exercise of skill. Exceptionally poor performances are typically caused by a heightened attention to self, in which the conscious mind tries to monitor the process of performance and in so doing interferes with the smooth, automatic, overlearned execution of skill (Baumeister, 1984). These disruptions, commonly called "choking under pressure," are often puzzling and distressing to individuals who find that they are unable to perform up to the level of their ability on precisely the occasions when they most want to do so. Choking under pressure may help explain the seeming contradiction between Csikszentmihalyi's observations about the exercise of skill in "flow" experiences and our general observation that loss of self involves letting go rather than controlling. Exercising skill may involve both a controlling and a conscious letting go of control—it is the overlearned, unconscious part of the mind that exercises control for maximum performance and satisfaction. The conscious mind must relinquish control, because if it insists on dominating the process, performance is impaired.

Escaping the self must be distinguished from mere escapism, as in interest in entertainments or other diversions. Television, movies, music, and other pastimes may appeal to people as pleasant distractions, but they are not specifically geared toward escaping from the self. To be sure, the self is probably forgotten when one is immersed in watching a show. These are not typically powerful methods for escaping the self, however, and probably most people have had the experience of being unable to attend to a television show or enjoy music while preoccupied with disturbing self-doubts arising from a recent, upsetting experience. Steele and Josephs (1990) have emphasized that people often combine alcohol use with such distractions in order to make escape fully effective; alcohol narrows the focus of attention, but if it is narrowly focused on the self, the result may be extra unpleasant. It is plausible that television and other such media do provide some escape from self for people who do not really need or crave escape; but people who want a reliable, effective means of forgetting themselves will probably find that distracting entertainments are not typically strong enough.

Relation to Other Phenomena

It could well be suggested that shrinking the self has important parallels in other psychological phenomena. The concept of transient depersonalization (Elliot, Rosenberg, & Wagner, 1984) has some similarities to the idea of shrinking the self. Elliot et al. found that transient depersonalization was correlated with low self-esteem, which could mean that it is a means of escaping from unpleasant thoughts about oneself, just as people may shrink the self to escape from an aversive conception of self. Elliot et al. also found an inverse relationship between transient depersonalization and self-awareness, which parallels the escape from self-awareness that occurs when shrinking the self. Another similar feature is the feeling of disconnection or unreality in transient depersonalization, which may be parallel to the loss of meaning in escape.

Despite these similarities, the concept of transient depersonalization has several differences from the shrinking of the self according to escape theory. Transient depersonalization was often described as "incidental" when it occurs or as odd, surprising experience, whereas shrinking the self is often far from an incidental or surprising result of the techniques people use to escape. Elliot et al. also failed to find any link between transient depersonalization and social anxiety, but according to escape theory anxiety is one major source of motivation for shrinking the self.

Another relevant phenomenon is the enforced transformation of self-awareness that occurs under brainwashing or in the aftermath of victimizing trauma. Heightened immediacy of awareness, self-blame, and other aspects of the calamity pattern of escape have been noted in the reactions of rape victims, for example (see Resick, 1983). Shrinking the self produces an emotionally numb state, which may be just what victims achieve with denial and other reactions to trauma (see Janoff-Bulman, 1989). Baumeister (1991b) has proposed that cognitive deconstruction following trauma may be a means of facilitating the construction of new interpretations that will, ideally, allow the victim eventually to integrate the experience into an acceptable view of self and world.

Brainwashing can be viewed as a forced deconstruction of the self. Brainwashing techniques often involve prolonged attacks on the egos or selves of the victims (Cushman, 1986), creating uncertainty about the self as well as negative affect. The former identity is linked to guilt and other afflictions, so the person wants to escape from it (see also Baumeister, 1986). Once the mental narrowing has occurred and meanings have been stripped away, there is a meaning vacuum that allows a new understanding of self and world to be accepted, which is the final stage of successful brainwashing (Cushman, 1986).

CONCLUSION

Although this volume is primarily concerned with substantive changes to the self, it is also necessary to consider changes to the phenomenal self. The phenomenal self—the portion of the self-concept that is present in awareness at any given time—changes inevitably through the course of each day, as different contexts, activities, and situations activate different aspects of the self. This chapter has been concerned, however, with a systematic pattern of shrinking the phenomenal self. Rather than merely moving awareness from one part of the self-concept to another, equally large and meaningful part, people sometimes try to shift the phenomenal self to a more restricted, meaningless, minimal aspect of self. Perhaps the extreme version was furnished by meditative exercises which focus attention on breathing. Although breathing is certainly a process of one's own body and thus attending to it is attending to oneself, it offers an exceptionally minimal definition of self. Being one who breathes invokes nothing profound, important, or meaningful—in fact, to be aware of self as a breathing organism is to be aware of self in a way that fails to distinguish oneself from any other person or animal alive on earth. It is hard to imagine any identity that identifies the person less.

We have proposed that people try to shrink their self-awareness for a variety of reasons that can be sorted into three main patterns. In the calamity pattern, people want to forget themselves because recent events reflect badly on the self and so thinking about oneself brings emotional distress. In the ego stress pattern, people desire to forget themselves now and then to be relieved of the burden of maintaining their identities. This pattern is akin to taking a vacation from oneself, in contrast to the calamity pattern, which is analogous to becoming numb to minimize suffering from torture or trauma. Lastly, the ecstasy pattern treats escape from self-awareness as a prerequisite for entering into desirable, blissful experiences.

Shrinking the self is necessary because people cannot force themselves to stop being aware of themselves. By restricting awareness of self to the physical body, such as mere movement and sensation in the immediate present, people can shed the complex trappings of identity and achieve the goals of the three motivations outlined in the preceding paragraph. The complex, symbolic, socially defined identity is forgotten, and the problems, stresses, implications, and other concerns are forgotten along with it. The individual may become acutely aware of self but only as a physical organism existing in the immediate present, and that view of self is largely free of the troubles and burdens that motivated the escape in the first place.

It seems initially counterintuitive to suggest that people might want to escape from self-awareness. Modern individuals, in particular, seem obsessed with expanding and constructing their identities, so shrinking the self seems to run counter to prevailing trends. It does. The modern self may be a great blessing in many respects, but it is also a burden, a risk, and a source of stress, as well as being just as great an obstacle to certain ecstatic experiences as it ever has been. Alcohol use, suicide, sexual masochism, and binge eating are only a few of the activities people use to shrink their identities down to the bare minimum. The wide range of things people do in order to escape from self-awareness is itself a powerful testimony to how powerful and prevalent the need is.

Forecasting the psychological structures of future generations is a risky and speculative business, but it seems likely that as long as the self remains such a powerful focus of cultural pressures and demands, the need for escapes from self will also continue to thrive. If society can change in a way that will reduce individualism and the attendant problems of selfhood, then escapist patterns may also diminish. The twentieth century has seen repeated patterns in various societies to get rid of modern individualistic patterns and return to more communal orientations. Typically these have had to be combined with brutal internal terror, such as in the fundamentalist movements in Iran and Cambodia and (indeed) the totalitarian and fascist utopias such as Nazi Germany and Communist Russia. Although the utopian dreams of such societies may have a significant appeal, the reality of daily life in them has ranged from repressive to repulsive. To our own American sensitivities, at least, it seems preferable to live in an individualistic society. The self may be a source of problems and stresses with occasionally disastrous consequences, but in general the cure seems worse than the disease.

REFERENCES

Baechler, J. (1979). *Suicides*. New York: Basic Books. Original work published 1975.

Baumeister, R. F. (1984). Choking under pressure: Self-consciousness and paradoxical effects of incentives on skillful performance. *Journal of Personality and Social Psychology*, 46:610–620.

_____. (1986). *Identity: Cultural change and the struggle for self*. New York: Oxford University Press.

_____. (1987). How the self became a problem: A psychological review of historical research. *Journal of Personality and Social Psychology*, 52:163–176.

_____. (1988). Masochism as escape from self. *Journal of Sex Research*, 25:28–59.

_____. (1989). *Masochism and the self*. Hillsdale, NJ: Erlbaum.

_____. (1990). Suicide as escape from self. *Psychological Review*, 97:90–113.

_____. (1991a). *Escaping the self: Alcoholism, spirituality, masochism, and other flights from the burden of selfhood*. New York: Basic Books.

_____. (1991b). *Meanings of life*. New York: Guilford Press.

Braudy, L. (1986). *The frenzy of renown: Fame and its history*. New York: Oxford University Press.

Buksbazen, C. (1976). Legacy of a suicide. *Suicide and Life-Threatening Behavior*, 6:106–122.

Califia, P. (1983). A secret side of lesbian sexuality. In *S and M: Studies in sadomasochism*, edited by T. Weinberg & G. Kamel (pp. 129–136). Buffalo, NY: Prometheus.

Carver, C. S., & Scheier, M. F. (1981). *Attention and self-regulation: A control theory approach to human behavior.* New York: Springer-Verlag.

Clebsch, W. A. (1979). *Christianity in European history.* New York: Oxford University Press.

Csikszentmihalyi, M. (1982). Toward a psychology of optimal experience. In *Review of personality and social psychology,* edited by L. Wheeler (vol. 2, pp. 13–36). Beverly Hills, CA: Sage.

Csikszentmihalyi, M. (1990). *Flow: The psychology of optimal experience.* New York: Harper & Row.

Cushman, P. (1986). The self besieged: Recruitment-indoctrination processes in restrictive groups. *Journal for the Theory of Social Behavior, 16:1–32.*

Dixon, T. M., & Baumeister, R. F. (1991). Escaping the self: The moderating effect of self-complexity. *Personality and Social Psychology Bulletin, 17:363–368.*

Duval, S., & Wicklund, R. A. (1972). *A theory of objective self-awareness.* New York: Academic Press.

Elliot, G., Rosenberg, M., & Wagner, M. (1984). Transient depersonalization in youth. *Social Psychology Quarterly, 47:115–129.*

Gibbons, F. X., & Wicklund, R. A. (1976). Selective exposure to self. *Journal of Research in Personality, 10:98–106.*

Goleman, D. (1988). *The meditative mind: The varieties of meditative experience.* New York: St. Martin's Press.

Greenberg, J., & Musham, C. (1981). Avoiding and seeking self-focused attention. *Journal of Research in Personality, 15:191–200.*

Hackworth, D. H., & Sherman, J. (1989). *About face: The Odyssey of an American warrior.* New York: Simon & Schuster.

Heatherton, T. F., & Baumeister, R. F. (1991). Binge eating as escape from self-awareness. *Psychological Bulletin, 110:86–108.*

Hendin, H. (1982). *Suicide in America.* New York: Norton.

Henken, V. J. (1976). Banality reinvestigated: A computer-based content analysis of suicidal and forced-death documents. *Suicide and Life-Threatening Behavior, 6:36–43.*

Higgins, E. T. (1987). Self-discrepancy: A theory relating self and affect. *Psychological Review, 94:319–340.*

Hull, J. G. (1981). A self-awareness model of the causes and effects of alcohol consumption. *Journal of Abnormal Psychology, 90:586–600.*

Hull, J. G., Levenson, R. W., Young, R. D., & Sher, K. J. (1983). Self-awareness-reducing effects of alcohol consumption. *Journal of Personality and Social Psychology, 44:461–473.*

Hull, J. G., & Young, R. D. (1983). Self-consciousness, self-esteem, and success-failure as determinants of alcohol consumption in male social drinkers. *Journal of Personality and Social Psychology*, 44:1097–1109.

Hull, J. G., Young, R. D., & Jouriles, E. (1986). Applications of the self-awareness model of alcohol consumption: Predicting patterns of use and abuse. *Journal of Personality and Social Psychology*, 51:790–796.

Janoff-Bulman, R. (1989). Assumptive worlds and the stress of traumatic events: Applications of the schema construct. *Social Cognition*, 7:113–136.

Jones, E. E., & Gerard, H. B. (1967). *Foundations of social psychology*. New York: John Wiley.

Kapleau, P. (1980). *The three pillars of Zen*. Garden City, NY: Doubleday Anchor.

Keegan, J. (1976). *The face of battle*. New York: Military Heritage Press.

Linehan, M. M., Goodstein, J. L., Nielsen, S. L., & Chiles, J. A. (1983). Reasons for staying alive when you are thinking of killing yourself: The Reasons for Living Inventory. *Journal of Consulting and Clinical Psychology*, 51:276–286.

Maris, R. (1981). *Pathways to suicide: A survey of self-destructive behaviors*. Baltimore, MD: Johns Hopkins University Press.

Maslow, A. H. (1968). *Toward a psychology of being*. New York: Van Nostrand.

Masters, W. H., & Johnson, V. E. (1970). *Human sexual inadequacy*. Boston, MA: Little, Brown.

Monat, A., Averill, J. R., & Lazarus, R. S. (1972). Anticipatory stress and coping reactions under various conditions of uncertainty. *Journal of Personality and Social Psychology*, 24:237–253.

Ogilvie, D. M., Stone, P. J., & Shneidman, E. S. (1983). A computer analysis of suicide notes. In *The psychology of suicide*, edited by E. Schneidman, N. Farberow & R. Litman (pp. 249–256). New York: Aronson.

Perrah, M., & Wichman, H. (1987). Cognitive rigidity in suicide attempters. *Suicide and Life-Threatening Behavior*, 17:251–262.

Resick, P. A. (1983). The rape reaction: Research findings and implications for intervention. *Behavior Therapist*, 6:129–132.

Rothberg, J. M., & Jones, F. D. (1987). Suicide in the U.S. Army: Epidemiological and periodic aspects. *Suicide and Life-Threatening Behavior*, 17:119–132.

Scarry, E. (1985). *The body in pain: The making and unmaking of the world*. New York: Oxford University Press.

Scott, G. G. (1983). *Erotic power: An exploration of dominance and submission*. Secaucus, NJ: Citadel Press.

Shafii, M. (1988). *Freedom from the self: Sufism, meditation, and psychotherapy*. New York: Human Sciences Press.

Steele, C. M., & Josephs, R. A. (1990). Alcohol myopia: Its prized and dangerous effects. *American Psychologist, 45:* 921–933.

Steele, C. M., & Southwick, L. (1985). Alcohol and social behavior I: The psychology of drunken excess. *Journal of Personality and Social Psychology, 48:*18–34.

Steenbarger, B. N., & Aderman, D. (1979). Objective self-awareness as a nonaversive state: Effect of anticipating discrepancy reduction. *Journal of Personality, 47:*330–339.

Stephens, B. J. (1985). Suicidal women and their relationships with husbands, boyfriends, and lovers. *Suicide and Life-Threatening Behavior, 15:*77–89.

Taylor, S. E., & Brown, J. D. (1988). Illusion and well-being: A social psychological perspective on mental health. *Psychological Bulletin, 103:*193–210.

Tishler, C. L., McKenry, P. C., & Morgan, K. C. (1981). Adolescent suicide attempts: Some significant factors. *Suicide and Life-Threatening Behavior, 11:*86–92.

Vallacher, R. R., & Wegner, D. M. (1985). *A theory of action identification.* Hillsdale, NJ: Erlbaum.

———. (1987). What do people think they're doing: Action identification and human behavior. *Psychological Review, 94:*3–15.

Weinberg, T., & Kamel, W. L. (Eds.) (1983). *S and M: Studies in sadomasochism.* Buffalo, NY: Prometheus.

Williams, J. M., & Broadbent, K. (1986). Autobiographical memory in suicide attempters. *Journal of Abnormal Psychology, 95:*144–149.

Zweig, P. (1980). *The heresy of self-love.* Princeton, NJ: Princeton University Press. Original work published 1968.

CHAPTER 6

Conceptualizing and Changing the Self from a Rational Therapy Perspective

Charles Zastrow

The two primary developers of rational therapy are Albert Ellis (1958) and Maxie Maultsby (1975, 1977). Rational therapy is now one of the most widely used approaches in psychotherapy to change unwanted emotions and dysfunctional behaviors. This chapter conceptualizes *self* from a rational therapy perspective, and also presents a theoretical approach for changing unwanted emotions, dysfunctional behaviors, and negative self-esteem. The chapter ends with raising, and then discussing, some issues and questions about the rational therapy perspective.

CONCEPTUALIZING *SELF*

Rational therapy recognizes that everyone has a biological self (composed of one's bodily elements) and a psychological self (which is essentially one's self-concept). Rational therapy focuses most on the psychological self, leaving the study of the biological self to other disciplines. (Rational therapy does assert there is considerable interaction between the biological self and the psychological self. For example, psychological stress does lead to stress-related illnesses in the biological self; and changes in the appearance or health of the biological self can have dramatic effects on self-concept. See also Chapter 12 in this volume by Toombs.)

Sections of this chapter are adapted with permission from: (a) Charles Zastrow, Rational Therapy, in *The Practice of Social work* (3rd ed.) (Chicago: The Dorsey Press, 1989), pp. 412–427; and (b) Charles Zastrow and Karen Kirst-Ashman, Assessing and Treating Unwanted Emotions, in *Understanding Human Behavior and the Social Environment* (2nd ed.) (Chicago: Nelson-Hall Publishers, 1990, pp. 264–272).

From a rational therapy perspective, our sense of self (our sense of who and what we are) refers to the general, ongoing sets of *self-talk* about the kind of person we are. Our self-talk is the set of evaluating thoughts we give ourselves about facts and events that happen to us.

Self-concept (or identity) development is a lifetime process. It begins during the early years and continues to change throughout our lifetime. During the early years, our sense of self is largely determined by the reactions of others.

A long time ago, Cooley (1902) discussed this early labeling process as resulting in the "looking-glass self"; that is, persons develop their self-concept (sense of who and what they are) in terms of how others relate to them. For example, if a neighborhood identifies a young boy as being a "troublemaker," a "delinquent," the neighbors are apt to relate to the youth as if he were not to be trusted, may accuse him of delinquent acts, and will label his semi-delinquent and aggressive behavior as being "delinquent." This labeling process, the youth begins to realize, also results in a type of prestige and status, at least from his peers. In the absence of objective ways to gauge whether he is, in fact, a "delinquent," the youth will rely on the subjective evaluations of others. Thus, gradually, as the youth is related to as being a "delinquent," he is apt to begin to perceive himself in that way and will begin to enact the delinquent role.

The labeling process undoubtedly has a substantial influence in shaping behavior. Yet, it fails to explain why children may be treated essentially the same, and yet engage in very different behavior, as well as develop substantially different self-concepts. We have all heard stories about two children raised essentially the same (in a ghetto or in an upper-class suburb) who develop vastly different lifestyles, with one becoming involved in a life of crime, while the other becomes a law-abiding, productive community leader. Why?

The following theory of self-concept development is adapted from the work of the Soviet psychologists Luria (1961) and Vygotsky (1962).

Phase I: Initially a child's behavior is determined by internal physical needs (e.g., hunger) and outside events (e.g., parental actions).

Phase II: The child begins to learn to control his (her) behavior in line with the verbal instructions and reactions of external agents (e.g., parents).

Phase III: The verbal instructions and reactions of external people lead to the development of elementary beliefs. Based on these elementary beliefs, the child begins to regulate some of his own actions through self-talk.

Phase IV: Future behavior patterns are then developed through an interaction of events and self-talk about those events. Repeated sets of self-talk become covert (i.e., go "underground," to use Vygotsky's term) and become attitudes, beliefs, and values.

Phase V: These attitudes, beliefs, and values form our sense of who and what we are. Our self-talk (based on our beliefs, attitudes, and values) about events that happen to us then largely controls our emotions and actions.

The diagram in Figure 6.1 shows how events and self-talk interact to form our self-concept.

Given the above theoretical material, let us return to the question of why, when two children have essentially the same experiences, they may develop very different personalities (that is, emotions and behaviors). The reason is that their self-talk about their experiences may vary.

For example, if an 8-year-old child is caught for shoplifting candy and is spanked by his parents, a wide range of self-talk is possible. If the child says, "I have done wrong. Stealing is wrong. Somehow I have got to restore my parent's trust in me," the child's inclinations to steal will be sharply reduced. However, if the child says the following to himself, shoplifting attempts are apt to continue: "Shoplifting is exciting. It's a way for me to get what I want. This is the first time I've been caught. Guess I was careless. I'll have to be more careful the next time." In a given situation, the self-talk of different people will vary because: (a) the values, beliefs, attitudes, and desires upon which self-talk is based will vary between individuals; and (b) each person has thousands of different values and beliefs, and in a particular situation, each person will somewhat haphazardly select only a few of these beliefs and values to base his self-talk upon.

FIGURE 6.1
Formation of Our Self-Concept

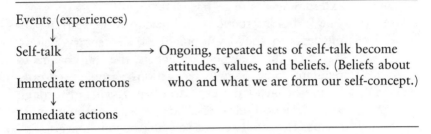

In summary, there are two components that largely determine the self-concept of any individual: (1) the events or experiences that a person has, and (2) the self-talk that a person gives himself about the experiences. Of these two components, self-talk is the key element in developing and perpetuating everyone's self-concept.

SELF-TALK DETERMINES OUR FEELINGS AND ACTIONS

It is erroneously believed by most people that our emotions and our actions are primarily determined by our experiences (that is, by events that happen to us). On the contrary, rational therapy asserts and has demonstrated (Ellis, 1979) that the primary cause of all our emotions and actions is what we tell ourselves about events that happen to us.

All feelings and actions occur according to the following format:

Events: (Or experiences)
↓
Self-talk: (Self-talk is the set of evaluating thoughts we give ourself about facts and events that happen to us.)
↓
Emotions: (May include remaining calm.)
↓
Actions:

This basic principle is not new. The Stoic philosopher Epictetus wrote in *The Enchiridion* in the first century A.D., "Men are disturbed not by things, but by the view which they take of them" (Ellis, 1979). A number of authorities have presented evidence that our self-talk (or cognitions) primarily causes our emotions (Beck, 1979; Burns, 1980; Dyer, 1976; Ellis, 1962; Foreyt & Rathjen, 1978; Guidano & Liotti, 1983; London & Nisbett, 1974; Schachter & Singer, 1962).

An example will illustrate the above process:

Event: A husband unexpectedly arrives home early and upon
| walking into his living room sees an acquaintance and
| his wife embracing.
↓

Self-talk: "My wife and this guy are having an affair—this is
| awful."
| "This guy is threatening my personal life."
| "This is morally wrong—the worst thing that could
| happen to me."
| "This guy is violating my rights—I've got to forcefully
| protect my rights."
↓

Emotion: Anger, rage, and a vengeful feeling.
↓

Action: Running at the acquaintance and physically getting
              into a fight

If, on the other hand, the husband remembers that his wife and the acquaintance are preparing to put on a romantic play at a nearby college, the following may occur:

Event: A husband unexpectedly arrives home early and upon
| walking into his living room sees an acquaintance and
| his wife embracing.
↓

Self-talk: "Well, apparently they're only practicing for the play."
| "I'll watch closely, but I don't think there is anything
| romantic occurring."
| "There is no reason for me to get upset and make a
| fool of myself."
↓

Emotion: Mildly emotionally aroused, somewhat wary, and a
| little jealous.
↓

Action: Casually making small talk with his wife and the ac-
              quaintance, while observing their interactions.

The most important point about the above process is that our self-talk determines how we feel and act; and, by changing our self-talk, we can change how we feel and act. Generally we cannot control events that happen to us, but we have the power to think rationally and thereby change *all* of our unwanted emotions and ineffective actions.

Frequently we do not have the power to control the events we encounter. However, we always have the capacity to tell ourselves rational thoughts about each of our experiences. John Lembo (1974, p. 9) notes:

> *We can think rationally or irrationally about* the things that will happen to us *and insist that we will not be a failure if our boss fires us or that we will be a worthless no-account if we are dismissed from our job; that nothing catastrophic will happen if our parents die or that it will be horrible and unbearable if they do die.*

Since we determine our feelings and our behaviors via self-talk, we are literally in control of our lives. If we are unhappy, unfulfilled, unsatisfied, frustrated, depressed, grief-stricken, or whatever, it is primarily our doing. Lembo (1974, p. 10) notes, "We have the ability to create a satisfying life for ourselves, and we will succeed in doing so if we rationally manage the thoughts we tell ourselves."

ADDITIONAL ASPECTS OF SELF-TALK

With repeated occurrences of an event, a person's emotional reactions to that event become nearly automatic, because the person rapidly gives himself or herself a set of self-talk statements gradually acquired through past experiences. Beck and Weishaar (1989, pp. 308–311) have coined the term *automatic thoughts* to refer to the phenomenon whereby a person, through continued experience with an event, instantaneously gives herself or himself a certain set of statements whenever that event occurs. For example, a few years ago I counseled a woman who became intensely emotionally upset every time her husband (who had a drinking problem) came home intoxicated. In examining this situation it became clear that because of repeated occurrences she would immediately give herself the following extensive self-talk upon seeing him inebriated:

Self-talk: "He's foolishly spending the money we desperately
| need in this family."
| "He is making a fool of himself and me in that condi-
| tion."
| "He's setting a terrible example for our children."
| "One of these days while drunk he's going to get into a
| serious accident, become incapacitated, and then what
| will we do?"
↓   "He loves drinking more than he loves me!"
Emotional   Anger, frustration, some depression, general unhappi-
reaction: ness.

Although automatic thoughts are difficult to change because the thinking processes have become an ingrained habitual response to a certain event, such automatic thoughts can be changed by the techniques described later in this chapter—including rational self-analysis, changing the distressing event, and enabling clients to identify and change their negative and irrational thinking patterns.

Another conceptualization of the self-talk approach is the assertion that a person may be aware, or unaware, of the self-talk that he or she is giving himself about a fact or event. If a person is having a discomforting emotion and is unaware of the underlying self-talk, then the focus of counseling initially needs to be on discovering this self-talk. Several years ago I counseled a married woman who expressed a strong desire to want to continue having extramarital affairs, but was afraid her husband would discover the affairs and end the marriage. Although she was fully aware of the emotional desire for having affairs, she was unaware of the self-talk generating this feeling. I probed into this area and got her to take a look (undoubtedly for the first time in her life) at the self-talk that was generating the emotional desire to have extramarital sex. Upon focusing her attention on this she gradually expressed and became aware of the following underlying self-talk, "I enjoy the feeling of being able to seduce someone who I am attracted to," "The people I seduce then feel somewhat obligated to me," and "The conquest of someone who is very attractive is three quarters of the thrill."

Another aspect of self-talk has been labeled as *layering* in which the emotional reaction (C) becomes a new event (A) by a person giving himself additional self-talk (B) about having the initial emotional reaction. Ellis (1973, p. 178) describes layering as follows:

> Once the individual becomes emotionally upset—or, rather, upsets himself!—another startling human thing frequently occurs. Most of the time, he *knows* that he is anxious, depressed, enraged, or otherwise agitated; and he also generally knows that his symptoms are undesirable and (in our culture) socially disapproved. For who approves or respects highly agitated or "crazy" people? He therefore makes his emotional Consequence (C) or symptom into another Activating Event (A).
>
> Thus he originally starts with something like "(A) I did poorly on my job today; (B) Isn't that horrible! What a worm I am for failing!" and he winds up with (C) feelings of anxiety, worthlessness, and depression. He now starts all over: "(A) I feel anxious and depressed, and worthless. (B) Isn't that horrible! What a worm I am for feeling anxious, depressed, and worthless!" Now he winds up with (C) even greater feelings of anxiety, worthlessness, and depression. Or, in other words, once he becomes anxious, he frequently makes himself anxious about being anxious. Once he becomes depressed, he makes himself depressed about *being* depressed. Et cetera! He now has two Consequences or symptoms for the price of one; and he often goes around and around, in a vicious cycle of (1) condemning himself for doing poorly at some task; (2) feeling guilty or depressed because of his self-condemnation; (3) condemning himself for his feelings of guilt and depression; (4) condemning himself for condemning himself; (5) condemning himself for seeing that he condemns himself and for still not stopping condemning himself; (6) condemning himself for going for psychotherapeutic help and still not getting better; (7) condemning himself for being more disturbed than other individuals; (8) concluding that he is indubitably hopelessly disturbed and that nothing can be done about it; and so on, and so forth.

Another conceptualization of the self-talk approach is that self-talk is related to attitudes, beliefs, and values. Although self-talk is often based on our attitudes, beliefs, and values, self-talk is distinct from these terms. Self-talk has a "here and now" quality as it represents those thoughts that we are giving ourselves at the present time. At any one point in time we hold thousands of beliefs, attitudes, and values, but our self-talk is only based on a fraction of our total set of attitudes and beliefs whenever we think about a fact or event. Our self-talk may also be generated by our needs, wants, desires, drives, and motives.

The last conceptualization of the self-talk approach that will be mentioned here is that, at times, a person's self-talk affects experiences that have not yet happened. In such instances the person's self-talk may become a self-fulfilling prophecy. A self-fulfilling prophecy occurs when a person's expectations (that is, self-talk about the future) of the outcome of an event makes the outcome more likely to happen than would otherwise have been true. Self-fulfilling prophecies occur frequently. A person who expects to have a miserable time at a social affair therefore puts little effort into conversing with others and ends up having a miserable time. If an individual expects a low grade on a statistics exam, he sees little value in studying hard and ends up performing poorly on the exam.

CHANGING UNWANTED EMOTIONS

There are only five ways to change an unwanted emotion, and only the first three of them are constructive. These three are getting involved in meaningful activity, changing the negative and irrational thinking which underlies the unwanted emotion, and changing the distressing event.

Meaningful Activity

The first constructive way is to get involved in some meaningful or enjoyable activity. When we become involved in activity that is meaningful, it provides satisfaction and structures and fills time, thereby taking our mind off a distressing event.

Practically all of us encounter day-to-day frustrations and irritations—having a class or two that are not going too well, having a job with irritations, or having a blah social life. If we go home in the evening and continue to think about and dwell on the irritations, we will develop such unwanted emotions as depression, anger, frustration, despair, or feeling of being a failure. (Which of these emotions we will have will directly depend on what we tell ourselves.)

By having an escape list of things we enjoy doing, we can nip unwanted emotions in the bud. Everyone should develop an escape list of things they enjoy doing: taking a walk, golf, going to a movie, tennis, shopping, needlework, visiting friends, and so on. By getting involved in things we enjoy, we take our mind off our day-to-day concerns and irritations. The positive emotions we will instead experience will directly stem from the things we tell ourselves about the enjoyable things we are doing.

In urging people to compile and use an escape list, the author is not suggesting that people should avoid doing something about trying to change unpleasant events. If something can be done to change an unpleasant event, all constructive efforts should be tried. However, we often do not have control over unpleasant events and cannot change them. Although we often cannot change unpleasant events, we always have the capacity to control and change what we tell ourselves about unpleasant events. It is this latter focus that is often helpful in learning to change our unwanted emotions.

Changing Self-Talk

A second approach to changing unwanted emotions is to identify and then change the negative and irrational thinking that leads to unwanted emotions. M. Maultsby (1975) developed an approach entitled Rational Self-Analysis (RSA) that is very useful for learning to challenge and change irrational thinking.

The goal in doing an RSA is to change any unwanted emotion (anger, love, guilt, depression, hate, and so on). A person seeking to change unwanted emotions via this approach first records on paper the event (or events) associated with the unwanted emotions. The person then specifies the self-talk statements (most of which are negative and irrational) that he or she is giving himself or herself about these events. The person next records the unwanted emotions that are being generated by the negative and irrational cognitions. The therapy process then begins by the person specifying, for each negative and irrational cognition, a rational and positive self-talk challenge that he or she is willing to give himself or herself. If these rational and positive self-talk challenges are continually used by the person to counter the problematic negative and irrational self-talk, the unwanted emotions will gradually subside.

In order to make a rational self-analysis work, a person has to put considerable effort into challenging the negative and irrational thinking with the rational challenges whenever he or she starts thinking negatively. With effort, a person can learn to change any unwanted emotion. This capacity is one of the most important abilities that people have. (Once a person learns and practices the process of writing out an RSA, he or she will be able to do the process in his or her head without having to write it out.)

The following material illustrates some of the negative and irrational self-talk, and the corresponding rational challenges, that a 23-year-old male gave himself after his partner of three years indicated she was ending their involvement:

Negative and irrational self-talk	Rational challenges
1. That bitch! she just wants to go out with other guys.	She's not a bitch. A bitch is a mother dog. Cindy is someone I really love and care about. She might want to go out with other guys even though she said this wasn't the case, not to mention it would be the logical thing to do if she wasn't going out with me. I had also said the same thing, that I wanted to date others earlier in our relationship.
2. I cannot live without her.	This is certainly not true. I lived well without her before I met her, and I can do the same in the future.
3. I'll never find anyone like her again.	There are over 2 million eligible women to date—surely some of those have characteristics I'll admire as much as the positives about Cindy.
4. I'm never going to get involved with anyone again.	Not too smart, especially if I want to get married some day. Besides, I know if I meet someone I really like I would go out with her. Besides that, I know there's a risk involved.

5.   I'm just going to treat girls like s— and take advantage of them.

This is not like me. I could never do this. Besides, it's not right to take things out on other people.

This process of challenging negative and irrational thinking *will* work in changing unwanted emotions if the person puts the needed effort into it. Just as dieting is guaranteed to lose weight, so is this approach guaranteed to change unwanted emotions. Both, however, require an effort and commitment to use the process in order to make it work.

Changing the Distressing Event

A third way to change unwanted emotions is to change the distressing event. Some distressing events can be changed by directly confronting the events and taking constructive action to change these events. For example, if we are let go from a job, we can seek another; when we find one we will feel better. Or, if we are receiving some failing grades, one way of constructively handling the situation is to meet individually with the instructors of these courses to obtain their suggestions on how to do better. If suggestions are received that appear practical and have merit, we will feel better.

Not all distressing events can be changed. For example, we may have a job that we need and be forced to interact with other employees who display behaviors we dislike. If we cannot change their behaviors, the only other constructive option is to bite the bullet and seek to adapt to the circumstances. However, when it is feasible and practical to change distressing events, we should seek to change these events; if we are successful we are apt to feel better because we will then give ourselves more positive self-talk.

DESTRUCTIVE WAYS TO CHANGE UNWANTED EMOTIONS

There are two other ways to change unwanted emotions which, unfortunately, some people turn to. One of these ways is by seeking to temporarily relieve intense unwanted emotions through the use of alcohol and other drugs. Unfortunately, many people seek to relieve unwanted emotions through the use of such mind-altering drugs as alcohol, cocaine, tranquilizers, and so on. When the effects of the drug wear off, a person's problems and unwanted emotions still remain, and there is a danger that through repeated use a person will become dependent on the drug.

The only other way to relieve unwanted emotions is a sure-fire way—a bullet to the head (or some other form of suicide). This way is the ultimate destructive approach to changing unwanted emotions.

ASSESSING AND CHANGING DEVIANT BEHAVIOR

Our thinking is not only the primary determinant of our emotions, but also of our actions, as depicted in the following diagram:

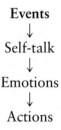

To demonstrate this principle, reflect on the last time you did something bizarre or unusual. What self-talk statements were you giving yourself (that is, what were you thinking) prior to and during the time when you did what you did?

Thinking processes primarily determine behavior. The reasons for unusual or dysfunctional behavior occurring can always be identified by determining what the perpetrator was thinking prior to and during the time when the act is being committed. Examples of cognitions that lead to dysfunctional behavior are the following:

> *Cognition:* A 17-year-old sees an unlocked Camaro and thinks "Hey, this is really a neat car to take a ride in. Let me cross the starting wires, and take it for a drive."
> *Behavior:* Car theft
> *Cognition:* A 27-year-old male is on his second date, is in his date's apartment, and thinks, "She is really sexy. Since I've now wined and dined her twice, it's now time for her to show her appreciation to me. She wants it as much as I do. I'll show her what a great lover I am. She may protest a little, but I'll overcome that

with force. Once we get involved sexually, she'll be emotionally attracted to me."

Behavior: Date rape

Cognition: A 31-year-old bartender thinks, "Cocaine gives me such a great high. Unfortunately I don't make the kind of money to buy as much as I need. I have no other choice but to buy more than I use, and then sell some of it for a profit."

Behavior: Drug trafficking

Cognition: A 16-year-old female who has run away from home thinks, "Now what am I going to do? Where am I going to stay? Where will I get enough money to eat? Maybe I can find some guys on the street who will give me a place to stay and some money. They'll probably want to jump on me—but that's O.K. That's better than going back home and being beaten by my father when he's drunk."

Behavior: Prostitution

Cognition: A 48-year-old bookkeeper of a retail computer firm thinks, "This is an awful financial mess I'm in. I've got so many bills: mortgage payments, gambling debts, and tuition payments for two kids in college. Hopefully I can win at the next poker game. But I need a stake. The only way to get a stake is to take a couple grand from this company and pay the money back in a few weeks. With me handling the books, no one will ever miss it."

Behavior: Embezzlement

It should be noted that the cognitions underlying each dysfunctional behavior may vary considerably among perpetrators. For example, possible cognitions for shoplifting a shirt might be the following. "This shirt would look really nice for the wedding I'm going to on Saturday. Since I'm buying a number of other items from this store, they still will make a profit from me even if I take this without paying for it." Another may be: "This will be a challenge to see if I can get away with taking this shirt. I'll put it on in the fitting room and put my own shirt and coat on over it, and no one will even see me walk out of the store with it. Since I've taken a number of things in the past, I'll act real casual as I walk out of the store." Or: "My son really needs a decent shirt. He doesn't have any nice ones to wear. I don't get enough money from AFDC to buy my children what they need. I know my son is embarrassed to wear the rags that he has. I'll just stick this shirt under my coat and walk out with it."

Assessing human behavior is largely a process of identifying the cognitions that underlie unwanted emotions or dysfunctional behavior. A deduction of the principle that thinking processes determine dysfunctional behaviors and unwanted emotions is that *in order to change dysfunctional behaviors or unwanted emotions it is necessary for the affected person to change his thinking patterns.* For example, Dan Barber's wife recently filed for divorce, after Dan discovered she had been having an affair with someone else for years. Dan gained custody of their 4½-year-old son. Last night Dan battered his son so severely he had to be hospitalized. When asked by the protective services worker why the abuse occurred, Dan indicated his thoughts at the time of the abuse:

"I can't take anymore of this."
"Here I have to take care of a kid that may not even be my own."
"This kid reminds me of the hurt that Mary has caused me. I have a right to even the score."
"This kid is willfully disobeying me—I've got to teach him a lesson."
"I can't stand this! I've got to shut this brat up!"
"My father beat me when I did wrong—that's the best way to show kids who's the boss."

For the physical abuse to stop, Mr. Barber must get help in changing such cognitions.

APPLICATION OF THE SELF-TALK APPROACH
TO CRIMINAL REHABILITATION

Crime is a comprehensive label covering a wide range of offenses: auto theft, arson, extortion, check forgery, drunkenness, prostitution, possession of narcotics, rape, sexual exhibition, and so on. Obviously, since the behavior exhibited by perpetrators of these crimes varies widely, the motives or causes underlying each must also vary widely. Without knowing why a crime occurs, it is extremely difficult—and perhaps impossible—to develop effective rehabilitation approaches.

Why do people commit criminal offenses? Zastrow and Navarre (1979) assert that "the reasons for any criminal act can be determined by identifying what the offender was telling him/herself prior to and during the time when the crime was being committed." This assertion is based on the notion that practically all actions by anyone are derived from thinking patterns. Examples of cognitions that lead to such crimes as car theft, date rape, drug trafficking, prostitution, and embezzlement have been specified earlier in this chapter.

If the self-talk approach is accurate in asserting that criminal behavior is primarily determined by criminal thinking processes, it then follows that through identifying what an offender was thinking prior to, and during, the time when he or she committed a criminal offense, we will then know why the offense was committed. This view is consistent with the emphasis in courts on identifying the motive for the offense. A motive is simply the set of cognitions (also called self-talk) that causes a person to commit a criminal offense.

The above conceptualization asserts that criminal behavior is primarily the result of cognitions related to the offenders' planning, execution, and justification of criminal activity. If this conceptualization is accurate, an important corollary is that *any intervention technique that is successful in rehabilitating criminal behavior is effective primarily because it changes offenders' cognitions from the planning, execution, and justification of criminal activities to the advantages of being law-abiding and to the negative consequences of criminal activity.* In other words, it appears that the key rehabilitative agent in the correctional system is changing the cognitions that lead to criminal activity so that offenders develop cognitions that lead them to seek to be law-abiding. Changing criminal thinking patterns has now become a major emphasis in many criminal rehabilitation programs (Allen & Bosta, 1981; Samenow, 1984, 1989; Yochelson & Samenow, 1985).

How can the cognitions of offenders be changed in a law-abiding direction? If criminal justice professionals want to rehabilitate offenders, the process is fairly simple to specify. The first step is to identify the cognitions that lead an offender to commit a criminal offense. The second and final step is to develop and apply a set of interventions designed to change such cognitions in a law-abiding direction.

The cognitions of an offender prior to and during the time that a criminal offense is committed can be determined in a variety of ways. One way is for the criminal justice professional to ask the offender what he or she was thinking and feeling prior to and during the time when the offense was committed. It may also be helpful to ask the offender some questions designed to obtain information about his or her life circumstances at that point in time.

Information can also be obtained from friends, relatives, and significant others about the offender's cognitions and circumstances at the time when the offense was committed. It may also be useful for criminal justice professionals to place themselves mentally in the life circumstances of the offender and then reflect on the kinds of cognitions that would lead such an individual to turn to crime. For example, if the offender is a 17-year-old female who has run away from home and is unemployed, it is fairly easy to identify (to some extent) the kinds of cognitions that would lead such an individual to resort to prostitution. (An excellent way for people preparing for a criminal justice career to develop their capacities to place themselves mentally into the thought processes of offenders is by role-playing, with others, a variety of roles.)

The second step of developing and applying a set of interventions to change the cognitions that lead to criminal behavior may or may not be easy. Obviously, what will work for one individual may not work for another. For a 17-year-old runaway who is starting to turn to prostitution the following are some of the options that may change the teenager's cognitions: placement in a runaway center (or foster home or group home) where counseling is provided; return to home, with the parents and the daughter receiving family therapy; arranging for the teenager to talk with a former prostitute who is able to convey the negative consequences of being a prostitute; arranging for the teenager to receive individual or group therapy or to attend a support group of other teenagers who are having similar problems; and helping the teenager to find suitable housing, to find lawful employment, and to become emancipated. In order for an intervention strategy to work, the strategy needs to be acceptable to the offender. If the offender is opposed to the strategy, he or she may find a way to undermine the intended rehabilitative effect.

Although this author is usually opposed to the use of punishment, punishment at times may change offenders' cognitions in a more law-abiding direction. For example, incarceration in a maximum security prison may lead some convicted offenders to decide that the threat of future imprisonment after release is a sufficient consequence for them to avoid further involvement in criminal activity. There are, however, a number of potential dangers in the use of punishment. Punishment is often counterproductive because it can generate hostility in the offender. Furthermore, punishment often has only temporary effects; when the offender realizes that he or she is no longer under surveillance, he or she may return to exhibiting dysfunctional behavior (Zastrow, 1988). Punishment through incarceration is further fraught with the danger of the prison serving as a "school for crime," in which inmates learn additional strategies for engaging in criminal activity from other inmates. Incarceration also has an adverse labeling effect because ex-convicts are often viewed by the public as being "untrustworthy," and therefore have considerable difficulty obtaining gratifying, lawful employment and being accepted in their home communities.

DEVELOPING POSITIVE SELF-ESTEEM

Negative self-esteem is directly determined by negative or irrational self-talk such as the following:

"I'm a failure."
"I can't accomplish anything I try."
"I'm inferior to other people."
"I'm not as competent, capable, or attractive as others."
"There's nothing left to live for."
"Bad things will always happen to me."
"I'll never find a mate, because I'm ugly."
"I'm terrible at math, so I'll never graduate from college."

One way for people who have low (also called negative) self-esteem to improve their self-esteem is to begin by writing out a Rational Self-Analysis (described earlier) in which they identify their negative cognitions about themselves and then also identify rational challenges to each of these negative cognitions. They will then gradually develop improved self-esteem *if* they seek to challenge their negative cognitions about themselves with their rational challenges *every time* they begin to think negatively about themselves.

THERAPY AS AN EDUCATIONAL PROCESS

Learning how to think rationally and to counter irrational and negative self-talk is seen as an educational process. Clients can learn how to analyze and change irrational self-talk in a variety of ways: instruction by the therapist; viewing videotapes and films on rational therapy; reading books and pamphlets; and by attending workshops or seminars on rational therapy. Ellis (1977) has demonstrated that the basic principles of how to analyze irrational self-talk and to think rationally can be successfully taught to elementary and secondary school students.

In therapy, the role of the therapist is to instruct clients on how to analyze the irrational self-talk underlying their unwanted emotions and irresponsible behavior. The therapist uses probes, confrontation, explanations, interpretations, humor, and suggestions to help clients discover their irrational thinking. Once clients become aware of their irrational self-talk, a rational therapist uses the techniques previously described in this chapter to help clients change their unwanted emotions, irresponsible behaviors, and negative self-esteem.

ISSUES AND UNANSWERED QUESTIONS

1. *Physiology of self-talk and emotions.* As yet we do not precisely know the physiological components of thinking, or of emotions. Our brain, of course, is important in enabling us to think. But, what precisely takes place in the brain that leads us to conceptualize every thought that we have? Are there other parts of the body involved in thinking? Thinking is related to memory. But what precisely is memory, and how do we "store" and "recall" experiences that we have? And, how are memory and thinking physiologically related?

Rational therapy theorizes that our self-talk primarily causes our emotions. But, again a number of physiological questions arise. What are the physiological processes involved in self-talk resulting in an emotion? What different physiological processes occur for such varied emotions as love, depression, grief, happiness, anger, frustration, sorrow, relaxation, hostility, fear, and so on? And, how, physiologically, do certain types of self-talk and certain kinds of emotional states influence our health? In a general fashion we know certain kinds of self-talk lead to the stress reaction, and that prolonged stress can cause psychosomatic illnesses. But, again, what are the specific physiological processes involved?

2. *Separating the effects of self-talk from the effects of physiological factors.* For people with injuries or abnormal conditions in the brain it is at times extremely difficult to separate the effects of their medical conditions from the effects of self-talk on their emotions and behaviors. Injuries of different areas of the brain will at times cause a change in the person's emotions and behaviors (White & Watt, 1973). Abnormal conditions of the brain can result from a wide range of factors, including brain tumors, disorders such as cerebral palsy, chronic alcoholic intoxication, Alzheimer's disease, general paresis, AIDS, and cerebral arteriosclerosis. Such medical conditions are a factor in causing confusion, incoherence, clouding of consciousness, loss of recent or past memory, reduction in reasoning capacities, listlessness, apathy, reduction in intellectual capacities, and sometimes perceptual changes. People with such medical conditions are at times fairly alert, and at other times they are confused.

While the above conditions tend to have permanent or long-lasting effects on thinking patterns and emotional reactions, there are also factors that can lead to temporary changes in mental activity—such as high fever, toxins or poisons, and the intake of drugs and alcohol.

Even with the presence of any of these factors, the self-talk that a person gives herself about these conditions will also affect that person's emotions and behaviors. Separating which effects are due to these other factors, and which are due to self-talk often is difficult.

3. *Nature versus nurture.* Nurture can be defined as the sum of the influences modifying the expression of the genetic potentialities of a person. The theory of human behavior presented in this chapter focuses on nurture determinants, since it states human behavior is determined by events and self-talk. This theory fails to include genetic factors, which obviously have some influence in determining human behavior.

4. *The importance of experiences or events themselves.* Some critics of rational therapy assert that experiences or events that happen to a person are as important (and perhaps even more important) in determining behavior than is the self-talk that people give themselves about such experiences. These critics point out that such events as poverty, discrimination, child abuse, overprotective

parents, inadequate education, and being victimized by crime are major determinants of human behavior.

5. *The difficulty of "reprogramming" negative and irrational self-talk.* At first glance the process of changing negative and irrational self-talk sounds fairly easy. However, often the change process is difficult, complex, and time consuming. For a variety of reasons, some people have difficulty in changing their "crooked" thinking in a more positive and rational direction.

Some individuals firmly believe that their unwanted emotions and dysfunctional behaviors are due to other causes (such as genetics or unconscious processes) than self-talk. Therefore, they generally put forth little effort in seeking to improve themselves by challenging and changing their negative and irrational cognitions.

Some individuals have difficulty in disputing their negative and irrational cognitions because these cognitions have a long-standing history and have become deeply ingrained patterns of thinking. For example, Carlos Gomez (22 years old) has low self-esteem as a result of two decades of self-downing thoughts that were reinforced by his parents calling him "stupid" and relating to him in a manner in which they conveyed that he was inferior. For Carlos to improve his self-esteem will require considerable effort to refute the long history of self-downing cognitions underlying his low self-esteem.

Sometimes negative and irrational self-talk is based on deeply held irrational beliefs. An example of such a belief is the idea that it is a dire necessity to be loved or approved by everyone for everything one does. (A more rational belief is to seek to do the things one wants to do as long as one does not hinder others.) To change "crooked" self-talk that is based on deeply held irrational beliefs is often difficult because the underlying deeply held irrational beliefs need to be identified and changed in a more positive and rational direction.

Being above average in intelligence is an asset in learning to "reprogram" negative and irrational self-talk. However, some persons who are highly intelligent but who have deeply held irrational beliefs may not be successful in changing their crooked cognitions because of their unwillingness to question the validity of their deeply held irrational beliefs.

Sometimes individuals are reluctant to change certain of their negative and irrational self-talk statements because such self-talk is leading to dysfunctional behavior that is giving them pleasure. Examples of dysfunctional behaviors that may be pleasurable include abuse of alcohol or other drugs, gambling, compulsive eating, and sexual abuse of others.

6. *Determining when self-talk is rational or good.* What is rational for one person may not be rational for another. The self-talk statement "I will become a professional baseball player" may be accurate and rational for someone with the essential athletic skills and desire to play professional baseball, but is probably irrational for those who do not. As a guideline for determining whether self-talk is irrational, Maultsby (1975) has indicated that thinking is irrational if it does one or more of the following:

a. Does not fit the facts. For example, you tell yourself no one loves you after someone has ended a romantic relationship—and you still have several close friends and relatives who love you.

b. Hampers you in protecting your life. For example, if you decide you can drive 30 miles to some place when you are intoxicated.

c. Hampers you in achieving your short- and long-term goals. For example, you want to do well in college and you have two exams tomorrow which you haven't studied for, but instead you decide to go out and party.

d. Causes significant trouble with other people. For example, you think you have a right to challenge anyone to a fight whenever you interpret a remark as being an insult.

e. Leads you to feel emotions that you do not want to feel.

According to Maultsby (1975, 1977) thinking is rational or "good" if any of the above negative consequences do not occur.

7. *The differences between self-talk and thoughts in general.* Self-talk has been defined as the set of evaluating thoughts we give ourselves about facts and events that happen to us. As indicated earlier, self-talk includes thoughts about future events. Does the term *self-talk* refer to *all* of our current thoughts, or to a more limited set of thoughts? If the latter, what are the boundaries that separate self-talk from other categories of thoughts? Answers to these critical questions have as yet not been advanced by the theoreticians who developed rational therapy.

8. *Boundaries of self-talk.* Self-talk appears to have immense effects on our lives, many of which have been summarized in this chapter. But what are the limits of the effects of self-talk? In reference to this question this author in another publication (Zastrow, 1979, pp. 327–328) presented the following example which highlights the unknown limits of the effects of self-talk:

> A college student recently asked if her mother's long-time concern about giving birth to a child with a "dwarf" arm might have led to her youngest being born with a malformed arm.
>
> The student mentioned her mother had been mildly concerned for a number of years that she would give birth to a child with a malformed arm. This young woman and her older brother were born without having such a malformation. However, shortly after the mother became pregnant the third time, a neighbor woman gave birth to a child with a malformed arm. This led the mother to have intense concerns that the child she was carrying would be born with a "dwarf" arm. When the child was born, it in fact was born with a "dwarf" arm.
>
> After I had given several lectures on the effects of self-talk in one of my classes, the student asked whether I thought this malformation was partly caused by self-talk, or was just a matter of coincidence.
>
> In truth, I answered I didn't know—and I still don't know. We know certain drugs (such as thalidomide and excessive drinking) can cause malformations. So can having certain illnesses, such as German measles, during the time when the mother is pregnant. There is also speculation that the mother's emotional state while pregnant can influence the emotional and physiological development of the unborn child (Ainsworth, 1966; Dunn, 1977). Is it possible that this mother's thoughts and fears about having a malformed child might have been a factor in the child being born with a malformed arm? . . .
>
> Daily I become aware of new ways in which my life, and that of others, is being influenced by self-talk. And, as I discuss the concept with others, the discussion usually ignites their relating to me specific incidents where their self-talk has had a powerful effect on them.
>
> At this point I frankly do not know what the boundaries are for the effects of self-talk. It may well be that we are only at the "tip of the iceberg" in understanding all of the effects of self-talk.

SUMMARY

Our self-concept is determined by what we think about ourselves. Our emotions and our feelings are also determined, primarily, by our cognitions. By changing our negative and irrational thinking in a more positive and rational direction, we will improve our self-esteem, gradually reduce our unwanted emotions, and curb our dysfunctional behaviors. Through learning to be a positive and rational thinker, we will be happier, healthier, and more productive.

If it is accurate (as this chapter asserts) that unwanted emotions, dysfunctional actions, and negative self-esteem primarily arise from negative and irrational self-talk, an important corollary is that any therapy technique that is successful in changing emotions, actions, or self-esteem is effective primarily because it changes a person's thinking from self-talk that is negative or irrational to self-talk that is more rational and positive. Thus it appears that restructuring thinking is the key psychotherapeutic agent in making positive changes in our self.

REFERENCES

Ainsworth, M. D., et al. (1966). *Deprivation of maternal care*. New York: Schocken Books.

Allen, B., & Bosta, D. (1981). *Games criminals play*. Sacramento, CA: RAE John.

Beck, A. T. (1979). *Cognitive therapy and emotional disorders*. New York: New American Library.

Beck, A. T., & Weishaar, M. E. (1989). Cognitive therapy. In *Current psychotherapies* (4th ed.), edited by R. Corsini & D. Wedding (pp. 285–320). Itasca, IL: F. E. Peacock.

Burns, D. D. (1980). *Feeling good: The new mood therapy*. New York: Morrow.

Cooley, C. H. (1902). *Human nature and the social order*. New York: Scribner's.

Dunn, J. (1977). *Distress and comfort*. Cambridge, MA: Harvard University Press.

Dyer, W. (1976). *Your erroneous zones*. New York: Funk & Wagnalls.

Ellis, A. (1958). Rational psychotherapy. *The Journal of General Psychology*, 58:35–49.

———. (1962). *Reason and emotion in psychotherapy*. New York: Lyle Stuart.

_____. (1973). Rational-emotive therapy. In *Current Psychotherapies,* edited by R. Corsini (pp. 167–206). Itasca, IL: F. E. Peacock.

_____. (1977). *How to raise an emotionally healthy, happy child.* Hollywood, CA: Wilshire Book Co.

_____. (1979). Rational-emotive therapy. In *Current Psychotherapies* (2nd ed.), edited by R. Corsini (pp. 185–229). Itasca, IL: F. E. Peacock.

Foreyt, J. P., & Rathjen, D. P. (Eds.) (1978). *Cognitive behavior therapy: Research and application.* New York: Plenum Press.

Guidano, V. P., & Liotti, G. (1983). *Cognitive processes and emotional disorders.* New York: Guilford Press.

Lembo, J. (1974). *Help yourself.* Niles, IL: Argus Communications.

London, H., & Nisbett, R. (1974). *Thought and feeling.* Chicago: Aldine.

Luria, A. (1961). *The role of speech in the regulation of normal and abnormal behavior.* New York: Liveright.

Maultsby, M. C., Jr. (1975). *Help yourself to happiness.* Boston: Herman Publishing.

_____. (1977). The ABC's of better emotional self-control. In *The personal problem solver,* edited by C. Zastrow & D. Chang (pp. 3–18). Englewood Cliffs, NJ: Prentice-Hall.

Samenow, S. (1984). *Inside the criminal mind.* New York: Times Books.

_____. (1989). *Before it's too late.* New York: Times Books.

Schachter, S., & Singer, J. E. (1962). Cognitive, social and physiological determinants of emotional state. *Psychological Review,* 69:379–399.

Vygotsky, L. (1962). *Thought and language.* Cambridge: MIT Press.

White, R. W., & Watt, N. F. (1973). *The abnormal personality* (4th ed.). New York: Ronald Press.

Yochelson, S., & Samenow, S. (1985). *The criminal personality—"The change process"* (vol. 2). New York: Jason Aronson.

Zastrow, C. (1979). *Talk to yourself: Use the power of self-talk.* Englewood Cliffs, NJ: Prentice-Hall.

_____. (1988). How to rehabilitate criminal offenders. *International Journal of Comparative and Applied Criminal Justice* (Winter):229–235.

_____. (1989). *The practice of social work* (3rd ed.). Chicago: Dorsey Press.

Zastrow, C., & Kirst-Ashman, K. (1990). *Understanding human behavior and the social environment* (2nd ed.). Chicago, IL: Nelson-Hall.

Zastrow, C., & Navarre, R. (1979). Self-talk: A new criminological theory. *International Journal of Comparative and Applied Criminal Justice,* 3(2):167–176.

CHAPTER 7

The Transtheoretical Model of Change

Diane Grimley
James O. Prochaska
Wayne F. Velicer
Linelle M. Blais
Carlo C. DiClemente

Today there are over four hundred theories of psychotherapy (Karasu, 1986), with the vast majority being intrapersonal in nature. These intrapersonal models have developed a tarnished reputation over the past decade or two. First of all, there has been considerable fragmentation in how theories analyze individuals and an overwhelming assortment of alternative and competing treatment protocols.

Historically, most intrapersonal theories have resulted in clinic-based interventions that are not only costly but also serve too few people. Emphasis has been placed on maximizing professional rather than public expertise. Furthermore, if fundamental forces that lead to behavior change are within individuals and if individuals fail to change, then it is all too easy to blame the person for not changing. "Failure to thrive" in therapy is usually attributed to the client. They weren't motivated enough. They were obsessive personalities. They had borderline characteristics. Finally,

This research was partially supported by Grants CA27821 and CA50087 from the National Cancer Institute. Requests for reprints or further information should be sent to James O. Prochaska, Ph.D., Cancer Prevention Research Consortium, University of Rhode Island, Kingston, RI. 02881-0808. (401) 792-2830.

and most importantly, intrapersonal models are largely theories of personality and psychopathology—theories of *why* people do not change. Few have been models of *how* people change.

As a result of the shortcomings of traditional intrapersonal models, we are left without a satisfactory understanding of how people intentionally change their own behavior. Whether we wish to intervene at the individual, interpersonal, organizational, or community levels, we ultimately need a more comprehensive explanation of how individuals go about changing maladaptive behaviors. In other words, we need to know *who* responds to *what* types of methods and *when*, if we are to assist persons in leading healthier lives. A more comprehensive model could potentially provide a synthesis of the diverse models of change and a framework for integrating them. Finally, a comprehensive model would need to cover the full course of change, from the time someone becomes aware that a problem exists to the point at which a problem has been modified. Most models of change have been action-oriented, that is, targeted for those individuals prepared to change. But there are many steps that precede and follow a person taking action toward modifying problem behaviors. Trying to decide how to best help someone to change includes taking into account where a particular person is in this cycle of change.

The Transtheoretical Model of Change, developed by Prochaska, DiClemente, Velicer, and colleagues, offers an alternate conceptualization of the structure of change. The model's focus is on the phenomena of intentional change, as opposed to societal, developmental, or imposed change. This eclectic approach utilizes integrative dimensions of change that occur across diverse systems of psychotherapy and across various phases of change. The basic model includes the stages of change as a temporal organizational structure; a set of independent variables that include the processes of change and the levels of change; and intermediate or dependent variables, including the pros and cons of change, self-efficacy, temptation, and environmental variables and behaviors specific to the problem areas.

It is important to recognize two key issues at this point. First, we view behavior as potentially determined by three powerful forces: (1) biological controls, (2) social controls, and (3) self-control. Biological controls can be very powerful, as is obvious in the case of addictive behaviors. Social systems are also assumed to be strongly influential. If people are struggling to change behaviors that objectively have them more under biological and/or social controls, then self-controls are going to have to be herculean for change to have a chance. The self-system is crucial in producing self-change. However, the self-system has a much better chance of succeeding if it is congruent with, and supported by, social and/or biological controls. Two against one tends to win.

As for the nature of the self-system, we have not bothered to articulate on such explicit over implicit assumptions regarding the self-system. We are not sure that it is necessary. But, without an adequate self-system, behavior becomes entirely determined by our biology and our society. Our work is to change behavior that is more self-determined, whatever the ultimate nature of "self" turns out to be.

The second point is that the Transtheoretical Model is a "template" of sorts that is translated or redefined across different problem behaviors. The model consists of general constructs and constructs specific to the problem behavior, which usually requires either minor or major changes in the wording of the items used in the assessment of these constructs.

The initial data for the model were derived from the area of smoking cessation, and much of the preliminary model testing involved this problem. Therefore, smoking cessation is employed as a prime example throughout this essay. We should add that the model has been applied successfully to a variety of behaviors, including exercise (Marcus, Rossi, Selby, & Niaura, 1992), sunscreen use (Rossi, 1992), weight control (Prochaska et al., in press), contraceptive and condom use (Grimley, Riley, Bellis, & Prochaska, 1992), HIV risk reduction (Redding, Rossi, Velicer, & Prochaska, 1989), mammography screening (Rakowski, Dube, Marcus, Prochaska, & Velicer, 1992), and dietary fat reduction (Rossi, Rossi, & Prochaska, 1990).

STAGES OF CHANGE

In cross-sectional and longitudinal studies of self-change, as well as in treatment studies, results indicate that individuals progress through specific stages as they struggle to reduce or remove problematic behaviors (DiClemente & Prochaska, 1982; DiClemente, Prochaska, Velicer, Fairhurst, Rossi, & Valesquez, 1991; Prochaska & DiClemente, 1983, 1984; Prochaska, DiClemente, Velicer, Ginpil, & Norcross, 1985).

The concept of *stages* is important for understanding change, in part because it reflects a temporal dimension in which change unfolds and includes a set of tasks needed for movement to the next stage. Although the time an individual spends in each stage may vary, the tasks to be accomplished in order to achieve successful movement to the next stage are assumed to be invariant. Stages may, therefore, represent an appropriate level of abstraction for understanding certain behavioral problems, such as smoking, obesity, psychological distress, and sedentary life-styles.

With respect to stability, a stage is somewhere between traits and states. Traits are typically construed as very stable but not very open to change. States, on the other hand, are very readily changed but typically lack stability. Other latent constructs, like "the working self-concept" (Markus & Nurius, 1986), self-efficacy, locus of control, barriers and facilitator, reinforcers and punishers, cues and consequences, cognitions and norms, all lack an inherent temporal dimension and/or a sense of directionality. In other words, the notion of stages suggests that individuals *pass* through each stage of change and cannot successfully leap from an early stage to a later one. It has been predicted that an individual who leaps to modifying a behavior without adequately thinking it through, or developing some plan of action, is at high risk for relapse (Prochaska, DiClemente, Velicer, & Rossi, 1992).

The stages were first identified in a study comparing smokers quitting on their own with smokers in two smoking cessation treatment programs (DiClemente & Prochaska, 1982). They were operationalized and developed further with a sample of outpatient therapy clients yielding four stages of change, precontemplation, contemplation, action, and maintenance (McConnaughy, Prochaska, & Velicer, 1983). A fifth stage between contemplation and action, labeled "preparation," has since been identified and validated (DiClemente et al., 1991; Velicer, Prochaska, Rossi, & Snow, 1992).

In the *precontemplation* stage, individuals are not intending to change their problem behavior in the foreseeable future. A six-month framework is usually used since it is assumed that this is about as far in the future people anticipate making specific behavior change. Individuals in this stage are often uninformed about the long-term consequences of their behavior, demoralized about their abilities to change, do not want to think about the problem, and/or defensive in response to social pressures to change. Precontemplation has been found to be the most stable stage, with some precontemplators never moving beyond this point in the change cycle. There is nothing in the stages of change model that suggests that precontemplators will automatically, dramatically, or discretely progress to the next stage of change. Rather, results (Prochaska, Velicer, Guadagnoli, Rossi, & DiClemente, 1991) show that of the nearly 200 smokers classified as precontemplators who were followed every six months for two years, approximately two-thirds remained in the precontemplation stage the entire time.

Contemplation is the stage in which people are aware that a problem exists and are seriously intending to change within the next six months. People in the contemplation stage have not yet made a commitment to take action and can remain stuck in this stage for long periods. In one study of self-changers, a group of 200 smokers remained in this relatively stable stage for two years without ever moving to significant action (DiClemente & Prochaska, 1982; Prochaska & DiClemente, 1984). The essence of the contemplation stage might be thought of as "knowing where you want to go, but not quite ready yet" (Prochaska, DiClemente, & Norcross, 1992).

Preparation is the stage in which individuals intend to take action in the near future, usually the next month. These individuals typically have developed a plan of action, have taken action in the past year, or have made some small behavioral change, such as reducing the number of cigarettes they smoke. This stage, then, has both intentional and behavioral criteria. Unlike precontemplation and contemplation, preparation is a transitional rather than stable stage, with individuals more likely to progress over the next 30 days.

Action is the stage during which overt behavioral changes have occurred within the past six months. The best behavioral change criterion available is one which health professionals agree places the person at low risk for this behavior. With smoking, individuals are not in the action stage if they reduce their smoking by 50 percent or have switched to low-tar and nicotine cigarettes. The action criterion is having quit smoking.

The action stage is the busiest of the five stages of change; individuals are actively engaged in eliminating their problem behavior by utilizing more processes of change than during any other stage. Not surprisingly, action is the least stable of the stages and carries the highest risks for relapse.

Maintenance is a period ranging from six months after the criterion has been reached until the problem behavior is finally terminated. Individuals in the maintenance stage are not just passively refraining from engaging in the problem, but are continuing to rely on their "bag" of behavioral and experiential skills necessary to prevent relapse. However, reliance on such techniques continues to decrease as the behavior in question becomes an increasingly less salient issue.

Preceding the five stages is *acquisition* and following them is *termination* (Velicer, Prochaska, Rossi, & Snow, 1992). Acquisition is the period during which a problem behavior is developed. To date, three stages of acquisition have been identified: precontemplation, decision making, and maintenance (Elder et al., 1990; Stern, Prochaska, Velicer, & Elder, 1987). Decision making combines both the cognitive and behavioral aspects of the three middle stages of cessation.

Termination is the period during which a problem behavior is entirely extinguished. Termination is defined by two criteria: (1) temptation to engage in the problem behavior across all previously tempting situations is zero; and (2) confidence in one's ability to not engage in the problem behavior across all previously tempting situations is 100 percent. With smoking cessation, for example, cross-sectional data on individuals in the maintenance stage for varying lengths of time indicate that confidence peaks after about 18 months of prolonged abstinence. Temptation, on the other hand, does not appear to bottom out until thirty-six to forty-eight months of abstinence (Prochaska & DiClemente, 1984). Recent smoking research reveals that even after twelve months of continuous abstinence, 37 percent of individuals will return to smoking. After five years of continuous abstinence, the risk for relapse falls to 7 percent (USDHHS, 1990). With a conservative time estimate, then, termination could safely be assumed for most people after five years of prolonged abstinence.

Progression through the stages is more often cyclical than strictly linear, with regression from the later stages of action or maintenance stages to an earlier stage. With smoking, successful self-changers make an average of three to four action attempts before they become long-term maintainers (Schachter, 1982).

Some relapsers feel like failures; they are embarrassed, ashamed, and guilty. These individuals become demoralized and resist thinking about behavior change. Approximately 15 percent of smokers who relapsed were found to have regressed back to the precontemplation stage (Prochaska & DiClemente, 1985).

Fortunately, research with self-changers indicates that the vast majority of relapsers (85 percent of smokers) recycle back to the contemplation or preparation stages (Prochaska & DiClemente, 1984). They begin to consider plans for their next action attempt while trying to learn from their mistakes. To take another example, 60 percent of unsuccessful New Year's resolvers make the same pledge the next year (Norcross, Ratzin, & Payne, 1989). This spiral model suggests that most relapsers do not revolve endlessly in circles and that they do not regress all the way back to where they began.

PROCESSES OF CHANGE

There are certain independent variables specific to a problem behavior. These can include external variables such as social pressure or internal variables such as demoralization. The conceptualization of the impact of these variables may be best thought of in terms of a "causal chain." These specific variables precede change by activating certain strategies that are a function of an individual's current stage of change.

What do individuals do to progress from one stage of change to the next? Since each stage requires certain tasks to be accomplished, specific behaviors are particularly important at certain stages of change. In a number of retrospective, cross-sectional, longitudinal, and intervention studies (DiClemente et al., 1991; DiClemente & Prochaska, 1982; Prochaska & DiClemente, 1983; Prochaska et al., 1985, 1991), different processes of change are emphasized at different stages of change. The processes of change represent a middle level of abstraction between the basic theoretical assumptions of a system of therapy and the techniques proposed by the theory. Processes of change are covert or overt activities individuals use to alter their experiences and/or environments in order to modify affect, behavior, cognitions, or relationships. Although there are a large number of coping activities, a limited set of processes represents the basic principles underlying these activities.

The change processes were first identified theoretically in a comparative analysis of the leading systems of psychotherapy (Prochaska, 1979). The processes were selected by examining recommended change techniques across different theories, which explains the term *transtheoretical*. Research with smokers has documented that naive self-changers used the same change processes that have been at the core of psychotherapy systems (DiClemente & Prochaska, 1982; Prochaska & DiClemente, 1984). Extensive validity and reliability data on the processes have been reported elsewhere (Prochaska et al., 1988; Rossi, 1992).

Table 7.1 presents the ten processes receiving the most theoretical and empirical support to date, along with their definitions and representative examples of specific interventions.

A common and finite set of change processes has been clearly revealed across such diverse problem areas as psychological distress, cigarette smoking, and obesity (Prochaska & DiClemente, 1985). In each problem area, the set of change processes accounted for nearly 70 percent of the variance in a principal component analysis of the Processes of Change Scale. There are striking similarities in the frequency with which the change processes were used across these problems. When processes were rank-ordered in terms of how frequently they were used for each of the problem behaviors, the rankings of the processes were nearly identical. Helping relationships, consciousness raising, and self-liberation, for example, were the three most frequently used processes across problems, whereas reinforcement management and stimulus control were the least used processes.

Significant differences do exist in the absolute frequency of use of the change processes across problem areas. Individuals relied more on helping relationships and consciousness raising for overcoming psychological distress than they did for either weight control or smoking cessation. Overweight individuals relied more on self-liberation and stimulus control than did distressed individuals (Prochaska & DiClemente, 1985).

TABLE 7.1

Titles, Definitions, and Representative Interventions of the
Processes of Change

Process	Definitions: Interventions
Consciousness raising	Increasing information about self and problem: observations, confrontations, interpretations, bibliotherapy
Self-reevaluation	Assessing how one feels and thinks about oneself with respect to a problem: value clarification, imagery, corrective emotional experience
Self-liberation	Choosing and commitment to act or belief in ability to change: decision-making therapy, New Year's resolutions, logotherapy techniques, commitment-enhancing techniques
Counterconditioning	Substituting alternatives for problem behaviors: relaxation, desensitization, assertion, positive self-statements
Stimulus control	Avoiding or countering stimuli that elicit problem behaviors: restructuring one's environment (e.g., removing alcohol or fattening foods), avoiding high-risk cues, fading techniques
Reinforcement management	Rewarding one's self or being rewarded by others for making changes: contingency contracts, overt and covert reinforcements, self-reward.
Helping relationships	Being open and trusting about problems with someone who cares: therapeutic alliance, social support, self-help groups
Dramatic relief	Experiencing and expressing feelings about one's problems and solutions: psychodrama, grieving losses, role-playing
Environmental reevaluation	Assessing how one's problem affects the physical environment: empathy training and documentaries
Social liberation	Increasing alternatives for nonproblem behaviors available in society: advocating for rights of repressed, empowering, policy interventions.

Most major systems of psychotherapy emphasize only two or three processes of change (Prochaska & DiClemente, 1984). Both clients and self-changers, however, utilize eight or ten processes of change (Norcross & Prochaska, 1986a, 1986b). One of the assumptions of the transtheoretical approach is that therapists should be at least as cognitively complex as their clients. In other words, they should be able to think and intervene in terms of a more comprehensive set of change processes. Two or three processes cannot do justice to all the knowledge being generated about the series of stages through which people progress and regress. At best, two or three processes can predict progress from one stage to the next (for example, precontemplation to contemplation). Other processes are necessary to predict other transitions. If we need clients to expand on what they learn in therapy, then we need to have therapy reflect the complexities of change rather than reduce it to a simple solution, such as the therapeutic relationship (Rogers), consciousness raising (Freud), counterconditioning (Wolpe), cognitive restructuring (Ellis), or contingency management (Skinner).

INTEGRATION OF STAGES AND PROCESSES

One of the most important findings to emerge from working with self-changers and therapy changers is that particular processes are emphasized during particular stages of change (DiClemente et al., 1991; Norcross, Prochaska, & DiClemente, 1991; Prochaska & DiClemente, 1983, 1984). The basic pattern of change processes across stages of change can best be represented by a mountain metaphor, "Mt. Change" (Prochaska & DiClemente, 1992; Prochaska et al., 1991). By integrating cross-sectional and longitudinal data, Prochaska et al. (1991) showed that the change processes followed a general curvilinear pattern of "climbing" from precontemplation to contemplation, "peaking" at about action, and then "descending" either to precontemplation levels or to somewhat higher levels if used as relapse prevention strategies during the maintenance stage.

Using the data as a point of departure, an interpretation of how particular processes can be applied or avoided at each stage of change has been offered (Prochaska, Norcross, Fowler, Follick & Abrams, 1992). During the precontemplation stage, individuals used eight of the change processes significantly less than people in any other stage. Precontemplators processed less information about their problems, devoted less time and energy to reevaluating themselves, and experienced fewer emotional reactions to the negative aspects of their problems. Furthermore, they were less open with significant others about their problems, and they did little to shift their attention, or their environment, in the direction of overcoming problems.

Individuals in the contemplation stage were most open to consciousness-raising techniques, such as observations, confrontations, and interpretations, and they were much more likely to use bibliotherapy and other educational techniques (Prochaska & DiClemente, 1984). Contemplators were also open to dramatic relief experiences, which raise emotions and lead to a lowering of negative affect if the person changes. As individuals became more conscious of themselves and the nature of their problems, they were more likely to reevaluate their values, problems, and themselves both affectively and cognitively. The more central their concerns were to their self-identity, the more their reevaluation involved altering their sense of self. Contemplators also reevaluated the effects their problematic behaviors had on their environments, especially the people with whom they were closest. They struggled with questions such as "How do I think and feel about living in a deteriorating environment that places my family and friends at increasing risk for disease, poverty, or imprisonment?"

Some of the cognitive, affective, and evaluative processes utilized in the contemplation stage continued during the preparation stage. In addition, individuals began to take small steps toward action. They used counterconditioning and stimulus control to begin reducing the number of cigarettes they smoked or to control the situations in which they relied on smoking (DiClemente et al., 1991).

During the action stage, people endorsed higher levels of self-liberation or willpower. They increasingly believed that they had the autonomy to change their lives in meaningful ways. Successful action also entailed effective use of behavioral processes, such as counterconditioning and stimulus control, in order to modify the conditional stimuli that frequently prompt relapse. Insofar as action was a particularly stressful stage, individuals relied increasingly on support and understanding from helping relationships (Prochaska & DiClemente, 1983, 1992; Prochaska et al., 1991).

Just as preparation for action was essential for success, so too was preparation for maintenance. The maintenance stage built on each of the processes that came before. Specific preparation for maintenance entailed an assessment of the conditions under which a person was likely to relapse and development of alternative responses for coping with such conditions, without resorting to self-defeating defenses and pathological responses. Perhaps most important was the sense that one was becoming the kind of person one wanted to be. Continuing to apply counterconditioning and stimulus control was most effective when it was based on the conviction that maintaining change supports a sense of self that was highly valued by oneself and at least one significant other (Prochaska, DiClemente, & Norcross, 1992).

Figures 7.1 and 7.2 illustrate the integration of the stages and processes of change for smoking cessation. Figure 7.1 reveals the frequency of use for dramatic relief, an earlier process. Figure 7.2 shows the frequency of use for stimulus control, one of the latter processes.

The integration of the stages and processes of change is an important guide to the development of more comprehensive therapy and self-help programs. In psychotherapy, for example, once a client's stage is clear, a psychotherapist would know which processes to apply to help the individual progress to the next stage. A therapist could also monitor which processes are being utilized and to what degree as the individual progresses through the stages and phases of therapy (Prochaska & DiClemente, 1984).

Since approximately two-thirds of the outcome variance in therapy is attributed to the client's efforts and one-third to the efforts of the therapist (Prochaska & Norcross, 1983), such monitoring should involve processes utilized between sessions as well as within sessions. Average outpatients spend about 99 percent of their waking week outside the clinical setting, which makes such an assessment seem critical (Prochaska et al., 1991).

For example, behaviorists and reality therapists have encouraged "homework" assignments for years. However, such actions reflect the use of one or two change processes that may be appropriate for clients who are in the preparation stage but may be entirely inappropriate for individuals in the earlier stages. Furthermore, homework assignments tend to be technique-oriented, whereas between-session work should be more process-oriented,

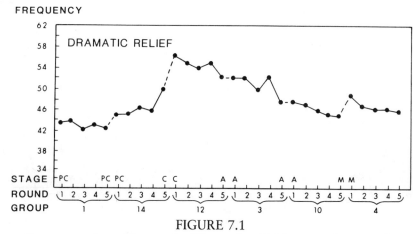

FIGURE 7.1

Frequency of use (T scores) of dramatic relief integrated across the stages of change.

since there are so many techniques for operationalizing processes. The Transtheoretical Model assumes that conscious and intentional change, guided by an adequate knowledge base of the stages and processes, is likely to be more effective than trial-and-error learning that lacks adequate representation of the processes of change.

DEPENDENT VARIABLES

Within the context of the Transtheoretical Model it can be seen that four critical movements occur: (1) from precontemplation to contemplation, (2) from contemplation to preparation, (3) from preparation to action, and (4) from action to maintenance. Existing criterion measures that focus on only target behaviors, such as smoking cessation, are appropriate for only one of these transitions: from preparation to action, when the person actually changes the behavior. Most interventions also focus on this transition (Prochaska & DiClemente, 1992). The other three transitions cannot be assessed with standard outcome measures. For example, the precontemplation-contemplation change will not involve a change in smoking status. What is expected to change is the attitudes and the intentions toward smoking cessation. Experiments with brief quitting attempts of less than twenty-four hours may occur, or information about the negative aspects of smoking will

FREQUENCY

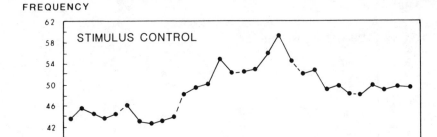

FIGURE 7.2

Frequency of use (T scores) of stimulus control integrated across the stages of change.

be processed (Velicer, DiClemente, Prochaska, & Brandenburg, 1985). In a similar manner, the transition from action to maintenance cannot be assessed with standard behavioral measures, since this will also involve no change in smoking status. The change will involve a lowering of the desire to smoke, an increase in the number of ways to cope with tempting situations, and the development of increased self-confidence (DiClemente, Prochaska, & Gibertini, 1985). Based on the need for more sensitive outcome measures, alternative constructs have been offered in the area of smoking that can easily generalize to other problem behaviors (Velicer, Rossi, Prochaska, & DiClemente, 1992). These constructs are decisional balance and self-efficacy.

Decisional Balance

Janis and Mann (1977) postulate eight categories for decision making: (1) instrumental benefits to self, (2) instrumental benefits to others, (3) approval by self, (4) approval by others, (5) instrumental cost to self, (6) costs to others, (7) disapproval by self, and (8) disapproval by others. This decision-making model has been tested with a number of behaviors (Prochaska et al., in press), with only two major categories consistently being found. Individuals seem to discriminate between the pros and cons of a decision. The

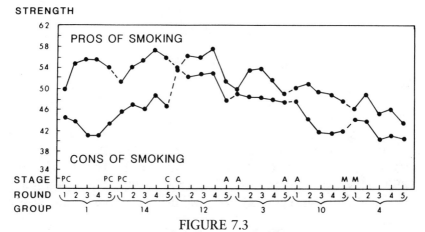

FIGURE 7.3

The strength of the pros and cons of smoking (T scores) integrated across the stages of change.

pros and cons are orthogonal factors; therefore, individuals can be high on one and low on the other, high on both, or low on both.

A decisional balance measure for smoking cessation was constructed to assess the pros and cons of smoking as they related to the stages of change (Velicer et al., 1985). The pros and cons are clearly relevant to precontemplation, contemplation, and preparation stages. In the initial stage of precontemplation, pros for smoking are high and the cons are quite low. The gap between the pros and cons narrows and shifts as individuals move from precontemplation to the later stages. However, during the action and maintenance stages, decisional balance considerations are less important as predictors for success (DiClemente et al., 1991; Prochaska et al., 1985). An illustrative example of the relationship between the pros and cons of smoking is presented in Figure 7.3.

The relationship of the pros and cons within stages is interesting; however, the pattern across stages is particularly revealing. The pros for smoking remain quite high throughout the first three stages of change. During the latter stages of preparation and action, the pros begin to decline in importance. The cons, on the other hand, increase in importance during contemplation to the point at which they equal the pros. At this point, these decisional considerations are in balance, which makes further movement unlikely. In the preparation stage, the cons clearly outweigh the pros.

During action, the cons remain higher than the pros, but they both decline in importance. Finally, during successful maintenance, these considerations continue to become less salient but remain with the decisional balance firmly established against smoking (DiClemente & Prochaska, 1982; DiClemente et al., 1991). The relationship between the stages of change and the pros and cons has been replicated across a wide range of behaviors (Prochaska et al., in press), including exercise (Marcus et al., 1992), sunscreen use (Rossi, 1992), radon gas testing (Rossi, 1992), contraceptive and condom use adoption (Grimley et al., 1992; Prochaska et al., 1990), HIV risk reduction (Redding et al., 1989), mammography screening (Rakowski et al., 1992), and dietary fat reduction (Rossi et al., 1990).

Self-Efficacy and Temptation

Just as the processes of change and the pros and cons can be integrated with the stages of change, so too can another important change variable. The concept of self-efficacy was presented by Bandura (1977, 1982) as an important mediator between knowledge and action. Research on addictive behavior (DiClemente, 1981, 1986; DiClemente & Hughes, 1990; DiClemente, Prochaska, & Gibertini, 1985; DiClemente et al., 1991; Velicer, DiClemente, Rossi, & Prochaska, 1990) has shown self-efficacy to be an important variable in understanding and predicting behavior change.

Self-efficacy is usually assessed by asking individuals to rate how confident they are that they will abstain from the problem behavior across a number of salient situations and experiences known to precipitate relapse. Responses are made on a 5-point scale in the Likert format and summed across situations to obtain an overall abstinence self-efficacy. Since an assessment of efficacy appears inadequate without some measure of salience of each of these cues, a separate, similar 5-point rating of temptation to engage in the behavior in each situation is also included. The resulting scores indicate that the degree to which an individual feels confident about changing a particular problem behavior and the level of temptation to engage in the problem behavior in specific situations are strongly related to the individual's current stage of change (DiClemente et al., 1985; DiClemente & Hughes, 1990; DiClemente et al., 1991).

Velicer et al. (1990) added to our understanding of self-efficacy by questioning the scoring of self-efficacy measures as a single scale and suggested that a higher-order factor could best explain the correlations found between efficacy variables. Structural modeling methods (Joreskog & Sorbom, 1984) produced results indicating that, with smoking behavior, there are two general factors—confidence and temptation—and three primary factors—positive/social, negative/affective, and habit/addictive. The conclusion was that the hierarchical model may be conceptualized as the structure that results from a model changing over time and that researchers should score measures of self-efficacy in two different ways. First, if employed as a general screening device to determine readiness for change, a single global score would be appropriate. Second, if employed during the course of treatment, three separate scores should be used to determine where relapse prevention efforts should be targeted for maximum effectiveness.

Across the stages for smoking cessation, efficacy scores vary significantly, with precontemplators reporting the lowest levels of self-efficacy and maintainers the highest. Efficacy evaluations have different implications in earlier stages of change, where individuals have not made a commitment to action and do not have modification performance feedback to use in their self-assessments. Abstinence efficacy for precontemplators of smoking is somewhat difficult to interpret. For these individuals, low self-efficacy scores can combine perceived inability and unwillingness. In the action stage, individuals can assess ability and confidence more directly.

The relationship between temptation and efficacy provides additional information that is stage-specific. Temptation scores are substantially and inversely related to efficacy evaluations ($r = -.60$). As we have seen with the pros and cons, efficacy and temptation interact across the stages of change. There is a rather large gap between low self-efficacy and high levels of temptation evaluations in precontemplation that narrows somewhat in contemplation and preparation stages. As individuals move into action, temptation and efficacy are in a precarious balance as efficacy increases rather dramatically and temptation decreases quite gradually. In maintenance, the precontemplation pattern is reversed, with temptation bottoming out and efficacy peaking and remaining high (DiClemente, 1986; DiClemente et al., 1991).

Self-efficacy is hypothesized to be a predictor of change. Research into the stages of change of smoking cessation (Prochaska et al., 1985) indicates that self-efficacy evaluations are quite relevant predictors of movement into action and maintenance, but do not emerge as relevant for earlier stage movement. These findings appear to reflect the fact that the construct of self-efficacy comes from a more action-oriented tradition (Social Learning Theory). Prediction of precontemplation and contemplation stage movement, on the other hand, seems to relate to decision making and cognitive processes of change, constructs developed in a tradition struggling with earlier stages of change. However, prediction of movement or outcome is only one possible predictive relationship.

A microanalysis of the relationship between self-efficacy and the stages suggests an interesting stage-specific link between efficacy and change process activity. Efficacy evaluations appear to modulate effort or coping activity, but not in a unidirectional manner. Higher efficacy scores among people in the precontemplation and contemplation stage were correlated with *greater* change process activity. However, in action and particularly maintenance stages, subjects' higher smoking abstinence self-efficacy correlated with *decreased* change process activity. Thus efficacy does appear to influence effort on specific change processes, dependent to some extent on stage status (DiClemente et al., 1985).

LEVELS OF CHANGE

Thus far, it may seem as if we have been discussing only how to approach a single, well-defined problem. However, human behavior change is not so accommodating and is not so simple a process. Although we can isolate certain symptoms and syndromes, these occur in the context of complex, interrelated levels of human functioning.

The next basic element of the transtheoretical approach addresses this issue. The Levels of Change represent a hierarchical organization of five interrelated levels of behavior problems: (1) symptom/situational problems; (2) maladaptive cognitions; (3) current interpersonal conflicts; (4) family/systems conflicts; and (5) intrapersonal conflicts.

Most systems of psychotherapy have attributed psychological problems to only one or two levels and focus interventions on these

TABLE 7.2
Integration of Levels, Stages, and Processes of Change

	Stages				
Levels	Precontemplation	Contemplation	Preparation	Action	Maintenance
Symptom/ Situational		Consciousness raising			
		Dramatic relief			
		Environmental reevaluation			
			Self-reevaluation		
			Self-liberation		
			Contingency management		
			Helping relationship		
					Counterconditioning
					Stimulus control
Maladaptive cognitions					
Interpersonal conflicts					
Family systems conflicts					
Intrapersonal conflicts					

levels. It is critical to the process of change that both the therapist and the client agree as to which level they attribute the problem and at which level, or levels, they are willing to engage in mutually as they work to change the problem behavior.

In the transtheoretical approach, initial intervention takes place at the symptom/situational level, since change tends to occur more quickly at this conscious and contemporary level of problems and since this level represents the primary reason for the individual's having entered therapy. The further down the hierarchy we focus, the further removed from awareness are the determinants of the problem likely to be. Moreover, as we progress down the levels, the further back in history are the determinants of the problem, and the more interrelated the problem is with the sense of self. Thus the prediction is that the deeper the level that needs to be changed, the longer and more complex therapy is likely to be and the greater the resistance of the client (Prochaska & DiClemente, 1984). Nor are these levels totally isolated from one another. Change at one level is likely to produce change at other levels. Symptoms often involve intrapersonal conflicts; maladaptive cognitions often reflect family/system beliefs or rules. In the transtheoretical approach, the complete therapist is prepared to intervene at any of the five levels of change, though the preference is to begin at the highest, most contemporary level that clinical assessment and judgment can justify.

In summary, the transtheoretical approach views successful self-change as the differential application of the processes of change at specific stages of change according to the problem level being addressed. Integrating the levels with the stages and processes of change provides a model for intervening hierarchically, as well as systematically, across a broad range of behavioral problems. Table 7.2 presents an overview of the integration of levels, stages, and processes of change.

APPLICATIONS OF THE TRANSTHEORETICAL MODEL

Great care has been taken to operationalize and validate each of the core constructs of the transtheoretical approach. These constructs are robust across different methodologies, different populations, and different problems. The stages, for example, have been identified and validated with a 32-item questionnaire applied to a range of patients entering psychotherapy (McConnaughy et al., 1983, 1989; Medeiros & Prochaska, 1992), alcoholics entering treatment (DiClemente & Hughes, 1990), and obese patients entering behavior therapy (Prochaska et al., in press). Brief 5-item algorithms have been used to validate stages of change for a broad range of problems, including smoking, cocaine use, risky sex, weight control, high-fat diets, exercise acquisition, sun exposure, radon exposure, and mammography screening (see Prochaska & DiClemente, 1992).

The ten processes of change have been replicated across a broad range of problems. These include smoking (Prochaska et al., 1985; 1988), psychological distress (DiClemente et al., 1991; Prochaska & DiClemente, 1985), weight control (Prochaska & DiClemente, 1985; Prochaska et al., in press), alcohol abuse (Snow, 1991), cocaine abuse (Rosenbloom, 1991), exercise acquisition (Marcus et al., 1992), and a variety of mental health disorders (Medeiros & Prochaska, 1992).

The systematic relationship between the stages of change and decisional balance has strong support with a number of diverse problems across diverse populations (see Prochaska et al., in press, for a review), as has the important change variable of self-efficacy (Velicer et al., 1990).

In a longitudinal analysis of subjects who progressed, regressed, and remained the same over a six-month period, discriminant functions predicted movement for the groups representing precontemplation, contemplation, action, and relapse stages. Predictors included the ten processes, two decision-making variables, and measures of self-efficacy and temptation, all variables open to change (Prochaska et al., 1985). When more static variables, such as age, education, smoking history, withdrawal symptoms, reasons for smoking, and health problems, were used as predictors, the results were much less pronounced (Wilcox, Prochaska, Velicer & DiClemente, 1985).

The Levels of Attribution and Change (LAC) Scale (Norcross & Magaletta, 1990; Norcross, Prochaska, Guadagnoli, & DiClemente, 1984; Norcross, Prochaska, & Hambrecht, 1985) is a highly reliable and valid instrument designed to assess the levels and loci of causal attributions about one's self-selected problems. The levels of change have received less empirical attention but have been replicated and validated with such problems as alcohol abuse (Begin, 1989), cocaine abuse (Rosenbloom, 1991), smoking (Norcross et al., 1984), and a mixture of DSM-III-R disorders (Medeiros & Prochaska, 1992; Penney, 1988).

This chapter concludes with some assertions concerning how the Transtheoretical Model of Change addresses such comprehensive questions as who changes, what changes, and when, where, why, and how changes occur. Specifically, the transtheoretical approach has focused on when changes occur, how changes occur, and what changes occur when problem behaviors are modified. The stage-of-change dimension indicates "when" people make particular changes in modifying problem behaviors. The processes of change address "how" people make particular changes when progressing from one stage to the next. The levels reveal "what" people need to change in order to overcome specific maladaptive behaviors.

"Where" people change has been assumed not to be a critical aspect of change. Whether people change in residential treatment centers, in outpatient therapy, in self-help groups, with self-help manuals, or at home working entirely on their own can have important practical implications, but does not appear to be a critical dimension for developing a comprehensive model of change.

"Why" people attempt to overcome problem behaviors relates to the important issue of motivation that many practitioners believe is the key to successful treatment. To date, the transtheoretical approach has not paid adequate attention to the question why some people attempt to change and others avoid change. Most sciences have progressed from adequately describing, then predicting, and, finally, explaining the phenomenon they study. Psychology has to leap to *why* questions before it has sufficiently answered the how, what, when, and where questions. We are not ready for such questions.

However, to date, decisional balance has been the variable that is most closely related to the issue of why some individuals change and others continue their maladaptive behavior. Data on decisional balance and informal observations suggest that motivations to change often vary with the stage an individual is in. Why someone begins to contemplate modifying high-risk behaviors, for example, can be different from why that person eventually takes action. Why someone makes continued efforts to maintain healthier actions can be different from why someone tries again after failing to maintain newly acquired health behaviors. Struggles to maintain behavior change may be based in part on a motivation to avoid failure. Returning to contemplation, rather than giving up, may be a result of one's motivation to be in control of one's own life, and not the belief that successful behavior change is beyond one's self-control. From a transtheoretical perspective, we assume that a comprehensive analysis of motivation to change will include an analysis of motivation at each stage of change and how motivation can be a dynamic phenomenon that fluctuates from one stage to the next.

"Who" changes in treatment and who fails have been traditionally addressed by the study of client characteristics. Such variables as age, gender, socioeconomic level, duration, frequency and intensity of the problem, intellectual functioning, psychological-mindedness, and degree of psychopathology are some of the client characteristics receiving considerable attention in the literature on therapy outcome (Luborsky, Chandler, Auerback, Cohen, & Bachrach, 1971; Meltzoff & Kornreich, 1970). The transtheoretical approach has not paid as much attention to such variables for several reasons. The most important reason is that such demographic, personality, and psychopathological variables tend to be traitlike and not particularly open to change or not likely to be under the client's or therapist's control. Decades of psychotherapy research on who benefits from treatment has done little to advance our knowledge of how we can help more people to change. This same research has often added to clinicians' pessimism about their abilities to assist whole classes, cultures, and communities of people overcome self-destructive problems. Until we develop more adequate models of treatment based on more comprehensive models of change, we really will not know the answers to who can change with maximum treatment, who can change with minimal treatment, who can change on their own, and who cannot, or will not, change regardless of what they, or we, try to do.

REFERENCES

Bandura, A. (1977). Self-efficacy: Toward a unifying theory of behavior. *Psychological Review, 84:*191–215.

———. (1982). Self-efficacy mechanism in human agency. *American Psychologist, 37:*122–147.

Begin, A. (1989). *Levels of attributions of male alcoholics, their significant others, and their therapists during the course of inpatient alcohol rehabilitation.* Unpublished doctoral dissertation, University of Rhode Island.

DiClemente, C. (1981). Self-efficacy and smoking cessation maintenance: A preliminary report. *Cognitive Therapy and Research, 5:*175–187.

———. (1986). Self-efficacy and addictive behaviors. *Journal of Social and Clinical Psychology, 4:*302–315.

DiClemente, C., & Hughes, S. (1990). Stages of change profiles in alcoholism treatment. *Journal of Substance Use, 2:*219–235.

DiClemente, C., & Prochaska, J. (1982). Self-change and therapy change of smoking behavior: A comparison of processes of change of cessation and maintenance. *Addictive Behaviors, 7:*133–142.

DiClemente, C., Prochaska, J., & Gibertini, M. (1985). Self-efficacy and the stages of self-change of smoking. *Cognitive Therapy and Research,* 9:181–200.

DiClemente, C., Prochaska, J., Velicer, W., Fairhurst, S., Rossi, J., & Velasquez, M. (1991). The process of smoking cessation: An analysis of precontemplation, contemplation and preparation stages of change. *Journal of Consulting and Clinical Psychology,* 59:295–304.

Elder, J., de Moor, C., Young, R., Wildey, M., Molgaard, C., Golbeck, A., Sallis, J., & Stern, R. (1990). Stages of adolescent tobacco-use acquisition. *Addictive Behaviors,* 15:449–454.

Grimley, D., Riley, G., Bellis, J., & Prochaska, J. (1992). *Assessing decision-making and contraceptive use of men and women for the prevention of pregnancy, STDs, and AIDS.* Manuscript under review.

Janis, I., & Mann, L. (1977). *Decision making: A psychological analysis of conflict, choice, and commitment.* New York: Free Press.

Joreskog, K., & Sorbom, D. (1984). *LISREL VI: User's guide.* Mooresville, IN: Scientific Software.

Karasu, T. (1986). The specificity versus nonspecificity dilemma: Toward identifying therapeutic change agents. *American Journal of Psychiatry,* 143:687–695.

Luborsky, L., Chandler, M., Auerback, A., Cohen, J., & Bachrach, H. (1971). Factors influencing the outcome of psychotherapy: A review of quantitative research. *Psychological Bulletin,* 75:145–185.

Marcus, B., Rossi, J., Selby, V., & Niaura, R. (1992). The stages and processes of exercise adoption and maintenance. *Health Psychology,* 11:386–395.

Markus, H., & Nurius, P. (1986). Possible selves. *American Psychologist,* 41:954–969.

McConnaughy, E., DiClemente, C., Prochaska, J., & Velicer, W. (1989). Stages of change in psychotherapy: A follow-up report. *Psychotherapy: Theory, Research and Practice,* 4:494–503.

McConnaughy, E., Prochaska, J., & Velicer, W. (1983). Stages of change in psychotherapy: Measurement and sample profiles. *Psychotherapy: Theory, Research and Practice,* 20:368–375.

Medeiros, M., & Prochaska, J. (1992). *Predicting premature termination from psychotherapy.* Manuscript submitted for publication.

Meltzoff, J., & Kornreich, M. (1970). *Research in psychotherapy.* New York: Atherton Press.

Norcross, J., & Magaletta, P. (1990). Concurrent validation of the levels of attribution and change (LAC) scale. *Journal of Clinical Psychology,* 46:618–622.

Norcross, J., & Prochaska, J. (1986a). Psychotherapists heal thyself—I: The psychological distress and self-change of psychologists, counselors, and laypersons. *Psychotherapy, 23:*102–114.

———. (1986b). Psychotherapists heal thyself—II: The self-initiated and therapy facilitated change of psychological distress. *Psychotherapy, 23:*345–356.

Norcross, J., Prochaska, J., & DiClemente, C. (1991). *The stages and processes of behavior change.* Manuscript submitted for publication.

Norcross, J., Prochaska, J., Guadagnoli, E., & DiClemente, C. (1984). Factor structure of the levels of attribution and change (LAC) scale in samples of psychotherapists and smokers. *Journal of Clinical Psychology, 40:*519–528.

Norcross, J., Prochaska, J., & Hambrecht, M. (1985). Levels of attribution and change (LAC) scale: Development and measurement. *Cognitive Therapy and Research, 9:*631–649.

Norcross, J., Ratzin, A., & Payne, D. (1989). Ringing in the New Year: The change processes and reported outcomes of resolution. *Addictive Behaviors, 14:*205–212.

Penney, D. (1988). *A comparison of psychotherapy-changers and self-changers in a naturalistic environment.* Unpublished doctoral dissertation, University of Rhode Island.

Prochaska, J. (1979). *Systems of psychotherapy: A transtheoretical analysis.* Homewood, IL: Dorsey Press.

Prochaska, J., & DiClemente, C. (1983). Stages and the processes of self-change of smoking: Toward an integrative model of change. *Journal of Consulting and Clinical Psychology, 51:*390–395.

———. (1984). *The transtheoretical approach: Crossing the traditional boundaries of therapy.* Homewood, IL: Dow Jones/Irwin.

———. (1985). Common processes of change for smoking, weight control, and psychological distress. In *Coping and substance abuse,* edited by S. Schiffman & T. Wills (pp. 345–346). New York: Academic Press.

———. (1992). Stages of change in the modification of problem behaviors. In *Advances in behavior modification,* edited by M. Herson, R. Eisler, & M. Miller (pp. 184–214). Sycamore, IL: Sycamore Press.

Prochaska, J., DiClemente, C., & Norcross, J. (1992). In search of how people change. *American Psychologist, 47:*1102–1114.

Prochaska, J., DiClemente, C., Velicer, W., Ginpil, S., & Norcross, J. (1985). Predicting change in smoking status for self-changers. *Addictive Behaviors, 10:*395–406.

Prochaska, J., DiClemente, C., Velicer, W., & Rossi, J. (1992). Criticisms and concerns of the transtheoretical model in light of recent research. *British Journal of Addiction, 87:*825–828.

Prochaska, J., Harlow, L., Redding, C., Rossi, J., & Velicer, W. (1990). *The stages of change model and HIV prevention.* Unpublished manuscript, University of Rhode Island.

Prochaska, J., & Norcross, J. (1983). Contemporary psychotherapists: A national survey of characteristics, theories, and practices. *Psychotherapy: Theory, Research and Practice, 20*:161–173.

Prochaska, J., Norcross, J., Fowler, J., Follick, M., & Abrams, D. (1992). Attendance and outcome in a work-site weight control program: Processes and stages of change as process and predictor variables. *Addictive Behaviors, 17*:35–45.

Prochaska, J., Velicer, W., DiClemente, C., & Fava, J. (1988). Measuring processes of change: Applications to the cessation of smoking. *Journal of Consulting and Clinical Psychology, 56*:520–528.

Prochaska, J., Velicer, W., Guadagnoli, E., Rossi, J., & DiClemente, C. (1991). Patterns of change: Dynamic topology applied to smoking cessation. *Multivariate Behavioral Research, 26*:83–107.

Prochaska, J., Velicer, W., Rossi, J., Goldstein, M., Marcus, B., Rakowski, W., Fiore, C., Harlow, L., Redding, C., Rosenbloom, D., & Rossi, S. (In press). *Health Psychology.*

Rakowski, W., Dube, C., Marcus, B., Prochaska, J., & Velicer, W. (1992). Assessing elements of women's decisions about mammography. *Health Psychology, 11*:111–118.

Redding, C., Rossi, J., Velicer, W., & Prochaska, J. (1989). *The pros and cons of safer sex: A measurement model.* Paper presented at the 97th annual meeting of the American Psychological Association, New Orleans, LA.

Rosenbloom, D. (1991). *A transtheoretical analysis of change among cocaine users.* Unpublished doctoral dissertation, University of Rhode Island.

Rossi, J. (1992). *Common processes of change across nine problem behaviors.* Paper presented at the 100th annual meeting of the American Psychological Association, Washington, DC.

Rossi, S., Rossi, J., & Prochaska, J. (1990, August). A stage model for reducing dietary fat. In J. O. Prochaska (Chair), *Stages of change: Extensions to new areas of behavior change.* Symposium presented at the 98th annual convention of the American Psychological Association, Boston, MA.

Schachter, S. (1982). Recidivism and self cure of smoking and obesity. *American Psychologist, 37*:436–444.

Snow, M. G. (1991). *A transtheoretical analysis of strategies used in the recovery process from alcohol problems.* Unpublished doctoral dissertation, University of Rhode Island.

Stern, R., Prochaska, J., Velicer, W., & Elder, J. (1987). Stages of adolescent cigarette smoking acquisition: Measurement and sample profiles. *Addictive Behaviors, 12:*319–329.

USDHHS. (1990). *The health benefits of smoking cessation.* U.S. Department of Health and Human Services. Office of Smoking and Health. DHHS Publication N. (CDC) 90-8416.

Velicer, W., DiClemente, C., Prochaska, J., & Brandenburg, N. (1985). A decisional balance measure for predicting smoking cessation. *Journal of Personality and Social Psychology, 48:*1279–1289.

Velicer, W., DiClemente, C., Rossi, J., & Prochaska, J. (1990). Relapse situations and self-efficacy: An integrative model. *Addictive Behaviors, 15:*271–283.

Velicer, W., Rossi, J., Prochaska, J., & DiClemente, C. (1992). *Criterion measurement model for addictive behaviors.* Manuscript under review.

Velicer, W., Prochaska, J., Rossi, J., & Snow, M. (1992). Assessing outcome in smoking cessation studies. *Psychological Bulletin, 111:*23–41.

Wilcox, N., Prochaska, J., Velicer, W., & DiClemente, C. (1985). Client characteristics as predictors of self-change in smoking cessation. *Addictive Behaviors, 10:*407–412.

CHAPTER 8

Pathways to Internalization: When Does Overt Behavior Change the Self-Concept?

Dianne M. Tice

The topic of self-concept change is of potentially great practical importance for understanding human development, adaptation, and growth, as well as for designing clinical techniques and other interventions to help people change. Although there may be powerful forces that resist self-concept change, it is apparent that sometimes such changes do occur. The challenge for researchers, therefore, is to identify the conditions under which self-concept change occurs and the processes that produce such change. This chapter presents a summary of the results of a research program designed to examine some conditions which effect and affect self-concept change.

This chapter will focus on one major process by which self-concept change occurs, namely, the internalization of behavior. It will formulate the questions about self-concept change in terms of the path from overt behavior to inner recognition and belief: How does the way one acts and behaves affect one's self-concept? Under what circumstances is a person's behavior likely to lead to a self-concept change? When a person acts in a certain way, what leads that person to think of himself or herself as being the type of person who characteristically behaves that way? If one desires to change one's self-concept, how can one use one's behavior to bring about such a change?

Examples of people who come to see themselves in a new light because of the way they behaved abound in literature and other media. One example can be found in Mario Puzo's novel *The Godfather*. The Godfather's son Michael (played by Al Pacino in the movie version) had high ideals and lived a clean, legitimate life in the beginning of the story. However, he got himself involved in family dealings once, and soon he came to accept himself as a vicious criminal. How could such a change in his self-concept occur? Part of it was undoubtedly the fact that he was involved in killing people and committing crimes, even if the initial impetus was high-minded family loyalty and self-defense and retaliation. Stories such as this suggest the lesson is that "you are what you do." Just as Michael Corleone's self-concept changed to fit his newly violent and illegal acts, so may other people's self-concepts shift to internalize the implications of their actions.

IMPETUS FOR CHANGE: SELF OR OTHER?

Do people have to be involved in attempts to change their own self-concepts, or can others induce a change without the individuals' consent or knowledge? It is quite apparent that some circumstances, such as therapy and brainwashing, are designed to promote personal change. And sometimes people clearly try to change each other. On the other hand, fears that people may be altered in significant ways without their consent or cooperation may be unfounded. At present, however, the best generalization seems to be that self-concepts are unlikely to change without the active cooperation of the people involved. If you want to change, others can help, but if you do not want to change, it will be difficult for others to induce such change.

One source of evidence for this conclusion comes from studies of brainwashing (Group for the Advancement of Psychiatry, 1957; see Baumeister, 1986, for review), which suggest that it is very difficult to change people against their will. Despite the sensational publicity and horror stories, few prisoners of war have genuinely converted to the cause of their enemies, even when determined efforts have been made to convert them. The Chinese attempts to indoctrinate American prisoners during the Korean War were largely ineffective at producing genuine change, although of course they could produce short-term compliance. In contrast, the Chinese reeducation efforts with their own citizens were much more effective, largely because those citizens were motivated to change.

Many understood that there was no going back and that their only chance for any semblance of normal life in the new Communist regime required them to become Communist believers, and they participated actively in the process of change.

A similar conclusion emerges from studies of conditioning processes. Dawson, Schell, Beers, and Kelly (1982) found that conditioning occurs only when people understand the critical relationship between the unconditioned and conditioned stimuli. Subjects in their experiment were told that they would hear some tones and receive some shocks, but were not told that they could predict the shocks based on the pattern of tones. Dawson et al. found that subjects who did not figure out the pattern showed no sign of arousal or anxiety (measured by psychophysiological recordings) in anticipation of the shock. When subjects were informed that the pattern of tones may predict the shock, most subjects figured out the pattern and showed signs of stress when they expected a shock. In short, subjects in this experiment became conditioned to respond aversively to the warning tone only after they understood the relationship between the shock and the tones. Dawson maintains that this research has implications for therapy; he advises therapists to actively engage their clients in the process of forming new associations that may be incompatible with previously held phobias.

Laboratory research provides additional confirmation for the assertion that it is difficult to effect a change in the self-concepts of people who do not want to change their self-concepts. There is now considerable evidence that people use a variety of strategies to maintain their self-concepts as they are, resisting change, especially change for the worse (Maracek & Mettee, 1972; Swann, 1983; Swann, 1987; Swann & Ely, 1984; Swann & Hill, 1982; Swann & Predmore, 1985; Swann & Read, 1981). For example, Swann and Hill (1982) found that people attempted to maintain their self-concepts even in the face of contradictory evidence. In a laboratory setting, they gave people personality feedback that was either discrepant from or consistent with their self-conceptions. They found that discrepant feedback produced self-concept changes only when the participants had no opportunity to reject or refute the feedback. If the participants had the opportunity to behave in a manner that discredited the feedback, they did so and subsequently displayed minimal self-concept change. In other words, given the opportunity, people monitor the feedback they receive and take active behavioral steps to undermine and refute feedback that threatens their existing self-conceptions. People resist information and influences that seek to change them.

Thus, for a demonstrated lasting effect to occur, people must normally be at least willing participants in self-concept change. They must want to be different, or at least they must willingly perform the behavior and must engage in the cognitive processing needed to interpret their own novel behavior as indicative of the kind of person they are.

Self-concept changes found in laboratory settings, however, often seem to occur without the individual's awareness, at least as long as people do not regard their own actions as lying outside the range of what they would normally consider acceptable. People often tend to resist influence if they see it coming (Swann & Hill, 1982), and so an attempt to change someone's self-concept is likely to succeed if he or she cooperates rather than resists. People who do not realize that they are being influenced to change their self-concepts may fail to resist simply because they see no need for resistance. Even so, self-concept change is not likely to succeed as a fully passive process. People must actively perform the behavior, process the information, and forge a new interpretation of themselves in order for self-concept change to succeed.

In this way, self-concept change is analogous to attitude change. Early studies of passive persuasion were set aside in the rush to study cognitive dissonance, which involved the person actively in changing his or her own attitudes. The essence of cognitive dissonance was that people would alter their attitudes to make them consistent with their own recent behavior—thus, attitude change under dissonance can be considered a form of internalization. (In fact, Aronson, 1969, noted that in much of the early dissonance literature, what was dissonant was not just any two cognitions, but cognitions about behavior and self-concept.) In most of the cognitive dissonance studies resulting in attitude change, people didn't realize they were being changed or were being influenced, and so they didn't resist—they changed. But dissonance required active participation. People had to feel that they actively chose to engage in the behavior, had to be led to interpret themselves as endorsing the new attitude, and so forth

(Davis & Jones, 1960; Linder, Cooper, & Jones, 1967; Kelley, 1967).

In sum, the impetus for change may come from outside the individual, but self-concept change seems to require active participation. It is extremely difficult to change someone's self-concept against his or her will, and some evidence suggests that people will generally tend to resist all efforts to change their self-concepts. Self-concept change is thus most likely to occur when the person does want to change and cooperates with the change process, or when the person fails to recognize that change may occur and hence unwittingly (but actively) participates in the process.

DEFINING INTERNALIZATION

The term *internalization* can be used to refer to self-concept changes that follow from overt behavior. In other words, internalization is a matter of bringing one's private concept of self into agreement with one's recent behavior (Festinger & Carlsmith, 1959). Internalization is thus a potentially important mechanism for self-concept change. Overt behavior becomes internalized, resulting in changes in the way the person sees himself or herself. These self-concept changes may potentially lead to changes in subsequent actions.

In purely conceptual terms, self-concept change can be understood as an alteration of the person's beliefs about the self. However, most psychologists would prefer to insist on a second criterion too, namely, behavioral change. The reason for this insistence is that what people say may be malleable and superficial, whereas change in behavior presumably reflects a more profound change of underlying structures. Thus researchers may be able to induce people to *say* they are different, but it is only when people *act* differently that researchers are confident that they mean it.

Hence it seems reasonable to accept both self-reported change in beliefs about the self and behavioral change as criteria for establishing that self-concept change has occurred. Clearly, these two criteria are not entirely unrelated, but they are not the same and in some cases may be quite independent. Thus, when people believe that change should occur and expect themselves to change, they may think that change has happened even if it hasn't. For example, Conway and Ross (1984) found that students who had enrolled in a study skills improvement course actually did not improve their study skills relative to a control group of students who were on the waiting list to get into the course. However, they believed that they had changed. They managed to maintain this conclusion by revising their impression of how poor their study skills had been before the program. That is, students who had completed the study skills course recalled their past performance as much worse than it actually had been, so that it appeared they had improved. The present could not be changed, but students' recall of their past supported their intuitive theory of improvement (change). An illusion of change was created to support their expectations.

Conversely, when people think they should remain the same and expect consistency, they may believe they are the same even if they have changed. For example, following attitude change, people incorrectly recall their past attitudes to have been the same as their present attitudes (Bem & McConnell, 1970; Goethals & Reckman, 1973; see also Ross & Conway, 1986).

In general, of course, people expect that they will remain the same, and consistency pressures form strong roadblocks to self-concept change. As noted above, Swann and Hill (1982) demonstrated that people tend to resist change and cling to existing self-conceptions. When people have firm, definite ideas about themselves, these will be especially difficult to alter and hence will resist change. But some ideas about the self are not yet firmly formed or may be in flux, and these unformed and changing self-views may be especially vulnerable to change.

SELF-PERCEPTION AND BIASED SCANNING

One way to alter people's self-views may be to first get them to behave in a different or unusual way. Assuming that people do observe their behavior and change their self-concepts to be in agreement with their behavior, then the crucial question becomes: How does this internalization occur? Self-perception theory (Bem, 1972) provides one important background for understanding self-concept change resulting from internalization of behavior. According to self-perception theory, people learn about themselves much the same way that they learn about others. People observe their own overt behavior and form generalizations or make inferences regarding that behavior in the same way they observe others' behaviors and draw inferences and generalizations about others. Of course, one has more opportunities to observe oneself than to observe others, so one has more information about oneself than one has about others.

It is quite clear that not all behaviors lead to revisions in the person's view of self (Swann & Hill, 1982; also Linder et al., 1967; Jones, Rhodewalt, Berglas, & Skelton, 1981). It is important, therefore, to identify the conditions under which internalization does occur. Self-perception theory offers some basis for predicting such conditions.

One crucial factor (suggested by self-perception theory) affecting shifts in the self-concept is the type of attribution the person makes for his or her behavior. An external or situational attribution is not likely to lead to self-concept change (see Kelley, 1967) or to subsequent behavior change. Only when people attribute their behavior to their own inner dispositions are they likely to use these actions as a basis for altering their views of themselves. For example, Grusec and her colleagues (Grusec, Kuczynski, Rushton, & Simutis, 1978; Grusec & Redler, 1980) have found that children who attributed their prosocial behavior to a trait were subsequently observed to engage in more prosocial behavior than children who attributed the same behavior to other, external factors.

The overjustification effect is another example of the importance of attributions in the self-perception process. The overjustification effect refers to the tendency for people to lose intrinsic interest in activities for which too much extrinsic reward is given. (The combination of intrinsic interest and extrinsic rewards is said to "overjustify" the activity.) Lepper, Greene, and Nisbett (1973) gave preschool children an opportunity to play with highly attractive new drawing equipment. One-third of the children were told that they were to play with the equipment in order to obtain a desirable prize. One-third of the children were not told anything about the prize while they played with the equipment, but were given the prize as a surprise at the end of the drawing session. In the last group of children, no prize was given or anticipated. Several days later, all three groups of children were allowed to use the drawing equipment if they wished, as one among several options. The researchers found that the group of children who had originally anticipated and received an external reward or prize for playing with the equipment played with it only about one half as much as children from the other two groups. Apparently, children who had anticipated the prize attributed their desire for playing with the equipment to the prize and not to the equipment itself. The internal versus external attribution was a crucial determinant of how they regarded themselves.

Similarly, in a study on consumer behavior, Dodson, Tybout, and Sternthal (1978) found that advertisements featuring extra come-ons or bonuses actually resulted in reduced loyalty to the brand after the special bonus offer was over. Apparently, consumers attributed their purchases to the extra bonus rather than to their preference for the product itself. Thus, attitude change occurs only when a person attributes his or her behavior to the self. When people behave in a manner that is discrepant from their self-concepts, self-concept change will only occur if they attribute their behavior to their own traits and not to some external, situational cause.

One particular elaboration of self-perception theory is biased scanning theory. People have large and complex self-concepts, and at any given time only one small part of it is present in awareness (Jones & Gerard, 1967). Situations, including laboratory manipulations, can bias the scanning of the self-concept, making some self-knowledge more salient than other self-knowledge. Such situations or events make you aware of yourself in a certain light; they bring out or emphasize things about you. Seeing yourself in this way stamps this vision of you into your memory. Biased scanning theory thus suggests one possible mechanism of internalization. Certain actions may make a certain view of the self—possibly a marginal or peripheral one—become salient, may cause it to be repeated in memory, until it evolves into a central aspect of the new view of self.

An important early study on self-perception and internalization was conducted by Fazio, Effrein, and Falender (1981). These researchers had subjects respond to questions that were loaded to pull for either introverted or extraverted behavior. A question like "What might you do to liven up a dull party?" would tend to cause people to remember their past extraverted actions and hence to think of themselves as an extravert, whereas a question like "What annoys you most about loud, crowded parties?" would probably cause people to think of themselves as an introvert. Fazio et al. (1981) found that responding to such questions affected their subjects' self-concepts. People who had been randomly assigned to answer the extravert questions later described themselves as extraverts, relative to the people who had been asked the introvert questions. When their subjects were subsequently given a chance to behave in a manner consistent with their self-concepts, subjects' actions conformed to these shifted self-conceptions.

These researchers explained their findings in terms of cognitive processes, specifically self-perception. They suggested that the loaded questions asked in the public interview made the subjects consider their own introverted or extraverted behavior in a biased manner. If the loaded questions pulled for extraverted responses, extraverted behavior was more salient to the subjects, whereas if the questions pulled for introverted responses, introverted behavior was more salient. As a result, subjects' self-conceptions shifted toward agreement with their behavior. In addition, the researchers secretly observed how their subjects responded to another person back in the waiting room, and they found that people behaved in ways consistent with the way they had recently been induced to view themselves: that is, people who had been asked the extravert questions were more likely to speak to others in the waiting room than were people who had been asked the introvert questions.

Subsequent work extended the findings of Fazio et al. (1981). Jones et al. (1981) and Rhodewalt and Agustdottir (1986) also found that induced behavior caused self-concepts to shift so as to reflect an internalization of the overt behavior, and they suggested two cognitive mechanisms for these self-concept shifts. First, cognitive dissonance (which arises from behaving in a manner inconsistent with one's beliefs about oneself) is reduced by changing the beliefs about the self. Second, in biased scanning, the induced behavior directs attention toward certain aspects of the self-concept, and so self-evaluations shift in the direction of the salient cognitions. In other words, to produce a large change in the self-concept, one could be induced to behave in a manner which is utterly inconsistent (or even the opposite of) the self-concept. For example, a person who believes that she is extremely outgoing may behave in a very shy manner in a given situation. Cognitive dissonance processes operate to reduce the large discrepancy between behavior and self-concept when the behavior is completely inconsistent with the self-concept; changes in the self-concept occur to reduce the dissonance produced by the discrepancy between behavior and the self-concept. Self-perception, on the other hand, operates when one's behavior is only mildly discrepant from the self-concept (in other words, the behavior is within one's latitude of acceptance). For example, a person who believes that she is moderately outgoing may behave in a highly outgoing manner. By the process of self-perception she may come to see herself as more outgoing than she originally did. (For a more complete explanation of the dissonance-produced versus self-perception-produced changes in the self-concept, see Rhodewalt, 1986.) Since people are likely to behave in a manner that is only mildly discrepant from their self-concepts rather than highly discrepant, most self-concept change is likely to be of this gradual, self-perception-induced biased scanning variety.

Thus the main model for how self-concepts change is based on biased scanning. The individual scans the accumulated information about himself or herself—but does so in a biased fashion that emphasizes certain traits and ignores evidence contradicting those traits. In this way, people can reach distorted conclusions about themselves which can gradually become entrenched, coloring subsequent self-perceptions and subsequent behavior. Situations that induce such biased scanning can thus help elicit self-concept change.

Although this model has emerged from laboratory research, it may explain some things that occur in therapy and other arenas of self-concept change. What some therapists do, perhaps, is to help clients to review what they have done, thought, and felt and to search for positive, constructive patterns. People may thus learn to see themselves in a new light as a result of the therapist's guidance, even though the therapist has not altered them but has merely called their attention to certain aspects of their own behavior.

In psychotherapy, of course, the therapist is instrumental in bringing about such change, for presumably the person comes to therapy because he or she is unable to accomplish the reconceptualization of self alone. Therapy thus relies heavily on the mediating role of someone other than the person who is changing. One might well ask whether this external mediation is unique to therapy; that is, is the involvement of other people helpful or even vital in self-concept change that occurs outside of therapy? The next section will examine the role of interpersonal circumstances in self-concept change.

PUBLIC CIRCUMSTANCES: SEEING ONESELF THROUGH ANOTHER'S EYES

The research reviewed in the previous section provided basic evidence for internalization; self-concept change was shown in both self-ratings and behavior. Biased scanning is a self-perception process in which behavior calls the individual's attention to certain aspects or potentialities of the self, which are then highly accessible and therefore exert a powerful influence on subsequent self-assessment. In principle, this pattern of self-perception occurs inside the individual and does not involve other people. In practice, however, the experiments designed to support the theory have invariably included the presence of other people to create public, interpersonal contexts. Thus there exists a discrepancy between the private, intrapsychic process in theory and the public, interpersonal setting in empirical practice. In other words, when I began reading the research literature on self-concept change, I noticed a serious gap between theory and data. Is internalization essentially something people do by themselves, or is it dependent on others' knowledge and presence?

It is plausible that the interpersonal aspect of the studies described above could strongly affect the internalization of behavior. Social interactions provide additional impact that may supplement the internalization produced by biased scanning. In keeping with a long tradition (Cooley, 1902; James, 1890; Mead, 1934), most researchers of the self acknowledge the importance of social interaction in constructing and modifying the self-concept (Baumeister, 1982, 1986; Gollwitzer, 1986; Rhodewalt, 1986; Schlenker, 1986; Wicklund & Gollwitzer, 1982). Because the self is publicly constructed and exists in relation to others, public events should have greater impact on the self-concept than private events. Public behavior implicates the self more than private behavior. Private behavior can be canceled, ignored, or forgotten, but public behavior cannot, because other people know about it. Public behavior may be more carefully monitored and processed than private behavior, resulting in greater internalization.

Public events have been shown to have more impact on self-evaluations than private events. For example, Baumeister and Jones (1978) found that public evaluations had greater impact on the self-concept (in the domain of the evaluation) than did private evaluations, and Greenberg and Pyszczynski (1985) found this was true even when the self-regard measures were considered to be private. Certainly in the attitude change literature, which to some extent serves as a model for self-concept change, the interpersonal context makes a difference. Baumeister and Tice (1984) found that subjects in a cognitive dissonance paradigm who had publicly performed the counterattitudinal behavior internalized the presented attitude to a greater degree than subjects whose presentations were private (see also Gaes, Kalle, & Tedeschi, 1978; Tedeschi, Schlenker, & Bonoma, 1971). If public behavior does have a greater impact on the self-concept than private behavior, then the internalization of a behavior may be more effective and powerful if the behavior is public than if it is private.

People do conform to the expectations of others. Research on the self-fulfilling prophecy demonstrates that people's behavior can be affected by another person's beliefs and expectations about them (Rosenthal & Jacobson, 1968; Snyder, Tanke, & Berscheid, 1977). Conforming to the expectations of others can lead to behavior change and hence to self-concept change (Darley & Fazio, 1980). You may begin to regard yourself differently as a result of how others regard you and treat you. Thus demonstrations of the impact of other people on the self-concept make it plausible that self-concept change is more than a simply private, intrapsychic process.

Even more fundamental, however, is that people are concerned with how others see them, and so the biased scanning process can receive a powerful boost from thinking that others are watching. That is, seeing yourself through other people's eyes can intensify the effect of certain behavior—can help stamp it into the self-concept. To do something out of character once, anonymously, invisibly, may have little or no lasting impact on how you regard yourself. But to do the same out-of-character action in front of hundreds of people may mark you for life.

Ultimately, the point is that people pay close attention to how they are perceived by others, because they care greatly and fundamentally about those perceptions. And so they seem to keep careful track of how their own behavior may come across to others. They may make errors, but they do monitor the process as best they can. Hence there may be a strong tendency for people to see their own behavior through the eyes of others who may be present, and this may intensify any biased scanning process.

Public behavior also *commits* the person in ways that private behavior does not, because other people know about the (public) behavior and can hold one responsible for it in the future. Public behavior cannot be canceled, ignored, or forgotten as readily as private behavior.

Thus there is plausible reason to think that early theories about self-concept change (in terms of self-perception and biased scanning) may only tell half the story. Researchers have generally explained evidence of internalization in terms of accessibility or salience of information to the self. Internalization was interpreted as occurring because subjects focused their attention on instances of their past behavior that supported their self-presentation. However, a full explanation may involve interpersonal factors and processes that go beyond these purely cognitive analyses. In theory, self-perception occurs within the individual and does not involve other people—but the experiments designed to test the theory invariably seem to have relied on the presence of other people to produce changes in self-concepts. This discrepancy between private, intrapsychic process in theory and public, interpersonal setting in empirical practice led to one of my own series of studies (Tice, in press).

The purpose of this set of studies was to examine whether performing an action *publicly* has any impact on the self-concept over and above the effects of performing the same behavior privately. I suggested that interpersonal factors provide the motivating force that makes self-concept change work, and salience and accessibility may be responsive to interpersonal cues.

The results of the first set of studies (Tice, in press) attest to the importance of public circumstances and interpersonal contexts for producing self-concept change. In two separate experiments, identical behaviors produced consistently stronger impact on the self-concept when they had been performed publicly than privately. Public circumstances were operationally defined as the potential presence and knowledge by someone else; that is, people answered the same loaded questions either anonymously (for a tape recording) or to a live other person. Public behaviors led to substantial shifts in self-descriptions and even to consistent behavioral change found on unobtrusive measures in subsequent situations. In contrast, the same behaviors had little or no apparent impact on the self-concept when they were performed in a private, anonymous context. Internalization of behavior in the public conditions was robust, unlike the effects in the private conditions.

In my first study, participants were induced to portray themselves in either an emotionally responsive or emotionally stable manner (or in an irrelevant manner in control conditions). The self-portrayals were either made in public, under highly identifiable conditions, or in private, under relatively anonymous conditions. Identical behaviors had greater impact on the self-concept when performed publicly rather than privately. That is, the first experiment indicated that the self-concept is more likely to change by internalizing public behavior than by internalizing behavior that is identical but lacks the interpersonal context. Using different self-portrayals, a second study replicated the findings of the first study and demonstrated that the self-concept change extends even to behavioral changes and even when participants are unaware of being observed (Tice, in press).

Schlenker, Dlugolecki, and Doherty (1992) likewise found that public, interpersonal behavior led to self-concept change and behavioral changes. They found that subjects who presented themselves as sociable to an interviewer demonstrated self-concept changes reflecting increased ratings in sociability and behavioral changes and resulting in an increase in sociable behavior (such as speaking sooner, more frequently, and longer than subjects who had not presented themselves as sociable). Schlenker et al. (1992) also found that public commitment to the identity portrayed in the self-presentation was the crucial antecedent of changes in the self-concept; biased self-perceptions were not sufficient to produce the changes. Directing subjects' thoughts toward congruent or incongruent prior experiences (thereby affecting the biased scanning of relevant information) had no impact on self-concept changes. Changes in self-concept were produced only when subjects had a public commitment to the behavior.

Thus, public, interpersonal behavior or public commitment to the new, desired identity appears to be very influential in affecting self-concept change. If one can change the public image of self first, the private self will follow along (as will behavior).

SOCIAL COMPARISON: SEEING ONESELF NEXT TO OTHERS

Thus far I have stressed the impact of interpersonal circumstances on self-concept change by showing that others' awareness intensifies the biased scanning process. There is another way in which other people can affect the internalization process. Self-perception often involves comparing oneself with others. When people do something that might lead them to question themselves, they often look to the behavior of others to learn the dimensions of what they did. Comparing one's actions with those of others in similar situations may be a powerful determinant of whether one's actions lead to lasting revisions of one's self-concept. After all, if everyone else would act the same way in the same situation, then there is no need to see your actions as reflecting anything special about you, and hence there is no need to revise your self-concept to accommodate your actions. By comparing one's behavior with that of others, one can begin to infer whether one's behavior was unique (thus suggesting something about oneself) or consensually typical (thus reflecting the situational forces).

I conducted a study to examine the effects of how knowledge about how other people had behaved in the same situation affected the internalization of behavior (Tice, 1987). In this study, all subjects were led to label a recent behavior as introverted and were then exposed to evidence about how similar others (people of the same gender and age with very similar personalities) and dissimilar others had behaved in the same situation. The behavior of dissimilar others had a greater impact on subjects' self-concepts than the behavior of similar others. Self-concept change was greatest when dissimilar others had behaved differently from the subject, which led subjects to see their own (introverted) behavior as reflecting dispositions. In contrast, when dissimilar others had behaved exactly the same as the subject, subjects attributed their behavior to the situation and did not internalize it. Variations in the behavior of similar others did not affect subsequent self-concept ratings or behavior. Dissimilar others seem to provide less ambiguous information than similar others about the dispositional attributions one can make about one's behavior, thus potentially facilitating self-concept change.

Similar others, on the other hand, may help one to maintain a stable self-concept (Caspi & Herbener, 1990; see also Buss, 1984; Newcomb, Koenig, Flacks, & Warwick, 1967). The behavior of similar others does not cause us to attribute our unique behavior to our personalities, and thus does not produce a large self-image shift. People choose to spend much of their time with similar others (Caspi & Herbener, 1990; Kandel, 1978; Newcomb, 1961), and this is likely to produce self-concept stability—not just because of normative pressure to conform, but simply for informational reasons.

Just as surrounding ourselves with similar others can result in less flexible self-concepts, so other environments may foster self-concept change. For example, the circumstances under which brainwashing is likely to occur (especially the "reeducation" camps that spring up following a military coup) may create conditions most suitable for inducing self-concept change. Taking citizens out of their normal environments and away from their family and friends, inducing them to repeatedly behave in a manner consistent with the new regime (such as writing denouncements of their past behavior, forbidding privacy, and controlling all information) may all increase the speed with which the self-concept change is likely to occur (Baumeister, 1986).

Major transition points in life have also been identified as being times when the individual is especially vulnerable to changes in the self-concept. For example, Harter (in press) reports that self-esteem is most likely to change at boundary points in life, like graduating from school or moving to a new place. Individuals are most likely to undergo an identity crisis (during which times major shifts in many aspects of the self-concept occur) during the college years, when individuals are in transition from an dependent status to a full adult status (Erikson, 1968; Marcia, 1966; Morash, 1980; Baumeister, Shapiro, & Tice, 1985).

OTHER VARIABLES AFFECTING SELF-CONCEPT CHANGE

Other aspects of the situation may also affect whether one's behavior is internalized and thus whether one's self-concept is affected. One of the studies I conducted (Tice, in press, study 3) suggested that several components of the situation affect the internalization of behavior and subsequent self-concept change. Having a choice about making the self-portrayal (that is, having the opportunity to refuse to behave in the requested manner, even though one does not choose to refuse), drawing on episodes from one's own past rather than relying on a script when behaving in the requested manner, and expecting future interaction with the audience (others who observed one behaving in the requested manner) all increased the internalization of a public behavior.

In a similar vein, individual differences may affect internalization of behavior. Some people may be more likely than others to change their self-concepts. Specifically, are people with one kind of personality more likely than others to internalize their behavior? One of the studies described above (Tice, in press, study 2) also assessed people on the trait of self-monitoring (Snyder, 1974). The construct of self-monitoring assesses the extent to which people monitor or regulate their behavior according to situational cues. High self-monitors are individuals who are sensitive to cues of situational appropriateness and regulate their behavior accordingly. Low self-monitors are individuals who behave more in accord with internal feelings and attitudes and are less influenced by the environment. When high and low self-monitors were induced to behave in either an introverted or an extraverted manner, high self-monitors were more likely to internalize their behavior and rate their self-concepts as being consistent with their prior behavior than were low self-monitors. Thus it may be easier to elicit a self-concept change in high self-monitors than in low self-monitors.

It is somewhat ironic that high self-monitors internalized their behavior more than low self-monitors in this study. High self-monitors are thought to regulate their expressive behavior in order to produce desired public appearances, but the high self-monitors themselves seem to come to believe some of their own presentations. High self-monitors are the behavioral chameleons, but perhaps their strategic public self-presentations are not just hypocritical staged acts. High self-monitors seem as influenced by their own behaviors as they want their audience to be.

SUMMARY

Self-concept change is not easy or common. Several forces exist to resist it. Change is the exception, not the norm. It is not surprising that therapists and others find it an uphill struggle when trying to alter how people view themselves!

Internalization provides one mechanism that does lead to self-concept change. People alter their self-conceptions to accommodate their recent actions. How internalization operates is an important question that research is beginning to answer. Both cognitive and interpersonal factors seem involved.

The cognitive aspect of the process seems to involve the way events make the person see himself or herself. Circumstances can cause people to act in unusual ways, and sometimes these circumstances can make these altered views of self become stable, central aspects of how people regard themselves.

Interpersonal factors seem to be decisive in determining whether these altered views of self have a lasting influence. People are very sensitive to the presence and attention of others, and so in public circumstances they seem to see themselves through the eyes of others—which raises the importance, salience, and commitment of the behavior. Self-concepts are thus likely to change to accommodate such public actions. In contrast, private and anonymous actions are relatively trivial and forgettable, because there is no interpersonal context, and such actions are much less likely to be internalized.

Another role of the interpersonal context involves social comparison. People evaluate their actions by comparing them with what others have done in similar circumstances. Perhaps ironically, comparisons with dissimilar others offer a more potent basis for changing one's self-concept than comparisons with similar others. People appear to be very sophisticated in their capacity to use information about others' behavior and their personal similarity in order to draw inferences about themselves from their own actions.

REFERENCES

Aronson, E. (1969). The theory of cognitive dissonance: A current perspective. In *Advances in experimental social psychology*, edited by L. Berkowitz (vol. 4). New York: Academic Press.

Baumeister, R. F. (1982). A self-presentational view of social phenomena. *Psychological Bulletin*, 91:3–26.

_____. (1986). *Identity: Cultural change and the struggle for self*. New York: Oxford University Press.

Baumeister, R. F., & Jones, E. E. (1978). When self-presentation is constrained by the target's knowledge: Consistency and compensation. *Journal of Personality and Social Psychology, 36:*608–618.

Baumeister, R. F., Shapiro, J. J., & Tice, D. M. (1985). Two kinds of identity crisis. *Journal of Personality, 53:*407–424.

Baumeister, R. F., & Tice, D. M. (1984). Role of self-presentation and choice in cognitive dissonance under forced compliance: Necessary or sufficient causes? *Journal of Personality and Social Psychology, 46:*5–13.

Bem, D. J. (1972). Self-perception theory. In *Advances in experimental social psychology,* edited by L. Berkowitz (vol. 6, pp. 1–62). New York: Academic Press.

Bem, D. J., & McConnell, H. K. (1970). Testing the self-perception explanation of dissonance phenomena: On the salience of premanipulation attitudes. *Journal of Personality and Social Psychology, 14:*23–31.

Buss, D. M. (1984). Toward a psychology of person-environment correspondence: The role of spouse selection. *Journal of Personality and Social Psychology, 47:*361–377.

Caspi, A., & Herbener, E. S. (1990). Continuity and change: Assortative marriage and the consistency of personality in adulthood. *Journal of Personality and Social Psychology, 58:*250–258.

Conway, M., & Ross, M. (1984). Getting what you want by revising what you had. *Journal of Personality and Social Psychology, 47:*738–748.

Cooley, C. H. (1902). *Human nature and the social order.* New York: Scribner's.

Darley, J. M., & Fazio, R. H. (1980). Expectancy confirmation processes arising in the social interaction sequence. *American Psychologist, 35:*867–881.

Davis, K. E., & Jones, E. E. (1960). Changes in interpersonal perception as a means of reducing cognitive dissonance. *Journal of Abnormal and Social Psychology, 61:*402–410.

Dawson, M. E., Schell, A. M., Beers, J. R., & Kelly, A. (1982). Allocation of cognitive processing capacity during human autonomic classical conditioning. *Journal Experimental Psychology: General, 111:*273–295.

Dodson, J. A., Tybout, A. M., & Sternthal, B. (1978). Impact of deals and deal retraction on brand switching. *Journal of Marketing Research, 15:*72–81.

Erikson, E. H. (1968). *Identity: Youth and crisis.* New York: Norton.

Fazio, R. H., Effrein, E. A., & Falender, V. J. (1981). Self-perceptions following social interactions. *Journal of Personality and Social Psychology, 41:*232–242.

Festinger, L., & Carlsmith, J. M. (1959). Cognitive consequences of forced compliance. *Journal of Abnormal and Social Psychology,* 58:203–210.

Gaes, G. G., Kalle, R. J., & Tedeschi, J. T. (1978). Impression management in the forced compliance situation: Two studies using the bogus pipeline. *Journal of Experimental Social Psychology,* 14:493–510.

Goethals, G. R., & Reckman, R. F. (1973). The perception of consistency in attitudes. *Journal of Experimental Social Psychology,* 9:491–501.

Gollwitzer, P. M. (1986). Striving for specific identities: The social reality of self-symbolizing. In *Public self and private self,* edited by R. F. Baumeister (pp. 143–159). New York: Springer-Verlag.

Greenberg, J., & Pyszczynski, T. (1985). Compensatory self-inflation: A response to the threat to self-regard of public failure. *Journal of Personality and Social Psychology,* 49:273–280.

Group for the Advancement of Psychiatry (1957). *Methods of forceful indoctrination: Observations and interviews.* New York: Author.

Grusec, J. E., Kuczynski, L., Rushton, J. P., & Simutis, Z. M. (1978). Modeling, direct instruction, and attributions: Effects on altruism. *Developmental Psychology,* 14:51–57.

Grusec, J. E., & Redler, E. (1980). Attribution, reinforcement, and altruism: A developmental analysis. *Developmental Psychology,* 16:525–534.

Harter, S. (In press). Causes and consequences of low self-esteem in children and adolescents. To appear in *Self-esteem: The puzzle of low self-regard,* edited by R. F. Baumeister. New York: Plenum.

James, W. (1890). *The principles of psychology.* New York: Holt.

Jones, E. E., & Gerard, H. B. (1967). *Foundations of social psychology.* New York: John Wiley.

Jones, E. E., Rhodewalt, F., Berglas, S., & Skelton, J. A. (1981). Effects of strategic self-presentation on subsequent self-esteem. *Journal of Personality and Social Psychology,* 41:407–421.

Kandel, D. B. (1978). Similarity in real-life adolescent friendship pairs. *Journal of Personality and Social Psychology,* 36:306–312.

Kelley, H. H. (1967). Attribution theory in social psychology. In *Strategic interaction and conflict,* edited by K. Archibald. Berkeley, CA: University of California, Institute of International Studies.

Lepper, M. R., Greene, D., & Nisbett, R. E. (1973). Undermining children's intrinsic interest with extrinsic reward: A test of the overjustification hypothesis. *Journal of Personality and Social Psychology,* 28:129–137.

Linder, D. E., Cooper, J., & Jones, E. E. (1967). Decision freedom as a determinant of the role of incentive magnitude in attitude change. *Journal of Personality and Social Psychology,* 6:245–254.

Maracek, J., & Mettee, D. R. (1972). Avoidance of continued success as a function of self-esteem, level of esteem certainty, and responsibility for success. *Journal of Personality and Social Psychology, 22:*90–107.

Marcia, J. E. (1966). Development and validation of ego-identity status. *Journal of Personality and Social Psychology, 3:*551–558.

Mead, G. H. (1934). *Mind, self, and society.* Chicago, IL: University of Chicago Press.

Morash, M. A. (1980). Working class membership and the adolescent identity crisis. *Adolescence, 15:*313–320.

Newcomb, T. M. (1961). *The acquaintance process.* New York: Holt, Rinehart, & Winston.

Newcomb, T. M. Koenig, K. E., Flacks, R., & Warwick, D. P. (1967). *Persistence and change: Bennington College and its students after twenty-five years.* New York: John Wiley.

Rhodewalt, F. (1986). Self-presentation and the phenomenal self: On the stability and malleability of the self-concept. In *Public self and private self,* edited by R. F. Baumeister (pp. 117–142). New York: Springer-Verlag.

Rhodewalt, F., & Agustdottir, S. (1986). Effects on self-presentation on the phenomenal self. *Journal of Personality and Social Psychology, 50:*47–55.

Rosenthal, R., & Jacobson, L. (1968). *Pygmalion in the classroom.* New York: Holt, Rinehart, & Winston.

Ross, M., & Conway, M. (1986). Remembering one's own past: The construction of personal histories. In *Handbook of motivation and cognition,* edited by R. M. Sorrentino & E. T. Higgins (pp. 122–144). New York: Guilford Press.

Schlenker, B. R. (1986). Self-identification: Toward an integration of the public and private self. In *Public self and private self,* edited by R. F. Baumeister (pp. 21–62). New York: Springer-Verlag.

Schlenker, B. R., Dlugolecki, D. W., & Doherty, K. (1992). *The impact of self-presentations on self-appraisals and behavior: The roles of commitment and biased scanning.* Unpublished manuscript, University of Florida.

Snyder, M. (1974). Self-monitoring of expressive behavior. *Journal of Personality and Social Psychology, 30:*526–537.

Snyder, M., Tanke, E., & Berscheid, E. (1977). Social perception and interpersonal behavior: On the self-fulfilling nature of social stereotypes. *Journal of Personality and Social Psychology, 35:*656–666.

Swann, W. B., Jr. (1983). Self-verification: Bringing social reality into harmony with the self. In *Social psychological perspectives on the self,* edited by J. Suls & A. G. Greenwald (vol. 2, pp. 33–66). Hillsdale, NJ: Erlbaum.

_____. (1987). Identity negotiation: Where two roads meet. *Journal of Personality and Social Psychology, 53:*1038–1051.

Swann, W. B., Jr., & Ely, R. J. (1981). A battle of wills: Self-verification versus behavioral confirmation. *Journal of Personality and Social Psychology, 46:*1287–1302.

Swann, W. B., Jr., & Hill, C. A. (1982). When our identities are mistaken: Reaffirming self-conceptions through social interaction. *Journal of Personality and Social Psychology, 43:*59–66.

Swann, W. B., Jr., & Predmore, S. C. (1985). Intimates as agents of social support: Sources of consolation or despair? *Journal of Personality and Social Psychology, 49:*1609–1617.

Swann, W. B., Jr., & Read, S. J. (1981). Self-verification processes: How we sustain our self-conceptions. *Journal of Experimental Social Psychology, 17:*351–372.

Tedeschi, J. T., Schlenker, B. R., & Bonoma, T. V. (1971). Cognitive dissonance: Private ratiocination or public spectacle? *American Psychologist, 26:*685–695.

Tice, D. M. (1987). *Similarity of others and dispositional versus situational attributions.* Unpublished dissertation, Princeton University.

_____. (In press). Self-presentation and self-concept change. *Journal of Personality and Social Psychology.*

Wicklund, R. A., & Gollwitzer, P. M. (1982). *Symbolic self-completion.* Hillsdale, NJ: Erlbaum.

PART 3

Experiences of Changing the Self

CHAPTER 9

Self-Change Experiences of Psychotherapists

John C. Norcross
Darren C. Aboyoun

Psychotherapists, by definition, study and modify human behavior; that is, they study *other* humans. The methods and principles of behavior change are rarely brought to bear on psychotherapists themselves (Norcross & Guy, 1989). And yet the personal qualities and interpersonal skills of the clinician account for at least as much treatment outcome as the specific techniques and theories employed (see Lambert, 1992).

The reasons for this external focus are multiple and explicable. It is certainly less threatening, individually and collectively, to look outward rather than inward. Anna Freud once made the telling observation that becoming a psychotherapist was one of our most sophisticated defense mechanisms: granting an aura of control and superiority as well as avoiding personal evaluation.

Until quite recently, practically no research was conducted on whether psychotherapists are successful practitioners of their own art. We simply did not know whether psychotherapists wisely utilize their professional knowledge in their own lives, whether they live, cope, and struggle like an average person despite their professional training and experience, or whether they use their professional stance to avoid exposing their vulnerabilities. If they are successful practitioners of their own art in self-change endeavors, then they would be rare among professionals: physicians are not necessarily healthier than the population at large, attorneys are not extraordinarily judicious in their private lives, and so forth (Gold-berg, 1992).

Whatever the reasons that therapists intensely scrutinize other humans rather than themselves, we believe this state of affairs requires correction. Consider that doctoral-level psychotherapists are among the most highly trained and experienced change agents. Yet we know so little, at least publicly, about how they change themselves or cope with their own distress. The tendency to view clinicians as not having lives outside the consulting room afflicts clients as well as psychotherapists. As Balint (1948) observed many years ago, a veil of secrecy and privacy is maintained over the psychotherapist's own life struggles and self-change; inquiry by independent third parties is strongly discouraged.

In this chapter we draw together and summarize the studies conducted from the transtheoretical perspective[1] related to the self-change experiences of psychotherapists. Building upon the Transtheoretical Model and measures presented in Chapter 7 by Grimley and colleagues, and elsewhere (e.g., Prochaska & DiClemente, 1992; Prochaska, DiClemente, & Norcross, 1992), we venture into the sensitive domain of clinicians' own life difficulties. From there we consider the efficacy of psychotherapists' self-change—their global outcomes, effective processes, and selected covariates. We then review four investigations that explored how psychotherapists attempt to change *clients* and how they attempt to change *themselves* with the identical problem. Next we examine how the self-change of behavior change "experts" differs from laypersons' self-change. Briefly we consider why some psychotherapists rely entirely on self-change whereas others pursue professional treatment and how therapists cope with stressful clients (as opposed to their own life difficulties). Finally, we integrate interrelated studies on the lasting lessons psychotherapists acquire from their personal psychotherapy regarding the behavior change enterprise.[2]

DEVALUATION OF SELF-CHANGE

Psychotherapists, like the majority of laypersons, devalue self-change. Although clinicians—like laypersons—routinely rely on their own change efforts without professional assistance from a peer, they persist in the unfortunate proclivity to focus on formal psychosocial intervention at the expense of natural self-initiated change. In addressing himself to this ironic imbalance in the profession, Watzlawick (1986, p. 93) offered the following observation:

> If that little green man from Mars arrived and asked us to explain our techniques for affecting human change, and if we then told him, would he not scratch his head (or its equivalent) in disbelief and ask us why we have arrived at such complicated, abstruse and farfetched theories, rather than first of all investigating how human change comes about naturally, spontaneously, and on an everyday basis?

Successful self-change is probably far more common and effective than heretofore anticipated by psychotherapists. First, as Schacter (1982) observes, people who do change themselves do not generally seek professional treatment. Professionals' views of the intractability of certain behavioral problems have been molded largely by the self-selected, hard-core group of people who, unable or unwilling to help themselves, go to psychotherapists for help, thereby becoming the available subjects for investigations. Second, inferences drawn from studies of therapeutic efficacy are invariably based on single attempts to change. Success rates with multiple change efforts are undoubtedly greater than with single attempts, with or without professional treatment. Third, the self-esteem, legal mandate, and economic survival of some psychotherapists are contingent on their unique ability to help people change; evidence for the efficacy of self-change is threatening and frequently dismissed.

Relatedly, many contemporary mental health approaches tend to "gloss . . . over the patient's attempts to define his problem in his own terms and the efficacy of using his own rationality to solve his problems" (Beck, 1976, p. 6). Beck speaks of a "subtle indoctrination" at the hands of the therapist derived from the widespread debasing of common sense. The self-changer's "confidence in the 'obvious' techniques he has customarily used in solving his own problems is eroded because he accepts the view that emotional disturbances arise from forces beyond his grasp. He can't hope to understand himself through his own efforts because his own notions are dismissed as shallow and unsubstantial."

PSYCHOTHERAPISTS' PROBLEMS

Several of our studies have found that a high percentage of psychotherapists have experienced psychological distress within the past
three years. Between 79 and 82 percent of the responding psychotherapists and 89 to 91 percent of the laypersons met the criteria
for high distress (Prochaska & Norcross, 1983b; Norcross & Prochaska, 1986a). Psychological distress or, more specifically, the
Nonspecific Psychological Distress Syndrome, is associated with
affective discomfort but is not indigenous to any particular mental
disorder (Mellinger et al., 1978, 1983). It has been called the
"fever of mental disorder" in that it indicates the presence of behavioral problems but does not localize or diagnose the disorder
(Dohrenwend, Shrout, Egri, & Mendelsohn, 1980; Vernon &
Roberts, 1981).

Psychotherapists' presenting complaints for therapy—what
troubles the troubleshooters—generally parallel those of the population at large. The three most frequent problems were marital
conflict (20 percent of the sample), depression (13 percent), and
anxiety (12 percent). These modal complaints—accounting for 45
percent of the sample—are consistent with the research indicating
that clinical practice exacts a negative toll on the practitioner, particularly in the forms of problematic anxiety, moderate depression,
and emotional underinvolvement with family members (Bermak,
1977; Cray & Cray, 1977; Daniels, 1974; Deutsch, 1985; Farber,
1983; Looney, Harding, Blottcky, & Barnhart, 1980; Norcross &
Prochaska, 1986a). Anxiety, depression, and marital conflict, then,
are psychotherapists' modal presenting problems for personal
treatment, as they are for their self-change efforts (Deutsch, 1985;
Norcross & Prochaska, 1986b).

In order to provide an anchor date and to determine provoking
agents, we asked for a particular event surrounding the distress
episode. The most frequent precipitants are shown in Table 9.1 for
both psychotherapists and laypersons.

Roughly 90 percent of the psychotherapists, doctoral-level psychologists and master-level counselors in this case, identified a
precipitating event for their psychological distress. The modal precipitant in each sample was an interpersonal problem, such as
dysfunctional marriages, disrupted relationships, and the like. Occupational problems represented the second most frequent precipi-

TABLE 9.1
Precipitating Event of Distress Episode

Precipitant	Psychotherapists (n = 171)	Laypersons (n = 82)
Relationship problems	28%	40%
Occupational difficulties	16	15
Family death	13	6
Family illness	10	9
Personal illness	5	6
Birth of child	8	1
Financial problems	2	2

tant; family deaths and illness were also prominent. Of course, this event need not represent a causal link, but nonetheless may be a perceived association. As Brown and Harris (1978) attest, these precipitants involve a wide variety of incidents. Some were unexpected but others had been eagerly sought, such as birth of a child; some were major catastrophes but others involved little more than a change in routine. These findings reinforce the fact that there is no single definition of a precipitant, but it is the *appraisal* of a situation that leads to distress (see Lazarus, 1966).

Reading through the descriptions of life events leaves no doubt that loss is the central feature of most events surrounding distress. Included in this group are death, marital separation, serious illnesses, relationship marital loss, and enforced changes of residence. All involve loss with life-threatening implications. Freud (1917/1957) made the point in "Mourning and Melancholia" that the object need not necessarily have died but simply have been lost as an object of love.

Psychotherapists are full of problems we do not expect to find in them. Their problems in living run the entire gamut of human concerns—abortions, affairs, divorce, alcoholism, murder of an old friend, a child's suicide, drug use, a sibling on trial for murder—to name just a few described by these psychotherapists. But perhaps we should not see such malaise among therapists as anything unusual. Burton (1972, p. x) adds reassuringly: "But the point is that to meliorate the distinctive problems of living, one has also to be human, and that means to have problems like everyone else."

Despite the enormous responsibilities of the profession, only *one* psychotherapist identified the precipitating event as a client problem, in this case, a suicide attempt. The remaining 170 therapists listed a nonpatient factor as the precipitant. Instead, the occupational hazards were related to supervisors, policies, promotions, salaries, and similar organizational plights. In the context of a psychotherapist's total life, patient conflicts emerge as a small source of distress; it was much more likely to result from extratherapy life problems.

This finding may not startle many experienced clinicians. However, in contrast to the prodigious research on in-therapy stress, it is perhaps a bit puzzling and ironic. Few studies have systematically studied the person of the psychotherapist *qua* person outside his or her professional world, thus underestimating real-life problems. Even the effects of therapists' personal characteristics are evaluated for their influence on clinical practice, rather than for their impact on the total person.

SELF-CHANGE EFFICACY: OUTCOMES AND STRATEGIES

We know relatively little of the nature and substance of psychotherapists' change experiences and even less of the comparative effectiveness of different ways of coping (Pearlin & Schooler, 1978). Historically, the paucity of comprehensive models and methodologies for self-change and the concomitant concentration on professional intervention have impeded their mutual facilitation. In the past decade, however, the Transtheoretical Model has made possible multidimensional comparisons of naturally initiated change attempts of clinically relevant disorders among psychotherapists and laypersons alike.

Global Outcomes

We first consider the self-reported coping outcomes of psychotherapists, restricted to those who attempted to change entirely on their own. In an extensive study (Norcross & Prochaska, 1986a, 1986b) involving nearly 200 psychotherapists, three items assessed the participants' perception of their self-change success during a singled distress episode: a confidence rating regarding use of the same self-change strategy during the next period of distress; a general success rating; and a symptom improvement rating. These items were based on Menaghan's (1982, 1983) analysis of the three most common indicators of coping effectiveness. In general, psychotherapists judged themselves to be moderately successful in their self-change. The group means for each outcome measure were greater than the scale midpoint, and on each measure 85 to 90 percent of the psychotherapists judged themselves to be successful.

One of the most impressive qualities of human beings is their ability to withstand personal loss and tragedy successfully. Despite serious setbacks such as death of a family member or a tragic personal illness, the vast majority of psychotherapists achieved a quality of life equivalent to or even exceeding their prior level. If self-reports are to be trusted, psychotherapists' self-change outcomes are impressive even by professional standards (Gurin, Veroff, & Feld, 1960). Not everyone readjusts, of course, but most do, and substantially on their own (Taylor, 1983).

Nonetheless, on two of the three outcome items the laypersons reported being significantly less successful than the psychotherapists. That is, the layperson outcome scores were significantly lower than the psychotherapists' scores, indicating that the laypersons generally rated their coping less efficacious.

Why might psychotherapists be more successful than laypersons? Several possibilities suggest themselves. The psychotherapists had an advantage in education, clinical experience, and socioeconomic status over laypersons. Psychotherapists may also possess a larger coping repertoire and be more selective and knowledgeable in their self-change strategies. Also, as discussed later in this chapter, the psychotherapists emphasized the change processes of using helping relationships more and self-blame and wishful thinking less than the laypersons. This pattern of self-change was predictive of positive outcome.

Effective Change Processes

A core question of our investigations has been "Are some change processes more adaptive and successful than others?"[3] As with psychotherapy research, conclusions about the effectiveness of self-change depend on the outcome criteria and time frame. And as emphasized in Chapter 7 of this volume, effective mechanisms of change are dependent on the stage of change. The following section pertains to efficacious change processes during the action stage; to our knowledge, effective self-change among psychotherapists in the precontemplation and contemplation stages has not been systematically evaluated.

Generalizing across studies, frequent use of wishful thinking, self-blame, and catharsis were negatively correlated with outcome. Conversely, stimulus control, helping relationships, self-liberation, contingency control, and counterconditioning processes were positively correlated with self-reported success. These results present an important, sensible, and face-valid pattern for efficacious coping.

Is it possible, then, to identify change processes that are particularly effective for the self-change of psychological distress? The answer is a qualified yes. It is apparent that the kinds of coping processes people bring to bear on their distress do make a difference. It is also equally apparent that there is no single self-change strategy so outstandingly effective that its possession alone would ensure an ability to fend off distress. There are appreciable outcome differences between self-change strategies, but at the same time, the effect of any single change process is rather modest. The findings suggest to us, as they have to others (Lazarus, 1980; Pearlin & Schooler, 1978), that possessing a particular weapon in one's arsenal is less important than having a variety of weapons. Effective self-change involves a wide repertoire and selective employment of coping process.

Successful change was characterized by increased utilization of several processes and decreased utilization of several others. "More" is not necessarily better; positive outcome seems to depend on selective or differential use of numerous change processes. The recommendations for self-changers during the action stage would thus be to maximize helping relationships, to restructure environments with stimulus control, to employ action processes such as counterconditioning and contingency control, to increase willpower and self-liberation, and to avoid excessive wishful thinking and self-blame. Considerable use of catharsis during the action stage, as opposed to the contemplation stage, is also to be avoided.

The positive impact of helping relationships and negative impact of excessive wishful thinking and self-blame have been demonstrated in earlier work. The availability of conducive interpersonal relationships diminishes the effect of personal disruptions on individual well-being and may act as a buffer between life events and distress (Mueller, 1980; Turner, 1981). By focusing on their not being able to change the way they feel and by ruminating about their problems, psychotherapists may accentuate the negative features of their situation. Such negative preoccupation and emotional release may reduce the decisiveness and effectiveness with which they cope with their distress (Coyne, Aldwin, & Lazarus, 1981). Intense self-blame may similarly distress the person further and paralyze adaptive resources.

Several correlates of successful self-change were unique to the psychologist sample. Medication use, for instance, was inversely associated with successful outcome. Psychologists may experience medication as a personal weakness, a retreat into biomedical solutions, or loss of self-control, at least for themselves if not for their patients. Reevaluating and reorganizing one's personal relations were also found to be beneficial for psychologists, as reflected in the positive correlations with the environmental reevaluation process. Why this is the case is not clear; however, psychologists apparently find interpersonal solutions effective for distress.

Selected Covariates

An effort was made to identify various correlates of successful self-change beyond the change processes. Accordingly, outcome measures in several studies have been correlated with germane distress and history variables. The severity and chronicity of the problem were consistently and negatively correlated with improvement. Specifically, problem severity accounts for 9 to 12 percent of the outcome. A similar state of affairs exists in research on psychotherapy-facilitated change. Severe distress can paralyze people by reducing their psychological resources, adaptive capacities, and social support systems. "The outstanding patient quality that foretells greater benefits from psychotherapy is psychological health, the opposite is what is termed psychiatric severity" (Luborsky, 1984, p. 54). In an extensive review of psychotherapy research, 68 studies were located in which severity-health was tried as an outcome predictor. Of these, 48 showed significant levels of prediction (Luborsky et al., 1971, 1980). In both therapy change and self-change, the less severe the distress, the more promising the prognosis.

THERAPISTS' CLIENT CHANGE VERSUS SELF-CHANGE

We became interested in the change processes that psychotherapists use in helping their *patients* overcome a behavioral disorder in relation to the change processes that psychotherapists use in helping *themselves* overcome the same disorder. For this purpose, we developed two forms of the Processes of Change Scale. The first form, *therapist-treat-client,* consisted of items with the prefix "I encourage my clients to," "I tell my clients that," or some similar therapy intervention. The second form, *therapist-treat-self,* contained items identical in context, numerical order, and use of first person singular but with a modified prefix of "I engage," "I use," or a similar self-intervention. Three studies employing this methodology have been published (Norcross & Prochaska, 1986b; Norcross, Prochaska, & Hambrecht, 1991; Prochaska & Norcross, 1983b).

An immediate question arose about the influence of clinicians' theoretical orientation, one of the most extensively researched variables in the psychotherapy outcome literature (Beutler, Crago, & Arizmendi, 1986). The results indicated that psychotherapists' clinical efforts with patients varied reliably as a function of orientation. Five orientations—cognitive-behavioral, eclectic, humanistic, (Freudian) psychoanalytic, and psychodynamic/neo-Freudian—received sufficient endorsement in the studies to warrant inclusion in the group analysis. Summarizing across the three studies, cognitive-behavior therapists report using significantly more counterconditioning, contingency control, and stimulus control than their psychoanalytic and psychodynamic colleagues. Psychodynamic and psychoanalytic therapists, on the other hand, report employing catharsis and the helping relationship significantly more frequently than their cognitive-behavioral counterparts. Humanistic therapists emphasize self-liberation more than non-like-minded therapists, and eclectics generally employ all the change processes in moderate dosage. Thus all the observed differences were consistent with theoretical prescription.

That the treatment of clients varies predictably with the psychotherapist's orientation is not surprising, and in fact, quite expected. The question then arose: Are psychotherapists equally influenced by theories in treating *themselves?*

Apparently not. No significant differences were observed among psychotherapists in their own self-change due to theoretical orientation. This pattern has now been replicated in four separate studies (Book, 1989; Norcross & Prochaska, 1986b; Norcross, Prochaska, & Hambrecht, 1991; Prochaska & Norcross, 1983b) involving different behavioral disorders and psychotherapist samples, and we have been unable to discern even a few significant differences expected by chance alone. In toto, these composite findings strongly argue for a considerable degree of similarity among psychotherapists in their own self-change.

At least three interpretations can be offered for this pattern of findings. Just as there are stable disparities in attributions for people in the roles of actors and observers (see Jones & Nisbett, 1971), so too do there appear to be robust differences in change strategies for people in the roles of clinicians and clients. In contrast to the classical "attribution effect," we might label this the "facilitation effect." In their roles as psychotherapists, people rely heavily on theories for facilitating change in others. In their role as self-changers, people are not apparently as influenced by theoretical prescriptions.

A second interpretation is a cynical perspective on the duplicity between psychotherapists' public careers and their personal lives. Psychotherapists may not avail themselves of what they offer their patients. Theoretical orientations may be for treatment-facilitated change of clients, not for self-initiated change of themselves. Negatively stated, one may *not* necessarily have to "practice what one preaches." As George Kelly (1955) noted, psychotherapists do *not* apply their theories reflexively; that is, they do not apply the same theories to their own behavior as psychologists that they use in understanding and treating patients.

The third and more positive explanation is that psychotherapists become more pragmatic, eclectic, and "secular" when they confront their own distress. This view is reminiscent of Fiedler's (1950a, 1950b) contention that experienced psychotherapists think quite similarly and of Wachtel's (1977) "therapeutic underground," an unofficial consensus of what experienced clinicians believe to be true. Also consistent with this explanation is evidence (Lazarus, 1971; Norcross & Prochaska, 1984; Norcross, Strausser, & Faltus, 1988) that the vast majority of behavior therapists choose *non*behavioral personal therapy. On a personal, if not a professional, level, clinicians may be taking the recent surge of psychotherapy integration to heart (Norcross & Goldfried, 1992).

In addition, this methodology offers a useful, albeit tentative, comparison between the attempts of psychotherapists to change themselves and to change their clients. A statistical test of the means is typically performed only on identical variables. Items constituting the two forms of the Processes of Change Scale were identical in content and order, but necessarily different in prefix. Consequently, it was decided that sufficient similarity existed between the two forms to permit the use of statistical tests in two studies.

In both studies, concerned respectively with psychological distress (Prochaska & Norcross, 1983b) and alcohol abuse (Norcross, Prochaska, Hambrecht, 1991), psychotherapists differed in the treatment of themselves and of their clients for the same disorder. Medication and helping relationships were recommended more frequently for patients than for themselves. Stimulus control, self-liberation, and punishment were favored more for therapists' self-change than for client change.

Precisely why it is that psychotherapists employ differential treatment strategies with themselves as compared with their patients cannot be conclusively determined. Five plausible explanations have been offered (Norcross, Prochaska, & Hambrecht, 1991).

1. Psychotherapists believe that some change processes good for the patient are not necessarily good for the practitioner. This interpretation suggests that psychotherapists may not avail themselves of what they offer their patients, which can be interpreted positively (for example, therapists make fine clinical discriminations based on individual need) or negatively (psychotherapists do not follow their own advice) (Royak-Schaler & Feldman, 1984).

2. Psychotherapists presume that they are healthier than their clientele and/or that their problems are generally less severe than those of their clients (although the study instructions controlled for the severity of the disorder).

3. Psychotherapists are aware that salient differences exist between change processes under clinical control and those under self-control. The processes emphasized for self-change, such as

stimulus control, self-liberation, and punishment, have greater potential for being brought under self-control. Conversely, medication and helping relationships—differentially favored for client change—are typically provided by professionals.

4. Psychotherapists perceive their own psychological change as involving less difficulty and distress than that of clients, as Mahoney, Norcross, Prochaska, and Missar (1989) previously found.

5. Clients presenting for professional treatment have already failed in their self-change endeavors. Psychotherapists, aware of the need for something new or different, use treatment processes different from those employed during the self-mediated change.

In any case, our multiple speculations concerning the mechanisms underlying these intriguing phenomena substantiate Edington's theory: The number of different hypotheses erected to explain a given phenomenon is inversely proportional to the available knowledge (Bloch, 1977). Detailed examination of the validity of these hypotheses would enlarge our understanding of psychotherapists' treatment of themselves and their clients.

THERAPISTS' VERSUS LAYPERSONS' SELF-CHANGE

We then wondered how psychotherapists' self-change, if unencumbered by theory, compared with laypersons' self-change. How do the behavior change "experts" treat themselves in comparison to educated laypersons? This question led to an examination of the change processes that laypersons and psychotherapists use to overcome their distress. Two comparative analyses of laypersons and psychologists were undertaken to discern which coping strategies differentiate professionals from nonprofessionals. One study (Norcross, Prochaska, & DiClemente, 1986) involved 270 laypersons and 158 psychologists; the other study (Norcross & Prochaska, 1986b), 94 laypersons, 83 psychologists, and 108 counselors.

In the first study, psychologists reported employing quantitatively more change processes than laypersons. The professionals used four of the six comparable processes more frequently than did their nonprofessional counterparts. Specifically, the former more frequently used of self-liberation, helping relationships, catharsis, and stimulus control in their self-change. On two processes—social liberation and medication—no significant differences were discerned between the two groups.

Although the utilization of self-change strategies was parallel (for example, helping relationship was used frequently and medication was used infrequently), they were not equivalent. Overall, psychologists appeared to "do more," in terms of both process activity and frequency of use. The differential use of the helping relationship and catharsis may attest to the relatively stronger social support network of the psychologist, as well as to the interpersonal emphasis of the profession. Compared with laypersons, the psychologists also reported more frequent use of self-liberation, a traditional "willpower" strategy, on the one hand, and stimulus control, a classical behavioral intervention, on the other. In short, the psychologists' coping repertoires were larger and more varied.

In the second study, we examined how psychotherapists and their layperson counterparts fared in use of fourteen change processes to combat distress. Five of the fourteen comparisons were statistically significant. The psychotherapists reported greater utilization of the helping relationship than laypersons. Conversely, the laypersons obtained higher mean scores on two problem-focused change processes—self-liberation and self-reevaluation—and two emotion-focused processes—wishful thinking and self-blame—than did the psychotherapists.

How does professional psychotherapists' coping compare with that of educated laypersons? On the one hand, psychotherapists use helping relationships significantly more frequently than laypersons. Predictably, psychotherapists would be expected to find interpersonal coping processes both satisfying and efficacious, whether it be for changing themselves or their patients. On the other hand, it would be naive and presumptuous to assume that psychotherapists simply "do more of everything." Indeed, the laypersons reported significantly more frequent use of four coping strategies in their self-change than psychotherapists, namely, self-liberation, self-reevaluation, wishful thinking, and self-blame. These processes are alike in that they all focus on the self, as opposed to others, and all involve internal cognitive strategies. In this sense, laypersons are more caught up in themselves than psychotherapists—an ironic twist indeed! Furthermore, two of the strategies (wishful thinking, self-blame) are more defense-oriented than action-oriented.

Although additional research is required to explicate these considerations fully, we speculate that experienced psychotherapists have learned several valuable lessons from their clinical work (Farber, 1983) which extend to their personal lives. As illustrated in the Vanderbilt Psychotherapy Project (Strupp & Hadley, 1979), many clinicians have learned to be integrative in treatment, whereas laypersons, even college professors specifically chosen for their interpersonal skills, tend to rely on a few techniques. Psychotherapists may have internalized advice for improving the therapeutic product: Emphasize the human element, minimize self-blame, avoid concentration on a single technique, and promote cognitive and experiential learning on a broad front (Strupp, 1981).

SELF-CHANGE VERSUS PERSONAL TREATMENT

Why do some psychotherapists rely entirely on self-change whereas others pursue professional treatment for distress? In one retrospective study (Norcross & Prochaska, 1986b), four variables consistently discriminated between the two groups. Clinicians seeking treatment were more likely to have experienced previous treatment and for a greater number of hours, had a longer (but not more severe) distress episode, and rated their self-change (before seeking therapy) as less successful. A return to personal therapy may be seen as both encouraging and discouraging: encouraging in that clinicians were satisfied with the efficacy of their previous treatment experiences, discouraging in that they may have had inadequate psychological resources and coping abilities to grapple with distress on their own. The latter interpretation is consistent with the lengthier average duration of distress despite no difference in severity.

Seeking treatment after relatively unsuccessful self-change is a common phenomenon. A study of college students' use of psychological services, for example, found that "the decision to actually use psychotherapy was likely to come only after ineffective attempts to cope with the problem one's self or with the help of a close friend or relative" (Farber & Geller, 1977, p. 306). Two noted psychologists (Goldfried & Davison, 1976, p. 9) put it a bit more directly: "To begin with, the very fact that the client has sought (professional) help is an open admission that he has been unable to adequately control certain aspects of his own life." Most of our therapeutic efforts are directed at unsuccessful self-changers.

It was also of interest to determine whether psychotherapists who sought treatment employed different change processes than the self-changers. They did not; for psychotherapists, change processes did not differ between those who sought psychotherapy and those who did not. Three possible reasons for the paucity of differences in change processes are that (1) clinicians have had extensive prior personal therapy, thus minimizing effects from this one brief period of treatment; (2) clinicians may be too knowledgeable, sophisticated, and experienced in these self-change processes; and, (3) as a group, the clinicians are more homogeneous than laypersons in terms of age, education, income, and employment.

DEALING WITH STRESSFUL CLIENTS

One study in the transtheoretical tradition focused on the client as a source of psychotherapist stress and identified the change strategies used by psychotherapists to deal with client-generated distress. The aim was to gain a better understanding of how seasoned therapists cope with stress experienced in working with difficult patients.

Factor-analyzing items from the Processes of Change Scale, the Ways of Coping Checklist (Aldwin et al., 1980), and two rationally created scales (humor, seeking inner peace), Medeiros and Prochaska (1988) found that 243 psychologists relied on six change strategies when confronted with difficult clinical encounters. *Self-reevaluation and wishful thinking* represented a critical evaluation of one's feelings coupled with a passive attitude toward the problem. *Humor* was the expression of amazement and perception of comedy in the situation. Attempts to engage in positive goal-directed behavior in response to the stressor was labeled *optimistic perseverance. Seeking social support* dealt with obtaining more information and direction from others. By contrast, *seeking inner peace* reflected attempts to achieve a tranquil state by focusing on neutral or positive thoughts within oneself. And clinicians using *avoidance* denied a thought, a fact, or its implication.

These findings revealed the means by which psychologists grapple with clinical stressors but not the adaptive mechanisms of doing so. Further analysis addressed the question of which, if any, of these change processes provided the therapist with effective strategies of mitigating the stress experienced in working with difficult clients. When self-report measures of effective self-change were used, the results found that the more psychologists employed self-reevaluation and wishful thinking, the more poorly they coped. As in the studies reviewed earlier in this chapter, self-reevaluation was highly correlated with increased intensity and longer duration of stress. Conversely, the more the psychologists relied on optimistic perseverance, the better they coped with client-generated stress.

LESSONS FROM PERSONAL TREATMENT

Many people use psychotherapy intermittently at times of need to supplement self-change, and psychotherapists are no exception. In dealing with the most distressing episode in the past three years (Norcross & Prochaska, 1986b), for instance, 43 percent of laypersons and 28 percent of the psychotherapists sought professional treatment. Treatment was typically not long-term; the median length ranged between 8 and 28 hours for three samples. The treatment received for this period of distress by laypersons represented 72 percent of their total personal psychotherapy; in 40 percent of the cases, this treatment constituted the only treatment they ever received. By contrast, the amount of treatment received by the psychotherapists constituted a small proportion of their lifetime therapy—18 percent on average.

This represents a brief return to personal therapy for practically all of these clinicians. We may speculate—and our own experiences support this—that previous lengthy work permits one to renew therapy comfortably with a limited focus on distressing life problems. Greenberg and Kaslow (1984, p. 20) argue that psychotherapists seeking treatment indicate that they "are, for the most part, consistent. They practice what they preach when they have problems in living, significant degrees of anxiety or depression, or other neurotic symptoms they seek help from highly respected colleagues." Moreover, seeking personal treatment implies that "they believe in what they are doing and they perceive therapy as a constructive measure that not only relieves symptoms but also leads to personal growth" (p. 20).

Overall, professional psychotherapists are avid therapy consumers. Approximately 75 percent of the psychologists, 67 percent of the psychiatrists, and 70 percent of the social workers have received personal therapy at least once during their lives (Henry, Sims, & Spray, 1973; Norcross, Strausser-Kirtland, & Missar, 1988). The number of discrete therapy episodes averages two: Approximately one-third of psychotherapists report each having one, two, and three (or more) episodes of personal treatment. The length of treatment varies with theoretical orientation (psychoanalysts the longest, behaviorists the shortest), but the average is between 100 and 200 hours and the median between 50 and 100.

Despite the profession's collective silence on personal therapy, practicing psychotherapists do in fact utilize the very service they provide. In three recent studies, over one-half of responding clinicians received personal psychotherapy *following* completion of formal training: 52 percent of psychoanalysts (Goldensohn, 1977), 55 percent of psychotherapists (Grunebaum, 1986), and 62 percent of psychologists (Guy, Poelstra, & Stark, 1988). It is an illusion—or perhaps a delusion—that most mental health professionals do not experience a need for personal therapy once they are in practice (Guy & Liaboe, 1988; Norcross, 1990).

Being such avid and informed consumers of psychotherapy themselves, psychotherapists are in a particularly advantageous position to provide recommendations on change mechanisms. Toward this end, in two studies (Norcross, Strausser-Kirtland, & Missar, 1988; Norcross, Dryden, & DeMichele, 1992), we asked psychotherapists to reflect on their personal treatment and briefly describe any lasting lessons they acquired concerning behavior change in general and about the practice of psychotherapy in particular. In an American study, 413 (or 81 percent) of the psychologists, psychiatrists, and social workers nominated at least one lasting lesson (a total of 604 lessons). In a British study, 375 clinical psychologists (or 99%) did so for a total of 560 lessons. The multifarious responses were content-coded, and the most frequent response categories are presented in Table 9.2. Note that these categories account for less than half of rich and diverse lessons.

Transatlantic convergence was evident in what contributes to successful behavior change. The four most common responses, in both countries, concerned the interpersonal relationship and dynamics of psychotherapy: warmth and empathy, transference and

TABLE 9.2
Psychotherapists' Lasting Lessons from Personal Treatment

Lesson	American (n = 604)	British (n = 560)	Total
Importance of the personal relationship, warmth, empathy in behavior change	84	85	169
Importance of transference/ countertransference	52	33	85
Need for more patience and tolerance	48	19	67
Therapists' use of self is essential	30	28	58
Know what it feels like to be in distress; see that everyone is human	14	43	57
Need for personal treatment among psychotherapists	26	31	57
Change attempts can be effective; resolve negative strategies and life problems	19	27	46
Change is gradual and painful, albeit possible	20	21	41

countertransference, patience and tolerance, use of self. Both British and American clinicians agreed that psychotherapy is useful and that behavior change is gradual and occasionally painful. Indeed, the lasting lessons explicated in Table 9.2, generated from lived clinical experiences as both patient and therapist, represent a *desiderata* for behavior change.

The modal enduring lesson taken by practicing psychotherapists from their own treatment concerned the importance of the helping, nurturing relationships—a recurring theme in this review of psychotherapists' self-change. The heightened awareness may well translate into clinical practice. The experience of personal therapy has been positively associated with the clinician's ability to display empathy, warmth, and genuineness (Peebles, 1980), and his or her increased emphasis on the personal relationship in therapy (Wogan & Norcross, 1985). This trend holds true for general samples of psychotherapists (McNair & Lorr, 1964; Sundland & Barker, 1967) as well as psychoanalytic (Strupp, 1955) and behavior (Norcross & Wogan, 1983) therapists.

CONCLUDING REMARKS

Reviewing these studies of the past decade have made us mindful of at least three lessons. First, most distressed individuals, psychotherapists included, do not bring their problems to mental health care providers, but grapple on their own or with the help of friends, family, and others. Therefore, theories of behavioral change must account for both naturally occurring self-change and professionally facilitated therapy change. We need to search for generic mechanisms of change without resorting to mystical explanations, such as "spontaneous recovery" (Lambert, 1976). Second, whatever therapeutic path we may choose, we might do well to follow the lead of the psychologists in these investigations by avoiding the single technique and the "either-or" dilemma, while emphasizing helping relationships and promoting cognitive and experiential learning on a broad front (Lazarus, Beutler, & Norcross, 1992).

Third, we are reminded of the major research challenge in self-change to establish conditional variables on which patterns of change depend, so that people can be grouped on the basis of similarities and differences for purposes of intervention. Our measurements and designs should identify processes of change that produce either positive or negative outcomes and the conditions effecting such outcomes. To the end that self-change interventions might become more differentiated with respect to types of patients and problems, we must continue to search for ways of improving self-change in real-life situations (Prochaska, DiClemente, & Norcross, 1992). This search requires more sophisticated thought than presently exists and a deep respect for the person who receives our help (Lazarus, 1983).

In closing, it should not be asking too much of psychotherapists to adhere to the Socratic dictum of "know thyself" as part of the arduous task of self-change. Before—and while—assisting others, they should know and ultimately heal themselves, be it by self-mediated or therapy-facilitated change.

NOTES

1.   We concern ourselves in this chapter solely to studies performed with the measures and assumptions of the Transtheoretical Model of Change. Readers interested in the broader topic of psychotherapists' personal experiences are re-

ferred to books by Corey and Corey (1989), Dryden and Spurling (1989), Goldberg (1986, 1992), Guy (1987), Kilburg, Nathan, and Thoreson (1986), Kottler (1986), Rippere and Williams (1985), and Scott and Hawk (1986).

2. The various studies discussed in this chapter involved four mutually exclusive groups of psychotherapists, all of whom were currently practicing psychotherapy. *Psychologists* refer to doctoral-level, licensed psychologists who belong to the American Psychological Association. *Psychiatrists* are physicians who are board-certified or board-eligible in psychiatry and who belong to the American Psychiatric Association. *Social workers* are master's-level therapists clinically registered by the National Association of Social Workers. *Counselors* possessed a master's degree in an area of counseling and are affiliated with the American Association for Counseling and Development.

Comparable groups of laypersons did not conduct psychotherapy and did not possess a graduate degree in psychology, medicine, counseling or social work, but had graduated from college. Laypersons were recruited through newspaper advertisements, requests in graduate courses, or random sampling telephone calls, depending on the particular study. All psychotherapists were recruited directly through mail questionnaires sent to randomly selected members of the respective professions. Specific recruitment methods and response rates can be found in the individual articles.

3. The processes of change (such as self-liberation, counterconditioning) and the stages of change (such as precontemplation, action) are defined and illustrated in Chapter 7 of this volume by Grimley and colleagues.

REFERENCES

Aldwin, C., Folkman, S., Schafer, C., Coyne, J., & Lazarus, R. S. (1980, August). *The ways of coping: A process measure.* Paper presented at the annual meeting of the American Psychological Association, Montreal, Canada.

Balint, M. (1948). On the psychoanalytic training system. *International Journal of Psycho-Analysis, 29:*163–173.

Beck, A. T. (1976). *Cognitive therapy and emotional disorders.* New York: International University Press.

Bermak, G. E. (1977). Do psychiatrists have special emotional problems? *The American Journal of Psychoanalysis, 37:*141–147.

Beutler, L. E., Crago, M., & Arizmendi, T. G. (1986). Research on therapist variables in psychotherapy. In *Handbook of psychotherapy and behavior change* (3rd ed.), edited by S. L. Garfield & A. E. Bergin. New York: John Wiley.

Bloch, A. (Ed.). (1977). *Murphy's law and other reasons why things go wrong.* Los Angeles: Price/Stern/Slogan.

Book, B. A. (1989). *Therapist heal thyself: Self-change processes and burnout among psychologists and social workers.* Unpublished doctoral dissertation.

274   EXPERIENCES OF CHANGING THE SELF

Brown, G. W., & Harris, T. (1978). *Social origins of depression: A study of psychiatric disorder in women*. New York: Free Press.

Burton, A. (1972). *Twelve therapists: How they live and actualize themselves*. San Francisco: Jossey-Bass.

Corey, M. S., & Corey, G. (1989). *Becoming a helper*. Pacific Grove, CA: Brooks/Cole.

Coyne, J. C., Aldwin, C., & Lazarus, R. S. (1981). Depression and coping in stressful episodes. *Journal of Abnormal Psychology, 90:*439–447.

Cray, C., & Cray, M. (1977). Stresses and rewards within the psychiatrist's family. *The American Journal of Psychoanalysis, 37:*337–341.

Daniels, A. K. (1974). What troubles the trouble shooters. In *The sociology of psychotherapy*, edited by P. M. Roman & H. M. Trice (pp. 191–214). New York: Aronson.

Deutsch, C. J. (1985). A survey of therapists' personal problems and treatment. *Professional Psychology: Research and Practice, 16:*305–315.

Dohrenwend, B. P., Shrout, P. E., Egri, G., & Mendelsohn, F. S. (1980). Nonspecific psychological distress and other dimensions of psychopathology. *Archives of General Psychiatry, 37:*1229–1236.

Dryden, W., & Spurling, L. (Eds.). (1989). *On becoming a psychotherapist*. London: Routledge.

Farber, B. A. (1983). Dysfunctional aspects of the therapeutic role. In *Stress and burnout in the human service profession*, edited by B. A. Farber (pp. 97–118). New York: Pergamon.

Farber, B. A., & Geller, J. D. (1977). Student attitudes toward psychotherapy. *Journal of American College Health Association, 25:*301–307.

Fiedler, F. E. (1950a). Comparison of therapeutic relationships in psychoanalytic, nondirective, and Adlerian therapy. *Journal of Consulting Psychology, 14:*426–445.

_____. (1950b). The concept of the ideal therapeutic relationship. *Journal of Consulting Psychology, 14:*239–245.

Freud, S. (1917/1957). Mourning and melancholia. In *The complete psychological works of Sigmund Freud* (standard edition, vol. 14), edited by J. Strachey. London: Hogarth.

Goldberg, C. (1986). *On being a psychotherapist*. New York: Gardner.

_____. (1992). *The seasoned psychotherapist*. New York: Norton.

Goldensohn, S. S. (1977). Graduates' evaluation of their psychoanalytic training. *Journal of the American Academy of Psychoanalysis, 5:*51–64.

Goldfried, M. R., & Davison, G. S. (1976). *Clinical behavior therapy*. New York: Holt, Rinehart & Winston.

Greenberg, S., & Kaslow, F. W. (1984). Psychoanalytic treatment for therapists, residents, and other trainees. In *Psychotherapy with psychotherapists*, edited by F. W. Kaslow. New York: Haworth.

Grunebaum, H. (1986). Harmful psychotherapy experiences. *American Journal of Psychotherapy, 40:165–176.*

Gurin, G., Veroff, J., & Feld, S. (1960). *Americans view their mental health*. New York: Basic Books.

Guy, J. D. (1987). *The personal life of the psychotherapist*. New York: John Wiley.

Guy, J. D., & Liaboe, G. P. (1988). Personal therapy for the experienced psychotherapist: A discussion of its usefulness and utilization. *The Clinical Psychologist, 39:20–23.*

Guy, J. D., Poelstra, P. L., & Stark, M. J. (1988). Personal distress and therapeutic effectiveness. *Professional Psychology: Research and Practice, 19:474–476.*

Henry, W. E., Sims, J. H., & Spray, S. L. (1973). *The public and private lives of psychotherapists*. San Francisco: Jossey-Bass.

Jones, E., & Nisbett, R. (1971). *The actor and the observer*. Morristown, NJ: General Learning Press.

Kelly, G. A. (1955). *The psychology of personal constructs*. New York: Norton.

Kilburg, R. R., Nathan, P. E., & Thoreson, R. W. (Eds.). (1986). *Professionals in distress*. Washington, DC: American Psychological Association.

Kottler, J. A. (1986). *On becoming a therapist*. San Francisco: Jossey-Bass.

Lambert, M. J. (1976). Spontaneous remission in adult neurotic disorders: A revision and summary. *Psychological Bulletin, 83:107–119.*

———. (1992). Psychotherapy outcome research: Implications for integrative and eclectic therapists. In *Handbook of psychotherapy integration*, edited by J. C. Norcross & M. R. Goldfried. New York: Basic Books.

Lazarus, A. A. (1971). Where do behavior therapists take their troubles? *Psychological Reports, 28:349–350.*

Lazarus, A. A., Beutler, L. E., & Norcross, J. C. (1992). The future of technical eclecticism. *Psychotherapy, 29:11–20.*

Lazarus, R. S. (1966). *Psychological stress and the coping process*. New York: McGraw-Hill.

———. (1980). The stress and coping paradigm. In *Competence and coping during adulthood*, edited by L. A. Bond & J. C. Rosen. Hanover, NH: University Press of New England.

————. (1983). The trivialization of distress. In *Preventing health risk behaviors and coping with illness,* edited by J. C. Rosen & L. J. Solomon. Hanover, NH: University Press of New England.

Looney, J. G., Harding, R. K., Blottcky, M. J., & Barnhart, F. D. (1980). Psychiatrists' transition from training to career: Stress and mastery. *American Journal of Psychiatry, 137:32–35.*

Luborsky, L. (1984). *Principles of psychotherapy.* New York: Basic Books.

Luborsky, L., Chandler, M., Auerbach, A., & Bachrach, H. (1971). Factors influencing the outcome of psychotherapy: A quantitative review. *Psychological Bulletin, 75:145–185.*

Luborsky, L., Mintz, J., Auerbach, A., Christoph, P., Bachrach, H., Todd, T., Johnson, M., Cohen, M., & O'Brien, C. P. (1980). Predicting the outcomes of psychotherapy: Findings of the Penn Psychotherapy Project. *Archives of General Psychiatry, 37:471–481.*

Mahoney, M. J., Norcross, J. C., Prochaska, J. O., & Missar, C. D. (1989). Psychological development and optimal psychotherapy: Converging perspectives among clinical psychologists. *Journal of Integrative and Eclectic Psychotherapy, 8:251–263.*

McNair, D. M., & Lorr, M. (1964). An analysis of professed psychotherapeutic techniques. *Journal of Consulting Psychology, 28:265–271.*

Medeiros, M. E., & Prochaska, J. O. (1988). Coping strategies that psychotherapists use in working with stressful clients. *Professional Psychology: Research and Practice, 19:112–114.*

Mellinger, G. D., Balter, M. B., Uhlenhuth, E. H., Cisin, I. H., Manheimer, D. I., & Rickles, K. (1983). Evaluating a household survey measure of psychic distress. *Psychological Medicine, 13:607–621.*

Mellinger, G. D., Balter, M. B., Uhlenhuth, E. H., Cisin, I. H., & Parry, H. J. (1978). Psychic distress, life crisis and use of psychotherapeutic medication: National Household Survey data. *Archives of General Psychiatry, 38:1045–1052.*

Menaghan, E. G. (1982). Measuring coping effectiveness: A panel study of marital problems and coping effectiveness. *Journal of Health and Social Behavior, 23:220–234.*

————. (1983). Individual coping efforts: Moderators between life stress and mental health outcomes. In *Psychosocial stress: Trends in theory and research,* edited by H. B. Kaplan. New York: Academic Press.

Mueller, D. P. (1980). Social networks: A promising direction for research on the relationship of social environment to psychiatric disorder. *Social Science and Medicine, 14:147–161.*

Norcross, J. C. (1990). Personal therapy for therapists: One solution. *Psychotherapy in Private Practice, 8:45–59.*

Norcross, J. C., Dryden, W., & DeMichele, J. T. (1992). British clinical psychologists and personal therapy: What's good for the goose? *Clinical Psychology Forum, 44:*29–33.

Norcross, J. C., & Goldfried, M. R. (Eds.). (1992). *Handbook of psychotherapy integration.* New York: Basic Books.

Norcross, J. C., & Guy, J. D. (1989). Ten therapists: The process of becoming and being. In *On becoming a psychotherapist,* edited by W. Dryden & L. Spurling (pp. 215–239). London: Travistock/Routledge.

Norcross, J. C., & Prochaska, J. O. (1984). Where do behavior (and other) therapists take their troubles?: II. *The Behavior Therapist, 7:*26–27.

———. (1986a). Psychotherapist heal thyself—I: The psychological distress and self-change of psychologists, counselors, and laypersons. *Psychotherapy, 23:*102–114.

———. (1986b). Psychotherapist heal thyself—II: The self-initiated and therapy-facilitated change of psychological distress. *Psychotherapy, 23:*345–356.

Norcross, J. C., Prochaska, J. O., & DiClemente, C. C. (1986). Self-change of psychological distress: Laypersons' vs psychologists' coping strategies. *Journal of Clinical Psychology, 42:*834–840.

Norcross, J. C., Prochaska, J. O., & Hambrecht, M. (1991). Treating ourselves vs. treating our clients: A replication with alcohol abuse. *Journal of Substance Abuse, 3:*123–129.

Norcross, J. C., Strausser, D. J., & Faltus, F. J. (1988). The therapist's therapist. *American Journal of Psychotherapy, 42:*53–66.

Norcross, J. C., Strausser-Kirtland, D. J., & Missar, C. D. (1988). The processes and outcomes of psychotherapists' personal treatment experiences. *Psychotherapy, 25:*36–43.

Norcross, J. C., & Wogan, M. (1983). American psychotherapists of diverse persuasions: Characteristics, theories, practices, and clients. *Professional Psychology: Research and Practice, 14:*529–539.

Pearlin, L. I., & Schooler, C. (1978). The structure of coping. *Journal of Health and Social Behavior, 19:*2–21.

Peebles, M. J. (1980). Personal therapy and ability to display empathy, warmth and genuineness in psychotherapy. *Psychotherapy: Theory, Research and Practice, 17:*252–262.

Prochaska, J. O., & DiClemente, C. C. (1992). The transtheoretical approach. In *Handbook of psychotherapy integration,* edited by J. C. Norcross & M. R. Goldfried. New York: Basic Books.

Prochaska, J. O., DiClemente, C., & Norcross, J. C. (1992). In search of how people change: Applications to addictive behaviors. *American Psychologist, 47:*1102–1114.

Prochaska, J. O., & Norcross, J. C. (1983a). Contemporary psychotherapists: A national survey of characteristics, practices, orientations and attitudes. *Psychotherapy, 20:*161–173.

_____. (1983b). Psychotherapists' perspectives on treating themselves and their clients for psychic distress. *Professional Psychology, 14:*642–655.

Rippere, V., & Williams, R. (Eds.). (1985). *Wounded healers: Mental health workers' experiences of depression.* New York: John Wiley.

Royak-Schaler, R., & Feldman, R. H. (1984). Health behaviors of psychotherapists. *Journal of Clinical Psychology, 40:*705–710.

Schacter, S. (1982). Recidivism and self-cure of smoking and obesity. *American Psychologist, 37:*436–444.

Scott, C. D., & Hawk, J. (Eds.) (1986). *Heal thyself: The health of health care professionals.* New York: Brunner/Mazel.

Strupp, H. H. (1955). The effect of the psychotherapist's personal analysis upon his techniques. *Journal of Consulting Psychology, 19:*197–204.

_____. (1981, April). *The future of time-limited dynamic psychotherapy: Research and clinical perspectives.* Distinguished lecture presented at the meeting of the Eastern Psychological Association, Boston, MA.

Strupp, H. H., & Hadley, S. W. (1979). Specific vs. nonspecific factors in psychotherapy: A controlled study of outcome. *Archives of General Psychiatry, 36:*1125–1136.

Taylor, S. E. (1983). Adjustment to threatening events: A theory of cognitive adaptation. *American Psychologist, 38:*1161–1173.

Turner, R. J. (1981). Social support as a contingency in psychological well-being. *Journal of Health and Social Behavior, 22:*357–367.

Vernon, S. W., & Roberts, R. E. (1981). Measuring nonspecific psychological distress and other dimensions of psychopathology. *Archives of General Psychiatry, 38:*1239–1247.

Wachtel, P. L. (1977). *Psychoanalysis and behavior therapy: Toward an integration.* New York: Basic Books.

Watzlawick, P. (1986). If you desire to see, learn how to act. In *The evolution of psychotherapy,* edited by J. K. Zeig. New York: Brunner/Mazel.

Wogan, M., & Norcross, J. C. (1985). Dimensions of therapeutic skills and techniques: Empirical identification, therapist correlates, and predictive utility. *Psychotherapy, 22:*63–74.

CHAPTER 10

Self and Self-Loss in Mystical Experience

Ralph W. Hood, Jr.

In the Western intellectual tradition the understanding of self has been intimately related to the understanding of God. Within the numerous varieties of Judeo-Christian faith tradition the notion that persons are created in God's image logically necessitated an understanding of God as crucial to an understanding of persons. Likewise, philosophical and scientific thought that emerged in opposition to the Judeo-Christian faith tradition could not escape the dilemma of unraveling the nature of God as part of unraveling the riddle of the human self. For instance, Feuerbach, the theologian of choice for both Marx and Freud, while arguing that "the consciousness of the infinite is nothing else than the consciousness of the infinity of the consciousness" (in Kung, 1980, p. 200), popularized what were to become "projection" views of God. Central to all such views is that the very existence of God is but a distorted and alienated perception of the human self.

Yet even this projected God image must be unraveled so that persons can be truly revealed to themselves. In the Marxian use of Feuerbach's theology, "religion is the opium of the people" (Marx, 1975, p. 39). Yet the preface to this famous quote reads, "Religious distress is at the same time the expression of real distress and also the protest against real distress. Religion is the sigh of the oppressed creature, the heart of a heartless world, just as it is the spirit of a spiritless condition" (Marx, 975, p. 39). For Marx the religious self is the estrangement of humankind's self, in all aspects, from its very nature, its "species being," and from itself in the total

279

ensemble of social relations, both intimate and institutional. Thus "to abolish religion as the illusory happiness of the people is to demand their real happiness" (Marx, 1975, p. 39). In a similar vein, Freud's (1961b) use of Feuerbach is exemplified in religion as illusion. Yet even here illusion contains a necessary truth. The truth is not of reality, now masked as an idealized cosmic drama, but instead of a self demanding that its desires be realized in the face of a harsh reality (Hood, 1992). Thus both Freud and Marx, the two great atheistic "cultural despisers" (to paraphrase Schleiermacher), popularized what many perceive as the inevitable antimony between religious and social scientific approaches to the understanding of self. Both religious and social scientific views of self occur within the shadow of God, as either reality or illusion. Yet as Grunbaum (1985) has emphasized, Freud's view of religion as illusion entails the commonsense assumption that persons know what desires remain central to self and are unfilled in reality. It is precisely these desires that Freud claimed the Judeo-Christian faith tradition perpetuated in ideological form as both individual and collective cultural projections. In a similar vein, Marx's claim that religion is the estranged realization of a person's selfhood entails that, as with Freud, "therapeutic" procedures are required so that the true image of self, distorted within religious conceptions of God, can be revealed. Hence, for both Freud and Marx the solution to the claim that persons are made in God's image is not simply to argue the obverse proposition as if reiterating Feuerbach's theology, but rather to argue for the therapeutic conditions under which the person's need to conceptualize self within or through God images (ideologically articulated within faith traditions) will disappear. As if to anticipate Wittgenstein (1961, p. 149), both Freud's individual and Marx's social therapies argue that the true realization of self results in the disappearance of the relevance of religious questions (the problem vanishes such that the question does not arise). In this sense, a religious self understood in God's image is replaced as it "withers away" under the therapeutic force of psychological and sociological understandings of self within various social scientific traditions.

In this chapter we shall first confront the reasons why the study of mysticism continually raises issues regarding the nature of self difficult to remove from their religious context. This is particularly the case when the claim is made that the loss of various empirical selves is seen as an almost therapeutic realization of a true self. Historically this newly realized self has been identified with the notion of a soul or transcendental self (often identified as now merged with God). Thus we shall discuss these claims at the psychological level, focusing upon the parallels between the debates of Hume and Kant and those of the Buddhist and Vedantic traditions regarding a transcendental self or soul. Although such debates might seem a diversion, we shall see that in the work of James these historical debates take on a contemporary relevance in the study of mysticism.

Our review of contemporary studies of mysticism, guided by the phenomenological insights of James and others, will demonstrate the empirical contribution that measurement and survey studies have made to the understanding of self and self-loss. Hopefully our earlier focus upon what some might perceive as merely philosophical or religious concerns will be seen as not irrelevant to an understanding of self as revealed in empirical studies of mystical experience.

PHILOSOPHICAL, PSYCHOLOGICAL, AND RELIGIOUS RELATIONSHIPS

William James and Phenomenology

Although many contemporary social scientists would choose neither classical Freudian nor Marxian theory to express the oppositional stance of the humanistic understanding of self to religious ones, many would accept the model inherent in our brief discussion above. That is to say, few social scientists are likely to think that religious conceptualizations of God are necessary to understanding a self supposedly contained in that image. An exception is in the study of mysticism, where both religious and scientific claims to the nature of self often meet. Indeed, they are often forced to meet on purely empirical grounds. Curiously, these empirical grounds are methodologically revealed in what James (1985, p. 393) referred to as "full facts," primarily in phenomenological treatments of mysticism. Thus, as we shall note shortly, much of the most fruitful discussion of self and self-loss in mysticism has been within phenomenologically oriented investigations or within positivistic, empirical investigations influenced by phenomenological works. Not surprisingly, many of these works applaud James as a phenomenologist of first rank despite typical textbook presentations of James as exemplifying American functionalist psychology (Edie, 1987; Levinson, 1981; Fontinell, 1986; Wilshire, 1968). However, as we shall soon see, it is not simply James's phenomenology of mysticism that dominates the literature. What is essential is that phenomenological methodologies be appreciated in the problematics that emerge in the empirical "full fact" investigation of self.

Hume and Kant on Self

It is historically the case that within both faith and philosophical traditions the problem of the existence of self emerged in a manner that set the context for contemporary empirical investigations of self within the social scientific study of mysticism. In the most general sense, the problem of self emerged within the Western intellectual tradition in the context of both ontological and metaphysical claims. In a modern context, the notion that a self "exists" in any verifiable scientific sense is at best problematic. The classic discussion of this is in Hume. His method is loosely phenomenological, and simply asserts that when one tries to locate the self in any reflexive empirical sense, no such self can be found. What is found, instead, is simple discrete perceptions. In Hume's words (1959, p. 239), "For my part, when I enter most intimately into what I call *myself*, I always stumble on some particular perception or other . . . I never catch *myself* at any time without a perception, and can never observe anything but the perception" (emphasis in original).

Hume's perplexity is widely shared by many contemporary social scientists. Whatever the self might or might not be, a self independent of the summation of a series of discrete perceptions is often claimed to be empirically unwarranted precisely because it is only the discrete perceptions that can be perceived. Simply put, for both Hume and many modern empirical self theorists, there is no substantial self or "soul" independent of reflexive self-perceptions. Perhaps the most pithy and succinct dismissal of any metaphysical claims to a substantial self within the Humean argumentative frame is Russell's (1957, p. 54) dismissal of any possibility of a self surviving death: "When I die, I shall rot, and nothing of my ego shall survive."

For purposes of this discussion, we shall refer to the Humean self as the *reflexive self*. Whether such a self requires no metaphysical claims to a substantial or what we shall term a *transcendent self* that is "witness" or is aware of such discrete perceptions is one of the continued debates with the Western intellectual tradition. Furthermore, as we shall soon see, it is also an issue that can be found within faith traditions. However, our point here is simply to introduce the empirical claim of Hume that simple self-reflection reveals no substantial self. A reflexive self composed of discrete perceptions is all Humean empiricism allows. Hume's position is that of many empirical psychologists influenced by positivism and operational measurement commitments who can find no "empirical evidence," much less warrant, for believing in a substantial or transcendental self.

Within the Western intellectual tradition, Humean skepticism has typically been seen as the inevitable outcome of a pure empiricism—one devoted to the building of constructs from bedrock facts of sense perception (Robinson, 1981). Yet critics of Hume quickly noted how common sense seems to demand an "owner" of such discrete perceptions. "I" and "myself" seem to be at least logically distinct concepts such that it is "I" as a transcendent self, substantial or not, that has the experiences recognized as "myself" (Hood & Morris, 1983, pp. 355–357). Furthermore, as Blose (1981) has emphasized, the possibility of a substantial self surviving bodily death is clearly empirically possible. Yet contemporary empirical psychologists are unlikely to be interested in a hypothesis of a substantial self empirically verified only upon death should the hypothesis be true, and not verified at all should the hypothesis be false, despite the conceptual logic of the validity of this very possibility (Blose, 1981; Fontinell, 1986). Kant (1964) best expressed this in postulating the logical necessity of a transcendental ego in response to Hume, claiming that things insofar as they are intelligible at all must be in terms of a consciousness of self. James noted that Kant's self or transcendental ego was a valid conceptual response to purely empirical claims to an associationist self arising spontaneously and empirically unified. Nevertheless, Kant's self had no positive attributes and, unlike Hume's reflexive self, did not appear in consciousness. It is precisely this that led Kant to claim its objectivity over Hume's mere subjective, empirical self. In Kant's (1964, p. 98) own words, "The transcendental unity of apperception is alone objectively valid; the empirical . . . contains only subjective validity." James argued against both Hume and Kant from a purely psychological perspective. Whereas Hume's empiricism is inadequate, Kant's critique of Hume is "metaphysical" and has no empirical force. James's quip is worth noting: "Although Kant's name for it—the 'original transcendental synthetic Unity of Apperception'—is so long our consciousness *about* it is, according to him, short enough" (James, 1981, p. 342, emphasis in original). We might note here that the fact that merely empirical knowledge leads to skepticism regarding absolutes, including a transcendental self, is well established in the Western intellectual tradition (see Robinson, 1981).

In sum, although Hume's position is in a modern sense "empirical," it ends in skepticism; although Kant's position allows for certainty, it is empirically unwarranted. Even Hume (1959, p. 239) laid the foundation for a possible empirical solution to a transcendental self when he admitted that others might perceive such a self though Hume could not. That such a self might exist in mystical states as a purely empirical phenomenon is to be considered later in this chapter. However, before presenting a Jamesian empirical solution to the debate between Hume and Kant on the nature of self, it will be helpful to note that this debate has parallels in faith traditions concerning the soul. James himself was sensitive to the fact that issues surrounding the self in psychology were suspicious to some positivists precisely because of their religious aroma. The psychologist's self had many characteristics of the religionist's soul. Yet in James's 1894 APA presidential address he stated, "It must be admitted that much of the reigning bias against the soul in so-called scientific circles is an unintelligent prejudice, traceable far more to a vague impression that it is theological superstition, than to exact logical grounds" (James, 1968a, p. 164). That this is still the case today can be illustrated by seeing the recent interest in self psychologists in Buddhist thought (Johannson, 1968; de Silva, 1979) less as a classic faith tradition than as a sophisticated introspective system of self psychology paralleling Hume.

Vedantic and Buddhist Parallels

If Kant was awakened from his dogmatic slumbers by Hume's skepticism, the Buddha simply turned away from earlier discussion of Kantianlike claims to a transcendent self within the Vedantic tradition. Vedantic thought argued that ultimate reality was Absolute Consciousness, or Pure Self, or *Brahman* (*Brahma* when personified). Each person had part of the Self within him or her (*atman/atta*). As such the Self is uncreated, eternal, and seeks union with Brahman. Complex theories arose as to the nature of *atta* or self, why this self was not fully realized, and what was the ultimate destiny of this self. Such talk we are likely to identify as mythical or religious and forms much of the early basis of the Hindu faith tradition. Yet the Sanskrit phrase "*tat tvam asi*," or "that thou art," is part of what Huxley (1944) claimed to be the "perennial philosophy" and parallels modern phenomenological works on mysticism claiming an identity between one's true self and an Absolute Consciousness (Earle, 1980; Hood, in press).

The Buddhist doctrine of *anatta* must be understood against the backdrop of Vedantic thought (see de Silva, 1979, pp. 11–29). The negative prefix *an* is typically interpreted in Humean fashion to mean nonsoul or nonself. In similar fashion, Buddhism is often interpreted to be a religion without a God. Although such simple claims are beyond the scope of this chapter, what is relevant is simply that Buddha, like Hume, found no soul or self in the sense of a *substantial self* within actual human experience. Unlike Hume, however, Buddha did not argue against a substantial self, but rather like James saw it as irrelevant empirically. Also, like both Freud and Marx, the Buddhist faith tradition is therapeutic in that debates and questions as to the origin, nature, and destiny of a substantial soul are not questions to be asked because no empirical answers can be given. The Buddhist solution to questions regarding a substantial soul as a "problem of life" pondered within the Vedantic tradition anticipates Wittgenstein: "The solution to the problem of life is seen in the vanishing of the problem" (Wittgenstein, 1961, p. 149).

Psychologists identifying themselves as empiricists are unlikely to be sympathetic to an in-depth consideration of issues raised in debates between Hume and Kant or their earlier parallels in debates between Buddha and the Vedantic tradition. The issue most likely to be engaged is what can be empirically established with respect to self, perhaps more clearly operationally defined and measured. Yet, as we shall see, James's (1968a, p. 168) largely ignored warning in his presidential address to the APA after the phenomenal success of his *Principles of Psychology* ("that book") must be reckoned with in any empirical treatment of self, and certainly in self and self-loss in mysticism: "I have become convinced since publishing that book that no conventional restriction *can* keep metaphysical and so-called epistemological inquiries out of the psychology books" (emphasis in original).

The Jamesian Solution

James's solution to the issue of a substantial self necessarily postulated by Kant's response to Hume is twofold. First, Hume's empiricism is inadequate since no experience of discrete events (even to reflexive consciousness) can result in their unity. Second, Kant's critique is unnecessary since it assumes one aspect of Hume's empiricism that is inadequate, namely, that only discrete events are experienced and not their connections. The unity Hume sought in vain in a substantial self and rightly rejected empirically is in the connections linking thoughts. Furthermore, since these connections are revealed empirically, the Kantian appeal to a transcendental ego as a nonempirical principle is unnecessary.

James (1968b, p. 195) evokes the doctrine of "radical empiricism" as his own self-admitted Weltanschauung to insist that one cannot admit into nor exclude from empirical science any element that is directly experienced. The reflection on this world of "pure experience" is best empirically revealed with phenomenological methods compatible with James's less formal introspective analyses of autobiographical and biographical textual material and everyday experience. The current renewed interest in James attests to his belated recognition as a phenomenologist (Edie, 1987; Levinson, 1981; Fontinell, 1986; Wilshire, 1968). With respect to our specific concern with self, James's phenomenological analysis of self experience sidesteps the Vedantic and Kantian claims to either the metaphysical or logical necessity of a *transcendental self* by simply showing that what we have called the *reflexive self* carries with it at every experienced moment its own self-identity as directly experienced even as it is, so to speak, dipped from the stream of consciousness. No Humean skepticism emerges because the self that exists knows itself in all of its sequential modes of existence. "Who owns the last self owns the self before the last, for what possesses the possessor possesses the possessed" (James, 1981, p. 322). Thus no *transcendental self* need be postulated insofar as the empirical facts are concerned as long as James's phenomenology is used and not simply Hume's self-reflection. James's conclusion applies only to Hume's incomplete empiricism, which fails to phenomenologically identify thinker and thought, self and reflexive self. However, James (1981, p. 324) concludes that "the passing Thought then seems to be the Thinker; and though there *may* be another non-phenomenal Thinker behind that, so far we do not seem to need him to express the facts" (emphasis in original).

The facts to be expressed are those of the Humean self. Empirically a Kantian solution to Hume's dilemma is not needed because there is no empirical dilemma. Hume's self at every instance is itself known and owned. As to the possibility of another, nonphenomenal self that appears in experience and hence becomes simultaneously both phenomenal and empirical, James and Hume were both open to it as at least a logical possibility. That this self appears in mystical experience, phenomenological and empirical research are in substantial agreement. Furthermore, it is this self that suggests the relevance of religious discourse, insofar as a nonphenomenal self is historically compatible with the notion of soul. Thus mysticism perpetually reminds even the nonmystic of the claim to a self that transcends the more limited conceptualizations of self typically identified in social scientific studies of self as either an agent of action or an object of reflective awareness, either to itself or others.

MEASUREMENT OF MYSTICAL EXPERIENCE

Contemporary empirical research on mysticism has benefited from the measurement of reported mystical experience based upon operationalization of phenomenologically derived criteria of mystical experience. Most common is the Mysticism Scale devised by Hood based upon Stace's seminal work (Hood, 1975; Stace, 1960). Basic to Stace's phenomenological analysis of mystical experience is a distinction between experience and its interpretation. Assuming that, at least at some levels, similar if not identical experiences can be differentially described, Stace derived a common core of mystical experience. This common core became the criteria operational in Hood's scale. Neither Stace's phenomenological analysis of mysticism nor the claim that experience can at least be partly divorced from interpretation is immune from criticism (Katz, 1978; Proudfoot, 1985). However, not only is Stace's phenomenological analysis of mysticism essentially congruent with a long line of such analyses starting with James (1985, pp. 301–339), but it is undisputed that the experience of unity central to Stace's phenomenological analysis of mysticism is in fact the essential phenomenological characteristic of mystical experience. Hood (1989a) has recently referred to this as the "unity thesis."

The Unity Thesis

Central to mystical experience is an experience of unity. Essentially this can be of two forms or varieties. Using Stace (1960) as a guide, we can refer to these as *extrovertive* or *introvertive*. In extrovertive mystical experiences the experience is of a unity with the multiplicity of experienced objects, including the self. "All is one" is a typical claim, and that "all" includes myself. The experience is perceptual, not simply conceptual. It entails the paradoxical claim of a multiplicity without distinction. It yields itself to a wide variety of interpretations, both within and outside faith traditions (Katz, 1983; Spilka, Hood, & Gorsuch, 1985, pp. 175–198; Stace, 1960, pp. 62–84).

In introvertive mystical experience, there is neither multiplicity nor distinction. An undifferentiated, contentless reality is experienced. Despite the paradoxical claim to an undifferentiated pure awareness, its report as characteristic of introvertive mysticism is well documented. Like extrovertive mysticism, introvertive mysticism has been variously interpreted both within and outside faith traditions (Katz, 1983; Spilka et al., 1985; Stace, 1960, pp. 111–123).

It is crucial to note that both extrovertive and introvertive mysticism entail an experience of loss of self. Stace (1960) argues that extrovertive mysticism may be preparatory to introvertive; Hood (1989b) argues that extrovertive mysticism is likely to follow and be possible because of introvertive experience. To date the empirical possibilities are unexplored, partly because of the inability to differentiate extrovertive and introvertive mysticisms in factor-analytic studies using largely mystically unsophisticated populations. Yet in both mysticisms, loss of self occurs. In extrovertive mysticism, the experience of self is altered such that it is one with what we might call the entire field of perception. This unity allows apparent distinctions to be united as "one." The fact that both self and nonpersonal objects can be united leads to the claim of an inner subjectivity to all, itself extensively discussed in the conceptual literature on mysticism. Perhaps the most common example of such inner subjective awareness to everything is in nature mysticism, where self and the natural world are seen as one, sharing an all-encompassing subjectivity. Typically this also is a noetic claim to have experienced one's true self (Zaehner, 1957).

In introvertive mysticism, self-loss, if anything, is even more complete, or at least without any content. There is pure consciousness, without any object. Roberts (1984) has recently aptly titled her book describing her own experiences *The Experience of No-Self*, a phrase which captures the phenomenological essence of introvertive mysticism. Furthermore, the identification of this "no-self" with pure consciousness is also a noetic claim to have realized one's true self. The claim is made, of necessity, after the experience, since during the experience there is no self-awareness, or perhaps better stated, no object of awareness. James (1985, p. 332) captured this essence in the language of his day: "In mystic states we both become one with the Absolute and we become aware of our oneness." In similar fashion, Stace (1960, pp. 124–125), using Jamesian language, notes, "We have everywhere found that the mystic having suppressed both empirical factors of the stream of consciousness, arrives at a pure ego or pure consciousness, and that the emergence of this pure ego *is* the introvertive experience" (emphasis in original). Here, in the context of mystical experience, both James and Stace suggest that, insofar as the facts of reported mystical experience are concerned, the fact that there may be a nonphenomenal thinker behind everyday experience is quite possible when that experience is mystical. Indeed, it is precisely this "nonphenomenal thinker" or "pure ego" that the self identifies with in the process of self-loss that is the introvertive mystical experience. Furthermore, it is worth emphasizing that at this level the claims are purely empirical insofar as the experience described is a Jamesian "full fact." Like the empiricist's sense perception, the mystic's experience is invulnerable at the level of brute reality. It is a noetic claim whose interpretation can be disputed but not the *that* of experience. In James's (1985, pp. 335–336) words, "Our own more 'rational' beliefs are based on evidence exactly similar in nature to that which the mystics quote for theirs."

EMPIRICAL EVIDENCE FOR MYSTICAL EXPERIENCE

Survey Research

Empirical evidence for the commonality of the report of mystical experience has mounted in recent years so much that it can be concluded with good assurance that mysticism is a common experience among normal populations. Bourque and Back (1974) employed the question "Would you say that you have ever had a 'religious or mystical experience'—that is, a moment of sudden religious insight awakening or insight?" in three separate Gallup polls in the 1960s. Overall, approximately one-third of the respondents answered in the affirmative, with progressive increases over time (30.5 percent in 1962; 31.8 percent in 1966; and 41.2 percent in 1967). They also have shown that social class determined the language of describing such experience, with lower classes and the less educated preferring the religious language of mainstream faith traditions, and the middle classes and the more educated preferring aesthetic language—this despite the fact that the basic experience is assumed to be identical, that only its interpretation should vary (Back & Bourque, 1970; Bourque & Back, 1968, 1969, 1974).

In a 1974 national sample of over fourteen hundred persons, Greeley (1974) used a more adequate question to tap the report of mystical experience, referring in almost Jamesian fashion to whether a person "felt as though you were very close to a powerful spiritual force that seemed to lift you out of yourself." Again, slightly more than a third of his sample responded affirmatively. Consistent with Greeley's data is a study by Wuthnow (1978) in which a sample carefully selected to be representative of residents of the Bay Area in California revealed 39 percent of respondents affirming an experience of "feeling that you were in harmony with the universe."

American survey research is consistent with cross-cultural data in Great Britain. In a regular omnibus survey in 1976 Hay and Morisy (1978) found that slightly more than a third of their sample affirmed being "aware of, or influenced by a power, whether referred to as God or not, which is different from their everyday selves." Likewise, using the specific Greeley question cited above, Hay and Morisy found remarkable consistency, with a 30.4 percent positive response rate to this question compared with Greeley's 35 percent.

However, one word of caution is relevant here. Survey data are notoriously difficult to interpret because a single question is open to numerous interpretations by respondents. For instance, Thomas and Cooper (1978) used the specific question employed by both Greeley (1974) and Hay and Morisy (1978) and obtained roughly equivalent affirmative response rates in a sample of persons selected from students and civic organizations (34 percent). However, when Stace's specific phenomenologically derived criteria of mysticism was used, only 2 percent fit the ideal pattern. This figure is closer to a figure of only approximately 6 percent experiences of unity reported by readers to solicitations from researchers at the Religious Experience Research Unit of Manchester College, Oxford, in response to written requests in a newspaper for descriptions of experiences to the Greeley and Hays and Morisy question above (Hardy, 1979). Thus, there is cross-cultural support for the claim that, in terms of a strict phenomenology of mysticism, perhaps many responses to survey questions such as noted above are not truly reporting mystical experiences of unity. A more apt assessment of mystical experiences is perhaps obtained by measurement studies concerned with more precise mystical measures.

Measurement Studies

Religious Experience Episodes Measure   Among measurement studies two scales have been widely used. First, initial efforts to tap into the phenomenology of mystical experience utilized brief descriptions of experiences culled from James's classic *Varieties of Religious Experience* (1985). The initial measure was named the Religious Experiences Episode Measure or REEM (Hood, 1970). It consisted of fifteen brief descriptions to which persons could respond on a 5-point scale regarding the extent to which they had had an experience similar to the one described. Later, Rosegrant (1976) modified this measure by reducing the number of descriptions by five, updating the language of the descriptions, and increasing the scale range from 5 to 9. This resulted in increased internal reliability for the REEM.

For our present purposes, studies employing the REEM have consistently showed mystical experiences to be related with positive aspects of religiousness. For instance, a person's REEM scores vary appropriately between faith traditions and ethnic groups that differentially emphasize mystical experiences (Hood, 1972; Hood & Hall, 1977). The REEM also relates in a meaningful conceptual fashion to the widely employed intrinsic/extrinsic distinction tapped by a variety of forms of the Allport and Ross Religious Orientation Scale (see Donahue, 1985; Gorsuch, 1988; Kirpatrick & Hood, 1990, for reviews relevant to this scale). Scores on the REEM correlate with intrinsic religiousness more strongly than extrinsic religiousness within faith traditions regardless of the extent to which the tradition emphasizes mystical and religious experiences (Hood, 1970). Insofar as only extrinsic religiousness is most consistently related to measures of psychological and social maladjustment, the positive relationship of the REEM to intrinsic religion is congruent with survey research suggesting the normality of reported mystical experience.

One drawback with the REEM is its consistent relationship to measures of religiosity. For instance, Hood (1970) reported correlation in the magnitude of +.40 between the REEM and self-reported religiosity even in relatively small samples ($N = 68$). Even with Rosegrant's updating of the language of the REEM, its religious connotation remains. Although this is fine with samples within most faith traditions, the effect of language on the willingness to report experiences is well established. It remains empirically possible that persons having mystical experiences will refuse to report these in religious language, even if that is their only option (Hood, 1976b; Morris & Hood, 1980).

Mysticism Scale   In order to overcome the limitations of the REEM, particularly its implicit religious language, Hood (1975) devised the Mysticism Scale or M Scale. This remains the most widely used scale in empirical studies of mysticism. Stace's (1960) phenomenology of mysticism, especially his common core, was used as a framework for generating scale items. The final form of this scale consists of 32 items representing both positively and negatively worded phrases tapping Stace's phenomenology of mysticism. Initial factor analysis of this scale resulted in two factors.

Factor I consists of 20 items interpreted as the minimal phenomenological properties of mysticism, none expressed in religious language. Most items refer to experiences of union, both introvertive or extrovertive, along with their associated phenomenologies.

This includes time and space variations characteristic of introvertive mysticism and inner subjectivity characteristic of extrovertive mysticism. We will refer to this factor as the *unity factor,* which includes the minimal phenomenological properties of mysticism.

Factor II consists of 12 items, primarily interpretative, including claims to knowledge and insight as well as to religious experience. We will refer to this as the *interpretation factor.*

Holm (1982) provided a replication of Hood's (1975) factor analysis based upon a Swedish translation of the Mysticism Scale. Identical factors emerged, suggesting the stability of both a unity and interpretive factor. Recently Caird (1988) has provided both a two- and a three-factor solution to the Mysticism Scale. His two-factor solution is identical to both Hood's and Holm's. His three-factor solution essentially allows for separation of the interpretative factor into separate knowledge and religious factors. This might prove useful in cases where interpretation of experience is such that even minimal religious language is unacceptable to those whose mystical experiences occur outside of faith traditions. Caird's three-factor solution could permit a noetic but non-religious interpretation of such experiences.

The Mysticism Scale has been shown to be related to a wide variety of indices ranging from measures of ego permissiveness to the absence of psychopathology and to positive indices of psychological health (see Spilka et al., 1985; Hood, 1985, for reviews). Furthermore, it has been possible to separate experiences of unity, whether extrovertive or introvertive (unity factor), from their interpretation (interpretation factor) and to find meaningful differential correlations. For instance, persons both within and outside faith traditions report mystical experiences in terms of unity, but, surprisingly, persons within faith traditions are more likely to use religious language to describe such experiences (Morris & Hood, 1980; Hood & Morris, 1981b). Nevertheless, insofar as either introvertive or extrovertive experiences of unity are emphasized, differential interpretations, especially in terms of religious language, may not reflect differential experiences of union at the minimal phenomenological level. Likewise, differential reports of experiences of union do not simply reflect familiarity with interpretative criteria of mysticism since persons equally knowledgeable regarding interpretative criteria of mysticism may still respond differentially to the experiential measures of actual reported mystical experience (Hood & Morris, 1981a). Unfortunately, factor-analytic studies fail to identify extrovertive and introvertive experiences of unity as independent factors. Perhaps this is due to the use of populations with limited mystical experience. There are good reasons to expect introvertive and extrovertive experiences to be differentiated as independent factors among more mystically experienced populations (Hood, 1989b). At this stage of our empirical knowledge, processes operating in experiences of unity, whether introvertive or extrovertive, are unknown, partly because of the failure to independently assess these experiences in measurement-based studies.

In summary, it is clear that the long debate within various philosophical and faith traditions regarding the meaning of mystical experience is fueled by an identifiable phenomenon at the empirical level. The report of mystical experience, whether in survey research or in responses to measurement scales, is both common and demonstrably related to a wide variety of psychological indices that suggest mystical experience to be a capacity of many healthy, normal persons. It clearly need not be religiously interpreted, although James's suggestion that particular "overbeliefs" may apply to mystical experience better than others cannot be ignored. We shall briefly return to this issue in closing. First, however, we must consider the conditions that trigger the mystical experience, cultivated or otherwise.

THE TRIGGERING OF MYSTICAL EXPERIENCE

Early psychological discussion of mysticism tended to be in the context of psychopathology. This was partly due to the fact that mysticism was usually interpreted as a religious phenomenon, itself typically viewed as psychopathology (Leuba, 1925). Continued interest in mysticism was shown primarily by the psychoanalysts, who unwittingly removed *mystical* from its necessary religious interpretation. For instance, Freud (1961b) responded to the Nobel prize laureate Rolland to the effect that, whatever the nature of mystical or "oceanic feelings," they had no necessary relationship to religious ideas. Still, despite conceptual inadequacies in this argument based largely upon inadequate appreciation of the phenomenology of mystical experience, psychoanalysis in general considers mysticism as a regressive and hence pathological experience, whether or not religiously interpreted (Hood, 1976a). James (1985) set the early exception by noting the normalcy of mysticism and its orthogonality to pathology. Mystics could be pathological as could anyone else, but mysticism was not itself pathological.

Following James's lead, the reemergence of the empirical psychology of religion in the 1960s has considered the factors contributing to the report of mystical experience, independent of psychopathology. Laski (1961) set the pattern by considering what she referred to as "triggers" of mystical experience. Her term *trigger* refers to conditions that release or permit mystical experience to occur, not to conditions deemed sufficient causes (Laski, 1961, p. 16). In this vein Laski is following the lead of James, who argued that passivity was a likely criterion of mysticism and that, despite efforts of attention to produce a mystic state, the actual phenomenology of mysticism includes an experience of control by a power other than one's self (James, 1985, pp. 302–303). Similar arguments have been made with respect to the paradox of mystical states in Zen, where the very effort to produce such states interferes with their attainment (Elwood, 1980). Nevertheless, intentional efforts to produce mystical experience are common both within and outside of faith traditions insofar as set and setting characteristics have been devised to facilitate such experiences. Ironically, such conditions will also help explain spontaneous mystical experiences, as we shall soon note. We will review the relevant literature insofar as assessments of mysticism have employed empirical measures congruent with the phenomenology of mysticism already noted.

Physiological Triggers

Probably the most massive literature surrounding the triggering of mystical states centers on alterations of physiology that facilitate such states. Such alterations can be as simple as dancing with the "swirling dervishes" of Sufi fame, or complex combinations of fasting, filtered light through stained glass windows, and the burning of incense within the various Judeo-Christian and Eastern meditative traditions, or the focusing of attention on sacred symbols in a hypnotic fashion common to almost all faith traditions. However, perhaps none of these stimulate as much controversy as the use of substances such as alcohol, mushrooms, tobacco, or synthesized chemicals used to trigger what are called either altered (Tart, 1969) or alternate (Zinberg, 1977) states of consciousness. This literature is immense and most relevant to issues regarding religious experience in general (Spilka et al., 1985; Wulff, 1991). However, specific studies concerning self-loss in mysticism are relatively few, despite their obvious importance.

Psychedelic Drugs   The classic study is a doctoral dissertation by Pahnke (1963, 1966) in which Stace's phenomenologically derived criteria were used to assess the outcome of 30 milligrams of psilocybin given to 10 experimental participants 90 minutes before hearing a Good Friday service composed of scriptural readings, music, and meditation conducted at Boston University's Marsh Chapel. Ten control participants received a placebo (200 milligrams of nicotinic acid) that would produce only minimal effects. In addition, all participants were further divided in groups of 4 with two team leaders knowledgeable about psychedelic drugs, only one of which had either the experimental or placebo drug. The experiment was double-blind. Within a week after the experiment all subjects completed a questionnaire, including responses to all of Stace's criteria for mysticism. For our purposes it is worthy to note that the experimental group significantly differed from the control on both introvertive and extrovertive mysticism. Sixty-two and 70 percent of the experimental group and only 7 and 8 percent of the control group, respectively, received the maximum possible scores on introvertive and extrovertive mysticism respectively.

This widely discussed and critiqued experiment (see Clark, 1969; Dittes, 1969; Wulff, 1991, pp. 184–188) must be understood in the general context of studies with psychedelic drugs in which reports of specifically mystical experiences are relatively rare (Masters & Houston, 1966; Spilka et al., 1985). However, it is clear that with proper set and setting physiological alteration of the body of various sorts can trigger mystical states. However, Hood (1977a) has shown that among persons reporting mystical experiences, only those outside mainstream American faith traditions are likely to have their experiences triggered by deviant triggers such as drugs. Greeley (1975) refused to include asking about drugs as triggers in his national survey precisely because of their deviant status. Identical experiences will be differentially evaluated according to whether or not they are perceived to be drug-triggered (Hood, 1980).

Precisely why specific physiology conditions facilitate mystical experiences is an immense area of controversial yet needed research. James recognized this, quoting extensively from the work of Blood and others involved in philosophical and psychological considerations of the "anesthetic revolution," and citing his own experience and evaluation of both alcohol and nitrous oxide. With respect to the former he stated: "The sway of alcohol over mankind is unquestionably due to its power to stimulate the mystical faculties of human nature. . . . Sobriety diminishes, discriminates and says no; drunkenness, expands, unites, and says yes" (James, 1985, p. 307). It is likely that such affirmations are more compatible with extrovertive than introvertive mysticism since the unity is most typically content-oriented.

Eroticism

Among the diverse triggers of mysticism, sexuality is as controversial a research area as psychedelic drugs. Yet no major faith tradition is without its erotic literature, and even a causal perusal of the mystical literature within secular or faith traditions reveals numerous sexual and erotic descriptions of mystical experience. Hood and Hall (1980) have reviewed this literature and categorized the dominant arguments linking erotic and mystical experiences into metaphorical, analogical, and identity views. They demonstrated that for females both sexual and mystical experiences tended to be congruently described with passive or communal adjectives. Likewise, Mallory (1977) has shown by sensitive questioning of Discalced Carmelite nuns that physiological experiences of sexual arousal are common during prayers eliciting mystical experiences. Similarly, Laski (1968, p. 145) notes that sexual love was a common trigger of mystical experience among her highly select sample, a finding consistent with Hood's (1977a) finding that sexual experience was reported as a trigger of mystical experiences among self-actualized persons outside of mainline faith traditions. Greeley's (1975) study also indicated sexual love to be a common trigger of mystical states. Descriptions of sexual union and the body are fundamental to discussions of what Brown (1959, p. 310) refers to as "Dionysian" or "bodily mysticisms." Deleuze and Guattari (1983, p. 5) succinctly capture the flavor of body mysticism in quoting from Miller's *Tropic of Cancer* "and my guts spilled out in grand schizophrenic rush, an evacuation that leaves me face to face with the Absolute." These serve as correctives to views of mysticism in which self-loss is interpreted outside the context of the body. Although such body mysticisms are beyond the scope of this chapter, the triggering of self-loss by sexuality is a common, if poorly researched, topic.

Sensory Isolation

It is a common occurrence in faith traditions to seek solitude and by so doing to attempt to trigger a wide variety of religious experiences. Whether the vision quest of Native Americans, the early isolationism of the desert fathers, or the structured contemplative tradition of Roman Catholicism, solitude has long been seen as a path in which the self finds its true nature. Typically, such experiences are full of imagery, and only insofar as such images are unified can we speak of an extrovertive mysticism. However, as with psychedelic drugs, spontaneous occurrences of truly mystical experiences, either extrovertive or introvertive, are rare in isolation studies. The classic example is in "sensory deprivation" in which the effects of minimal sensory input were investigated (Schultz, 1965). More recently, Lilly (1956, 1977) has perfected the isolation tank as a device to facilitate various modes of alternative awareness. In two studies specifically using isolation tanks to elicit religious imagery it was found that religious imagery could be facilitated by proper set conditions and that, regardless of set conditions, intrinsically oriented subjects reported some religious imagery, although it is not clear that such images are unified in an extrovertive mysticism (Hood & Morris, 1981b). However, under appropriate suggestions of contemplative prayer within isolation tanks, intrinsic persons report unity experiences of an introvertive type (Hood, Morris, & Watson, 1990). This suggests that sensory isolation and an intense "turning within" are a trigger of mysticism, particularly introvertive. These findings are congruent with studies documenting solitary introspection (either prayer or meditation) as a frequent trigger of mystical experiences (Goleman, 1977; Hood, 1977a; Hood, Morris, & Watson, 1989). Interestingly, it also has been shown that introspective techniques are equally facilitative as triggers for mystical states for persons within and outside mainline faith traditions. The distinction between such groups is in the interpretation given to such states, not in the introspective processes that trigger them (Hood, 1976a). Also, it is worth noting that focused introspective techniques, whether meditation or prayer, shade into hypnotic phenomena known to correlate with measures of mystical experience (Hood, 1973).

Set and Setting Incongruities

We shall end triggers of mystical experience with the well-documented fact that mysticism, especially extrovertive mysticism, is frequently triggered by experiences in nature (Laski, 1968). Furthermore, many isolation experiences occur in nature, such as during expeditions in which parties are stranded. Reports of alternate states of consciousness are common under such conditions, as are (less frequently) mystical experiences. Indeed, one classification of types of mysticism is "nature mysticism," where one's self is seen as totalized within the nature context, often suddenly and spontaneously and often in what are perceived as stressful conditions. Rosegrant (1976) noted that nonstressful nature experiences were triggers of mystical experiences, as measured by his modification of the REEM discussed above. More recently, in two closely related quasi-experimental studies, Hood (1977b, 1978) has suggested that it is not the absence or presence of stress in nature settings per se that triggers mysticism but rather their incongruity. In particular, Hood suggested that when either personal anticipatory stress or the actual nature setting stress is incongruent, mystical experiences can be triggered. Adolescent males placed within both stressful and nonstressful nature settings indicated mystical experiences only if they stressfully anticipated what turned out to be a nonstressful nature event or found themselves in a stressful nature setting they had anticipated to be nonstressful. Such stress set/setting incongruity has been interpreted as permitting the sudden recognition of transcending limits or a reversal of figure and ground effect such that mystical experience occurs, and may also be the process operating in enlightenment with the Zen tradition (Elwood, 1980). This incongruity hypothesis is compatible with other general explanations of the effect of mystical triggers, such as Deikman's (1966) hypothesis of deautomization, in which sudden awareness of atypical perceptions of reality and self are possible once routine processing of information is transcended, for whatever reason. It further suggests that any disruptions in expectations can suddenly force into awareness alternatives, one of which is a broader self than the one normative in the context before the disruption. What processes might operate in such sudden transformation is an open empirical question.

CONCLUSION

We have fairly exhaustively covered at least the range of studies congruent with James's and Stace's phenomenology of mystical experience. That such experiences of self-loss occur is without doubt a simple empirical fact. That they are almost typical is also well documented, leading Scharfstein (1973) to make reference to "everyday mysticism." Furthermore, measurement studies have proven useful in relating mysticism to a wide variety of triggering conditions. However, the explanation and theoretical excursion into mysticism must be in terms of the phenomenology of consciousness that it entails. Returning to James's resolution of the debate between Hume and Kant, we can note that his initial disagreement with Kant's resolution to Hume's skepticism is in the empirical realm of phenomenologically revealed facts. Kant's transcendental unity of apperception seemed a rather hollow solution to Hume's misguided empiricism. Yet, as we confront mystical states of self-loss, the empirical facts are expanded. Now the self is itself seen as but part of a whole, another self it had not known before. This new unity is authoritative for those who experience it, and for others but a curious claim, akin to that of color to the blind. Still, as James (1985, p. 338) noted, "The existence of mystical states absolutely overthrows the pretension of non-mystical states to be the sole and ultimate dictators of what we may believe." If psychology is to develop empirically, the phenomenological investigation of mysticism must be taken into account (Staal, 1975). Thus, what some might perceive as methodological limitations of studies based upon self-report must be tempered with the possibility that, insofar as states of awareness are concerned, methodologies based upon self-report are essential. Careful reading of the studies reviewed above will reveal that self-reports are neither uncritically accepted nor immune from criticism. Still, as in more phenomenologically rooted investigations, the wide variety of methodologies employed in the study of mysticism at some point must link with self-report. Here the issues of self psychology interact with philosophical and faith traditions based upon a common empiricism rooted in the phenomenology of self-loss. If the religious aroma of self psychology emerges once again in the study of mysticism, perhaps this time it will lead to mutual enrichment (Hood, 1989b). As James noted, the empirical facts may require more. Perhaps mystical states point to, if not define, what that more is.

REFERENCES

Back, K. W., & Bourque, L. B. (1970). Can feelings be enumerated? *Behavioral Science, 15:*487–496.

Blose, B. L. (1981). Materialism and disembodied minds. *Philosophy and Phenomenological Research, 42:*59–74.

Bourque, L. B., & Back, K. W. (1968). Values and transcendental experiences. *Social Forces, 47:*34–48.

———. (1969). Social correlates of transcendental experiences. *Sociological Analysis, 30:*151–163.

———. (1974). Language, society, and subjective experience. *Sociometry, 34:*1–21.

Brown, N. O. (1959). *Life against death.* Middletown, CT: Wesleyan University Press.

Caird, D. (1988). The structure of Hood's mysticism scale: A factor analytic study. *Journal for the Scientific Study of Religion, 27:*122–126.

Clark, W. H. (1969). *Chemical ecstasy: Psychedelic drugs and religion.* New York: Sheed Ward.

Deikman, A. J. (1966). De-automatization and the mystic experience. *Psychiatry, 29:*329–343.

Deleuze, G., & Guattari, F. (1983). *Anti-Oedipus.* Minneapolis: University of Minnesota Press.

de Silva, L. A. (1979). *The problem of self in Buddhism and Christianity.* New York: Barnes & Noble.

Dittes, J. E. (1969). Psychology of religion. In *The handbook of social psychology,* edited by G. Lindzey & E. Aronson (vol. 5, 2nd ed., pp. 602–659). Reading, MA: Addison-Wesley.

Donahue, M. J. (1985). Intrinsic and extrinsic religiousness: Review and meta-analysis. *Journal for the Scientific Study of Religion, 48:*400–419.

Earle, W. (1980). *Mystical reason.* Chicago: Regnery Gateway.

Edie, J. M. (1987). *William James and phenomenology.* Bloomington: Indiana University Press.

Elwood, R. S., Jr. (1980). *Mysticism and religion.* Englewood Cliff, NJ: Prentice-Hall.

Fontinell, E. (1986). *Self, God, and immortality: A Jamesian investigation.* Philadelphia: Temple University Press.

Freud, S. (1961a). *Civilization and its discontents,* translated by J. Strachey. New York: Norton.

_____. (1961b). *The future of an illusion,* translated by J. Strachey. New York: Norton.

Goleman, D. (1977). *The varieties of meditative experience.* New York: Dutton.

Gorsuch, R. L. (1988). Psychology of religion. *Annual Review of Psychology, 39*:201–221.

Greeley, A. (1974). *Ecstasy: A way of knowing.* Englewood Cliffs, NJ: Prentice-Hall.

_____. (1975). *The sociology of the paranormal: A reconnaissance.* Beverly Hills, CA: Sage.

Grunbaum, A. (1985). *The foundations of psychoanalysis.* Berkeley: University of California Press.

Hardy, A. (1979). *The spiritual nature of man.* Oxford: Clarendon Press.

Hay, D., & Morisy, A. (1978). Reports of ecstatic, paranormal, or religious experience in Great Britain and the United States: A comparison of trends. *Journal for the Scientific Study of Religion, 17*:255–268.

Holm, N. G. (1982). Mysticism and intense experiences. *Journal for the Scientific Study of Religion, 21*:260–276.

Hood, R. W., Jr. (1970). Religious orientation and the report of religious experience. *Journal for the Scientific Study of Religion, 9*:285–291.

_____. (1972). Normative and motivational determinants of reported religious experience in two Baptist samples. *Review of Religious Research, 13*:92–196.

_____. (1973). Hypnotic susceptibility and reported religious experience. *Psychological Reports, 33*:549–550.

_____. (1975). The construction and preliminary validation of a measure of reported mystical experience. *Journal for the Scientific Study of Religion, 14*:29–41.

_____. (1976a). Conceptual criticisms of regressive explanations of mysticism. *Review of Religious Research, 17*:179–188.

_____. (1976b). Mystical experience as related to present and anticipated patterns of future church participation. *Psychological Reports, 39*:1127–1136.

_____. (1977a). Differential triggering of mystical experience as a function of self actualization. *Review of Religious Research, 18*:264–270.

———. (1977b). Eliciting mystical states of consciousness with semistructured nature experience. *Journal for the Scientific Study of Religion,* 16:155–163.

———. (1978). Anticipatory set and setting: Stress incongruities as elicitors of mystical experience in solitary nature situations. *Journal for the Scientific Study of Religion,* 17:279–287.

———. (1980). Social legitimacy, dogmatism, and the evaluation of intense experiences. *Review of Religious Research,* 21:184–194.

———. (1985). Mysticism. In *The Sacred in a Secular Age,* edited by P. Hammond (pp. 285–297). Berkeley: University of California Press.

———. (1989a). Mysticism, the unity thesis, and the paranormal. In *Exploring the paranormal,* edited by G. K. Zollschan, J. F. Schumaker, & G. F. Walsh (pp. 117–130). Great Britain: Prism Press.

———. (1989b). The relevance of theologies for religious experiencing. *Journal of Psychology and Theology,* 17:336–342.

———. (1992). Mysticism, reality, illusion, and the Freudian critique of religion. *The International Journal for the Psychology of Religion,* 2:141–159.

———. (In press). A Jamesean look at self and self loss in mysticism. *Journal of the Psychology of Religion.*

Hood, R. W., Jr., & Hall, J. R. (1977). Comparison of reported religious experience in Caucasian, American Indian, and Mexican American samples. *Psychological Reports,* 41:657–658.

———. (1980). Gender differences in the description of erotic and mystical experience. *Review of Religious Research,* 21:195–207.

Hood, R. W., Jr., & Morris, R. J. (1981a). Knowledge and experience criteria in the report of mystical experience. *Review of Religious Research,* 23:76–84.

———. (1981b). Sensory isolation and the differential elicitation of religious imagery in intrinsic and extrinsic persons. *Journal for the Scientific Study of Religion,* 20:261–273.

———. (1983). Toward a theory of death transcendence. *Journal for the Scientific Study of Religion,* 22:353–365.

Hood, R. W., Jr., Morris, R., & Watson, P. J. (1989). The differential report of prayer experience and religious orientation. *Review of Religious Research,* 31:39–45.

———. (1990). Quasi-experimental elicitation of the differential report of religious experience among intrinsic and indiscriminately pro-religious types. *Journal for the Scientific Study of Religion,* 29:164–172.

Hume, D. (1959). *A treatise on human nature* (vol. 1). New York: E. P. Dutton.

Huxley, A. (1944). *The perennial philosophy.* New York: Harper & Row.

James, W. (1968a). The knowing of things together. Presidential address, American Psychological Association, Princeton, December, 1894. In *The writings of William James,* edited by J. J. McDermott (pp. 152–168). New York: Modern Library.

_____. (1968b). A world of pure experience. In *The writings of William James,* edited by J. J. McDermott (pp. 194–214). New York: Modern Library.

_____. (1981). *The works of William James: The principles of psychology* (vol. 1), edited by F. H. Burkhardt. Cambridge: Harvard University Press.

_____. (1985). *The works of William James: The varieties of religious experience,* edited by F. H. Buckhardt. Cambridge: Harvard University Press.

Johannson, R.E.A. (1970). *The psychology of nirvana.* New York: Anchor.

Kant, I. (1964). *Critique of pure reason,* translated by J.M.D. Meiklejohn. New York: E. P. Dutton.

Katz, S. T. (Ed.) (1978). *Mysticism and philosophical analysis.* New York: Oxford University Press.

_____. (1983). *Mysticism and religious traditions.* New York: Oxford University Press.

Kirpatrick, L. A., & Hood, R. W., Jr. (1990). Intrinsic-extrinsic religious orientation: The boon or bane of contemporary psychology of religion. *Journal for the Scientific Study of Religion, 29:*442–462.

Kung, H. (1980). *Does God exist?* New York: Doubleday.

Laski, M. (1961). *Ecstasy.* New York: Greenwood.

Leuba, J. H. (1925). *The psychology of religious mysticism.* New York: Harcourt Brace.

Levinson, H. S. (1981). *The religious investigations of James.* Chapel Hill: University of North Carolina Press.

Lilly, J. C. (1956). Mental effects of reduction of ordinary levels of physical stimuli on intact healthy persons. *Psychiatric Research Reports, 5:*1–9.

_____. (1977). *The deep self.* New York: Warner.

Mallory, M. M. (1977). *Christian mysticism transcending techniques.* Amsterdam, Holland: Van Gorcum Assen.

Marx, K. (1975). Contribution to the critique of Hegel's philosophy of law. In *Marx and Engles on religion.* Moscow: Progress Publishers.

Masters, R.E.L., & Houston, J. (1966). *The varieties of psychedelic experience.* New York: Holt, Rinehart & Winston.

Morris, R. J., & Hood, R. W., Jr. (1980). Religious and unity criteria of Baptists and Nones in the report of mystical experience. *Psychological Reports, 46:*728–730.

Pahnke, W. N. (1963). Drugs and mysticism: An analysis of the relationship between psychedelic drugs and mystical experience. Unpublished doctoral dissertation, Harvard University.

———. (1966). Drugs and mysticism. *International Journal of Parapsychology, 8:295–314.*

Proudfoot, W. (1985). *Religious experience.* Berkeley: University of California Press.

Roberts, B. (1984). *The experience of no-self.* Boulder, CO: Shambahla.

Robinson, D. (1981). *An intellectual history of psychology* (rev. ed.). New York: Macmillan.

Rosegrant, J. (1976). The impact of set and setting on religious experience in nature. *Journal for the Scientific Study of Religion, 15:301–310.*

Russell, B. (1957). *Why I am not a Christian.* New York: Simon & Schuster.

Scharfstein, B. (1973). *Mystical experience.* Indianapolis, IN: Bobbs-Merrill.

Schultz, D. P. (1965). *Sensory restriction.* New York: Academic Press.

Spilka, B., Hood, R. W., Jr., & Gorsuch, R. (1985). *The psychology of religion: An empirical approach.* Englewood Cliffs, NJ: Prentice-Hall.

Staal, F. (1975). *Exploring mysticism.* Berkeley: University of California Press.

Stace, W. (1960). *Mysticism and philosophy.* Philadelphia: Lippincott.

Tart, C. T. (Ed.). (1969). *Altered states of consciousness.* New York: John Wiley.

Thomas, L. E., & Cooper, P. E. (1978). Measurement and incidence of mystical experience: An exploratory study. *Journal for the Scientific Study of Religion, 17:433–437.*

Wilshire, B. (1968). *William James and phenomenology: A study of "The Principles of Psychology."* Bloomington: Indiana University Press.

Wittgenstein, L. (1961). *Tractatus logico-philosophicus,* translated by D. F. Pears & B. F. McGuinnes. New York: Routledge & Kegan Paul.

Wulff, D. M. (1991). *Psychology of religion: Classic and contemporary views.* New York: John Wiley.

Wuthnow, R. (1978). *Experimentation in American religion.* Berkeley, CA: University of California Press.

Zaehner, R. C. (1957). *Mysticism, sacred and profane.* London: Oxford University Press.

Zinberg, N. (Ed.). (1977). *Alternate states of consciousness.* New York: Free Press.

CHAPTER 11

Minority Identity and Self-Concept: The American Indian Experience

John M. Dodd
J. Ron Nelson
Bonnie Henderson Hofland

Ethnic affiliation has a profound impact on the experiences and opportunities proffered by society. Those experiences and opportunities surely affect self-concept in a myriad of ways. For example, persons who look and act like the majority are afforded all the rights, privileges, and benefits of education, whereas nonmajority persons, even with appropriate education, may face job ceilings and other barriers that impede full participation and achievement (Fordham & Ogbu, 1986). When this lack of opportunity is recognized, aspiration and enthusiasm for education are diminished. It is only reasonable to assume that these experiences and expectations have an effect on both academic and nonacademic self-concept.

The basis for federal Indian policy was a policy of assimilation designed to make American Indian persons indistinguishable from

F. M. Dodd, a non-Indian person who took the time to learn the Iowa language, demonstrated interest in and respect for American Indian people, and shared countless tales about Indian people with a son is acknowledged for providing the genesis for interest which took years to develop. Nellie L. Hamilton Eby, Assiniboine; Will Henderson and Faron L. Running Crane, Blackfeet; Lance C. Hogan and William Spint, Crow; and Richard Murphy, Iowa, are acknowledged for their help and suggestions.

other Americans (Harmon, 1990). Even today some American Indian religious practices are still considered illegal (Plummer, 1992). Despite efforts to assimilate American Indian people and some immigrant groups, the United States did not become a melting pot for these people. Persons from different identifiable ethnic groups have not become majority culture look-alikes, nor do they act the same or feel alike. One interesting contradiction is that some of these immigrant groups have been encouraged to keep intact their ethnic identity and feelings and beliefs about themselves even after generations of life in the United States. The Saint Patrick's Day celebrations so evident in many cities in the United States are certainly evidence of retention of ethnic identity and pride.

Forecasts of future population trends suggest even greater ethnic diversity in the future. One-third of public school students will be members of minority groups by 1995, and those "minority students" will be the majority in public schools in four states ("Forecast . . . ," 1991). Indeed, thirty-three states already have kindergarten through high school enrollments of 20 percent or more minority students, and minority enrollment has increased in forty-four states in the last five years. All twenty-five of our nation's largest city school systems have "majority minorities" (Sleeter, 1991). Such diversity makes it necessary to understand the effects of minority group and ethnic affiliation experiences on self-concept development.

Clearly not all minority groups experience life in the United States in the same ways, and not all ethnic groups are treated the same. Most recent Eurocentric ethnic groups cannot be recognized on sight as members of minority groups. As groups, they also came to the United States voluntarily. In essence, they initially chose their minority status, and their future generations need not be viewed as members of a minority group.

The experience is different, although voluntary, for minority groups such as Hispanic immigrants from Cuba or Mexico and Indians from India. Their dark skin, and of course their language, frequently make them readily identifiable. Yet they chose to come to this country and become minority group members. The rewards of this choice seem to outweigh the disadvantages brought by minority status. Ogbu (1988) characterizes these groups as having primary cultural differences. Such immigrants see the cultural and language differences as barriers to be overcome to achieve their goals.

There are other minority groups who were brought into what is commonly known as "the American society" involuntarily through slavery or conquest. Ogbu (1988) describes their differences as secondary cultural differences which arise after members of one population have begun to participate in institutions controlled by members of another population. Involuntary minorities do not interpret their experiences as a longed-for opportunity.

Many black Americans whose ancestors were forced to come to the United States as slaves have had their status and appearance viewed as inferior from the time they came to this country. Most black people were segregated in ghettos leading to segregated schools, which were generally accepted throughout the nation less than a half-century ago. Economic disparity continues to foster de facto segregation in spite of legal gains prohibiting discrimination. Black people were clearly relegated to menial positions and experienced discrimination from the moment of their arrival in the United States.

The involuntary minority experience of American Indian peoples, whose ancestors were the first inhabitants of the Americas, is still different. They were free people whose homeland was encroached on by ever-increasing numbers of uninvited persons of ethnic, cultural, and linguistic origins different from their own. Like black people they were segregated, but they attempted to reserve for themselves comparatively small tracts of land called "reservations." These reservations tended to become diminished in size as disease, starvation, or other adversities forced American Indian people to sell additional land.

American Indian people wanted to remain in their own nations and live among persons who shared the same cultural and linguistic heritage and values. Additionally, American Indians were not one people, but many tribes who wanted to remain free and separate within their own Indian nations.

Ancestors of the persons called "American Indian" people inhabited the land now known as the United States, although they did not own it or have legal title to it in the same way European invaders had owned land. Owning the land was unimaginable, just as owning the sun might be unimaginable to us today (Lipinski, 1989). The land was used by all of its inhabitants—human and animal alike—and they were inextricably bound together with the land, which provided for their needs. Fedullo (1992) explains that the people and the people's land are inseparable. He quotes a Navajo young man as saying, "Us Navajos are just an extension of the land; we are a form of it" (Fedullo, 1992, p. 154). He then explains that for Navajos, when sheep and horses are added, there is "a perfect harmony of earth, animal and human" and adds a modern element—the pick-up truck—which is a present-day essential on many reservations. In a discussion of native religions, Hultkrantz (1987, p. 24) says, "They care about the trees, because they give evidence of the supernatural; they care about the animals, because they may represent spirits; they care about the vast lands because they may reveal God." Theirs was a communal existence, and nature and natural events kept all in harmony. To destroy that balance and harmony was to invite disaster.

American Indian people had clear expectations for appropriate behavior. There was an educational system with clear expectations, which was maintained by elders who were respected and had responsibility for communicating values and expectations. They told tales about what people had done and what were the outcomes of such behavior. The elders defended the value of family through deeds and not simply by words or thought (Red Horse, 1980). Deeds elicited approval, and that approval enhanced the way American Indian youth felt about themselves as demonstrated by their accomplishments. For example, the Crow parents and grandparents followed a principle of readiness just as teachers of beginning reading are taught to do, watching for clues that revealed interest, and then they provided the appropriate materials and relaxed supervision (Voget, 1984).

Coopersmith (1981) says that self-images are based largely on the way an individual is treated by significant people, including parents, teachers, and peers. A clear system for valuing appropriate deeds was in place for American Indian peoples. That system was destroyed when youngsters were taken unwillingly to boarding schools without elders to model and reinforce appropriate deeds. Coopersmith (1981) indicates that domination, rejection, and severe punishment result in low self-esteem. That was the experience given to young Indian children who experienced shame by having their hair cut and their clothing destroyed and replaced by inappropriate and strange clothing. They were punished for speaking their own language, maintaining their religious beliefs, or in any way engaging in activities their elders had taught them were appropriate. That is certainly clear evidence of rejection and domination.

PRESENT-DAY AMERICAN INDIAN PEOPLE

Persons who had been forcibly taken to boarding schools and punished for being Indian were to become the parents and grandparents of the modern-day child. As one might expect, numerous effects of those experiences remain.

Examination of the present experience of the first Americans reveals the results of the loss of a way of life and some loss of identity. They are unlikely to refer to themselves as Native Americans or American Indians unless they are referring collectively to groups of Indian peoples because their identity comes from their tribal affiliation, and differences between various Indian nations are enormous (Bryan, 1985). Contrary to popular stereotype, most do not live on reservations, although the reservations are a source of identity for the majority and home to many.

First Americans, once thought to be a vanishing race, increased by more than one million persons between 1950 and 1980 (Bureau of the Census, 1988). However, they have not fared well educationally. Their school dropout rate is greatest of all ethnic groups. It was reported that 56 percent of American Indian people aged 25 and over had completed four years or more of high school, compared with 67 percent in the total population (Hillabrant, Romano, & Stang, 1992). Of those who go to college, 65 percent leave without a degree (Chavers, 1991).

American Indian people are numerically the smallest minority group in the United States, representing only 0.8 percent of the nation's population (*Chronicle of Higher Education Almanac*, 1992). However, in 1987 American Indian persons were awarded only 0.4 percent of the total number of bachelor's degrees and not quite 0.3 percent of the total number of doctoral degrees in the United States (American Council on Education, 1989).

Although American Indian people are frequently referred to as one group, they are really many distinct tribes, bands, and nations with separate language, philosophies, worldviews, values, and beliefs. Indeed, it has been pointed out that they include at least four hundred distinctly identifiable ethnicities lumped into a catch-all term of *Native American* or *American Indian* (Churchill, 1985). Approximately five hundred Indian tribes and bands were identified in the 1980 census (Bureau of the Census, 1988). Explaining that there is no one generic American Indian and that Indian groups vary culturally, linguistically, and technologically, Medicine (1985) points out that the common theme shared by all American Indian cultures is postcontact decimation, destruction of native life-styles and languages, and subordination of aboriginal people. Presently American Indian persons range from those persons who have retained their language and traditional values to persons who have been assimilated (Bearcrane, Dodd, Nelson, & Ostwald, 1990). Fedullo (1992) indicates that there are no reservation Indian people who are totally acculturated into the mainstream and none who are totally traditional, with all Indian people falling somewhere between the two extremes. Whereas some have become bicultural persons who are able to function in either culture, others are marginal persons who exemplify neither their own tribal cultures nor the majority culture. Undoubtedly self-concept and self-esteem vary along the continuum from assimilation, to maintenance of language and customs and values, to the development of biculturalism.

The American Indian population is young, with the largest number ranging between 25 and 29 years of age (Bureau of the Census, 1990), compared with the median age of the general population of 32.9 (Bureau of the Census, 1990). Attesting to large families, children under 5 years of age make up 7 percent of the general population, and children under 5 years of age among American Indian or Aleut make up 11 percent of their total population. They do not live as long as other Americans. Only approximately 6 percent of American Indians were 65 years or older in 1990, compared with 12.6 percent of the total population.

Descriptions of American Indian children are difficult to obtain. Indeed, it has been pointed out that the most prominent feature about information on the American Indian student in contemporary culture is the lack of information (Lipinski, 1989), and there is virtually no research on American Indian women (Medicine, 1988). Information about nonreservation American Indian children is almost nonexistent, but they are more heterogeneous than children who share traditions, ethnic affiliation, and language on reservations.

The reservation American Indian child has good chances of having unemployed parents, since unemployment recently has averaged approximately 35 percent on reservations (Bureau of the Census, 1988). Similarly, the American Indian child has good chances of living in poverty as measured by present standards, since 28 percent of the total Indian population lived in poverty in 1979 compared with about 12 percent in the general population (Bureau of the Census, 1988). Frequently there is a lack of jobs for American Indian people on reservations, and many of the jobs that are available provide employment for women. The men who retain a traditional warrior image may be devastated when women must provide the financial support for the family. This situation may lead to problems within families, and it clearly affects the way persons view themselves. On the other hand, decisions to leave reservations may lead American Indian people to real poverty—depriving them of the support of the extended family and their own cultural heritage. However, sharing is inherent in American Indian value systems, and traditionally Indian people have considered themselves in poverty only if they have had nothing left they could give to others (Lipinski, 1989).

The reader is reminded that there is a great deal of heterogeneity among Indian peoples and differences between tribal groupings. Most American Indian people identify themselves by tribal affiliation rather than by the collective designation of *American Indian* or *Native American people*. For example, Fedullo (1992) describes asking a young Navajo man to imagine he was something he was not. The young man said he would pretend he was an Indian. Similarly, when a professor whispered to a Crow college senior that a telephone call was from our nation's capital, Washington, D.C., the student responded without hesitation that his nation's capital is Crow Agency. However, information about American Indian persons will be briefly summarized because self-concept is derived from the way one experiences the world, and many non-Indian persons react to American Indian people without regard to their tribal affiliation.

LANGUAGE

Some American Indian persons speak excellent standard English, but many do not. The reasons for language differences are many and varied. When the federal policy was assimilation, young Indian children were often taken to boarding schools, where there was an attempt to force them to become like the white majority. They were punished for all evidence of maintaining their own Indian ways. Indeed, they were taught by word and deed that being Indian was despicable, which had negative effects on self-concepts.

They were forbidden to speak their own language, even being punished for doing so. Although the aim was to produce standard English speakers, the evidence today suggests that the procedure was not efficient. It has been pointed out that sufficient development of a first language before introducing the second language can facilitate learning a second language (Cummins, 1979). In contrast, suppressing a first language while being submerged in a new one may contribute to the development of inadequate language skills. Persons who have a first language other than English can profit from bilingual programs. However, many American Indian persons have not been provided such programs.

Parents whose first language was their traditional tribal language taught their children only English. However, since they were teaching their weaker language, the children often developed smaller vocabularies than those who learned English from persons for whom it was the dominant language. Still other youngsters learned English from adults who were members of different tribes that spoke a different tribal language. Therefore, they were forced to communicate in a common but less developed language, English.

Additionally, many reservations are isolated, and language usage has been developed which serves to communicate on the reservation without difficulty. This isolation and the use of Indian words, phrases, word order, or just innovation create what is known as "reservation English," which is not the standard English used in schools.

One anonymous college student who is an inhabitant of the Crow nation described his language as follows:

> While I do not speak the Crow language one could not say that I had been an English speaker either. My language was based upon the English language, but was more of a language that had been learned by Indians and so had an Indian flavor to it. My language was "Indian English." Indian English was my fault. I live on the Crow Reservation and have grandparents who

speak the Crow language, but I chose to ignore my own language and speak a foreign language.

COMMUNITY

Traditionally American Indian persons have been judged by their group contribution rather than their individual contributions (Hynd & Garcia, 1979; Flores, 1985–86; Little Soldier, 1989). These group values, which differ from the early competitiveness instilled in children within the majority culture, obviously contribute to a different source of self-esteem. It has been pointed out that even the idea of personal property may be foreign to Indian children because the family is accustomed to sharing whatever they have (Little Soldier, 1989). Thus competitive curricula and grading systems which encourage achievement among white middle-class schoolchildren may be counterproductive with American Indian children, who would be far more comfortable with cooperative and group learning activities.

TIME

Life in the United States is dominated by the clock. The clock tells us when to turn on the television set, when to go to the airport, when to leave for work, and how many minutes to play at recess or how many minutes to use for the coffee break at work, as well as when we should stop all of those activities. Traditionally, American Indian people viewed time as a continuum with no real beginning or end (Little Soldier, 1989). Thus, for American Indian children it may be surprising to learn that there is a set time to begin or end activities. As one might expect, it has been reported that both American Indian reservation elementary schoolchildren (Burd, Dodd, & Grassl, 1981) and adolescents (Anderson, Burd, Dodd, & Keller, 1980) did not estimate how much time tasks would require for completion as efficiently as their non-Indian counterparts. Admirably, American Indian people might view stopping and talking with a friend as more important than keeping an appointment (Morgan, Guy, & Cellini, 1986). However, those differences in attitude toward time have been viewed in an ethnocentric manner by persons in the majority society, resulting in the somewhat disparaging term *Indian time*. It has also been responsible for failure experiences in school when tasks are not completed by teachers' deadlines. Clearly the use of time affects the way one feels about self.

ATTRIBUTION

When persons are placed in situations in which they have no control over the outcome of events, they may develop "learned helplessness" (Seligman, 1975). Since many American Indian persons live in conditions over which they have no control, it is not surprising that American Indian people develop learned helplessness, which may be masked as complacency (Dodd, Ostwald, & Rose, 1991). From cradle to grave the American Indian people are addressed, guided, and molded according to others' values. The Bureau of Indian Affairs has a Trust Responsibility to provide housing, schools, and hospitals, all of which have been used to manage and control American Indian people. They often live on reservations where no jobs are available. Despite their efforts to obtain employment, they are unable to get a job. Clearly this experience leads to feelings of helplessness. They can also expect to experience prejudice not elicited by their own behavior. Stereotypes about American Indian people abound (Stedman, 1982).

American Indian persons have been reported to attribute failure to a lack of ability (Powers & Rossman, 1983). In one comparative study of ethnic differences in locus of control, it was reported that American Indian persons were more externally controlled than Hispanics or whites (Graves, 1967). These findings stand to reason: American Indian people have been able to exert very little control over their own destiny since their land has been occupied by non-Indian persons.

SCHOOLS

Eurocentric schools, an equalizer for middle-class white children, may enable children from the majority culture to overcome even the effects of poverty or parental lack of education; however, they are experienced differently by children of involuntary minority status. Tales of Abraham Lincoln's rise to the presidency from his rail-splitting days simply do not inspire American Indian children to want to learn what is taught in schools. The books read in schools are infrequently about American Indian people and their success. All too frequently the teachers are white persons who do not dress like the children's parents, do not look like their family members, and do not speak like family members. The research base, if any, for the methods and procedures the teachers employ is almost sure to have been obtained from non-Indian data.

Hall (1976) proposes a paradigm for comparing cultures, suggesting that cultures vary along a continuum in the degree to which their communicative messages are contextualized. High-context cultures do not require a great deal of verbalization to communicate messages, whereas low-context cultures require a great deal of verbalization. According to Westby and Rouse (1985), mainstream culture is toward the lower end of the continuum, whereas American Indian children are more likely to come from a high-context culture. However, most of the language of the school reflects a low-context culture, and facts are obtained apart from context. Thus the meaning must be obtained from words alone. Children who are used to a highly contextualized system of communication fail to gather sufficient meaning from words alone. Such experiences affect the self-concept and the way one views school experiences.

Tharp (1989) reports that it may be distracting to American Indian children to have the teacher interrupt to elicit comments about a book being read rather than listening to the entire story. Additionally, non-Indian teachers are more likely to respond more quickly and speak more rapidly than the adults American Indian children know. Language has a cadence, and American Indian people may speak more slowly than non-Indian people, with pauses for thinking and reflection (Dodd et al., 1991). The amount of time the teacher waits for a student to respond to a question and the amount of time the teacher waits following a student response has been referred to as "wait time." The teacher may actually interrupt an American Indian child who is accustomed to a longer wait time. Rowe (1987) indicates that invisible students, particularly minority students, become more visible when wait time is increased. However, when a teacher continues before a youngster has responded, it may help the American Indian youngster incorporate into his or her self-concept that his or her response is not valued.

American Indian people had an educational system through which children were well educated in skills for maturity (Szasz,

1989). They were taught endurance and patience, and they learned to cultivate a lively sense of humor. They felt good about themselves when they had assumed the values being taught and were accorded praise and respect for those appropriate behaviors. Their educational system provided three main focuses. They were taught about survival, how one related with all things in the world. They were taught the proper way to act and behave according to the tribal norms. Additionally, they were taught spirituality, which provided their philosophy of life.

American Indian people saw Euro-American schooling as an addition and not a replacement of their own educational system, which included hunting, fishing, and gathering in addition to interpersonal skills for survival. Their educational methodology included role modeling, apprenticeship training, and group consensus (LaFramboise & Rowe, 1983). Elders told tales about other young people and how they had behaved and what the effects of such behavior were. These tales provided models for behaving in approved ways.

Testing

Tests, testing procedures, and test norms are based on the majority culture. For example, high verbal scores on intelligence tests may indicate high academic ability. However, the converse may not be true: low verbal scores do not necessarily indicate low ability. Rather, it may be an indicator of a language difference and a predictor of the ability to function in an English-language setting (Bailey & Harbin, 1980; Hynd & Garcia, 1979).

A system of interdependence and mutual obligation has helped Indian people maintain identity and culture (Hall, 1991). However, tests designed to require competition with peers which necessitate comparison with others do not fit in with traditional American Indian beliefs about the interconnectedness of persons. Dana (1984) reports that some American Indian students may have been taught that self-disclosure to a stranger results in a loss of self-control. Thus efforts made to establish rapport with American Indian children, which include a mutual exchange of self-disclosed information, may be unwelcome (Stock, 1987). Therefore, to comply with the expectations of testors might be evidence that the child has a poor self-concept.

Classroom Control

Non-Indian teachers may exercise control within classrooms differently than American Indians. Contrary to the children's experience at home, the non-Indian teacher may attempt to control all communicative activity and function like a switchboard through whom most verbal expression is directed and who allocates turns at speaking (Erickson & Mohatt, 1977). In contrast, in Erickson and Mohatt's (1977) description of an Indian teacher's distinction between teachers' time and students' time, the loci of social control was not made sharply. Rather, social control was distributed as a shared quantity. Needless to say, being treated in school with less respect than one expects affects how one feels about oneself in school settings.

FAMILY

Hall (1991) indicates that the most important unit in Native American culture is the family. American Indian families are structurally open and may include several households along both vertical and horizontal lines (Light & Martin, 1986): that is, they may extend out among present generations and not just back through parents and grandparents. A particular strength of American Indian cultures is this extended family, which involves many persons in rearing children. Family welfare is considered more important than individual welfare, and rearing children is an entire family's responsibility. It is not uncommon to find grandparents, aunts, uncles, cousins, or even friends of the family rearing a child. Although this may be interpreted by persons who do not understand American Indian cultures as evidence of neglect or inability to care for a child, this does not have to be the case, nor does it necessarily indicate a lack of emotional attachment. It may reflect the close family ties between the parents and the person rearing the child. To permit another to rear a child may require a very strong self-concept and conviction that to do so would be better for the child or for the person entrusted with such an important responsibility.

Although American Indian children may on occasion be abused or neglected, Congress passed the Indian Child Welfare Act (ICWA) (1978), which recognized the extended family system. The ICWA requires that when foster placement or adoption is needed, the first placement priority must be within the extended family. If that is not possible, the ICWA's next priority is with the tribe itself.

TRADITIONAL ATTITUDES TOWARD CHILDREN

The traditional American Indian way of educating children has been viewed as permissive by persons who do not understand the system. Hynd and Garcia (1979) point out that American Indian children are accorded the same degree of respect as adults. Traditionally, American Indian children have been disciplined quietly without harsh verbal or physical expression. This may be especially true when a child is reared by older parents or grandparents.

American Indian children experience a great deal of freedom and participation with adults. For example, it is common to see American Indian children, even very young ones, running freely at traditional settings such as pow wows, hand games, feasts, ceremonies and athletic events. Whether hand games are being played or a pow wow is taking place, children are present and have freedom to take part or play together. Children take part in pow wows just as adults do—by dancing. Such positive experiences of equality and respect affect how one feels about self in those settings.

DISABILITIES

American Indian people are reported to have numerous health problems and high rates of some disabilities. For example, American Indian children have been reported to have a higher incidence of otitis media, an infection of the middle ear, than other youngsters (Goinz, 1984; McShane & Mitchell, 1979; Scaldwell & Frame, 1985). Furthermore, otitis media is associated with educational problems (McShane & Mitchell, 1979; Thielke & Shriberg, 1990). Nickoloff (1983) reports a higher incidence of hearing problems among Indian persons than other ethnic groups. American Indian people are also reported to have a high incidence of diabetes, which can lead to other health problems (Pine, 1988). Indeed, the Pima Indian people have the highest rate of diabetes in the world (Heckler, 1985). The high rate of alcoholism among Indian persons is well documented (May, 1986; Young, 1987). One study reports that American Indian persons were overrepresented tenfold in a youth chemical dependency unit (Query, 1985).

O'Connell (1987) reports that American Indian persons are proportionately identified more frequently with learning disabilities than any other group. These experiences may encourage American Indian people to expect fewer abilities and more disabilities than other people.

SUICIDE

American Indian adolescents have been reported to take their own lives at about twice the rate of white adolescents (Harras, 1987). In one study of American Indian adolescents (Blum, Harmon, Harris, & Resnick, 1992), it was reported that 26.9 percent had attempted suicide. American Indian people, who have been faced with assimilation and destruction of their culture, could view suicide as the ultimate act of freedom, although authors presenting information on the possible reasons for suicide have not kept up with the steady escalation of suicide rates in the American Indian population (LaFramboise & Bigfoot, 1988). Perhaps Baumeister and Boden (see Chapter 5 in this volume) would interpret this as the ultimate escape from self which is chosen by American Indian adolescents. Nevertheless, the high incidence of suicide and attempts to prevent it have been addressed frequently (Claymore, 1988; Miller & Schoenfeld, 1971; Peters, 1981). May (1987) reviews forty studies on suicide among American Indian groups and points out that American Indian suicides are predominantly among young males. He further points out that women and older people have low suicide rates. Additionally, the suicides are carried out with particularly lethal or violent methods. Tribes undergoing rapid change and those with loose social integration rather than conformity to tribal culture have high suicide rates. Regardless of the reasons for suicide, it is certain that positive self-esteem is not among the causal factors.

ACCIDENTAL DEATHS

Heckler (1985) reports that American Indian people have the highest rate of accidental deaths. Motor vehicles account for the majority of these accidental deaths. These deaths have a devastating effect on families, necessitating frequent adjustment to losses. Deaths and accidents increase the likelihood of instability within families, when family stability is an essential basis for one's self-concept.

PRESENT-DAY EXPERIENCES

American Indian people continue to experience negative treatment on a continuum ranging from misunderstanding to overt prejudice. One example can be found in communities near or even on reservations, often referred to as "Indian towns." The non-Indian inhabitants of Indian towns make frequent disparaging comments about Indian people—and to them. "Drunken Indian" conveys derogatory meaning and lack of positive expectations to the townspeople. Both Indian and non-Indian people have seen American Indian men and women reeling or even lying down sleeping on the ground because of the effects of too much alcohol, which was introduced to American Indian people along with other "gifts of civilization." Gone are the signs that said "No dogs or Indians allowed," but the attitudes and feelings which were responsible for the existence of those signs seem to have lingered.

Even without evidence of the effects of alcohol, the American Indian experience may include walking down the street without being recognized by a smile, greeting, or nod—even from persons who know who they are. To an outside observer, it may seem as though they are nonpersons. Inside a store, the experience may be different. An observer might notice that the American Indian presence is acknowledged and every move watched with suspicion. The white owners and the other customers seem to anticipate theft.

In and near these Indian towns, older and somewhat dilapidated automobiles may be referred to as "reservation" or "Indian" cars. The prevalence of such cars, often filled to capacity, on and near reservations is noticeable. Those older cars, necessitated by low income and poor road conditions, may be responsible for the high rate of accidental deaths. Their designation as Indian or reservation cars conveys the notion that inferiority is good enough for American Indian people.

Since many American Indian youngsters have not achieved well in schools in those "Indian towns," a negative expectation can become established. When it is, American Indian students may not be encouraged to take college preparation classes even though they have the ability and perhaps even plans to attend college. Frequently American Indian youngsters have been taught to respect authority and might not be willing to question the advice or to counter the implied message "You are not college material."

Other examples of negative experience are more subtle, such as the experience of a student who attends the state university and whose surname might be Running Crane but finds that his transcript is issued to "Mr. Runningcrane." Or a student named John Rides at the Door may find the instructor reading his name as "John Door." These examples are probably based on misunderstanding. However, a large part of identity is symbolized by name. Historically American Indian people viewed names as very important, with each name selected carefully for each person (Bryan, 1985). However, early Europeans ignored that fact and frequently gave Indian people European names, which convey no meaning. Even tribal names were changed. For example, the Amskapi Pikuni are called Blackfeet, and the Absalokas are called Crow. These changes would be similar to telling American people they are no longer Americans because now they are olas altas. Such changes and distortions of name imply that there must be something wrong or inappropriate about the original name.

SELF-CONCEPT AND PROBLEMS WITH THE PSYCHOSOCIAL CONSTRUCTS

Studying the self-concept of American Indian persons encounters serious obstacles because the psychosocial constructs may be inadequately conceptualized for American Indian children and youth. Although the work of Erikson (1959) serves as a useful model for understanding identity processes for Anglo youth (see Chapter 1 by Hamachek in this volume), there appears to be no adequate conceptual formulations for American Indian children and youth. Ogbu's typology (castlike, immigrant, and autonomous) for describing minority youth has been illuminating, but it is inadequate for linking internal psychological processes with those environmental effects described earlier. The psychological processes articulated are those that relate to developmental tasks generally, and others are linked to adaptations required as a function of the specific sociocultural conditions of a particular minority group. Although this typology links the individual's status with experiences as a minority group member, it fails to account for individual social experiences (Trueba, 1988). Racial and ethnic conceptual models traditionally have been driven by pathology rather than by normal development processes.

PROBLEMS ASSOCIATED WITH THE MEASUREMENT OF PSYCHOLOGICAL CONSTRUCTS AMONG AMERICAN INDIAN AND OTHER MINORITIES

There are a number of methodological concerns associated with the measurement of psychological constructs among American Indian people (Spencer & Markstrom-Adams, 1990). The primary and obvious problem is that most instruments are administered in English, which is a major problem for many American Indian tribal members, for whom English is a second language. This is a problem even if the individual's dominant language is nonstandard English, because instruments are usually normed on middle-class white populations, who employ standard English. Thus there is a problem with nonequivalence in items, words, and performance requirements for American Indian youngsters (Beiser, 1981).

The problem of nonequivalence across ethnic groups is further compounded by the lack of homogeneity across tribes. Because there are more than three hundred American Indian tribes in the United States alone (May, 1987), cultural, geographic, linguistic, and economic differences exist among American Indian tribes. As a result, measurement of psychosocial constructs among tribes is problematic.

Related to these measurement problems, the psychosocial constructs may only represent attributes that are desirable in the dominant society but not within the American Indian cultures (Spencer & Markstrom-Adams, 1990). Furthermore, these constructs may not generalize across cultures (Lonner, 1987) and, in the case of American Indians, across tribes.

Bienvenue (1978) proposes a dual-socialization model for American Indians. Within this model, both the cultural values and those of the dominant culture play critical roles in the socialization of American Indian people, suggesting that self-evaluation needs to be researched in terms of a series of self-concept traits. In a study comparing Native and Euro-Canadian students, she reports that the Native group generally expressed less favorable self-evaluations than the dominant group for characteristics most likely to be evaluated according to standards established by the dominant culture. Those standards were generally characteristics considered important for success and achievement. On the other hand, in terms of such traits as kind, happy, pleasant, friendly, and unselfish, the native students did not differ from their Euro-Canadian counterparts.

Many of the studies available suggest that American Indian persons' self-concepts are less positive than the self-concept of the majority culture. However, tests designed to assess self-concept are likely to assess attributes important to the self-concept of white children but not to American Indian children (Rotenberg & Cranwell, 1989). Certainly the high suicide and alcoholism rates would support the conclusion that American Indian people have difficulties with identity and self-esteem. However, the studies typically have been conducted employing measurement tools and norms devised within the majority culture and reflecting the problems described above.

Martinez and Dukes (1987) investigated race and gender in relationship to self-esteem in regard to satisfaction with self and intelligence. Their results indicated that Native Americans had lower levels of self-esteem in regard to both intelligence and satisfaction with self than white persons did. However, contrary to their expectations, American Indian females did not appear to have a greater sense of intellectual inferiority than American Indian males.

Rotenberg and Cranwell (1989) employed an open self-description measure to compare self-concepts of American Indian and white children. The results supported the existence of differences between American Indian and white children on specific attributes of self-concept. They suggested that the attributes measured as parts of self-concept are not equally important for the two groups. For example, their data revealed that American Indian children showed a greater external orientation than white children.

Otis (1983) conducted a study that compared values of American Indian students, which included Hupa, Paiute, Apache, Hopi, Papago, and Pima tribal groups, with those of non-Indians. He found that within the tribal groups there were far more value similarities than differences. They ranked terminal and instrumental values in different orders than did their non-Indian peers and teachers.

As Fordham and Ogbu (1986) point out, subordinate minorities develop a sense of collective identity which is oppositional to the social identity of white Americans. This oppositional frame of reference helps to maintain boundaries, and to "act white" is negatively sanctioned. Unfortunately, learning to follow standard academic practices may be equated with "acting white," and academic success may be viewed as a subtractive process, which would mean the loss of one's own American Indian self-concept. Therefore, to do well in school can be interpreted as "acting white." Such persons are sometimes called "apples" by other American Indian people to indicate that they are like Indians on the outside but their identity is really white on the inside.

INTERPRETING SELF-CONCEPT ACCORDING
TO CULTURAL VALUES

To obtain concrete examples of problems that might exist in interpreting self-concept, we asked a male adult member of a plains Indian tribe whose first language was an Indian language to write the five characteristics or traits which would make up an ideal person. These were considered to be the characteristics whose possession or demonstration would make one feel good about oneself.

Because he cautioned that the list was his own and might not be generalized to others, other members of the same tribe were asked the same questions and responded similarly. Examples from the list are used below to illustrate how a behavior might be shown as evidence of a positive self-concept among one American Indian group but the same behavior might be interpreted as evidence of a poor self-concept among non-Indian populations.

For example, an American Indian child might proudly wear a new sweater to school shortly after a birthday or Christmas. In each of the following days the sweater might be worn by siblings or friends. A teacher, accustomed to teaching non-Indian children who have been taught from an early age to take care of "number one," might react with sympathy and feel that the youngster lacked enough self-confidence to exert his own ownership of the new apparel. However, the child might indeed be exhibiting evidence of a good self-concept because he is sharing and showing care or concern for the larger group. The child is behaving according to the tribal ideals.

The same teacher might observe the youngster who has just expressed his point of view in a class discussion while he quietly listens while other youngsters express opinions contrary to his own. The teacher or another observer from a different cultural background might interpret this behavior as a lack of assertiveness or insecurity in regard to his opinions, and therefore evidence of a "poor" self-concept. However, the youngster is indicating a good and positive self-concept because he is exhibiting respect for others and showing his respect by permitting each person to speak until he or she has had his or her say.

On still another occasion, the same teacher might ask a question and be pleased as hands are waved vigorously in the air. However, she might observe that the youngster who has been reared with traditional values does not raise a hand and wave it eagerly. The teacher again might interpret this as unsureness or an unwillingness to try answering or a lack of understanding or information. Again, the teacher or observer might interpret this as evidence of a poor self-concept. However, this is not the case. The youngster is providing evidence of a good self-concept because he is behaving in a socially sanctioned manner, carefully thinking over the answer and weighing the various options before speaking. He is exhibiting the ability to think and speak only after careful consideration because words once uttered can never be brought back.

In still another example, the teacher may observe a youngster who has been offered a number of colored pencils who takes only two while the other youngsters take one of each color available. The teacher might interpret this as meaning the child believes he is entitled to less than others and interpret it as evidence of a poor self-concept. However, the youngster again is exhibiting a good and appropriate self-concept because he is practicing the culturally sanctioned quality of humility and takes no more than he needs. In another era, the hunter might spare killing a number of fine animals and exhibiting his prowess with the bow or a rifle because he takes only what is needed.

Finally, the teacher or other observer might see the other youngsters giving evidence of extreme exuberance and interpret that as enjoying winning or enjoying a special activity, while the traditional American Indian youngster remains comparatively quiet. This may be interpreted as passivity and therefore evidence of a poor self-concept. However, the youngster is indeed providing evidence of a positive self-concept because he is providing evidence of having and displaying all of his emotions and not letting one emotion dominate.

The aforementioned examples show that the response to questions or reactions to situations or even selection of nonverbal and "culture-fair" pictorial responses might reveal erroneous information about self-concepts. Moreover, these examples were selected from only one tribal group, and adding other groups might double or quadruple the possible interpretations of the same responses.

However, the examples illustrate how the different values of American Indian cultures can clash with the values of the majority culture. Since many persons with whom American Indian people come into contact view the world ethnocentrically, their words and deeds may convey to American Indian persons that their values are wrong or inferior. If your values are wrong, it is an invitation to devalue yourself, leading to the development of a negative self-concept.

ENHANCING IDENTITY AND SELF-ESTEEM

The experiences of American Indian people make it abundantly clear that previous and, to some extent, current federal policies have not been helpful to American Indian people. There is something horribly debilitating about being kept dependent and having decisions affecting oneself made by other persons. Recently one American Indian person explained that the one thing the diverse groups of American Indian people have in common is their experience with the Bureau of Indian Affairs. The tone of voice made it abundantly clear that this shared experience had not been positive.

Duster (1991) points out that, except for American Indian people, there is no such thing as an American without a hyphen. That is, there are Mexican-Americans or Irish-Americans, but the real Americans were the first Americans. He also points out that generations of immigrants have struggled to balance both sides of the hyphen, and many find comfort in an identification with an old country.

Despite generations of facing deliberate attempts to destroy their linguistic and cultural heritage and replace it with a new identity, many American Indian people have retained their traditional convictions and attitudes. It is time for federal policies and persons within the majority society to recognize the importance of maintaining cultural integrity.

It is recognized that many standard practices have not worked well with American Indian people. One reason is that American Indian people have traditionally maintained a great deal of respect for individuality and the uniqueness of each individual. Good Tracks (1973) points out that any kind of intervention is contrary to American Indian people's adherence to the principle of self-determination or noninterference. He says that American Indian society will not allow interference or meddling even if it is designed to keep another from doing something foolish or dangerous. Nearly all agencies which have come in contact with American Indian people have done just that—attempted to change Indian people to make them more like non-Indian people to save them from the "folly" of their own ways and beliefs.

Since coercive attempts have been traditionally viewed as rude and inappropriate, they have not been successful. American Indian people have seemed to go along with the coercion, only to fail to conform to the expected behavior. This may be interpreted to mean that American Indian persons have failed to understand, whereas the reality is that they are ignoring or escaping from inappropriate and rude behavior.

Policymakers seem to have failed to understand the delicacy and sensitivity required for interpersonal relations with American Indian people. For example, Good Tracks (1973) indicates that it is not appropriate to urge people to attend a social gathering one is planning. That is interfering with free choice. Rather, if people know the gathering is being planned, it is safe to assume that they will come if they want to attend.

Therefore, to effect positive change in the self-esteem of American Indian people, it is essential to provide an opportunity for genuine self-determination. To have succumbed to coercion is to lose respect for oneself. However, to choose the same course of action when it is available is to maintain self-respect and enhance positive feelings about the self. The increased enrollment of American Indian persons in college, from 84,000 in 1980 to 103,000 in 1990 (*Chronicle of Higher Education Almanac*, 1992), is one example of movement toward self-determination. As American Indian people join the ranks of physicians, teachers, lawyers, and other professions, they increase the chance of having their voices heard and heeded. They also increase the chance of young American Indian people knowing successful role models.

Similarly, in discussing the substance abuse programs for American Indian people which appeared to be most viable and in which clients were enthusiastic participants, Weibel-Orlando (1989) report that they were self-generated. Members of the community had decided to do something about the program rather than have involvement imposed. Additionally, the leaders were tribal leaders or other important people to the American Indian people, and the members were both clients and healers. They also saw themselves as a community structure alternative to the drinking culture. Again, self-determination appeared to be at the heart of the successful programs.

American Indian people had a system which provided for the development of positive self-concepts. It makes sense to encourage the use of these culturally relevant systems as they have evolved within particular tribal groups. For example, in traditional American Indian society children experienced a network of caring adults (Brendtro, Brokenleg, & Van Bockern, 1991). They honored their relationships through the use of extended families, seeing themselves as related to virtually all persons with whom they had regular contact. Relationships were manufactured so that any who might be left out would feel included among a gathering of relatives. Children were taught that the relationships provided harmony and to alter that harmony could invite tragedy. The other emphases besides belonging were a spirit of mastery, independence, and generosity.

The policy of assimilation appears to be giving way to the practice of self-determination. When American Indian people have a genuine opportunity to employ their own cultural practices, they have been able to demonstrate success. A good example is the development of tribally controlled colleges, which are known to provide culturally relevant programs and to teach tribal history, languages, and cultural practices (Boyer, 1989–90). Their recognition of the American Indian cultural heritage and their use of traditional values along with current knowledge and skills has provided a means of maintaining identity without giving up self-determination. Blum et al. (1992) point out that strategies that build on community identity and culture are more likely to succeed than externally imposed solutions. They emphasize that programs that promote role models of accomplishment increase the likelihood of challenging the prevailing sense of hopelessness.

Other examples of programs designed to enhance identity and self-concept are taking place on the Blackfeet reservation in Montana. The Blackfeet language had been nearly exterminated, but an effort was initiated among the Indian people to reintroduce it. Today in schools the youngsters are proudly studying their own language, in addition to English, as they learn to take pride in themselves and their culture. The pictures displayed in classrooms and other rooms at the school are pictures of the Blackfeet elders and tribal council members, and also some people of other tribes. Each classroom has been supplied with a Blackfeet flag. The Blackfeet Community College has established a conference, Days of the Blackfeet, which extends information about and pride in the traditional Blackfeet culture to the entire community.

Across the mountains in Montana on the Flathead reservation, home of the Confederated Salish and Kootenai Tribes, Salish Kootenai College offers courses in both Salish and Kootenai. Established as a two-year community college, the college led the way in providing access to college for persons with disabilities. Faculty and administration also developed a four-year bachelor's degree to address the needs of American Indian people with disabilities. American Indian people and others are taught to assist with their rehabilitation while still respecting the traditional ways of noninterference, respect for individuality without being singled out, and using the ways of the extended family and sense of community. Nearby the Confederated Salish and Kootenai Tribes built and run a resort, KwaTaqNuk, on Flathead Lake to employ its people and get a share of tourist dollars. American Indian people have numerous newspapers, which provide a tribal voice. These publications frequently address information not covered in other newspapers, and they also report news about their own tribes or others from the standpoint of American Indian people. There are countless other efforts throughout the nation, initiated by American Indian people, which recognize their cultural and linguistic heritage and help to restore pride, respect, and feelings of competency.

As Duster (1991) points out, in regard to ethnic groups the options may have been too narrowly defined as either assimilation or retreat into ethnic enclaves. Rather, cultural pluralism, which includes collective problem solving by persons from many different backgrounds without viewing one as superior or more correct, may produce superior results. Public schools which afford genuine respect and recognition of various ethnic groups and which offer the opportunity to maintain cultural identity and values without coercion can serve as the beginning of healthy self-esteem for all ethnic groups.

REFERENCES

American Council on Education Office of Minority Concerns. (1989). *Eighth annual status report: Minorities in higher education.* Washington, DC: Author.

Anderson, B., Burd, L., Dodd, J., & Keller, K. (1980). A comparative study in time estimating. *Journal of American Indian Education, 19:*1–4.

Anonymous Crow college student. (1991). *My language.*

Bailey, D. B., & Harbin, G. L. (1980). Nondiscriminatory evaluation. *Exceptional Children, 46:*590–596.

Bearcrane, J., Dodd, J. M. Nelson, J. R., & Ostwald, S. W. (1990). Educational characteristics of Native American culture. *The Rural Educator, 11:*1–5.

Beiser, M. (1981). Mental health of American Indian and Alaska Native children: Some epidemiological perspectives. *White Cloud Journal, 2:*37–47.

Bienvenue, R. M. (1978). Self-evaluations of Native and Euro-Canadian students. *Canadian Ethnic Studies, 10:*97–105.

Blum, R. W., Harmon, B., Harris, L., & Resnick, M. D. (1992). American Indian—Alaska native youth health. *Journal of the American Medical Association, 267:*1637–1644.

Boyer, P. (1989–90). The Tribal college: Teaching self-determination. *Community Technical and Junior College Journal, 60:*24–29.

Brendtro, L. K., Brokenleg, M., & Van Bockern, S. V. (1991). The circle of courage. *Beyond Behavior, 2:*5–11.

Bryan, W. L. (1985). *Montana's Indians: Yesterday and tomorrow.* Helena: Montana Magazine, Inc.

Burd, L., Dodd, J. M., & Grassl, P. (1981). A comparison of reservation Native American and other public school children's time estimation skills. *Child Study Journal, 11:*247–252.

Bureau of the Census. (1988). *We the First Americans.* Washington, DC: U.S. Government Printing Office.

———. (1990). Census of population and housing summary tape file 1C United States summary. Washington, DC: U.S. Department of Commerce.

Chavers, D. (1991). Indian education: Dealing with disaster. *Principal*, 70:28–29.

Chronicle of Higher Education Almanac. (1992). Washington, DC: The Chronicle of Higher Education.

Churchill, W. (1985). The situation of indigenous populations in the United States: A contemporary perspective. *Wicazo Sa Review*, 1:30–35.

Claymore, B. J. (1988). A public health approach to suicide attempts on a Sioux reservation. *American Indian and Alaska Mental Health Research*, 1:19–24.

Coopersmith, S. (1981). *Self-esteem inventories.* Palo Alto: Consulting Psychologists Press.

Cummins, J. (1979). Linguistic interdependence and the educational development of bilingual children. *Review of Educational Research*, 49:222–225.

Dana, R. H. (1984). Intelligence testing of American Indian children: Sidesteps in quest of ethical practice. *White Cloud Journal*, 3:35–43.

Dodd, J. M., Ostwald, S. W., & Rose, P. M. (1991). Cultural pluralism: A necessary consideration for rehabilitation personnel. *National Association of Rehabilitation Professionals in the Private Sector Journal and News*, 6:103–108.

Duster, T. (1991). Understanding self-segregation on the campus, *Chronicle of Higher Education*, 38:B1–B2.

Erickson, E. H. (1959). *Childhood and education* (2nd ed.). New York: Norton.

Erickson, F., & Mohatt, G. (1977). The social organization of participation structures in two classrooms of Indian students. Department of Indian Affairs and Northern Development, Ottawa, Ontario. (ERIC Document reproduction Service No. ED 192 935)

Fedullo, M. (1992). *Light of the feather: Pathways through contemporary Indian America.* New York: William Morrow.

Flores, J. F. (1985–86). Alcoholism treatment and the relationship of Native American cultural values to recovery. *The International Journal of Addictions*, 20:1707–1726.

Fordham, S., & Ogbu, J. U. (1986). Black students' school success: Coping with the "burden" of acting white. *The Urban Review*, 18:176–206.

Forecast: Third of students will be minorities by 1995. (1991, September). *Billings Gazette*, p. 8A.

Goinz, J. B. (1984). Otitis media among preschool and school age Indian children in MI, MN and WI. *Hearing Instruments*, 35:16–18.

Good Tracks, J. G. (1973). Native American non-interference. *Social Work*, 18:30–34.

Graves, T. D. (1967). Psychological acculturation in a triethnic community. *Southwestern Journal of Anthropology, 23:*336–350.

Hall, E. T. (1976). *Beyond Culture.* Garden City, NY: Anchor Press.

Hall, M. (1991). Gadugi: A model of service-learning for Native American communities. *Phi Delta Kappan, 72:*754–757.

Harmon, A. (1990). When is an Indian not an Indian: The "Friends of the Indian" and the problems of Indian identity. *Journal of Ethnic Studies, 18:*95–123.

Harras, R. (1987). *Issues in adolescent health: Suicide.* Division of Medical Systems Research and Development Monograph Series, Washington, DC: U.S. Department of Health and Human Services.

Heckler, M. M. (1985). Report of the secretary's task force on black and minority health: Executive summary. U.S. Department of Health and Human Services. Washington, DC: U.S. Government Printing Office.

Hillabrant, W., Romano, M., & Stang, D. (1992). Native American education at a turning point: Current demographics and trends. In *Indian Nations at risk: Listening to the people. Summaries of papers commissioned by the Indian Nations at Risk Task Force of the U.S. Department of Education,* edited by P. Cahape & C. R. Howley (pp. 6–9). Charleston, WV: ERIC Clearing House on Rural and Small Schools.

Hultkrantz, A. (1987). *Native religions of North America: The power of visions and fertility.* San Francisco: Harper.

Hynd, G. W., & Garcia, W. I. (1979). Intellectual assessment of the Native American student. *The School Psychology Digest, 9:*446–454.

Indian Child Welfare Act of 1978, 25 U.S.C. Congress 1901 (1978).

LaFramboise, T. D., & Bigfoot, D. S. (1988). Cultural and cognitive considerations in the prevention of American Indian adolescent suicide. *Journal of Adolescence, 11:*139–153.

LaFramboise, T. D., & Rowe, W. (1983). Skills training for bicultural competence: Rationale and application. *Journal of Counseling Psychology, 30:*589–595.

Light, H. K., & Martin, R. E. (1986). American Indian families. *Journal of American Indian Education, 26:*1–5.

Lipinski, T. A. (1989). The role of vocational counseling for the American Indian student. *Rural Special Education Quarterly, 10:*31–37.

Little Soldier, L. (1989). Cooperative learning and the Native American student. *Phi Delta Kappan, 71:*161–163.

Lonner, W. J. (1987). Introduction to the special issue. *Journal of Cross Cultural Psychology, 18:*379–382.

Martinez, R., & Dukes, R. L. (1987). Race, gender, and self-esteem among youth. *Hispanic Journal of Behavioral Sciences, 9:*427–443.

May, P. A. (1986). Alcohol and drug misuse prevention programs for American Indians: Needs and opportunities. *Journal of Studies of Al-*

cohol, 47:187–195.

———. (1987). Suicide and self-destruction among American Indian youths. *American Indian and Alaska Native Health Research,* 1:52–69.

McShane, D., & Mitchell, J. (1979). Middle ear disease, hearing loss and educational problems of American Indian children. *Journal of American Indian Education,* 19:7–11.

Medicine, B. (1985). Child socialization among Native Americans: The Lakota (Sioux) in cultural context. *Wicazo Sa Review,* 1:23–28.

———. (1988). Native American (Indian) women: A call for research. *Anthropology and Education Quarterly,* 19:86–92.

Miller, S. I., & Schoenfeld, L. S. (1971). Suicide attempt patterns among the Navajo Indians. *International Journal of Psychiatry,* 17:189–193.

Morgan, C. O., Guy, E., & Cellini, H. (1986). The rehabilitation of disabled Native Americans. *Journal of Rehabilitation,* 52:25–31.

Nickoloff, E. G. (1983). Vocational rehabilitation of the hearing impaired Native American. *Journal of Rehabilitation of the Deaf,* 16:16–21.

O'Connell, J. C. (Ed.). (1987). *A study of the special problems and needs of American Indians with handicaps both on and off the reservation* (vol. 1). Flagstaff: Northern Arizona University Native American Research and Training Center; Tucson: University of Arizona Native American Research and Training Center.

Ogbu, J. U. (1988). Cultural diversity and human development. *New Directions for Child Development,* 42:11–28. San Francisco: Jossey-Bass.

Otis, M. G., Jr. (1983). *A comparative study of American Indian students' values.* Ann Arbor, MI: University Microfilms International Dissertation Information Service.

Peters R. (1981). Suicidal behavior among Native Americans: An annotated bibliography. *White Cloud Journal,* 2:9–20.

Pine, C. J. (1988). Diabetes and behavior: American Indian issues. In *Behavioral health issues among American Indians and Alaska Natives: Explorations on the frontiers of the biobehavioral sciences,* edited by S. M. Manson & Norman G. Dinges (*vol. 1,* pp. 94–115). Denver: The National Center for American Indian and Alaska Mental Health Research.

Plummer, M. (1992, July 24). Exception to the rule: Indian religious freedom. *Char-Koosta News,* pp. 1, 2.

Powers, S., & Rossman, M. H. (1983). *Attribution factors of Native American and Anglo community college students.* (ERIC Document Reproduction Service ED No. 235 991)

Query, J. N. (1985). Comparative admission and follow-up study of American Indians and whites in a youth chemical dependency unit on the north central plains. *International Journal of the Addictions,* 20:489–502.

Red Horse, J. G. (1980). American Indian elders: Unifiers of Indian families. *The Journal of Contemporary Social Work,* 6:490–493.

Rotenberg, K. J., & Cranwell, F. R. (1989). Self-concept in American Indian and White children: A cross-cultural comparison. *Journal of Cross-Cultural Psychology,* 20:39–53.

Rowe, M. B. (1987). Wait time: Slowing down may be a way of speeding up. *American Educator,* 47:38–43.

Scaldwell, W. A., & Frame, J. E. (1985). Prevalence of otitis media in Cree and Ojibway school-children in six Ontario communities. *Journal of American Indian Education,* 25,1–5.

Seligman, M. E. (1975). *Helplessness.* San Francisco: Freeman.

Sleeter, C. E. (1991). *Empowerment through multicultural education.* Albany, NY: State University of New York Press.

Spencer, M. B., & Markstom-Adams, C. (1990). Identity processes among racial and ethnic minority children in America. *Child Development,* 61:290–310.

Stedman, R. W. (1982). *Shadows of the Indian: Stereotypes in American culture.* Norman, OK: University of Oklahoma Press.

Stock, L. (1987). Native Americans: A profile. *Journal of Visual Impairment and Blindness,* 81:152.

Szasz, M. C. (1989). Listening to the Native voice: American Indian schooling in the twentieth century. *Montana: The Magazine of Western History,* 39:42–53.

Tharp, R. G. (1989). Psychocultural variables and constraints: Effects on teaching and learning in schools. *American Psychologist,* 44:349–359.

Thielke, H. M., & Shriberg, L. D. (1990). Effects of recurrent otitis media on language, speech and educational achievement in Menominee Indian children. *Journal of American Indian Education,* 29:25–35.

Trueba, H. T. (1988). Culturally based explanations of minority students' academic achievement. *Anthropology and Education Quarterly,* 19:270–287.

Voget, F. W. (1984). *The Shoshoni-Crow Sun Dance.* Norman, OK: University of Oklahoma Press.

Weibel-Orlando, J. (1989). Hooked on healing: Anthropologists, alcohol and intervention. *Journal of the Society for Applied Anthropology,* 48:148–155.

Westby, C. E., & Rouse, G. R. (1985). Culture in education and the instruction of language learning-disabled students. *Topics in Language Disorders,* 5:15–28.

Young, T. J. (1987). Inhalant use among American Indian youth. *Child Psychiatry and Human Development,* 18:36–46.

CHAPTER 12

Disability and the Self

S. Kay Toombs

As a person living with chronic, progressive multiple sclerosis, I have had some occasion to reflect upon the relation between physical disability and the self. I was 30 years old when I was first diagnosed with M.S. In the beginning my illness was characterized by discrete attacks—the loss of vision in one or other eye, the loss of sensation in a leg, the sudden weakness of one or more limbs. Such attacks were sometimes followed by complete remissions; at other times they abated, leaving me with a new or increased disability. In the past several years there have been fewer acute episodes (except for a recurrent optic neuritis which periodically robs me of sight). Rather there has been a slow, but relentless, progression of disability, in the course of which I have lost the full use of my legs, a good deal of trunk and upper body strength (requiring me to wear a brace to keep upright), my sense of balance, and normal voluntary control of my bowels and bladder. Since I can no longer walk, I use a motorized scooter or wheelchair for mobility.

In treating my disorder, clinical medicine makes the assumption that my physical body is quite distinct from my self, that my disability is a purely physical affair and, to the extent that it affects my self at all, such effects represent accidental rather than substantive changes in the self. Furthermore, since self is conceived to be extrinsic to body, it is deemed beyond the province of medicine and of little or no concern in the therapeutic endeavor.

In this essay I shall suggest that a phenomenological analysis of the experience of disability poses a challenge to these assumptions of clinical medicine. (In the interests of time, I shall confine my exploration to disability arising from the loss of motility and shall

337

not here include sensory and visual disorders.) In particular, I shall argue that, in effecting a fundamental change in the lived body, permanent disability incorporates a profound transformation of the self—a transformation which must be taken into account not only in the clinical encounter but in the personal and social response to disability.

THE EXPERIENCE OF DISABILITY

In considering disability it is helpful briefly to reflect upon the experience of embodiment (Sartre, 1956; Merleau-Ponty, 1962). As an embodied subject, I do not experience my body primarily as an object among other objects of the world. Rather than being an object for me-as-subject, my body as-it-is-lived represents my particular point of view on the world (Merleau-Ponty, 1962, p. 70). I am embodied not in the sense that I "possess" a body (in the same way that I "possess" or "have" a house, a car, or a dog), but in the sense that I EXIST (or live) my body. In this respect, the lived body is not the objective, physiological body which can be seen by the microscope but the body that exists in the act of seeing (Toombs, 1992, pp. 51–81; Toombs, 1988, pp. 201–226). Furthermore, the lived body is the basic scheme of orientation, the center of one's system of coordinates. I experience myself as the Here, over against which everything else is There. As orientational locus, the body orients me to the world around by means of my senses and positions the world in accord with my bodily placement (Husserl, 1982, pp. 116–117; Husserl, 1989, pp. 165–166; Schutz, 1962, pp. 222–226). Additionally, the lived body is the locus of my intentions. I actively engage the world through the medium of my body. Not only do I find myself within the world, but I continually organize it in terms of my projects, and so forth. As orientational and intentional locus, the lived body represents not simply my bodily being but my *being-in-the-world*. My embodying organism is always experienced as "in the midst of environing things, in this or that situation of action, positioned and positioning relative to some task at hand" (Zaner, 1981, p. 97).

In this respect, surrounding objects present themselves as invitations to my body's possible actions. For instance, a book is encountered as an object "to be read" or "to be replaced on the shelf," a chair as that which is "to sit on" or, perhaps, "to walk around in order to get to the door." The surrounding world is thus structured in various strata of reality—the world within actual reach, the "manipulatory sphere" (the sector of the world which I can modify directly by movements of my body or with the help of artificial extensions such as tools) and the world within potential reach (the world of my potential working acts) (Schutz, pp. 223ff). As the "manipulatory sphere," surrounding space represents a space of action. From my center outward the world around me arranges itself into zones of near and far goals.

Moreover, the lived body manifests one's being-in-the-world, not only as orientational and intentional locus, but additionally in the sense that distinct bodily patterns (such as walking, talking, gesturing, and so forth) express one's unique bodily existence. That is, one develops a certain corporeal style, a certain bodily bearing which identifies the lived body as peculiarly "me." Sexual, motor, and other patterns express one's mode of existing (Merleau-Ponty, 1962, p. 150). Furthermore, not only do I recognize such bodily patterns as peculiarly my own but, additionally, such patterns represent my self-presentation to others.

An understanding of the lived body as orientational and intentional locus provides some important insights into the experience of disability. To begin with, the character of surrounding space changes with the onset of disability. Rather than representing the arena of possible action, space is encountered as the restriction of possibilities. In the normal course of events locomotion continually opens up space, allowing one freely to change position and move toward objects in the world. Loss of motility anchors one in the Here, engendering a heightened sense of distance between oneself and surrounding things. What might formerly have been regarded as "near" is now experienced as "far." When I could walk, for instance, the distance from my office to the classroom (about 30 yards) was unremarkable. As my mobility decreased, the classroom appeared "near" to the office on the way to the lecture but "far" from it on the return journey. Today (if I were to be without my motorized scooter) the distance to traverse would appear immense—beyond attainable reach. In this respect, as Straus (1982, p. 152) has noted, man in his motility orients himself beyond the actual toward the possible. Loss of motility obstructs the capacity to "possibilize."

The manipulatory sphere is disrupted in another way. With the onset of motor dysfunction mundane objects which were formerly grasped as "utilizable" (as "invitations" to the body's possible action) now present themselves as "obstacles" to the body. Motor dysfunction causes a disturbance in the various and varied interactions between lived body and world. Consequently, the very nature of one's being-in-the-world is transformed. For the person with a tremor, for example, not only is it the case that the distance between the cup and one's lips is "far," but the cup represents a concrete problem which must be solved (how to raise the cup to one's lips without spilling the contents, dropping it, and so forth). For a person like myself with nonfunctioning legs and weakened muscles, furniture (which was hitherto largely taken for granted and unnoticed) now presents a particular challenge to the body. (I cannot, for instance, get up from a chair which has no arms, raise myself from a deep sofa, turn over, and get out of a king-size bed.) Thus, for those with disabilities, familiar objects (such as stairs, doors, tools) represent concrete experiences of bodily limitation and the frustration of intentionality. One's engagement in the world is effortful whereas hitherto it had been effortless.

In this regard it is important to note that the position of objects in relation to one's body is defined not merely by spatial coordinates but in relation to axes of practical reference. "The cup of coffee is *next to* my papers" means I must be careful not to upset it as I reach for the telephone. "The chair is *to the right of* the desk" means I must walk around it when I make my way to the door. We encounter surrounding space always as *functional* space—that milieu within which we carry out our various activities—and functional space is disturbed with loss of motility.

Furthermore, physical space itself assumes a restrictive character. Slopes may be too steep to climb, pathways too uneven to walk on, doorways too narrow to navigate with a wheelchair. Consequently, people with physical disabilities necessarily come to view the world through the medium of their damaged bodies. I well remember, for example, that my first impression of the Lincoln Memorial was not one of awe at its architectural beauty but rather dismay at the number of steps to be climbed.

This bodily perception (this seeing-through-the-body) is, of course, not limited to those with disabilities. Even if not physically incapacitated, one encounters a narrowed passageway through which one must pass not primarily as a space with certain measurable dimensions but rather as a "restrictive potentiality" for the body requiring modification of one's actions (Merleau-Ponty, 1962, p. 143). (One knows without thinking about it that one must turn sideways in order to proceed past the obstruction.) Rather than representing merely objective locations, points in space mark the varying range of one's gestures and actions. What is perhaps remarkable about this seeing-through-the-body in disability is that such "seeing" renders explicit one's being as a being-in-the-world. A problem with the lived body is a problem with the environment because world and body represent a unified system.

The loss of equilibrium which often accompanies motor disability further alters the character of surrounding space. In the taken-for-grantedness of everyday life, the surrounding world for the most part represents a stable, nonthreatening environment. We run down the stairs or stride along the sidewalk confident in the knowledge not only that our legs will function but that our senses will provide us with the necessary information to negotiate obstacles. We are oriented toward the world and the objects in it. To lose one's sense of balance is to become powerfully disoriented within the world. For instance, it is never to know for certain that one can maintain one's position in space. One may suddenly, unexpectedly, fall backwards or pitch forwards. One may intend to get out of a chair but, on standing, immediately fall back down again. Furthermore, being "unbalanced" or "off balance" is to be vulnerable within the world. The inability to control physical movement means bumping into objects rather than successfully going around them, banging against walls, hitting oneself on a doorway as one lurches through it.

With loss of balance even open space may be experienced as potentially threatening. Objects at least provide support. (Indeed, one way to compensate for loss of balance is to negotiate space by holding on to furniture and walls.) To be faced with a wide-open area is a frightening experience for those with poor balance. (To give some idea of what this is like: think of the childhood experience of learning to ice-skate. Do you remember standing at the edge of the rink, faced with what appeared to be an immense expanse of ice, knowing there was nothing to hold on to once you let go of the barrier—and knowing also that you couldn't control your wayward legs once you ventured out on to the ice?)

Loss of motility thus exerts a centripetal force, anchoring one in the Here and obstructing one's capacity to move outward toward the world. This powerful pull to the center also manifests itself in the forced attention to body. In the normal course of events we engage the world THROUGH the medium of our bodies but it is the worldly engagement itself that is the object of our attention. As Sartre (1956, pp. 425–430) points out, at the level of lived body, the body is that which is perpetually "forgotten" or "surpassed" in carrying out my projects in the world. While the lived body is always present, always the center of reference of my world, it is the "inapprehensible given," a center which is indicated but never grasped as such.

If I am writing a letter, for example, I am not aware of the movements of my arm or the way in which my fingers grasp the pen; rather, my attention is directed at the task at hand (the writing of the letter). With loss of function the body itself becomes thematic to consciousness. If I have trouble grasping the pen, I am preoccupied with the ineffectiveness of my hand or the clumsiness of my fingers. Rather than being directed outward, my attention is called back to the malfunctioning body or, more particularly, to a specific body part. Furthermore, the damaged body necessarily becomes a precondition of one's plans and projects, in that body and environment must always be taken into account. For example, if one uses a wheelchair for mobility, a routine excursion to someone's house, to the theater, to a restaurant, or to the grocery store requires that one first check if one can get into the building (are there steps, is it wheelchair accessible, is there adequate parking, and so forth). In this sense the lived body (rather than being that which is routinely overlooked in carrying out one's projects in the world) manifests itself as an *insistent presence* which remains always at the fringes of one's consciousness.

This centripetal force manifests itself not only in the constriction of space but also in the constriction of the temporal horizon (Toombs, 1990, pp. 227–241). Just as lived spatiality is characterized by an outward directedness, a purposiveness and intention, so time is experienced not as a static present but as a moving toward the future. Normally we act in the Now in light of anticipations of what is to come, more or less specific goals which relate to future possibilities. This gearing into the future is obstructed with disability. In the first place the sheer physical demands of impaired embodiment ground one in the present moment, requiring a disproportionate attention to the Here and Now. One is forced to concentrate on the present moment and the present task, rather than focusing on the next moment. In addition, in the case of progressive disability, the future assumes a distant and problematic character. Forthcoming projects may have to be deferred, goals modified or abandoned. Disability truncates the forward directionality of time, pulling one back to an enduring present.

As noted, the lived body manifests one's being-in-the-world, not only as orientational and intentional locus, but additionally in the sense that distinct bodily patterns express one's unique bodily existence, identifying the lived body as peculiarly "me." A permanent alteration of motor function affects a concurrent change in body style, a transformation in the mode of existing in one's body. The development of a limp, a tremor, or a paralytic limb transforms corporeal style. The disabled individual is acutely aware of this change in body display—a change which is at once unfamiliar and uncomfortable. One feels no longer "at home" in one's body. For example, even after a couple of years, I still have difficulty accepting my disordered patterns of movement and posture as my own. To catch sight of myself in a full-length mirror is to experience a shock of nonrecognition, a sense of puzzlement. Is that person who is moving so strangely really ME?

The change in body style is particularly significant when it involves the loss of upright posture. Upright posture is a crucial element in the constitution of lived spatiality and in the possible modes of communication and performance (Straus, 1966). Furthermore, the ability to stand upright (to stand on "one's own two feet") is directly related to autonomy. Indeed, not only does the loss of upright posture engender feelings of dependency in oneself, but it causes others to treat one as dependent. I have noticed, for example, that whenever I am in my wheelchair strangers invariably address themselves to my husband and refer to me in the third person. "Where would SHE like to sit?" "What would SHE like to eat?" "Can SHE get out of the wheelchair?"

Upright posture and motility are integral elements in the many forms of social interaction and expression which we take for granted—shaking hands in greeting, waving to an acquaintance, standing facing one another "eye to eye," gesturing, and so forth. Disturbance of these usual modes of communication results in a concurrent disruption of the social world. A transformation in body style is not only discomforting to the person who develops a disability but a source of discomfort to others. The person with a paralytic arm finds others embarrassed at the loss of function. How does one shake hands in greeting? Eyes are typically averted from the individual with a severe tremor. Rather than being effortless, social interaction becomes awkward.

I am particularly aware of the disruption in social interaction accompanying loss of upright posture whenever I attend stand-up gatherings (receptions and so forth). In my scooter or wheelchair I am approximately three and a half feet tall, and, for the most part, the conversation takes place above my head. When speaking to a standing person, I have to "look up" at them and they "down" at me. This gives me the ridiculous sense of being a child again surrounded by very tall adults. There is more than figurative significance to such expressions as "to look down on" and "to look up to." In constantly "looking up" to others and being "looked down on," one feels oneself concretely diminished in person as well as in body. Consequently, disability exerts a centripetal force in another sense. The disturbance it creates in ordinary social interaction engenders a powerful impulse to withdraw from the social arena.

TRANSFORMATION OF THE SELF

I should now like to consider the impact of disability upon the self. It should be noted, of course, that the concept of Self is notoriously difficult to delineate. However, in this essay, I am not concerned with evaluating different psychological or philosophical theories regarding this concept. Rather, I am concerned with the everyday manner in which we experience our selves and the impact of disability upon this commonsense experience.

The fundamental change in one's being-in-the-world which occurs with permanent disability engenders a concurrent transformation in one's sense of self. As has been noted, loss of motility disrupts one's engagement in the surrounding world, frustrates purposiveness and intentionality, and obstructs the human capacity to "possibilize." These losses strike at the very core of the self. Our sense of who we are is intimately related to the roles we occupy, professional and personal (wife, lover, teacher, tennis player, and so forth), and to the personal goals and aspirations which are of greatest importance to us. With disability roles may be annihilated altogether (one can no longer be a tennis player without functioning legs) or they may be severely disrupted (I can, for instance, no longer carry out many of the activities which were part and parcel of my role as wife prior to the onset of my disability). This permanent disruption of role strikes at the very core of that personal identity which we fashion for ourselves. As Robert Murphy remarked about his own experience of disability:

> From the time my tumor was first diagnosed through my entry into wheelchair life, I had an increasing apprehension that I had lost much more than the full use of my legs. I had also lost a part of my self . . . it was a change for the worse, a diminution of everything I used to be. (Murphy, 1987, p. 85)

Furthermore, there is an intimate relationship between the self and those important goals and projects toward which one strives. To know what my goals and projects are is, in some sense, to know *ME*. The change in being-in-the-world which is manifested in disability poses a direct threat to the pursuit of life goals. Not only is it the case that physical abilities to engage the world are restricted, but, just as importantly, the effortful nature of this engagement erodes the will to continue. A deep sense of fatigue accompanies the ongoing demands of impaired embodiment. This fatigue is not only physical (although it is surely that) but also existential. There is a powerful impulse to withdraw, to relinquish the commitment to projects, to view them as no longer relevant. This impulse is exacerbated by the change in temporal significance. The preoccupation with the present disrupts one's ability to project toward future goals. The loss of the future which occurs with progressively disabling disorders makes it particularly hard to resist the temptation to relinquish future goals.

In this respect it is important to note that the onset of permanent disability engenders a major disruption in the life narrative of the patient. Each of us constructs a unique life narrative, a personal biography which incorporates not only past and present but a reference to future anticipations of what we will become. The substantive change in being-in-the-world represents not simply an episode in the life narrative, but rather a major transformation of the narrative. Indeed, it necessitates the construction of a new life narrative.

The changes in body style which inevitably accompany disability also reflect a change in self. Not only do bodily patterns of walking, talking, gesturing, and so forth identify the lived body as peculiarly "mine," but such patterns represent my self-presentation to others. Thus the newly disabled person finds corporeal style alien, self-presentation irrevocably altered.

In this respect, it is important to note that it is the CHANGE in body style which precipitates the transformation in one's sense of self. If one is congenitally disabled, one's *disordered* pattern of movement represents one's corporeal identity, as the following quote from a disabled woman illustrates:

> She [her mother] made numerous attempts over the years of my childhood to have me go for physical therapy and to practice walking more "normally" at home. I vehemently refused all her efforts. She could not understand why I would not walk straight. . . . My disability, with my different walk and talk and my involuntary movements, having been with me all my life, was part of me, part of my identity. With these disability features, I felt complete and whole. My mother's attempt to change my walk, strange as it may seem, felt like an assault on myself, an incomplete acceptance of all of me, an attempt to make me over. (Asch & Fine, 1988, pp. 25–26)

Since the disordered pattern of movement did not represent a change in body style, it did not represent a change in this woman's manner of being-in-the-world.

It should be noted that the changes in body style which occur with motor disability almost invariably result in the loss of self-esteem since they present a negative body image in a culture which places great emphasis on physical fitness, sexuality, and youth. Bodily integrity, physical grace, and ease are all attributes which count toward the ideal of attractiveness. Consequently, the person who staggers, wears a brace, uses crutches or a cane, is far from the ideal. Indeed, studies have shown that the attitudes of the non-disabled toward persons with disabilities are overwhelmingly negative in our society (Asch & Fine, 1988, pp. 15–16). Thus the change in lived body causes a diminution of the self which is magnified by debasement from others.

All of the foregoing (disruption of role, modification or abandonment of projects, transformation of the life narrative, change in self-presentation) result in a fundamental disruption of the self as a social being. We are not simply isolated individuals; we are individuals who are members of a community. We find ourselves always at the center of a web of interrelationships with others—some intimate (family, loved ones, friends), some less close (professional colleagues, associates, neighbors), some even more distant (casual acquaintances, strangers). The change in one's being-in-the-world disturbs this web of relationships. Those with whom a newly disabled person shares a common past find it hard to adjust to the new self. The relationship has to be redefined, reconstituted. This is true of even the most intimate relationships. In the case of relations with strangers, I have already noted the disruption in social interaction caused by disability.

The phenomenological analysis of embodiment thus suggests that a person who experiences significant and permanent physical disability cannot avoid a concurrent change in the self because disability (1) transforms bodily identity (irrevocably altering bodily patterns that hitherto signified my body as peculiarly "me"); (2) alters self-presentation to others (disrupting one's sense of the public self); (3) affects personal and professional roles (engendering—at least initially—a profound sense of ambiguity on the part of the disabled person since one's sense of self-identity is often intimately related to one's engagement in such roles); (4) disrupts future projects, personal goals, and aspirations (thus posing a threat not only to the present but to the future self—the self that one had planned to become); and (5) disrupts the social self (one's experience of the self as a social being).

Is there then no choice involved in this self transformation? Is the individual completely helpless in light of the changes in the lived body noted above? Can one choose *not* to change the self in spite of the global effects of lived body disruption which are intrinsic to the experience of disability? Although I do not believe that one can avoid the process of self transformation altogether (given profound and permanent changes in one's manner of being-in-the-world), I would suggest that there is, nevertheless, an element of choice involved in such a self transformation. That is, choice is involved in the fashioning of a new self—in deciding how to be in light of the change in embodiment. In this respect, the person who experiences serious illness or disability is forced to confront the issue of selfhood—explicitly to ask the question "Who am I?" "What am I to become?" in an urgent and concrete way. Often this is an opportunity (unwelcome though it may be) to reevaluate personal values, to make conscious decisions about what is really important in one's life. The recognition that there IS some choice involved in the process of self transformation (albeit a choice which is necessarily influenced by the nature of the disability) is vital. To feel that one is completely without choice is to feel helpless—and thereby to lose the will to redefine the self in a positive fashion. As a person living with progressively increasing disability, an illness for which there is no cure, and a future fraught with uncertainty, I experience the concrete loss of choices on a daily basis. Yet I still retain the freedom to decide how to integrate my ever-changing way of being into my life plan. The recognition that one has this freedom is of vital importance because it allows one to retain some level of control over one's situation—regardless of what that situation might be.

IMPLICATIONS FOR MEDICAL PRACTICE

An understanding of disability as the disruption of *lived body* has important implications for medical practice. Modern scientific medicine has—for the most part—adopted a mechanistic paradigm of body (a dualistic notion which separates mind and body). The physical machinelike body is thus assumed to be extrinsic to the essential self. Consequently, according to the prevailing biomedical model of illness, disability is conceived as a purely physical affair. The problem is seen to be an anatomical or physiological disorder to be corrected or ameliorated by standard modes of therapy—surgery, drugs, and so forth. The emphasis is on the objective manifestation of the disease state, on explaining the disorder in strictly somatic or quantitative terms without reference to the personhood of the patient. As Robert Murphy (1987, p. 87) has noted, medical people thus "have a penchant for looking primarily at the biological aspects of health." Accordingly some consider a paralytic to be doing well "if he has no skin breakdowns, is not visibly depressed, and has clear bowels and bladder." In focusing exclusively on bodily systems, organs, structures, and functions, medicine effectively separates the person from his or her body. That is, the physical body is considered by medicine (in Sartre's terms) as an "in-itself" rather than as a lived body "in situation" engaged in the world.

The foregoing phenomenological analysis clearly suggests that disability is much more than simply the dysfunction of the biological body. Rather, physical disability is experienced by the patient as the disruption of *embodiment*. In particular, it is noted that the lived experience of the body is of the body as one's being-in-the-world and any permanent change in the body is experienced as a transformation of such being. The implications for clinical medicine are several:

1. The recognition that permanent or chronic disability represents a total disruption of the patient's manner of being-in-the-world motivates a shift from an exclusive preoccupation with the biological body to a heightened concern for lived body disruption. In particular, if one is to address the impact of disability upon the self, it is vital to focus concretely upon such factors as the constriction of space and time with the goal of extending the patient's range of possible actions and restoring, to the extent possible, the capacity to "possibilize."

In this regard Merleau-Ponty (1962, p. 143) notes that in the normal course of events, through the performance of habitual tasks, as embodied individuals we incorporate objects into our bodily space. For example, the woman who habitually wears a hat with a long feather intuitively allows for the feather when going through a doorway. Similarly, the blind man's stick becomes an extension of body that increases its range. The point of the stick becomes "an area of sensitivity, extending the scope and active radius of touch, and providing a parallel to sight" (Merleau-Ponty, 1962, p. 143). Individuals with motor disabilities can likewise learn to extend their bodily space and range through the incorporation of such aids as crutches, walkers, wheelchairs, and so forth, and they should be encouraged to view such aids as extensions of bodily space, rather than as symbols of disability. In this respect, it is interesting to note that physicians usually spend little time discussing with patients specific ways in which to ameliorate lived body disruption. Rather, the overwhelming focus is on the disease process, on the manner in which the patient's experience manifests itself in terms of "objective," quantitative clinical data (Stetten, 1981, pp. 458–60; Rabin, 1982, pp. 506–509).

2. The awareness that physical disability represents a fundamental change in the patient's being-in-the-world (a change which incorporates an alteration in the experience of surrounding space,

the perception of time, the interrelationships between body and environment, and so forth) forces one to recognize that such lived body disruption cannot simply be relegated to the purely "psychological," rather than "physical," aspect of the patient's condition. That is, *it is vital to recognize the significance of the lived body as intentional and orientational locus.* Thus, although the psychologist may well be helpful (especially if the patient is suffering from, say, a "depressive disorder"), it cannot be assumed that lived body disruption is exclusively the domain of the psychologist, rather than the physician. Indeed, if one is to address such disruption effectively (and thus aid the patient in addressing the experience of self transformation), it requires the assistance of other healers, including physical therapists, occupational therapists, social workers, pastors, and so forth, and the involvement of patients who have experienced such lived body disruption in their own lives.

3. An integral element of the experience of disability (and the concurrent self transformation) is the loss of the capacity to "possibilize" through changes in temporal significance (loss of the future, preoccupation with the present, and so forth). It is therefore imperative that physicians (and others involved in the healing process) recognize and directly address the disruption of temporality. For instance, it is important to note that fear for the future is *necessarily* a part of progressively degenerative diseases such as multiple sclerosis and, furthermore, that such fear can be one of the most debilitating aspects of such illness. Indeed, a newly diagnosed patient may become so preoccupied with the imagined future threat that he or she acts in the present *as if* already severely incapacitated. Patients should be assisted in addressing such fears in a realistic fashion. Fears for the future are almost always concrete: "Will I be able to get from my office to the classroom?" "Will I be able to continue on with my job?" "Will I be able to sit at my desk all day?" Once such concrete fears are explicitly recognized and explored, practical strategies can be developed to deal with them. Such strategies can be as simple as ensuring that patients have an accurate understanding of their situation (that they are not unnecessarily pessimistic about the future), making patients aware of mechanical aids, exploring new ways to accomplish tasks, discussing such factors as the rearrangement of the patient's daily timetable in order to compensate for debilitating fatigue, and so on. To directly address such concrete fears is to put the patient back in

control of his or her situation and, thereby, to minimize the global sense of uncertainty which is a part of progressive disabling disease.

In this regard, it would be a mistake to assume that the patient's preoccupation with the future is a pathological fear. Rather, I believe it would be unreasonable *not* to be concerned about the future in face of the radical uncertainty which a progressively disabling disease represents. I have been interested to note, however, that in the eighteen years since my diagnosis no neurologist has ever asked me if I am afraid or even if I am concerned about the future. This simply underscores the fact that the neurologist's primary focus is upon "objective clinical data" rather than lived body disruption.

4. The recognition that the essential change in being-in-the-world represents a transformation of the self reveals that an important therapeutic goal is to assist those faced with physical disability in their efforts to reconstruct or redefine their changed selves. Indeed, to ignore the transformation of the self is to discount the major impact of disability.

5. An important goal in training programs in medicine and allied health professions should be to expand the prevailing biomedical model of illness and disability to include an understanding of the lived body and lived body disruption. Such an understanding might be developed in a number of ways. For instance, an intensive effort should be made to encourage students to focus on the patient's clinical narrative, in addition to the medical history (Toombs, 1992, pp. 103–110). The clinical narrative is the patient's story of what the illness or disability means in the context of his or her particular life situation. Such a narrative is necessarily concerned with lived body disruption. The medical history, on the other hand, focuses exclusively on the medical "facts" of the case—symptoms, disease etiology, prognosis, modes of treatment, and so forth.

The focus on clinical narratives can be developed in a formal way. For example, students can be directed to study published clinical narratives alongside the textbook descriptions of disease. Thus a student learning about Parkinson's disease would read not only a textbook on neurological disease but also a work such as Oliver Sacks's *Awakenings* (Sacks, 1983). In this book Sacks reports how he asked his patients with Parkinsonism to describe what life was like for them. In their narratives the patients tell of profound disruptions in the experience of space and time—details which are found in no medical textbook but which immeasurably enrich one's understanding of Parkinsonism. (Indeed, one might argue that without this information, one's knowledge of Parkinson's disease is inadequate.) There are many such published accounts of illness and disability which provide an invaluable source of information for professionals.

Additionally, students should witness and participate in numerous in-depth face-to-face interviews with individuals who are willing to share the personal experience of illness or disability. One such endeavor has been reported by Dr. Rita Charon at Columbia University (Charon, 1989). Charon teaches a course for second-year medical students which introduces them to the voice and the world of the patient. An important exercise in the course is to have the students interview a patient with chronic illness. The patient is invited to relate the story of the illness and students are directed to focus on the patient's own understanding of the illness and its impact on daily life. Following the interview students are required to write an account of the patient's illness using the narrative voice of the patient. Students comment that writing the stories allows them to feel something of the patient's experience, and comparing the stories written from the same interview demonstrates to them the selectiveness of attention and the personal contribution of the hearer (Charon, 1989, p. 137).

Another important goal should be to sustain and develop students' imaginative faculties through continuing involvement in the humanities. For instance, at Baylor University I teach an interdisciplinary course which relates the humanities and health care. In this course colleagues from the English and biology departments join me (philosophy) in exploring with the students such topics as suffering, death, illness, disability, caregivers, the physician-patient relationship, pain, aging, sexuality, and mental illness. During the course of the semester we read major classic and contemporary works in all three disciplines (literature, philosophy, and medicine), including such authors as Tolstoy, Sartre, Chekhov, Kafka, Unamuno, Plato, Osler, William Carlos Williams, Selzer, and Lewis Thomas. We encourage the students explicitly to consider how these works illuminate the experience of illness and lived body disruption, as well as the manner in which they provide important insights into their future task as professionals.

SOCIAL RESPONSE TO DISABILITY

In providing the insight that disability is experienced as the disruption of lived body (the transformation of one's being-in-the-world), the phenomenological analysis assists the nondisabled person better to understand and empathize with the disabled person's struggle for a sense of identity. In particular, certain aspects of the struggle become prominent.

1. The change in character of surrounding space (the effortful nature of engagement in the world, the constriction to the Here, the restrictive character of physical space) which represents the loss of the ability to "possibilize" is an integral element of permanent and progressive disability. This experience is, however, not limited to permanent disability. Indeed, we all experience this change on a temporary basis when we are immobilized through illness. For example, if one is confined to bed with an attack of the flu, the world shrinks to the confines of one's room, the bathroom which appeared "near" to the bed in health appears "far" from it now that one is ill, projects which demanded one's attention in normal circumstances become irrelevant, friends and colleagues recede into the distance, the workplace seems a "world" away. Once one regains one's health this experience is easily passed over and forgotten. Nevertheless, it does provide the basis for empathic understanding of the permanently disabled person's loss of ability to "possibilize." How would it feel if this experience were to continue on indefinitely, if it were to become one's "normal" existence?

2. In encountering the restrictive character of physical space, persons with disabilities come to view the world through the medium of their dysfunctional bodies. It is interesting to note that those who have close contact with a person who has some kind of physical limitation begin to view the world through the eyes of the disabled individual. For instance, friends and colleagues who are in the habit of accompanying me now "encounter" objects such as curbs, narrow doorways, and steps as "obstacles" which prevent me (and others like me) from making our way about the world.

In this respect it is important to note the extent to which the restrictive character of physical space for the motor disabled is exacerbated by the fact that until very recently all of our architecture was constructed and designed for people with working legs. Physical barriers such as curbs, steps, swinging doors, narrow doorways, stairs, uneven surfaces, and so forth prevent access to houses, to the subway, to stores, theaters, restaurants, hotels, offices, educational facilities, and so on. Consequently, a disabled person never knows for sure if it will be possible to visit such places and use these facilities unless he or she first makes inquiries. More often than not there are physical barriers preventing access. This is not simply a logistical problem (although it is surely that). As the foregoing analysis reveals, it is a problem that affects the disabled person's self directly to the extent that he or she can no longer participate fully in the life of the community or engage in activities that were hitherto important. In addition, such restrictions cause the individual to feel restricted, thus "handicapped." It is therefore of great importance that we, as a society, recognize the manner in which such physical barriers intensify the disabled person's struggle for a sense of identity and that we take concrete steps to remove such barriers. The recent legislation contained in the Americans With Disabilities Act should be helpful in this regard, provided, of course, that such legislation is enforced. However, as individuals, we need to be much more sensitive to the difficulties that the disabled face on a day-to-day basis.

3. A prominent aspect of the struggle for self-identity is the change in corporeal identity—a change which is particularly disquieting because of cultural attitudes toward the disabled and societal values with regard to the "ideal" body. The loss of self-esteem which accompanies this permanent change in body image can be readily understood if one reflects upon more mundane lived experiences. For instance, one has only to spend a day in a hospital bed, or an hour in a wheelchair, to experience concretely the loss of independence and feelings of dependency that accompany the loss of upright posture. Furthermore, from time to time, in everyday life we may all experience our bodies in a negative fashion—for instance, in fleeting regrets that one's rotund appearance does not "measure up" to another's svelte frame, or in the discomforting experience that we are "no longer as young as we used to be." Such mundane experiences provide insights into the profound loss of self-esteem which is necessarily an integral element in disabling

disorders. Moreover, one is forced to recognize the extent to which the response of others contributes to this loss of self-esteem.

PERSONAL RESPONSE TO DISABILITY

A final word on the nature of disability and the self. I have argued, of course, against the notion that there is an essential self quite distinct from one's physical body. In so doing, I have suggested that the fundamental change in being-in-the-world which occurs with permanent or progressive motor dysfunction is not simply a bodily change which bears no relation to personhood. Rather the transformation in body effects a concurrent transformation of self, in that it annihilates or significantly alters personal roles, disrupts life projects, alters self-presentation, and fundamentally changes one's relations with the world and with others. In arguing this position, I am concerned to say that catastrophic illness or accident resulting in permanent disability represents not simply a modification of the self but the acquisition of a new identity.

This distinction is important in a number of respects. To suggest that permanent disability represents simply a modification of the self is to take the view that physical incapacity represents a change in the quality of life but not a fundamental transformation in one's whole way of being. Consequently, in this view, one is tempted to view the desired response to disability as being that of "transcendence." The disabled person is encouraged to "transcend" or "overcome" physical dysfunction in the sense of "setting it aside" (viewing it as peripheral to existence) and carrying on with life as "normally" as possible ("normally" meaning in a manner as close to one's prior mode of living as possible). Thus, in this view, the occurrence of disability is seen to represent a temporary interruption—rather than a radical break—in the life plan. Following the onset of disability, the individual is expected to RESUME life, albeit in a changed fashion. In other words, there is an assumption that it is possible to remain essentially the same person even though one's being-in-the-world is irrevocably altered.

The task is significantly different, however, once one recognizes disability as a fundamental transformation of one's being. Rather than "transcendence," the goal is "incorporation." That is, the task for the disabled individual is to incorporate disability into a newly defined self (recognizing it to be a central rather than peripheral factor of existence). Instead of attempting to preserve the old self (an impossible task given the change in embodiment), one is involved in a radical reconstruction of the self. One does not simply RESUME life, following the onset of disability; one reconstitutes self-identity in integrating one's changed way of being into a new life plan. Indeed, I would suspect that one of the factors which predicts whether a person will make an adaptive or a nonadaptive response to disability is whether or not the individual is willing to engage in this process of integration. The individual who refuses to "relinquish" the former self, who does not accept a changed way of being-in-the-world, is likely to find it difficult to redefine the self in a positive manner. Indeed, disability may have the effect of making the self more malleable, in the sense that an adaptive response to disability requires a certain openness to possibility—an acknowledgement that the self is less stable (more subject to change) than one might formerly have believed.

An interesting question concerns the manner in which this task of reconstructing the self differs in the case of disability caused by sudden catastrophic accident or trauma, as opposed to disability caused by irreversible, progressive, and immobilizing disease. I do not intend to develop the answer to this question in detail here. I do, however, suspect that the reconstruction of the self in the case of progressive disease differs in the sense that there are no clearly defined parameters of disability with which one can come to terms. Consequently, the individual must redefine the self again and again in light of ongoing and increasing impairment.

REFERENCES

Asch, A., & Fine, M. (1988). Introduction: Beyond pedestals. In *Women with Disabilities,* edited by M. Fine & A. Asch. Philadelphia: Temple University Press.

Charon, R. (1989). Doctor-patient/reader-writer: Learning to find the text. *Soundings, 72*:137–152.

Husserl, E. (1982). *Cartesian meditations: An introduction to phenomenology,* translated by D. Cairns. The Hague: Martinus Nijhoff.

———. (1989). *Ideas pertaining to a pure phenomenology and to a phenomenological philosophy: Studies in the phenomenology of constitution,* translated by R. Rojcewicz & A. Schuwer. Dordrecht, Holland: Kluwer Academic Publishers.

Merleau-Ponty, M. (1962). *Phenomenology of perception,* translated by C. Smith. London: Routledge & Kegan Paul.

Murphy, R. F. (1987). *The body silent.* New York: Henry Holt.

Rabin, D. (1982). Occasional notes: Compounding the ordeal of ALS: Isolation from my fellow physicians. *The New England Journal of Medicine, 307:506–509.*

Sacks, O. (1983). *Awakenings.* New York: E. P. Dutton.

Sartre, J. P. (1956). *Being and nothingness: A phenomenological essay on ontology,* translated by H. E. Barnes. New York: Pocket Books.

Schutz, A. (1962). On multiple realities. In *The Problem of Social Reality,* edited by M. Natanson. Vol. 1 of *Alfred Schutz: Collected Papers.* The Hague: Martinus Nijhoff.

Stetten, D. (1981). Coping with blindness. *The New England Journal of Medicine, 305:458–460.*

Straus, E. (1966). *Phenomenological psychology. Selected papers,* translated by E. Eng. New York: Basic Books.

———. (1982). *Man, time and world: Contributions to anthropological psychology,* translated by D. Moss. Pittsburgh: Duquesne University Press.

Toombs, S. K. (1988). Illness and the paradigm of lived body. *Theoretical Medicine, 9:201–226.*

———. (1990). The temporality of illness: Four levels of experience. *Theoretical Medicine, 11:227–241.*

———. (1992). *The meaning of illness: A phenomenological account of the different perspectives of physician and patient.* Dordrecht, The Netherlands: Kluwer Academic Publishers.

Zaner, R. M. (1981). *The context of self: A phenomenological inquiry using medicine as a clue.* Athens, OH: Ohio University Press.

SUBJECT INDEX

Academic achievement, 72–74, 92–93, 307
Action identification theory, 150, 153
Adult development, 42–51
Affective (emotional) components of the self (see also Depression):
  reduction of, 152
  self-awareness and, 146–147, 157–158
  techniques of changing, 183–187
African-Americans, 309
Agentic self (see also Self-as-subject), 5–6, 90, 97, 101
Alcohol "myopia," 154–155
Alcohol use (see also Drug use):
  among Native Americans, 320, 322
  and effects on self-awareness, 154–155, 297
  as self escape, 8, 154–155, 186–187
  treatment for, 220–222, 264
Alienation, 90–91
Allport, G. W., 128
Americans With Disabilities Act, 354
Attitude change, 232–233, 240
Attributions, 235–236, 316

Being-in-the-world, 338–340, 343–347, 349
Behavior change (see also Self-talk, Transtheoretical model):
  across the lifespan, 61
  processes of, 207–210
  public versus private, 239–242
  self and, 10–11, 27, 233–246
  stages in, 10, 203–207

transtheoretical model of, 201–223
Behavior therapists, 263
Biased scanning theory, 236–241, 243
Binge eating (see Eating disorders)
Bodily self (see also Disability), 15–16, 26, 151–152, 161, 168–169, 175, 338–344, 348–352, 355
Brainwashing, 168, 230–231, 244
Branden, N., 111
Buddhism, 284–286

Calamity (effects on self of), 146–147
Cognitive dissonance, 232–233, 237–238, 240
Cohen, A. K., 91–92
Collective self-esteem, 75
Conditioning, 231
Continuity of self, 233–234, 244, 355–356
Cooley, C. H. (see Reflected appraisals, Self)
Core sense of self (see Continuity of self)
Criminal behavior, 9, 189–192
Cultural effects on self, 311–332

Death (see Self, Suicide)
Decisional balance, 214–216
Delinquency (juvenile):
  and delinquent subculture, 5, 11, 91–93
  as derogated self, 91–92, 94–95
  as "performance," 93–94
  changing the self in, 89–107

359

AUTHOR INDEX